Testing Web Security

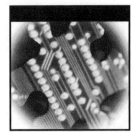

Testing Web Security
Assessing the Security of Web Sites and Applications

Steven Splaine

Wiley Publishing, Inc.

Publisher: Robert Ipsen
Editor: Carol Long
Developmental Editor: Scott Amerman
Managing Editor: John Atkins
New Media Editor: Brian Snapp
Text Design & Composition: Wiley Composition Services

Designations used by companies to distinguish their products are often claimed as trademarks. In all instances where Wiley Publishing, Inc., is aware of a claim, the product names appear in initial capital or ALL CAPITAL LETTERS. Readers, however, should contact the appropriate companies for more complete information regarding trademarks and registration.

This book is printed on acid-free paper. ∞

Published by Wiley Publishing, Inc., Indianapolis, Indiana
Published simultaneously in Canada

For general information on our other products and services, please contact our Customer Care Department within the United States at (800) 762-2974, outside the United States at (317) 572-3993 or fax (317) 572-4002.

Wiley also publishes its books in a variety of electronic formats. Some content that appears in print may not be available in electronic books.

Library of Congress Cataloging-in-Publication Data:
0-471-23281-5

Printed in the United States of America

10 9 8 7 6 5 4 3 2 1

*To my wife Darlene and our sons, Jack and Sam,
who every day remind me of just how fortunate I am.*

*To the victims and heroes of September 11, 2001,
lest we forget that freedom must always be vigilant.*

Contents

Acknowledgments xv
Foreword xix
Preface xxi

Part One An Introduction to the Book 1

Chapter 1 Introduction 3
    The Goals of This Book 4
    The Approach of This Book 5
    How This Book Is Organized 6
    Terminology Used in This Book 7
        Hackers, Crackers, Script Kiddies, and Disgruntled Insiders 8
        Testing Vocabulary 9
    Who Should Read This Book? 11
    Summary 11

Part Two Planning the Testing Effort 13

Chapter 2 Test Planning 15
    Requirements 15
        Clarifying Requirements 16
        Security Policies 17
    The Anatomy of a Test Plan 18
        Test Plan Identifier 20
        Introduction 20
        Project Scope 20

Change Control Process 21
Features to Be Tested 22
Features Not to Be Tested 22
Approach 23
Pass/Fail Criteria 26
Suspension Criteria and Resumption Requirements 27
Test Deliverables 27
Environmental Needs 32
Configuration Management 33
Responsibilities 35
Staffing and Training Needs 36
Schedule 37
Project Closure 38
Planning Risks and Contingencies 38
Issues 40
Assumptions 40
Constraints and Dependencies 40
Acronyms and Definitions 40
References 41
Approvals 41

Master Test Plan (MTP) 41

Summary 42

Part Three Test Design **45**

Chapter 3 **Network Security** **47**

Scoping Approach 48

Scoping Examples 50
Hotel Chain 50
Furniture Manufacturer 50
Accounting Firm 51
Search Engine 52
The Test Lab 52
Suspension Criteria 53

Device Inventory 53

Network Topology 56
Device Accessibility 56

Validating Network Design 57
Network Design Reviews 58
Network Design Inspections 59

Verifying Device Inventory 59
Physical Location 60
Unauthorized Devices 61
Network Addresses 62

Verifying Network Topology 65
    Network Connections 65
    Device Accessibility 66
Supplemental Network Security 68
    Network Address Corruption 69
    Secure LAN Communications 71
    Wireless Segments 71
    Denial-of-Service (DoS) Attacks 73
Summary 77

Chapter 4   System Software Security 79
Security Certifications 80
Patching 81
Hardening 83
Masking 86
Services 88
Directories and Files 95
UserIDs and Passwords 97
    Manual Guessing of UserIDs and Passwords 99
    Automated Guessing of UserIDs and Passwords 101
    Gaining Information via Social Engineering 103
    Disgruntled Employees Committing Illicit Acts 103
User Groups 103
Summary 105

Chapter 5   Client-Side Application Security 107
Application Attack Points 107
Client Identification and Authentication 108
    Relying upon What the User Knows: The Knows-Something
        Approach 109
    Relying upon What the User Has: The Has-Something Approach . .110
    Relying upon What the User Is: The Biometrics Approach 114
User Permissions 115
    Functional Restrictions 116
    Data Restrictions 117
    Functional and Data Cross-Related Restrictions 117
Testing for Illicit Navigation 118
    HTTP Header Analysis 118
    HTTP Header Expiration 118
    Client-Side Application Code 119
    Session IDs 119
    Navigational Tools 119

Client-Side Data 120
  Cookies 121
  Hidden Fields 123
  URLs 123
  Local Data Files 123
  Windows Registry 123

Secure Client Transmissions 124
  Digital Certificates 124
  Encryption Strength 125
  Mixing Encrypted and Nonencrypted Content 126
  Avoiding Encryption Bottlenecks 127

Mobile Application Code 129
  ActiveX Controls 130
  Java Applets 130
  Client-Side Scripts 132
  Detecting Trojan Horse Mobile Code 133

Client Security 135
  Firewalls 136
  Browser Security Settings 137
  Client Adaptive Code 140
  Client Sniffing 141

Summary 142

Chapter 6 Server-Side Application Security **143**

Common Gateway Interface (CGI) 144
  Language Options 145
  Input Data 146
  Permissions and Directories 147
  Scalability 148

Third-Party CGI Scripts 149

Server Side Includes (SSIs) 151

Dynamic Code 155
  Viewing the Template 156
  Single Point of Failure 156
  System Commands 157
  Demonstration Scripts 157
  Helpful Error Messages 158

Application Code 158
  Compileable Source Code 158
  Noncompileable Source Code 158
  Copyrights 159
  Helpful Error Messages 160
  Old Versions 160

Input Data 160
   Invalid Data Types 161
   Invalid Ranges 161
   Buffer Overflows 162
   Escape Characters 169

Server-Side Data 170
   Data Filenames 173
   Data Tripwires 173
   Data Vaults 174
   WORMs 174
   Data Encryption 175
   Data Deception 175
   Data Islands 176
   Distributed Copies 176
   Fragmented Data 176
   Database Management System (DBMS) Enforced Constraints 177
   Filtered Indexes 178

Application-Level Intruder Detection 179

Summary 180

Chapter 7   **Sneak Attacks: Guarding against the Less-Thought-
of Security Threats** **181**

Combatting Social Engineers 181
   Tricks by Telephone 182
   Tricks by Email 182
   Tricks by Traditional Mail 183
   Tricks in Person 184

Twarting Dumpster Divers 185
   Proper Disposal of Paper 185
   Cleaning Up Brainstorms 186
   Proper Disposal of Electronic Hardware .186

Defending against Inside Accomplices 188
   Preventative Measures and Deterrents 188
   Detective Measures 189
   Corrective and Prosecutive Measures 190

Preventing Physical Attacks 192
   Securing a Facility 192
   Securing Hardware 194
   Securing Software 195
   Securing Data 196

Planning against Mother Nature 197

Guarding against Sabotage 197

Summary 198

Chapter 8   Intruder Confusion, Detection, and Response 199

Intruder Confusion 200
Dynamic Defenses 200
Deceptive Defenses 201
Honey Pots 201
Evaluating Intruder Confusion 203

Intrusion Detection 204
Intrusion Detection Systems (IDSs) 205
Audit Trails 207
Tripwires and Checksums 209
Malware 210
Monitoring 213

Intrusion Response 216
Confirmation of Intrusion 217
Damage Containment 217
Damage Assessment and Forensics .217
Damage Control and Recovery 219
System Salvage and Restoration 221
Notification 223
Retaliation and Prosecution 223
Policy Review 224

Summary 225

Part Four   Test Implementation 227

Chapter 9   Assessment and Penetration Options 229

Staffing Options 230
Do It Yourself (DIY) 230
Outsourcing 231
Combination of In-House and Outsourced Testing 240

Tools for Testing 240
Manual Approach 240
Automated Approach 241
Tool Evaluation 242

Summary 249

Chapter 10   Risk Analysis 251

Recycling 252
Asset Audit 252
Fault Trees and Attack Trees 253
Gap Analysis 255

Test Priority 256
Device Inventory 256

Threats 257
Business Impact 262
Risk Likelihood 266
Calculating Relative Criticality 267
Identify and Assign Candidate Tests 267
Priority Modifiers 268
Test Schedule 272
Failure Mode, Effects, and Criticality Analysis (FMECA) 273

Summary 274

Epilogue **277**

Part Five   Appendixes **279**

**Appendix A   An Overview of Network Protocols, Addresses,
and Devices** **281**

Network Protocols 281
Application Layer 283
Presentation Layer 283
Session Layer 284
Transport Layer 284
Network Layer 284
Data Link Layer 285
Physical Layer 285
Security-Minded Network Protocols 286

Network Addresses 286
Dynamic IP Addresses 287
Private IP Addresses 287
Multiple IP Addresses 288
IP-less Devices 288
Misdirecting Host Names 288

Network Devices 289
Repeater 289
Hub 289
Bridge 289
Gateway 289
Switch (Switching Hub) 290
Router 290
Brouter 290
Network Controller 290
Load Balancer 290
Servers 291

Firewalls 292
Firewall Types 292
Firewall Configurations 294

Appendix B SANS Institute Top 20 Critical Internet Security Vulnerabilities **299**

Appendix C Test-Deliverable Templates **301**

Template Test Status/Summary Report .301

Template Test Incident Report 303

Template Test Log 304

Additional Resources **307**

Books 307

Computer Forensics 307

Configuration Management 308

Disaster Recovery 308

Internet Law 308

Miscellaneous 309

Network Design 309

Risk Analysis 309

Security 310

Software Engineering 313

Testing (General) 313

Testing (Web) 315

Web Sites 315

Chapter 1: Introduction 315

Chapter 2: Test Planning 316

Chapter 3: Network Security 317

Chapter 4: System Software Security 319

Chapter 5: Client-Side Application Security 321

Chapter 6: Server-Side Application Security 323

Chapter 7: Sneak Attacks: Guarding against the Less Thought of
Security Threats 325

Chapter 8: Intruder Confusion, Detection, and Response 325

Chapter 9: Assessment and Penetration Options 328

Chapter 10: Risk Analysis 330

Appendix A: An Overview of Network Protocols, Addresses, and
Devices 330

Appendix B: SANS Institute Top 20 Critical Internet Security
Vulnerabilities 331

Appendix C: Test-Deliverable Templates .331

News and Information 332

Index **333**

Acknowledgments

The topic of Web security is so large and the content is so frequently changing that it is impossible for a single person to understand every aspect of security testing. For this reason alone, this book would not have been possible without the help of the many security consultants, testers, webmasters, project managers, developers, DBAs, LAN administrators, firewall engineers, technical writers, academics, and tool vendors who were kind enough to offer their suggestions and constructive criticisms, which made this book more comprehensive, accurate, and easier to digest.

Many thanks to the following team of friends and colleagues who willingly spent many hours of what should have been their *free time* reviewing this book and/or advising me on how best to proceed with this project.

James Bach	Joey Maier
Rex Black	Brian McCaughey
Ross Collard	Wayne Middleton
Rick Craig	Claudette Moore
Dan Crawford	David Parks
Yves de Montcheuil	Eric Patel
Mickey Epperson	Roger Rivest
Danny Faught	Martin Ryan
Paul Gerrard	John Smentowski
Stefan Jaskiel	John Splaine
Jeff Jones	Herbert Thompson
Philip Joung	Michael Waldmann

A special thank-you goes to my wife Darlene and our sons Jack and Sam, for their love and continued support while I was writing this book. I would especially like to thank Jack for understanding why Daddy couldn't go play ball on so many evenings.

Professional Acknowledgment

I would like to thank everyone who helped me create and then extend Software Quality Engineering's Web Security Testing course (www.sqe.com), the source that provided much of the structure and content for this book. Specifically, many of SQE's staff, students, and clients provided me with numerous suggestions for improving the training course, many of which were subsequently incorporated into this book.

Foreword

As more and more organizations move to Internet-based and intranet-based applications, they find themselves exposed to new or increased risks to system quality, especially in the areas of performance and security. Steven Splaine's last book, *The Web Testing Handbook*, provided the reader with tips and techniques for testing performance along with many other important considerations for Web testing, such as functionality. Now Steve takes on the critical issue of testing Web security.

Too many users and even testers of Web applications believe that solving their security problems merely entails buying a firewall and connecting the various cables. In this book, Steve identifies this belief as the *firewall myth*, and I have seen victims of this myth in my own testing, consulting, and training work. This book not only helps dispel this myth, but it also provides practical steps you can take that really will allow you to find and resolve security problems throughout the network. Client-side, server-side, Internet, intranet, outside hackers and inside jobs, software, hardware, networks, and social engineering, it's all covered here. How should you run a penetration test? How can you assess the level of risk inherent in each potential security vulnerability, and test appropriately? When confronted with an existing system or building a new one, how do you keep track of everything that's out there that could conceivably become an entryway for trouble? In a readable way, Steve will show you the ins and outs of Web security testing. This book will be an important resource for me on my next Web testing project. If you are responsible for the testing or security of a Web system, I bet it will be helpful to you, too.

Rex Black
Rex Black Consulting
Bulverde, Texas

Preface

As the Internet continues to evolve, more and more organizations are replacing their *placeholder* or *brochureware* Web sites with mission-critical Web applications designed to generate revenue and integrate with their existing systems. One of the toughest challenges facing those charged with implementing these corporate goals is ensuring that these new storefronts are safe from attack and misuse.

Currently, the number of Web sites and Web applications that need to be tested for security vulnerabilities far exceeds the number of security professionals who are sufficiently experienced to carry out such an assessment. Unfortunately, this means that many Web sites and applications are either inadequately tested or simply not tested at all. These organizations are, in effect, playing a game of *hacker roulette*, just hoping to stay lucky.

A significant reason that not enough professionals are able to test the security of a Web site or application is the lack of introductory-level educational material. Much of the educational material available today is either high-level/strategic in nature and aimed at senior management and chief architects who are designing the high-level functionality of the system, or low-level/extremely technical in nature and aimed at experienced developers and network engineers charged with implementing these designs.

Testing Web Security is an attempt to fill the need for a straightforward, easy-to-follow book that can be used by anyone who is new to the security-testing field. Readers of my first book that I coauthored with Stefan Jaskiel will find I have retained in this book the checklist format that we found to be so popular with *The Web Testing Handbook* (Splaine and Jaskiel, 2001) and will thereby hopefully make it easier for security testers to ensure that the developers and network engineers have implemented a system that meets the explicit (and implied) security objectives envisioned by the system's architects and owners.

Steven Splaine
Tampa, Florida

An Introduction to the Book

CHAPTER 1

Introduction

The following are some sobering statistics and stories that seek to illustrate the growing need to assess the security of Web sites and applications. The 2002 Computer Crime and Security Survey conducted by the Computer Security Institute (in conjunction with the San Francisco Federal Bureau of Investigation) reported the following statistics (available free of charge via www.gocsi.com):

- Ninety percent of respondents (primarily large corporations and government agencies) detected computer security breaches within the last 12 months.

- Seventy-four percent of respondents cited their Internet connection as a frequent point of attack, and 40 percent detected system penetration from the outside.

- Seventy-five percent of respondents estimated that disgruntled employees were the likely source of some of the attacks that they experienced.

The following lists the number of security-related incidents reported to the CERT Coordination Center (www.cert.org) for the previous 4½ years:

- 2002 (Q1 and Q2)—43,136
- 2001—52,658
- 2000—21,756
- 1999—9,859
- 1998—3,734

In February 2002, Reuters (www.reuters.co.uk) reported that "hackers" forced CloudNine Communications—one of Britain's oldest Internet service providers (ISPs) —out of business. CloudNine came to the conclusion that the cost of recovering from the attack was too great for the company to bear, and instead elected to hand over their customers to a rival ISP.

In May 2002, CNN/Money (www.money.cnn.com) reported that the financing division of a large U.S. automobile manufacturer was warning 13,000 people to be aware of identity theft after the automaker discovered "hackers" had posed as their employees in order to gain access to consumer credit reports.

The Goals of This Book

The world of security, especially Web security, is a very complex and extensive knowledge domain to attempt to master—one where the consequences of failure can be extremely high. Practitioners can spend years studying this discipline only to realize that the more they know, the more they realize they need to know. In fact, the challenge may seem to be so daunting that many choose to shy away from the subject altogether and deny any responsibility for the security of the system they are working on. "We're not responsible for security—somebody else looks after that" is a common reason many members of the project team give for not testing a system's security. Of course, when asked who the somebody else is, all too often the reply is "I don't know," which probably means that the security testing is fragmented or, worse still, nonexistent.

A second hindrance to effective security testing is the naive belief held by many owners and senior managers that all they have to do to secure their internal network and its applications is purchase a firewall appliance and plug it into the socket that the organization uses to connect to the Internet. Although a firewall is, without doubt, an indispensable defense for a Web site, it should not be the only defense that an organization deploys to protect its Web assets. The protection afforded by the most sophisticated firewalls can

---

THE FIREWALL MYTH

The *firewall myth* is alive and well, as the following two *true* conversations illustrate. Anthony is a director at a European software-testing consultancy, and Kevin is the owner of a mass-marketing firm based in Florida.

   Anthony: We just paid for someone to come in and install three top-of-the-line firewalls, so we're all safe now.
   Security tester: Has anybody tested them to make sure they are configured correctly?
   Anthony: No, why should we?

   Kevin: We're installing a new wireless network for the entire company.
   Security tester: Are you encrypting the data transmissions?
   Kevin: I don't know; what difference does it make? No one would want to hack us, and even if they did, our firewall will protect us.

be negated by a poorly designed Web application running on the Web site, an oversight in the firewall's configuration, or a disgruntled employee working from the inside.

This book has two goals. The first goal is to raise the awareness of those managers responsible for the security of a Web site, conveying that a firewall should be *part* of the security solution, but not *the* solution. This information can assist them in identifying and planning the activities needed to test *all* of the possible avenues that an intruder could use to compromise a Web site. The second goal is aimed at the growing number of individuals who are new to the area of security testing, but are still expected to evaluate the security of a Web site. Although no book can be a substitute for years of experience, this book provides descriptions and checklists for hundreds of tests that can be adapted and used as a set of candidate test cases. These tests can be included in a Web site's security test plan(s), making the testing effort more comprehensive than it would have been otherwise. Where applicable, each section also references tools that can be used to automate many of these tasks in order to speed up the testing process.

The Approach of This Book

Testing techniques can be categorized in many different ways; white box versus black box is one of the most common categorizations. Black-box testing (also known as *behavioral testing*) treats the system being tested as a black box into which testers can't see. As a result, all the testing must be conducted via the system's external interfaces (for example, via an application's Web pages), and tests need to be designed based on what the system is expected to do and in accordance with its explicit or implied requirements. White-box testing assumes that the tester has direct access to the source code and can look into the box and see the inner workings of the system. This is why white-box testing is sometimes referred to as *clear-box, glass-box, translucent,* or *structural* testing. Having access to the source code helps testers to understand how the system works, enabling them to design tests that will exercise specific program execution paths. Input data can be submitted via external or internal interfaces. Test results do not need to be based solely on external outputs; they can also be deduced from examining internal data stores (such as records in an application's database or entries in an operating system's registry).

In general, neither testing approach should be considered inherently more effective at finding defects than the other, but depending upon the specific context of an individual testing project (for example, the background of the people who will be doing the testing—developer oriented versus end-user oriented), one approach could be easier or more cost-effective to implement than the other. Beizer (1995), Craig et al. (2002), Jorgensen (2002), and Kaner et al. (1999) provide additional information on black-box and white-box testing techniques.

Gray-box testing techniques can be regarded as a hybrid approach. In other words, a tester still tests the system as a black box, but the tests are designed based on the knowledge gained by using white-box-like investigative techniques. Gray-box testers using the knowledge gained from examining the system's internal structure are able to design more accurate/focused tests, which yield higher defect detection rates than those achieved using a purely traditional black-box testing approach. At the same time,

---

GRAY-BOX TESTING

Gray-box testing incorporates elements of both black-box and white-box testing. It consists of methods and tools derived from having some knowledge of the internal workings of the application and the environment with which it interacts. This extra knowledge can be applied in black-box testing to enhance testing productivity, bug finding, and bug-analyzing efficiency.
Source: Nguyen (2000).

---

however, gray-box testers are also able to execute these tests without having to use resource-consuming white-box testing infrastructures.

Wherever possible, this book attempts to adopt a gray-box approach to security testing. By covering the technologies used to build and deploy the systems that will be tested and then explaining the potential pitfalls (or vulnerabilities) of each technology design or implementation strategy, the reader will be able to create more effective tests that can still be executed in a resource-friendly black-box manner.

This book stops short of describing platform- and threat-specific test execution details, such as how to check that a Web site's Windows 2000/IIS v5.0 servers have been protected from an attack by the Nimda worm (for detailed information on this specific threat, refer to CERT advisory CA-2001-26—www.cert.org). Rather than trying to describe in detail the specifics of the thousands of different security threats that exist today (in the first half of 2002 alone, the CERT Coordination Center recorded 2,148 reported vulnerabilities), this book describes generic tests that can be extrapolated and customized by the reader to accommodate individual and unique needs. In addition, this book does not expand on how a security vulnerability could be exploited (information that is likely to be more useful to a security abuser than a security tester) and endeavors to avoid making specific recommendations on how to fix a security vulnerability, since the most appropriate remedy will vary from organization to organization and such a decision (and subsequent implementation) would generally be considered to be the role of a security designer.

How This Book Is Organized

Although most readers will probably find it easier to read the chapters in sequential order, this book has been organized in a manner that permits readers to read any of the chapters in any order. Depending on the background and objectives of different readers, some may even choose to skip some of the chapters. For example, a test manager who is well versed in writing test plans used to test the functionality of a Web application may decide to skip the chapter on test planning and focus on the chapters that describe some of the new types of tests that could be included in his or her test plans. In the case of an application developer, he or she may not be concerned with the chapter on testing a Web site's physical security because someone else looks after that (just so long as someone actually does) and may be most interested in the chapters on application security.

To make it easier for readers to hone in on the chapters that are of most interest to them, this book has been divided into four parts. Part 1 is comprised of this chapter and provides an introduction and explanation of the framework used to construct this book.

Chapter 2, "Test Planning," provides the material for Part 2, "Planning the Testing Effort," and looks at the issues surrounding the planning of the testing effort.

Part 3, "Test Design," is the focus of this book and therefore forms the bulk of its content by itemizing the various candidate tests that the testing team should consider when evaluating what they are actually going to test as part of the security-testing effort of a Web site and its associated Web application(s). Because the testing is likely to require a variety of different skill sets, it's quite probable that different people will execute different groups of tests. With this consideration in mind, the tests have been grouped together based on the typical skill sets and backgrounds of the people who might be expected to execute them. This part includes the following chapters:

Chapter 3: Network Security

Chapter 4: System Software Security

Chapter 5: Client-Side Application Security

Chapter 6: Server-Side Application Security

Chapter 7: Sneak Attacks: Guarding against the Less-Thought-of Security Threats

Chapter 8: Intruder Confusion, Detection, and Response

Having discussed what needs to be tested, Part 4, "Test Implementation," addresses the issue of how to best execute these tests in terms of who should actually do the work, what tools should be used, and what order the tests should be performed in (ranking test priority). This part includes the following chapters:

Chapter 9: Assessment and Penetration Options

Chapter 10: Risk Analysis

As a means of support for these 10 chapters, the appendix provides some additional background information, specifically: a brief introduction to the basics of computer networks as utilized by many Web sites (in case some of the readers of this book are unfamiliar with the components used to build Web sites), a summarized list of the top-20 critical Internet security vulnerabilities (as determined by the SANS Institute), and some sample test deliverable templates (which a security-testing team could use as a starting point for developing their own customized documentation).

Finally, the resources section not only serves as a bibliography of all the books and Web sites referenced in this book, but it also lists other reference books that readers interested in testing Web security may find useful in their quest for knowledge.

Terminology Used in This Book

The following two sections describe some of the terms used in this book to describe the individuals who might seek to exploit a security vulnerability on a Web site—and hence the people that a security tester is trying to inhibit—and the names given to some of the more common deliverables that a security tester is likely to produce.

Hackers, Crackers, Script Kiddies, and Disgruntled Insiders

The term *computer hacker* was originally used to describe someone who really knew how the internals of a computer (hardware and/or software) worked and could be relied on to come up with ingenious workarounds (*hacks*) to either fix a problem with the system or extend its original capabilities. Somewhere along the line, the popular press relabeled this term to describe someone who tries to acquire unauthorized access to a computer or network of computers.

The terminology has become further blurred by the effort of some practitioners to differentiate the skill levels of those seeking unauthorized access. The term *cracker* is typically used to label an attacker who is knowledgeable enough to create his or her own hacks, whereas the term *script kiddie* is used to describe a person who primarily relies on the hacks of others (often passed around as a script or executable). The situation becomes even less clear if you try to pigeonhole disgruntled employees who don't need to gain unauthorized access in order to accomplish their malicious goals because they are already authorized to access the system.

Not all attackers are viewed equally. Aside from their varying technical expertise, they also may be differentiated by their ethics. Crudely speaking, based on their actions and intentions, attackers are often be categorized into one of the following color-coded groups:

White-hat hackers.   These are individuals who are authorized by the owner of a Web site or Web-accessible product to ascertain whether or not the site or product is adequately protected from known security loopholes and common generic exploits. They are also known as *ethical hackers*, or are part of a group known as a *tiger team* or *red team*.

Gray-hat hackers.   Also sometimes known as *wackers*, gray-hat hackers attack a new product or technology on their own initiative to determine if the product has any new security loopholes, to further their own education, or to satisfy their own curiosity. Although their often-stated aim is to improve the quality of the new technology or their own knowledge without directly causing harm to anyone, their methods can at times be disruptive. For example, some of these attackers will not inform the product's owner of a newly discovered security hole until they have had time to build and publicize a tool that enables the hole to be easily exploited by others.

HACKER

Webster's II New Riverside Dictionary **offers three alternative definitions for the word** *hacker*, **the first two of which are relevant for our purposes:**
   1a. Computer buff
   1b. One who illegally gains access to another's electronic system

---

COLOR-CODING ATTACKERS

The reference to colored hats comes from Hollywood's use of hats in old black-and-white cowboy movies to help an audience differentiate between the good guys (white hats) and the bad guys (black hats).

Black-hat hackers. Also known as *crackers*, these are attackers who typically seek to exploit known (and occasionally unknown) security holes for their own personal gain. *Script kiddies* are often considered to be the subset of black-hatters, whose limited knowledge forces them to be dependent almost exclusively upon the tools developed by more experienced attackers. Honeynet Project (2001) provides additional insight into the motives of black-hat hackers.

Of course, assigning a particular person a single designation can be somewhat arbitrary and these terms are by no means used consistently across the industry; many people have slightly different definitions for each category. The confusion is compounded further when considering individuals who do not always follow the actions of just one definition. For instance, if an attacker secretly practices the black art at night, but also publicly fights the good fight during the day, what kind of hatter does that make him?

Rather than use terms that potentially carry different meanings to different readers (such as hacker), this book will use the terms *attacker*, *intruder*, or *assailant* to describe someone who is up to no good on a Web site.

Testing Vocabulary

Many people who are new to the discipline of software testing are sometimes confused over exactly what is meant by some of the common terminology used to describe various software-testing artifacts. For example, they might ask the question, "What's the difference between a test case and a test run?" This confusion is in part due to various practitioners, organizations, book authors, and professional societies using slightly different vocabularies and often subtly different definitions for the terms defined within their own respective vocabularies. These terms and definitions vary for many reasons. Some definitions are embryonic (defined early in this discipline's history), whereas others reflect the desire by some practitioners to push the envelope of software testing to new areas.

The following simple definitions are for the testing artifacts more frequently referenced in this book. They are not intended to compete with or replace the more verbose and exacting definitions already defined in industry standards and other published materials, such as those defined by the Institute of Electrical and Electronics Engineers (www.ieee.org), the Project Management Institute (www.pmi.org), or Rational's Unified Process (www.rational.com). Rather, they are intended to provide the reader with a convenient reference of how these terms are used in this book. Figure 1.1 graphically summarizes the relationship between each of the documents.

Test plan. A *test plan* is a document that describes the *what, why, who, when*, and *how* of a testing project. Some testing teams may choose to describe their entire testing effort within a single test plan, whereas others find it easier to organize

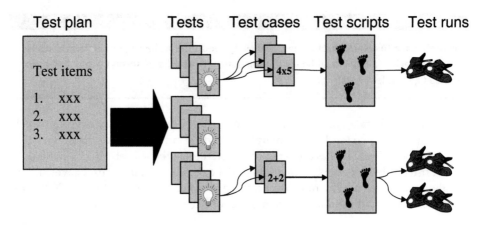

Figure 1.1   Testing documents.

groups of tests into two or more test plans, with each test plan focusing on a different aspect of the testing effort.

To foster better communication across projects, many organizations have defined test plan templates. These templates are then used as a starting point for each new test plan, and the testing team refines and customizes each plan(s) to fit the unique needs of their project.

Test item.   A *test item* is a hardware device or software program that is the subject of the testing effort. The term *system under test* is often used to refer to the collection of all test items.

Test.   A *test* is an evaluation with a clearly defined objective of one or more test items. A sample objective could look like the following: "Check that no unneeded services are running on any of the system's servers."

Test case.   A *test case* is a detailed description of a *test*. Some tests may necessitate utilizing several test cases in order to satisfy the stated objective of a single test. The description of the test case could be as simple as the following: "Check that NetBIOS has been disabled on the Web server." It could also provide additional details on how the test should be executed, such as the following: "Using the tool nmap, an external port scan will be performed against the Web server to determine if ports 137–139 have been closed."

Depending on the number and complexity of the test cases, a testing team may choose to specify their test cases in multiple test case documents, consolidate them into a single document, or possibly even embed them into the test plan itself.

Test script.   A *test script* is a series of steps that need to be performed in order to execute a test case. Depending on whether the test has been automated, this series of steps may be expressed as a sequence of tasks that need to be performed manually or as the source code used by an automated testing tool to run the test. Note that some practitioners reserve the term *test script* for automated scripts and use the term *test procedure* for the manual components.

Test run.   A *test run* is the actual execution of a test script. Each time a test case is executed, it creates a new instance of a test run.

Who Should Read This Book?

This book is aimed at three groups of people. The first group consists of the owners, CIOs, managers, and security officers of a Web site who are ultimately responsible for the security of their site. Because these people might not have a strong technical background and, consequently, not be aware of all the types of threats that their site faces, this book seeks to make these critical decision makers aware of what security testing entails and thereby enable them to delegate (and fund) a security-testing effort in a knowledgeable fashion.

The second group of individuals who should find this book useful are the architects and implementers of a Web site and application (local area network [LAN] administrators, developers, database administrators [DBAs], and so on) who may be aware of some (or all) of the security factors that should be considered when designing and building a Web site, but would appreciate having a checklist of security issues that they could use as they construct the site. These checklists can be used in much the same way that an experienced airplane pilot goes through a mandated preflight checklist before taking off. These are helpful because the consequences of overlooking a single item can be catastrophic.

The final group consists of the people who may be asked to complete an independent security assessment of the Web site (in-house testers, Q/A analysts, end users, or outside consultants), but may not be as familiar with the technology (and its associated vulnerabilities) as the implementation group. For the benefit of these people, this book attempts to describe the technologies commonly used by implementers to build Web sites to a level of detail that will enable them to test the technology effectively but without getting as detailed as a book on how to build a Web site.

Summary

With the heightened awareness for the need to securely protect an organization's electronic assets, the supply of available career security veterans is quickly becoming tapped out, which has resulted in an influx of new people into the field of security testing. This book seeks to provide an introduction to Web security testing for those people with relatively little experience in the world of information security (*infosec*), allowing them to hit the ground running. It also serves as an easy-to-use reference book that is full of checklists to assist career veterans such as the growing number of certified information systems security professionals (CISSPs) in making sure their security assessments are as comprehensive as they can be. Bragg (2002), Endorf (2001), Harris (2001), Krutz et al. (2001 and 2002), Peltier (2002), the CISSP Web portal (www.cissp.com), and the International Information Systems Security Certifications Consortium (www.isc2.org) provide additional information on CISSP certification.

Planning the
Testing Effort

Test Planning

Failing to adequately plan a testing effort will frequently result in the project's sponsors being unpleasantly surprised. The surprise could be in the form of an unexpected cost overrun by the testing team, or finding out that a critical component of a Web site wasn't tested and consequently permitted an intruder to gain unauthorized access to company confidential information.

This chapter looks at the key decisions that a security-testing team needs to make while planning their project, such as agreeing on the scope of the testing effort, assessing the risks (and mitigating contingencies) that the project may face, spelling out any rules of engagement (terms of reference) for interacting with a production environment, and specifying which configuration management practices to use. Failing to acknowledge any one of these considerations could have potentially dire consequences to the success of the testing effort and should therefore be addressed as early as possible in the project. Black (2002), Craig et al. (2002), Gerrard et al. (2002), Kaner et al. (1999, 2001), the Ideahamster Organization (www.ideahamster.org), and the Rational Unified Process (www.rational.com) provide additional information on planning a testing project.

Requirements

A common practice among testing teams charged with evaluating how closely a system will meet its user's (or owner's) expectations is to design a set of tests that confirm whether or not all of the features explicitly documented in a system's requirements specification have been implemented correctly. In other words, the objectives of the testing effort are dependent upon on the system's stated requirements. For example, if the system is required to do 10 things and the testing team runs a series of tests that confirm that the system can indeed accurately perform all 10 desired tasks, then the system will typically be considered to have *passed*. Unfortunately, as the following sections seek to illustrate, this process is nowhere near as simple a task to accomplish as the previous statement would lead you to believe.

Clarifying Requirements

Ideally, a system's requirements should be clearly and explicitly documented in order for the system to be evaluated to determine how closely it matches the expectations of the system's users and owners (as enshrined by the requirements documentation). Unfortunately, a testing team rarely inherits a comprehensive, unambiguous set of requirements; often the requirements team—or their surrogates, who in some instances may end up being the testing team—ends up having to clarify these requirements before the testing effort can be completed (or in some cases started). The following are just a few situations that may necessitate revisiting the system's requirements:

Implied requirements.   Sometimes requirements are so obvious (to the requirements author) that the documentation of these requirements is deemed to be a waste of time. For example, it's rare to see a requirement such as "no spelling mistakes are to be permitted in the intruder response manual" explicitly documented, but at the same time, few organizations would regard spelling mistakes as desirable.

Incomplete or ambiguous requirements.   A requirement that states, "all the Web servers should have service pack 3 installed," is ambiguous. It does not make it clear whether the service pack relates to the operating system or to the Web service (potentially different products) or which specific brand of system software is required.

Nonspecific requirements.   Specifying "strong passwords must be used" may sound like a good requirement, but from a testing perspective, what exactly is a strong password: a password longer than 7 characters or one longer than 10? To be considered strong, can the password use all uppercase or all lowercase characters, or must a mixture of both types of letters be used?

Global requirements.   Faced with the daunting task of specifying everything that a system should not do, some requirements authors resort to all-encompassing statements like the following: "The Web site must be secure." Although everyone would agree that this is a good thing, the reality is that the only way the Web site could be made utterly secure is to disconnect it from any other network (including the Internet) and lock it behind a sealed door in a room to which no one has access. Undoubtedly, this is not what the author of the requirement had in mind.

Failing to ensure that a system's requirements are verifiable before the construction of the system is started (and consequently open to interpretation) is one of the leading reasons why systems need to be reworked or, worse still, a system enters service only for its users (or owners) to realize in production that the system is not actually doing what they need it to do. An organization would therefore be well advised to involve in the requirements gathering process the individuals who will be charged with verifying the system's capability. These individuals (ideally professional testers) may then review any documented requirement to ensure that it has been specified in such a way that it can be easily and impartially tested.

More clearly defined requirements should not only result in less rework on the part of development, but also speed the testing effort, as specific tests not only can be designed earlier, but their results are likely to require much less interpretation (debate). Barman (2001), Peltier (2001), and Wood (2001) provide additional information on writing security requirements.

Security Policies

Documenting requirements that are not ambiguous, incomplete, nonquantifiable, or even contradictory is not a trivial task, but even with clearly defined requirements, a security-testing team faces an additional challenge. Security testing is primarily concerned with testing that a system *does not do* something (negative testing)—as opposed to confirming that the system can do something (positive testing). Unfortunately, the list of things that a system (or someone) should not do is potentially infinite in comparison to a finite set of things that a system should do (as depicted in Figure 2.1). Therefore, security requirements (often referred to as *security policies*) are by their very nature extremely hard to test, because the number of things a system should not do far exceeds the things it should do.

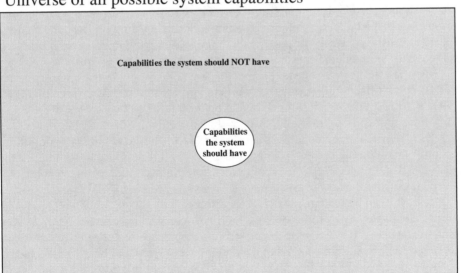

Universe of all possible system capabilities

Capabilities the system should NOT have

Capabilities the system should have

Figure 2.1 System capabilities.

When testing security requirements, a tester is likely to have to focus on deciding what negative tests should be performed to ascertain if the system is capable of doing something it *should not do* (capabilities that are rarely well documented—if at all). Since the number of tests needed to prove that a system does not do what it isn't supposed to is potentially enormous, and the testing effort is not, it is critically important that the security-testing team not only clarify any vague requirements, but also conduct a risk analysis (the subject of Chapter 10) to determine what subset of the limitless number of negative tests will be performed by the testing effort. They should then document exactly what (positive and negative tests) will and will not be covered and subsequently ensure that the sponsor of the effort approves of this proposed scope.

The Anatomy of a Test Plan

Once a set of requirements has been agreed upon (and where needed, clarified), thereby providing the testing team with a solid foundation for them to build upon, the testing team can then focus its attention on the test-planning decisions that the team will have to make before selecting and designing the tests that they intend to execute. These decisions and the rationale for making them are typically recorded in a document referred to as a *test plan*.

A test plan could be structured according to an industry standard such as the Institute of Electrical and Electronics Engineers (IEEE) Standard for Software Documentation—Std. 829, based on an internal template, or even be *pioneering* in its layout. What's more important than its specific layout is the process that building a test plan forces the testing team to go through. Put simply, filling in the blank spaces under the various section headings of the test plan should generate constructive debates within the testing team and with other interested parties. As a result, issues can be brought to the surface early before they become more costly to fix (measured in terms of additional resources, delayed release, or system quality). For some testing projects, the layout of the test plan is extremely important. For example, a regulatory agency, insurance underwriter, or mandated corporate policy may require that the test plan be structured in a specific way. For those testing teams that are not required to use a particular layout, using an existing organizational template or industry standard (such as the Rational's Unified Process [RUP]) may foster better interproject communication. At the same time, the testing team should be permitted to customize the template or standard to reflect the needs of their specific project and not feel obliged to generate superfluous documentation purely because it's suggested in a specific template or standard. Craig et al. (2002) and Kaner et al. (2002) both provide additional guidance on customizing a test plan to better fit the unique needs of each testing project.

A test plan can be as large as several hundred pages in length or as simple as a single piece of paper (such as the one-page test plan described in Nguyen [2000]). A voluminous test plan can be a double-edged sword. A copiously documented test plan may contain a comprehensive analysis of the system to be tested and be extremely helpful to the testing team in the later stages of the project, but it could also represent the proverbial *millstone* that is hung around the resource neck of the testing team, consuming ever-increasing amounts of effort to keep up-to-date with the latest project developments or risk becoming obsolete. Contractual and regulatory obligations aside, the testing team should decide at what level of detail a test plan ceases to be an aid and starts to become a net drag on the project's productivity.

The testing team should be willing and able (contractual obligations aside) to modify the test plan in light of newly discovered information (such as the test results of some of the earlier scheduled tests), allowing the testing effort to hone in on the areas of the system that this newly discovered information indicates needs more testing. This is especially true if the testing effort is to adopt an iterative approach to testing, where the later iterations won't be planned in any great detail until the results of the earlier iterations are known.

As previously mentioned in this section, the content (meat) of a test plan is far more important that the structure (skeleton) that this information is hung on. The testing team should therefore always consider adapting their test plan(s) to meet the specific needs of each project. For example, before developing their initial test plan outline, the testing team may wish to review the test plan templates or checklists described by Kaner et al. (2002), Nguyen (2000), Perry (2000), Stottlemyer (2001), the Open Source Security Testing Methodology (www.osstmm.org), IEEE Std. 829 (www.standards .ieee.org), and the Rational unified process (www.rational.com). The testing team may then select and customize an existing template, or embark on constructing a brand-new structure and thereby produce the test plan that will best fit the unique needs of the project in hand.

One of the most widely referenced software-testing documentation standards to date is that of the IEEE Std. 829 (this standard can be downloaded for a fee from www.standards.ieee.org). For this reason, this chapter will discuss the content of a

---

IEEE STD. 829-1998 SECTION HEADINGS

For reference purposes, the sections that the IEEE 829-1998 standard recommends have been listed below:

a) Test plan identifier
b) Introduction
c) Test items
d) Features to be tested
e) Features not to be tested
f) Approach
g) Item pass/fail criteria
h) Suspension criteria and resumption requirements
i) Test deliverables
j) Testing tasks
k) Environmental needs
l) Responsibilities
m) Staffing and training needs
n) Schedule
o) Risks and contingencies
p) Approvals

security test plan, in the context of an *adapted* version of the IEEE Std. 829-1998 (the 1998 version is a revision of the original 1983 standard).

Test Plan Identifier

Each test plan and, more importantly, each version of a test plan should be assigned an identifier that is unique within the organization. Assuming the organization already has a documentation configuration management process (manual or automated) in place, the method for determining the ID should already have been determined. If such a process has yet to be implemented, then it may pay to spend a little time trying to improve this situation before generating additional documentation (configuration management is discussed in more detail later in this chapter in the section *Configuration Management*).

Introduction

Given that test-planning documentation is not normally considered exciting reading, this section may be the only part of the plan that many of the intended readers of the plan actually read. If this is likely to be the case, then this section may need to be written in an executive summary style, providing the casual reader with a clear and concise understanding of the exact goal of this project and how the testing team intends to meet that goal. Depending upon the anticipated audience, it may be necessary to explain basic concepts such as why security testing is needed or highlight significant items of information buried in later sections of the document, such as under whose authority this testing effort is being initiated. The key consideration when writing this section is to anticipate what the targeted reader wants (and needs) to know.

Project Scope

Assuming that a high-level description of the project's testing objectives (or goals) was explicitly defined in the test plan's introduction, this section can be used to restate those objectives in much more detail. For example, the introduction may have stated that security testing will be performed on the wiley.com Web site, whereas in this section, the specific hardware and software items that make up the wiley.com Web site may be listed. For smaller Web sites, the difference may be trivial, but for larger sites that have been integrated into an organization's existing enterprise network or that share assets with other Web sites or organizations, the exact edge of the testing project's scope may not be obvious and should therefore be documented. Chapter 3 describes some of the techniques that can be used to build an inventory of the devices that need to be tested. These techniques can also precisely define the scope of the testing covered by this test plan.

It is often a good idea to list the items that will *not* be tested by the activities covered by this test plan. This could be because the items will be tested under the auspices of another test plan (either planned or previously executed), sufficient resources were unavailable to test every item, or other reasons. Whatever the rationale used to justify a particular item's exclusion from a test plan, the justification should be clearly documented as this section is likely to be heavily scrutinized in the event that a future security failure occurs with an item that was for some reason excluded from the testing effort. Perhaps because of this concern, the "out of scope" section of a test plan may generate more debate with senior management than the "in scope" section of the plan.

Change Control Process

The scope of a testing effort is often defined very early in the testing project, often when comparatively little is known about the robustness and complexity of the system to be tested. Because changing the scope of a project often results in project delays and budget overruns, many teams attempt to freeze the scope of the project. However, if during the course of the testing effort, a situation arises that potentially warrants a change in the project's scope, then many organizations will decide whether or not to accommodate this change based on the recommendation of a change control board (CCB). For example, discovering halfway through the testing effort that a mirror Web site was planned to go into service next month (but had not yet been built) would raise the question "who is going to test the mirror site?" and consequently result in a change request being submitted to the CCB.

When applying a CCB-like process to changes in the scope of the security-testing effort in order to provide better project control, the members of a security-testing CCB should bear in mind that unlike the typical end user, an attacker is not bound by a project's scope or the decisions of a CCB. This requires them to perhaps be a little more flexible than they would normally be when faced with a nonsecurity orientation change request. After all, the testing project will most likely be considered a failure if an intruder is able to compromise a system using a route that had not been tested, just because it had been deemed to have been considered out of scope by the CCB.

A variation of the CCB change control process implementation is to break the projects up into small increments so that modifying the scope for the increment currently being tested becomes unnecessary because the change request can be included in the next scheduled increment. The role of the CCB is effectively performed by the group responsible for determining the content of future increments.

THE ROLE OF THE CCB

The CCB (also sometimes known as a *configuration control board*) is the group of individuals responsible for evaluating and deciding whether or not a requested change should be permitted and subsequently ensuring that any approved changes are implemented appropriately.

In some organizations, the CCB may be made up of a group of people drawn from different project roles, such as the product manager, project sponsor, system owner, internal security testers, local area network (LAN) administrators, and external consultants, and have elaborate approval processes. In other organizations, the role of the CCB may be performed by a single individual such as the project leader who simply gives a nod to the request. Regardless of who performs this role, the authority to change the scope of the testing effort should be documented in the test plan.

Features to Be Tested

A system's security is only as strong as its weakest link. Although this may be an obvious statement, it's surprising how frequently a security-testing effort is directed to only test some and not all of the following features of a Web site:

- Network security (covered in Chapter 3)
- System software security (covered in Chapter 4)
- Client-side application security (covered in Chapter 5)
- Client-side to server-side application communication security (covered in Chapter 5)
- Server-side application security (covered in Chapter 6)
- Social engineering (covered in Chapter 7)
- Dumpster diving (covered in Chapter 7)
- Inside accomplices (covered in Chapter 7)
- Physical security (covered in Chapter 7)
- Mother nature (covered in Chapter 7)
- Sabotage (covered in Chapter 7)
- Intruder confusion (covered in Chapter 8)
- Intrusion detection (covered in Chapter 8)
- Intrusion response (covered in Chapter 8)

Before embarking on an extended research and planning phase that encompasses every feature of security testing, the security-testing team should take a reality check. Just how likely is it that they have the sufficient time and funding to test everything? Most likely the security-testing team will not have all the resources they would like, in which case choices must be made to decide which areas of the system will be drilled and which areas will receive comparatively light testing. Ideally, this selection process should be systematic and impartial in nature. A common way of achieving this is through the use of a risk analysis (the subject of Chapter 10), the outcome of which should be a set of candidate tests that have been prioritized so that the tests that are anticipated to provide the greatest benefit are scheduled first and the ones that provide more marginal assistance are executed last (if at all).

Features Not to Be Tested

If the testing effort is to be spread across multiple test plans, there is a significant risk that some tests may drop through the proverbial cracks in the floor, because the respective scopes of the test plans do not dovetail together perfectly. A potentially much more dangerous situation is the scenario of an entire feature of the system going completely untested because everyone in the organization thought someone else was responsible for testing this facet of the system.

Therefore, it is a good practice to not only document what items will be tested by a specific test plan, but also what features of these items will be tested and what features will fall outside the scope of this test plan, thereby making it explicitly clear what is and is not covered by the scope of an individual test plan.

Approach

This section of the test plan is normally used to describe the strategy that will be used by the testing team to meet the test objectives that have been previously defined. It's not necessary to get into the nitty-gritty of every test strategy decision, but the major decisions such as what levels of testing (described later in this section) will be performed and when (or how frequently) in the system's life cycle the testing will be performed should be determined.

Levels of Testing

Many security tests can be conducted without having to recreate an entire replica of the system under test. The consequence of this mutual dependency (or lack of) on other components being completed impacts when and how some tests can be run.

One strategy for grouping tests into multiple testing phases (or levels) is to divide up the tests based on how complete the system must be before the test can be run. Tests that can be executed on a single component of the system are typically referred to as *unit-* or *module-level* tests, tests that are designed to test the communication between two or more components of the system are often referred to as *integration-*, *string-* or *link-level* tests, and finally those that would benefit from being executed in a full replica of the system are often called *system-level* tests. For example, checking that a server has had the latest security patch applied to its operating system can be performed in isolation and can be considered a unit-level test. Testing for the potential existence of a buffer overflow occurring in any of the server-side components of a Web application (possibly as a result of a malicious user entering an abnormally large string via the Web application's front-end) would be considered an integration- or system-level test depending upon how much of the system needed to be in place for the test to be executed and for the testing team to have a high degree of confidence in the ensuing test results.

One of the advantages of unit-level testing is that it can be conducted much earlier in a system's development life cycle since the testing is not dependent upon the completion or installation of any other component. Because of the fact that the earlier that a defect is detected, the easier (and therefore more cheaply) it can be fixed, an obvious advantage exists to executing as many tests as possible at the unit level instead of postponing these tests until system-level testing is conducted, which because of its inherent dependencies typically must occur later in the development life cycle.

Unfortunately, many organizations do not conduct as many security tests at the unit level as they could. The reasons for this are many and vary from organization to organization. However, one recurring theme that is cited in nearly every organization where unit testing is underutilized is that the people who are best situated to conduct this level of testing are often unaware of what should be tested and how to best accomplish this task. Although the *how* is often resolved through education (instructor-led training, books, mentoring, and so on), the *what* can to a large part be addressed by documenting the security tests that need to be performed in a unit-level checklist or more formally in a unit-level test plan—a step that is particularly important if the people who will be conducting these unit-level tests are not members of the team responsible for identifying all of the security tests that need to be performed.

Dividing tests up into phases based upon component dependencies is just one way a testing team may strategize their testing effort. Alternative or complementary strategies include breaking the testing objectives up into small increments, basing the priority and type of tests in later increments on information gleaned from running earlier tests (an *heuristic* or *exploratory* approach), and grouping the tests based on who would actually do the testing, whether it be developers, outsourced testing firms, or end users. The large variety of possible testing strategies in part explains the proliferation of testing level names that are in practice today, such as unit, integration, build, alpha, beta, system, acceptance, staging, and post-implementation to name but a few. Black (2003), Craig et al. (2002), Kaner et al. (2001), Gerrard et al. (2002), and Perry (2000) provide additional information on the various alternate testing strategies that could be employed by a testing team.

For some projects, it may make more sense to combine two (or more) levels of testing into a single test plan. The situation that usually prompts this test plan cohabitation is when the testing levels have a great deal in common. For example, on one project, the set of unit-level tests might be grouped with the set of integration-level tests because the people who will be conducting the tests are the same, both sets of tests are scheduled to occur at approximately the same time, or the testing environments are almost identical.

Relying on only a single level of testing to capture all of a system's security defects is likely to be less efficient than segregating the tests into two (or more) levels; it may quite possibly increase the probability that security holes will be missed. This is one of the reasons why many organizations choose to utilize two or more levels of testing.

When to Test

For many in the software industry, testing is the activity that happens somewhere in the software development life cycle between coding and going live. Security tests are often some of the very last tests to be executed. This view might be an accurate observation of yesterday's system development, when development cycles were measured in years and the tasks that the system was being developed to perform were well understood and rarely changed, but it most certainly should not be the case today.

In today's world of ever-changing business requirements, rapid application development, and extreme programming, testing should occur throughout the software development life cycle (SDLC) rather than as a single-step activity that occurs toward the end of the process, when all too often too little time (or budget) is left to adequately test the product or fix a major flaw in the system.

When to Retest

Although many foresighted project managers have scheduled testing activities to occur early in the development cycle, it is less likely that as much thought will be given to planning the continuous testing that will be needed once the system goes live. Even if the functional requirements of a system remain unchanged, a system that was deemed secure last week may become insecure next week. The following are just a few examples of why this could happen:

- A previously unknown exploit in an operating system used by the system becomes known to the attacker community.

- Additional devices (firewalls, servers, routers, and so on) are added to the system to enable it to meet higher usage demands. Unfortunately, these newly added devices may not have been configured in exactly the same way as the existing devices.

- A service pack installed to patch a recently discovered security hole also resets other configuration settings back to their default values.

- Due to the large number of false alarms, the on-duty security personnel have become desensitized to intruder alerts and subsequently do not respond to any automated security warnings.

- User-defined passwords that expire after a period of time and were originally long and cryptic have become short, easy to remember, and recycled.

- Log files have grown to the point that no free disk space is left, thereby inhibiting the capability of an intruder detection system to detect an attack.

Security testing should not be regarded as a one-time event, but rather as a recurring activity that will be ongoing as long as the system remains active. The frequency with which the retests occur will to a large part be driven by the availability of resources to conduct the tests (cost) and the degree to which the system changes over time. Some events may, however, warrant an immediate (if limited in scope) retest. For example, the organization may decide to upgrade the operating system used by a number of the servers on the Web site, or a firewall vendor releases a "hot fix" for its product.

What to Retest

As a starting point, the testing team should consider each test that was utilized during the system's initial testing effort as a potential candidate for inclusion into a future set of tests that will be reexecuted on a regular basis after the system goes into production (sometimes referred to as a *postdeployment regression test set*) to ensure that vulnerabilities that were supposedly fixed (or never existed) do not subsequently appear.

For tests that have been automated, there may be very little overhead in keeping these tests as part of a regression test set, especially if the automated test script is being maintained by another organization at no additional cost, which may well be the case

---

THE REGRESSION TEST SET

Regression tests are usually intended to be executed many times and are designed to confirm that previously identified defects have been fixed and stay fixed, that functionality that should not have changed has indeed remained unaffected by any other changes to the system, or both.

for a security assessment tool (such as those listed in Table 9.4) that an organization has a maintenance agreement for, or is available free of charge.

With regard to manual tests, the determination as to whether or not to repeat a test will to a large part depend upon how problems previously detected by the test were fixed (and consequently what the likelihood is that the problem will reappear). For example, if the testing team had originally found that weak passwords were being used and the solution was to send an email telling everyone to clean up their act, then chances are within a couple of userID/password cycles, weak (easy to remember) passwords will again start to show up, necessitating the testing team to be ever vigilant for this potential vulnerability. If, on the other hand, a single user-sign-on system was implemented with tough password requirements, then the same issue is not likely to occur again and therefore may not warrant the original tests being included in future regression tests.

Pass/Fail Criteria

A standard testing practice is to document the expected or desired results of an individual test case prior to actually executing the test. As a result, a conscious (or subconscious) temptation to modify the pass criteria for a test based on its now known result is avoided.

Unfortunately, determining whether security is good enough is a very subjective measure—one that is best left to the project's sponsor (or the surrogate) rather than the testing team. Making a system more secure all too often means making the system perform more slowly, be less user-friendly, harder to maintain, or more costly to implement. Therefore, unlike traditional functional requirements, where the theoretical goal is absolute functional correctness, an organization may not want its system to be as secure as it could be because of the detrimental impact that such a secure implementation would have on another aspect of the system. For example, suppose a Web site requires perspective new clients to go through an elaborate client authentication process the first time they register with the Web site. (It might even involve mailing user IDs and first-time passwords separately through the postal service.) Such a requirement might reduce the number of fraudulent instances, but it also might have a far more drastic business impact on the number of new clients willing to go through this process, especially if a competitor Web site offers a far more user-friendly (but potentially less secure) process. The net result is that the right amount of security for each system is subjective and will vary from system to system and from organization to organization.

Instead of trying to make this subjective call, the testing team might be better advised to concentrate on how to present the findings of their testing effort to the individual(s) responsible for making this decision. For example, presenting the commissioner of a security assessment with the raw output of an automated security assessment tool that had performed several hundred checks and found a dozen irregularities is probably not as helpful as a handcrafted report that lists the security vulnerabilities detected (or suspected) and their potential consequences if the system goes into service (or remains in service) as is.

If an organization's testing methodology mandates that a pass/fail criteria be specified for a security-testing test effort, it may be more appropriate for the test plan to use a criteria such as the following: "The IS Director will retain the decision as to whether the total and/or criticality of any or all detected vulnerabilities warrant the rework and/or retesting of the Web site." This is more useful than using a dubious pass criteria such as the following: "95 percent of the test cases must pass before the system can be deemed to have passed testing."

Suspension Criteria and Resumption Requirements

This section of the test plan may be used to identify the circumstances under which it would be prudent to suspend the entire testing effort (or just portions of it) and what requirements must subsequently be met in order to reinitiate the suspended activities. For example, running a penetration test would not be advisable just before the operating systems on the majority of the Web site's servers are scheduled to be upgraded with the latest service pack. Instead, testing these items would be more effective if it was suspended until after the servers have been upgraded and reconfigured.

Test Deliverables

Each of the deliverables that the testing team generates as a result of the security-testing effort should be documented in the test plan. The variety and content of these deliverables will vary from project to project and to a large extent depend on whether the documents themselves are a *by-product* or an *end product* of the testing effort.

As part of its contractual obligations, a company specializing in security testing may need to provide a client with detailed accounts of all the penetration tests that were attempted (regardless of their success) against the client's Web site. For example, the specific layout of the test log may have been specified as part of the statement of work that the testing company proposed to the client while bidding for the job. In this case, the test log is an end product and will need to be diligently (and time-consumingly) populated by the penetration-testing team or they risk not being paid in full for their work.

In comparison, a team of in-house testers trying to find a vulnerability in a Web application's user login procedure may use a screen-capture utility to record their test execution. In the event that a suspected defect is found, the tool could be used to play back the sequence of events that led up to the point of failure, thereby assisting the tester with filling out an incident or defect report. Once the report has been completed, the test execution recording could be attached to the defect (providing further assistance to the employee assigned to fix this defect) or be simply discarded along with all the recordings of test executions that didn't find anything unusual. In this case, the test log was produced as a by-product of the testing effort and improved the project's productivity.

Before a testing team commits to producing any deliverable, it should consider which deliverables will assist them in managing and executing the testing effort and which ones are likely to increase their documentation burden. It's not unheard of for testing teams who need to comply with some contractual documentary obligation to write up test designs and creatively populate test logs well after test execution has been completed.

The following sections provide brief overviews of some of the more common deliverables created by testing teams. Their relationships are depicted in Figure 2.2.

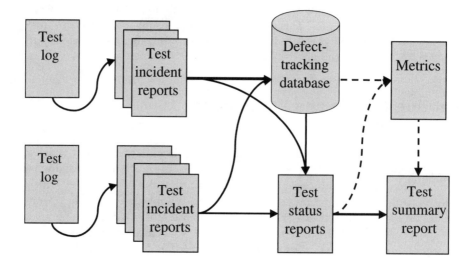

Figure 2.2   Testing deliverables.

Test Log

The test log is intended to record the events that occur during test execution in a chronological order. The log can take the form of shorthand notes on the back of an envelope, a central database repository manually populated via a graphical user interface (GUI) front end, or a bitmap screen-capture utility unobtrusively running in the background taking screen snapshots every few seconds. Appendix C contains a sample layout for a test log.

Test Incident Report

An incident is something that happens during the course of test execution that merits further investigation. The incident may be an observable symptom of a defect in the item being tested, unexpected but acceptable behavior, a defect in the test itself, or an incident that is so trivial in nature or impossible to recreate that its exact cause is never diagnosed.

The test incident report is a critical project communication document because the majority of incidents are likely to be investigated by someone other than the person who initially observed (and presumable wrote up) the incident report. For this reason, it is important to use a clear and consistent report format and an agreement be reached between representatives of those who are likely to encounter and report the incidents and those who are likely to be charged with investigating them. Appendix C contains an example layout of a test incident report.

Although the exact fields used on the report may vary from project to project, depending on local needs, conceptually the report needs to do one thing: accurately document the incident that has just occurred in such a way that someone else is able to understand what happened, thereby enabling the reader to thoroughly investigate the incident (typically by trying to reproduce it) and determine the exact cause of the event. Craig et al. (2002) and Kaner et al. (1999) provide additional information on the content and use of test incident reports.

Defect-Tracking Reports

A defect differs from an incident in that a defect is an actual flaw (or bug) in the system, whereas an incident is just an indicator that a defect may exist. At the moment an incident is initially recorded, it is typically not clear whether this incident is the result of a defect or some other cause (such as a human error in the testing). Therefore, it's a common practice to include incident reports that have not yet been investigated along with identified defects in a single defect-tracking report. In effect, a guilty-until-proven-innocent mentality is applied to the incidents.

The question of who should be assigned ownership of a defect (who is responsible for making sure it is resolved) may be a politically charged issue. Often the testing team has the task of acting as the custodian of all known incident and defect reports. To make managing these reports easier, most testing teams utilize an automated tool such as one of those listed in Table 2.1.

Using a commercial defect-tracking tool (such as one of the tools listed in Table 2.1) or an in-house-developed tool typically enables the testing team to automatically produce all sorts of defect-tracking reports. Examples include project status reports showing the status of every reported incident/defect; progress reports showing the number of defects that have been found, newly assigned, or fixed since the last progress report was produced; agendas for the next project meeting where defect-fixing priorities will be assessed; and many interesting defect statistics.

Just because a tool can produce a particular report does not necessarily mean that the report will be useful to distribute (via paper or email). Too many reports produced too frequently can often generate so much paper that the reports that are truly useful get lost in the paper shredder. Therefore, a testing team should consider what reports are actually going to be useful to the team itself and/or useful methods of communication to individuals outside of the testing team, and then document in this section of the test plan which reports they initially intend to produce. If the needs of the project change midway through the testing effort, requiring new reports, modifications to existing ones, or the retirement of unneeded ones, then the test plan should be updated to reflect the use of this new set of reports.

Metrics

Some defect metrics are so easy to collect that it's almost impossible to avoid publishing them. For example, the metrics of the number of new incidents found this week, the mean number of defects found per tested Web page, or the defects found per testing hour are easily found and gathered. The problem with statistics is that they can sometimes cause more problems than they solve. For instance, if 15 new bugs were found this week, 25 last week, and 40 the previous week, would senior management then determine that based on these statistics that the system being tested was nearly

Table 2.1 Sample Defect-Tracking Tools

NAME	ASSOCIATED WEB SITE
Bug Cracker	www.fesoft.com
Bugbase	www.threerock.com
BugCollector	www.nesbitt.com
Buggy	www.novosys.de
BUGtrack	www.skyeytech.com
BugLink	www.pandawave.com
Bugzilla	www.mozilla.org
ClearQuest	www.rational.com
D-Tracker	www.empirix.com
Elementool	www.elementool.com
PT BugTracker	www.avensoft.com
Razor	www.visible.com
SWBTracker	www.softwarewithbrains.com
Team Remote Debugger	www.remotedebugger.com
Team Tracker	www.hstech.com.au
TestDirector	www.mercuryinteractive.com
TestTrack Pro	www.seapine.com
Visual Intercept	www.elsitech.com
ZeroDefect	www.prostyle.com

ready for release? The reality could be quite different. If test execution was prioritized so that the critical tests were run first, moderately important tests were run next, and the low-priority tests were run last, then with this additional information, it would be revealed that the unimportant stuff works relatively well compared to the system's critical components. This situation is hardly as desirable as might have been interpreted from the numbers at first glance.

Before cracking out metric after metric just because a tool produces it or because it just seems like the right thing to do, the testing team should first consider the value of these metrics to this project or to future projects. Moller et al. (1993) cites six general uses for software metrics: (1) goal setting, (2) improving quality, (3) improving productivity, (4) project planning, (5) managing, or (6) improving customer confidence. More specific goals may include identifying training needs, measuring test effectiveness, or pinpointing particularly error-prone areas of the system. If a proposed metric is not a measure that can be directly used to support one or more of these uses, then it runs the risk of being irrelevant or, worse still, misinterpreted. Black (2002, 2003), Craig et al. (2002), and Kan (1995) provide additional information on collecting and reporting software-testing metrics.

This section of the test plan can be used to document what metrics will be collected and (optionally) published during the testing effort. Note that some metrics associated with process improvement may not be analyzed until after this specific project has been completed. The results are then used to improve future projects.

Test Summary Report

The *test summary report*—also sometimes known as a *test analysis report*—enables the testing team to summarize all of its findings. The report typically contains information such as the following:

- A summary of the testing activities that actually took place. This may vary from the originally planned activities due to changes such as a reduction (or expansion) of testing resources, an altered testing scope, or discoveries that were made during testing (this will be especially true if extensive heuristic or exploratory testing was utilized).

- A comprehensive list of all of the defects and limitations that were found (sometimes euphemistically referred to as a *features list*). The list may also include all the significant incidents that could still not be explained after investigation.

- High-level project control information such as the number of hours and/or elapsed time expended on the testing effort, capital expenditure on the test environment, and any variance from the budget that was originally approved.

- Optionally, an assessment of the accumulative severity of all the known defects and possibly an estimation of the number and severity of the defects that may still be lurking in the system undetected.

- Finally, some test summary reports also include a recommendation as to whether or not the system is in a good enough state to be placed into or remain in production. Although the ultimate decision for approval should reside with the system's owner or surrogate, often the testing team has the most intimate knowledge of the strengths and weaknesses of the system. Therefore, the team is perhaps the best group to make an objective assessment of just how good, or bad, the system actually is.

The completion of the test summary report is often on a project plan's critical path. Therefore, the testing team may want to build this document in parallel with test execution rather than writing it at the end of the execution phase. Depending upon how long test execution is expected to take, it may be helpful to those charged with fixing the system's vulnerabilities to see beta versions of the report prior to its final publication. These beta versions often take the form of a weekly (or daily) status report, with the test summary report ultimately being the very last status report. Appendix C contains an example layout of a test summary report.

Environmental Needs

A *test environment* is a prerequisite if the security-testing team wants to be proactive and attempt to catch security defects before they are deployed in a production environment. In addition, tests can be devised and executed without worrying about whether or not executing the tests might inadvertently have an adverse effect on the system being tested, such as crashing a critical program. Indeed, some tests may be specifically designed to try and bring down the target system (a technique sometimes referred to as destructive testing). For example, a test that tried to emulate a denial-of-service (DoS) attack would be much safer to evaluate in a controlled test environment, than against a production system (even if in theory the production system had safeguards in place that should protect it against such an attack).

It would certainly be convenient if the testing team had a dedicated test lab that was an exact full-scale replica of the production environment, which they could use for testing. Unfortunately, usually as a result of budgetary constraints, the test environment is often not quite the same as the production environment it is meant to duplicate (in an extreme situation it could solely consist of an individual desktop PC). For example, instead of using four servers (as in the production environment) dedicated to running each of the following components—Web server, proxy server, application server, and database server—the test environment may consist of only one machine, which regrettably cannot be simultaneously configured four different ways. Even if a test environment can be created with an equivalent number of network devices, some of the devices used in the test lab may be cheap imitations of the products actually used in the production environment and therefore behave slightly differently. For example, a $100 firewall might be used for a test instead of the $50,000 one used in production.

If the test environment is not expected to be an exact replica of the production environment, consideration should be given to which tests will need to be rerun on the production system, as running them on the imperfect test environment without incident will not guarantee the same results for the production environment. A second consideration is that the test environment could be too perfect. For example, if the implementation process involves any steps that are prone to human error, then just because the proxy server in the test lab has been configured to implement every security policy correctly does not mean that the production version has also been implemented correctly.

In all probability, some critical site infrastructure security tests will need to be rerun on the production environment (such as checking the strength of system administrators' passwords, or the correct implementation of a set of firewall rules). If the Web site being tested is brand-new, this extra step should not pose a problem because these tests can be run on the production environment prior to the site going live. For a Web site that has already gone live, the security-testing team must develop some *rules of engagement* (*terms of reference*) that specify when and how the site may be prodded and probed, especially if the site was previously undertested or not tested at all. These rules serve as a means of eliminating false intruder alarms, avoiding accidental service outages during peak site usage, and inadvertently ignoring legitimate intruder alarms (because it was thought that the alarm was triggered by the security-testing team and not a real intruder).

Configuration Management

Configuration management is the process of identifying (what), controlling (library management), tracking (who and when), and reporting (who needs to know) the components of a system at discrete points in time for the primary purpose of maintaining the integrity of the system. A good configuration management process is not so obtrusive, bureaucratic, or all encompassing that it has a net negative effect on development or testing productivity, but rather speeds such activities.

Developing, testing, or maintaining anything but the most simplistic of Web sites is virtually impossible without implementing some kind of configuration management process and should therefore be a prerequisite for any significant testing effort, and consequently be addressed by the associated test plan. For example, a Webmaster may choose to install an operating system service pack midway through a penetration test, or a developer may directly perform a quick fix on the Web application in production. Both decisions can cause a great deal of confusion and consequently prove to be quite costly to straighten out.

Many organizations have become accustomed to using a configuration management tool to help them manage the ever-increasing number of software components that need to be combined in order to build a fully functional Web application. A typical source code promotion process would require all developers to check in and check out application source code from a central development library. At regular intervals, the configuration manager (the build manager or librarian) baselines the application and then builds and promotes the application into a system-testing environment for the testing team to evaluate. If all goes well, the application is finally promoted into the production environment. Note that some organizations use an additional staging area between the system-testing and production environments, which is a particularly useful extra step if for any reason the system test environment is not an exact match to the production environment. Table 2.2 lists some sample configuration management tools that could be used to assist with this process.

A second area of software that is a candidate for configuration management (potentially using the same tools to manage the application's source code) would be the test scripts and test data used to run automated tests (sometimes collectively referred to as *testware*). This is a situation that becomes increasingly important as the size and scope of any test sets grow.

It is less common to see a similar configuration management process being applied to system software installation and configuration options. For example, the current set of servers may have been thoroughly tested to ensure that they are all configured correctly and have had all the relevant security patches applied, but when new servers are added to the system to increase the system's capacity or existing servers are reformatted to fix corrupted files, the new system software installations are not exactly the same as the configuration that was previously tested; it can be something as simple as two security patches being applied in a different order or the installer forgetting to uncheck the install sample files option during the install.

Rather than relying on a manual process to install system software, many organizations now choose to implement a configuration management process for system software by using some sort of disk replication tool. (Table 2.3 lists some sample

Table 2.2   Sample Configuration Management Tools

TOOL	ASSOCIATED WEB SITE
ChangeMan	www.serena.com
ClearCase	www.rational.com
CM Synergy	www.telelogic.com
Endevor/Harvest	www.ca.com
PVCS	www.merant.com
Razor	www.visible.com
Source Integrity	www.mks.com
StarTeam	www.starbase.com
TRUEchange	www.mccabe.com
Visual SourceSafe	www.microsoft.com

Table 2.3   Sample Disk Replication Tools

TOOL	ASSOCIATED WEB SITE
Drive2Drive	www.highergroundsoftware.com
Ghost	www.symantec.com
ImageCast	www.storagesoftsolutions.com
Image MASSter/ImageCast	www.ics-iq.com
LabExpert/RapiDeploy	www.altiris.com
OmniClone	www.logicube.com
PC Relocator	www.alohabob.com

software- and hardware-based disk replication tools.) The process works something like the following: a master image is first made of a thoroughly tested system software install. Then each time a new installation is required (for a new machine or to replace a corrupted version), the replication tool copies the master image onto the target machine, reducing the potential for human error.

One undesirable drawback of disk replication tools is their dependence on the target machine having the same hardware configuration as the master machine. This would be no problem if all the servers were bought at the same time from the same vendor. However, it would be problematic if they were acquired over a period of time and therefore use different device drivers to communicate to the machine's various hardware components.

Unfortunately, due to the lack of automated tools for some platforms, some devices still need to be configured manually—for example, when modifying the default network traffic filtering rules for a firewall appliance. Given the potential for human error, it's imperative that all manual installation procedures be well documented and the installation process be regularly checked to ensure that these human-error-prone manual steps are followed closely.

Before embarking on any significant testing effort, the security-testing team should confirm two things: that all of the Web site and application components that are to be tested are under some form of configuration management process (manual or automated) and that under normal circumstances these configurations will not be changed while test execution is taking place. Common exceptions to this ideal scenario include fixing defects that actually inhibit further testing and plugging newly discovered holes that present a serious risk to the security of the production system.

If the items to be tested are not under any form of configuration management process, then the security-testing team should not only try to hasten the demise of this undesirable situation, but they should also budget additional time to handle any delays or setbacks caused by an unstable target. Also, where possible, the team should try to schedule the testing effort in a way that minimizes the probability that a serious defect will make its way into production, especially one that results from a change being made to part of the system that had already been tested and wasn't retested.

Brown et al. (1999), Dart (2000), Haug et al. (1999), Leon (2000), Lyon (2000), and White (2000) all provide a good starting point for those attempting to define and implement a new configuration management process.

Responsibilities

Who will be responsible for making sure all the key testing activities take place on schedule? This list of activities may also include tasks that are not directly part of the testing effort, but that the testing team depends upon being completed in a timely manner. For instance, who is responsible for acquiring the office space that will be used to house the additional testers called for by the test plan? Or, if hardware procurement is handled centrally, who is responsible for purchasing and delivering the machines that will be needed to build the test lab?

Ideally, an escalation process should also be mapped out, so that in the event that someone doesn't fulfill their obligations to support the testing team for whatever reason, the situation gets escalated up the management chain until it is resolved (hopefully as quick and painless as possible).

Another decision that needs to be made is how to reference those responsible for these key activities. Any of the reference methods in Table 2.4 would work.

When listing these activities, the testing team will need to decide on how granular this list of things to do should be. The more granular the tasks, the greater the accountability, but also the greater the effort needed to draft the test plan and subsequently keep it up to date. The test plan also runs the risk of needlessly duplicating the who information contained in the associated test schedule (described later in this chapter in the section *Schedule*).

Table 2.4   Options for Referencing Key Personnel

KEY PERSON REFERENCED BY . . .	EXAMPLE
Company level	The xyz company is responsible for conducting a physical security assessment of the mirror Web site hosted at the London facility.
Department level	Network support is responsible for installing and configuring the test environment.
Job/role title	The application database administrator (DBA) is responsible for ensuring that the database schema and security settings created in the test environment are identical to those that will be used in the production environment.
Individual	Johnny Goodspeed is responsible for testing the security of all application communications.

Staffing and Training Needs

If outside experts are used to conduct penetration testing (covered in more detail in Chapter 9), is it cost effective for the internal staff to first conduct their own security tests? If the outside experts are a scarce commodity—and thus correspondingly expensive or hard to schedule—then it may make sense for the less experienced internal staff to first run the easy-to-execute security assessment tests; costly experts should only be brought in after all the obvious flaws have been fixed. In effect, the in-house staff would be used to run a set of comparatively cheap *entry-criteria tests* (also sometimes referred to as *smoke tests*) that must pass before more expensive, thorough testing is performed.

One consideration that will have a huge impact on the effectiveness of any internally staffed security-testing effort is the choice of who will actually do the testing. The dilemma that many organizations face is that their security-testing needs are sporadic. Often extensive security-oriented testing is not needed for several months and then suddenly a team of several testers is needed for a few weeks. In such an environment, an organization is going to be hard pressed to justify hiring security gurus and equally challenged to retain them. An alternative to maintaining a permanent team of security testers is to appropriate employees from other areas such as network engineers, business users, Web masters, and developers. Unfortunately, many of these candidates may not be familiar with generic testing practices, let alone security-specific considerations. This could result in a longer-lasting testing effort and less dependable test results.

For organizations that maintain a permanent staff of functional testers, Q/A analysts, test engineers, or other similarly skilled employees, one possible solution is to train these individuals in the basics of security testing and use them to form the core of a temporary security-testing team. Such a team would, in all probability, still need to draw upon the skills of other employees such as the firewall administrators and DBAs in order to conduct the security testing. But having such a team conduct many of the security tests that need to be performed may be more cost effective than outsourcing the entire testing task to an outside consulting firm. This would be especially beneficial for the set of tests that are expected to be regularly rerun after the system goes into production.

The degree to which some (or all) of the security-testing effort can be handled in house to a large extent depends on the steepness of the learning curve that the organization's employees will face. One way to reduce this learning curve is to make use of the ever-growing supply of security-testing tools. The decision on how much of the testing should be done in house and what tools should be acquired will therefore have a major impact on how the security-testing effort is structured. These topics are expanded on further in Chapter 9.

Schedule

Unless the testing effort is trivial in size, the actual details of the test schedule are probably best documented in a separate deliverable and generated with the assistance of a project-scheduling tool such as one of those listed in Table 2.5.

Table 2.5 Sample Project-Scheduling Tools

NAME	ASSOCIATED WEB SITE
Easy Schedule Maker	www.patrena.com
FastTrack Schedule	www.aecsoft.com
GigaPlan.net	www.gigaplan.com
ManagePro	www.performancesolutionstech.com
Microsoft Project	www.microsoft.com
Niku	www.niku.com
OpenAir	www.openair.com
PlanView	www.planview.com
Proj-Net	www.rationalconcepts.com
ProjectKickStart	www.projectkickstart.com
Project Dashboard	www.itgroupusa.com
Project Office	www.pacificedge.com
Time Disciple	www.timedisciple.com
Various	www.primavera.com
Xcolla	www.axista.com

With the scheduling details documented elsewhere, this section of the test plan can be used to highlight significant scheduling dates such as the planned start and end of the testing effort and the expected dates when any intermediate milestones are expected to be reached.

Since many testing projects are themselves subprojects of larger projects, a factor to consider when evaluating or implementing a scheduling tool is how easy it is to *roll up* the details of several subprojects into a larger master project schedule, thereby allowing for easier coordination of tasks or resources that span multiple subprojects.

Project Closure

Although itmight be desirable from a security perspective to keep a security-testing project running indefinitely, financial reality may mean that such a project ultimately must be brought to closure (if only to be superseded by a replacement project).

When winding down a security testing project, great care must be exercised to ensure that confidential information (such as security assessment reports or a defect-tracking database that contains a list of all the defects that were not fixed because of monitory pressures) generated by the testing effort does not fall into the wrong hands. This is especially relevant if going forward nobody is going to be directly accountable for protecting this information, or if some of this information was generated by (or shared with) third parties.

The test plan should therefore outline how the project should be decommissioned, itemizing important tasks such as who will reset (or void) any user accounts that were set up specifically for the testing effort, making sure no assessment tools were left installed on a production machine, and that any paper deliverables are safely destroyed.

Planning Risks and Contingencies

A planning risk can be any event that adversely affects the planned testing effort (the schedule, completeness, quality, and so on). Examples would include the late delivery of application software, the lead security tester quitting to take a better-paid job (leaving a huge gap in the testing team's knowledge base), or the planned test environment not being built due to unexpected infrastructure shortages (budget cuts).

The primary purpose of identifying in the test plan the most significant planning risks is to enable contingency plans to be proactively developed ahead of time and ready for implementation in the event that the potential risk becomes a reality. Table 2.6 lists some example contingency plans.

For any given risk, typically numerous contingencies could be considered. However, in most cases, the contingencies can be categorized as either extending the time required for testing, reducing the scope of the testing (for example, reducing the number of test items that will be tested), adding additional resources to the testing effort, or reducing the quality of the testing (for example, running fewer or less well designed tests), thereby increasing the *risk* of the system failing. These contingency categories can be illustrated by the *quality trade-off triangle* depicted in Figure 2.3. Reducing one side of the triangle without increasing at least one of the other sides reduces the quality of the testing (as represented by the area inside the triangle).

Table 2.6 Example Contingency Plans

PLANNING RISK	CONTINGENCY PLAN
Midway through the testing effort, Microsoft releases a new service pack for the operating system installed on a large number of the servers used by the Web site.	Don't install the service pack. (Keep the scope the same.)
	Install the service pack and reexecute any of the test cases whose results have now been invalidated. (More time or resources are needed.)
	Install the service pack, but don't change the test plan. (The quality of the testing is reduced.)
	Redo some of the highly critical tests that have been invalidated and drop some of the lower, as-yet-unexecuted tests. (The quality of the testing is reduced.)
The production environment upgrades its firewall to a more expensive/ higher-capacity version.	Do nothing, as the test environment becomes less like the production environment. (The quality of the testing is reduced.)
	Buy a new firewall for the test environment. (Increase resources.)
	Reduce firewall testing in the test environment and increase testing in the production environment. (Change the scope of the testing.)
The entire testing team wins the state lottery.	Make sure you are in the syndicate.

Figure 2.3 Quality trade-off triangle.

None of these options may sound like a good idea to senior management and they may decide that all these contingencies are unacceptable. Unfortunately, if management does not make a proactive contingency decision, the decisions (and their consequences) do not go away. Instead, they are implicitly passed down to the individual members of the testing team. This results in unplanned consequences such as a tester unilaterally deciding to skip an entire series of tests, skimping on the details of an incident report (requiring the incident investigator to spend more time trying to recreate the problem), or working extra unpaid hours (while at the same time looking for another job). None of these consequences are likely to be more desirable than the options that senior management previously decided were unacceptable.

Issues

Many people may hold the view that each and every issue is merely a risk that needs to be mitigated by developing one or more contingencies, resulting in any issues that the testing team faces being documented in the "planning risks" section of the test plan.

Alternatively, issues that have highly undesirable or impractical contingencies (such as a huge increase in the cost of the testing effort), maybe siphoned off from the planning risks section and thereby highlighted in their own section, allowing management to focus on these unresolved issues.

Assumptions

In a perfect world, a test plan would not contain any assumptions, because any assumption that the testing team had to make would be investigated to determine the validity of the assumption. Once thoroughly researched, the assumption would be deleted or transferred to another section (such as the *Planning Risks* section).

Unfortunately, many assumptions may not be possible to prove or disprove because of the time needed to investigate them, or because the people who could confirm the assumption are unwilling to do so. For example, the testing team may need to assume that the information provided by bug- and incident-tracking center Web sites (such as those listed in Table 4.2) is accurate, because the effort needed to reconfirm this information would take too long and consume too many resources.

Constraints and Dependencies

The testing team may find it useful to list all the major constraints that they are bound by. Obvious constraints include the project's budget or the deadline for its completion. Less obvious constraints include a corporate "no new hires" mandate (which means that if the testing is to be done in house, it must be performed using the existing staff), or a corporate procurement process that requires the testing team to purchase any hardware or software that costs more than $1,000 through a central purchasing unit (a unit that typically runs six to eight weeks behind).

Acronyms and Definitions

This section of the test plan can be used to provide a glossary of terms and acronyms referenced by the test plan and are not normally found in the everyday language of the plan's anticipated readership.

References

It's generally considered a good practice to include a summary list of all the other documents that are referenced, explicitly or implicitly, by the test plan (such as the project schedule or requirements documentation). Placing the list in its own section towards the end of the test plan will improve the readability of this section—and hence improve the chances that it is actually used.

Approvals

A test plan should identify two groups of approvers. The first group will be made up of those individuals who will decide whether or not the proposed test plan is acceptable and meets the security-testing needs of the organization, whereas the second group (which may be composed of the same individuals as the first group) will decide whether or not the deliverables specified in the test plan and subsequently produced and delivered by the testing team (for example, the test summary report) are acceptable.

Being asked to approve something is not the same as being kept informed about it. There may be additional interested parties (*stakeholders*) who need to be kept informed about the ongoing and ultimate status of the testing project, but do not really have the organizational power to approve or disapprove any of the deliverables listed in the test plan. For example, the configuration management librarian may need to know what the testing team needs in terms of configuration management support, but it is unlikely to be able to veto a particular set of tests. Rather than listing these individuals as approvers, it may be more accurate to identify them as stakeholders and indicate that their acceptance of the test plan merely indicates that they believe they have been adequately informed of the testing project's plans.

Master Test Plan (MTP)

For small simple testing projects, a single, short test plan may be all that is needed to sufficiently convey the intended activities of the testing team to other interested parties. However, for larger projects, where the work may be divided across several teams working at separate locations for different managers and at different points in the system's development, it may be easier to create several focused test plans rather than one large all-encompassing plan. For example, one plan may focus on testing the physical security of the computer facilities that the Web site will be housed in, another may describe the penetration testing that will be performed by an outsourced security-testing firm, and a third may concentrate on the unit-level tests that the Web application development team is expected to do.

If multiple test plans will be used, the activities within each plan need to be coordinated. For instance, it does not make sense for all of the test plans to schedule the creation of a common test environment; instead, the first plan that will need this capability should include this information. The higher the number of test plans, the easier it is to manage each individual plan, but the harder it becomes to coordinate all of these distributed activities, especially if the organization's culture does not lend itself to nonhierarchical lines of organizational communication.

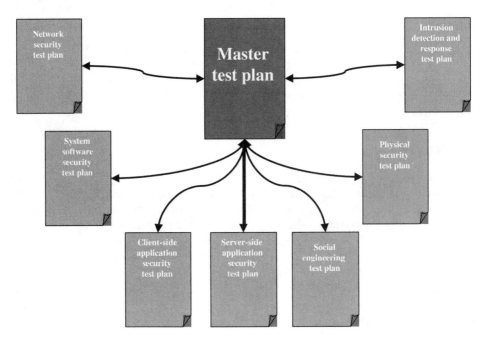

Figure 2.4   MTP.

One solution to the problem of multiple test plan coordination that many practitioners choose to utilize is the master test plan (MTP). The MTP is a test plan that provides a high-level summary of all the other test plans, thereby coordinating and documenting how the entire security-testing effort has been divided up into smaller, more manageable units of work (as depicted in Figure 2.4).

A by-product of defining multiple test plans is that such an approach may facilitate several security-testing teams working in parallel, which provides a significant advantage when working in Web time. Additionally, having several documented and well-scoped groups of tests makes outsourcing some or all of the testing effort much more controllable.

As is the case with each individual test plan, it is often the process of developing an MTP rather than the actual end product that is of greater help to the testing team. Creating the MTP should facilitate discussions on what testing objectives should be assigned to each individual test plan as part of an overall scheme, rather than relying on the recognizance of head-down individuals working in isolation on separate test plans. Craig et al. (2002) and Gerrard (2002) provide additional information on the concept of a master test plan.

Summary

Whether a person chooses to use a test plan format based on an industry standard, an internal template, or a unique layout customized for this specific project, the test plan and its associated documents should be reviewed to make sure that it adequately addresses the test-planning considerations summarized in Table 2.7.

Table 2.7   Test-Planning Consideration Checklist

YES	NO	DESCRIPTION
☐	☐	Have the system's security requirements been clarified and unambiguously documented?
☐	☐	Has the goal (and therefore scope) of the testing effort been clearly defined?
☐	☐	Have all the items (and their versions) that need to be tested been identified?
☐	☐	Have any significant items that will not be tested been listed?
☐	☐	Has a change control process for the project been defined and have all the individuals who will approve changes to the scope of the testing been identified?
☐	☐	Have all the features that need to be tested been identified?
☐	☐	Have any significant features that will not be tested been listed?
☐	☐	Has the testing approach (strategy) been documented?
☐	☐	Have the criteria (if any) by which the system will be deemed to have passed security testing been documented?
☐	☐	Have the criteria (if any) for halting (and resuming) the testing effort been documented?
☐	☐	Have the deliverables that the testing effort is expected to produce been documented?
☐	☐	Have all the environmental needs of the testing effort been researched and documented?
☐	☐	Has a configuration management strategy for the items that are to be tested been documented?
☐	☐	Has a configuration management strategy for the test scripts and test data (testware) been documented?
☐	☐	Have responsibilities for all the testing activities been assigned?
☐	☐	Have responsibilities for all the activities that the testing effort is dependent upon been assigned?
☐	☐	Have staffing needs been identified and resourced?
☐	☐	Have any training needs been identified and resourced?
☐	☐	Has a test schedule been created?

(continues)

Table 2.7   Test-Planning Consideration Checklist (*continued*)

YES	NO	DESCRIPTION
☐	☐	Have the steps necessary to bring the project to a graceful closure been considered?
☐	☐	Have the most significant planning risks been identified?
☐	☐	Have contingency plans for the most significant planning risks been devised and approved?
☐	☐	Have all issues, assumptions, constraints, and dependencies been documented?
☐	☐	Have any unusual acronyms and terms been defined?
☐	☐	Have any supporting documents been identified and cross-referenced?
☐	☐	Have those individuals responsible for approving the test plans been identified?
☐	☐	Have those individuals responsible for accepting the results of the testing effort been identified?
☐	☐	Have those individuals who need to be kept informed of the testing effort's plans been identified?

PART

Three

Test Design

Network Security

When asked to assess the security of a Web site, the first question that needs to be answered is, "What is the scope of the assessment?" Often the answer is not as obvious as it would seem. Should the assessment include just the servers that are dedicated to hosting the Web site? Or should the assessment be expanded to include other machines that reside on the organization's network? What about the routers that reside *upstream* at the Web site's Internet service provider (ISP), or even the machines running legacy applications that interface to one of the Web applications running on the Web site? Therefore, one of the first tasks the testing team should accomplish when starting a security assessment is to define the scope of the testing effort and get approval for the scope that they have proposed.

This chapter discusses how a security assessment effort can be scoped by referencing a set of network segments. The network devices attached to these segments collectively form the *network under test*. Adding the physical locations used to house these devices, the business process aimed at ensuring their security, and the system software and applications that run on any of these devices may then form the collection of test items that will ultimately comprise the system that will be tested by the security-testing effort. Figure 3.1 graphically depicts this relationship.

The subsequent sections of this chapter explains an approach that may be used by the testing team to ensure that the network defined by the scoping effort has been designed and implemented in a manner that minimizes the probability of a security vulnerability being exploited by an attacker (summarized in Figure 3.5).

Many of the networking terms used in this chapter may not be readily familiar to some readers of this book. Appendix A provides a basic explanation of what each of the network devices referenced in this chapter does and gives an overview of the

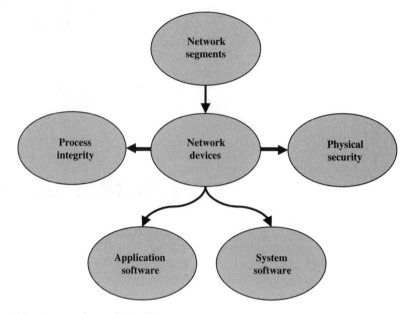

Figure 3.1   Scope of security testing.

networking protocols used by these components to communicate to each other across the network. Readers who are unfamiliar with what a firewall does or what the Transmission Control Protocol/Internet Protocol (TCP/IP) is should review this appendix first before continuing with the rest of this chapter. For those readers looking for a more detailed explanation of networking concepts, the following books provide a good introduction to this topic: Brooks 2001, Nguyen 2000, and Skoudis 2001.

Scoping Approach

A security assessment can be scoped in several ways. The assessment can focus entirely on the software components that compromise a single Web application or restrict itself to only testing the devices that are dedicated to supporting the Web site. The problem with these and other similar approaches is that they ignore the fact that no matter how secure a single component is (software or physical device), if the component's neighbor is vulnerable to attack and the neighbor is able to communicate to the allegedly secure component unfettered, then each component is only as secure as the most insecure member of the group. To use an analogy, suppose two parents are hoping to spare the youngest of their three children from a nasty stomach bug that's currently going around school. The parents would be deluding themselves if they thought that their youngest child would be protected from this threat if he were kept home from school and his older sisters still went to school. If the elder siblings were eventually infected, there would be little to stop them from passing it on to their younger brother.

The approach this book uses to define the scope of a security assessment is based on identifying an appropriate set of network segments. Because the term *network segment* may be interpreted differently by readers with different backgrounds, for the purposes of defining the testing scope, this book defines a *network segment* as a collection of networked components that have the capability to freely communicate with each other—such as several servers that are connected to a single network hub.

Many organizations choose to use network components such as firewalls, gateways, proxy servers, and routers to restrict network communications. For the purposes of defining a testing scope, these components can be considered to represent candidate boundaries for each of the network segments. They can be considered this way because these devices give an organization the opportunity to partition a large network into smaller segments that can be insulated from one another (as depicted in Figure 3.2), potentially isolating (or delaying) a successful intrusion.

The scope of a security assessment can therefore be documented by referencing a collection of one or more network segments. For some small Web sites, the scope could be as simple as a single multipurpose server and a companion firewall appliance. For larger organizations, the scope could encompass dozens (or even hundreds) of servers and appliances scattered across multiple network segments in several different physical locations.

Depending upon how the network engineers and local area network (LAN) administrators have (or propose to) physically constructed the network, these network segments may be easily referenced (for example, stating that the scope of the testing effort will be restricted to the network segments ebiz.tampa, crm.tampa, and

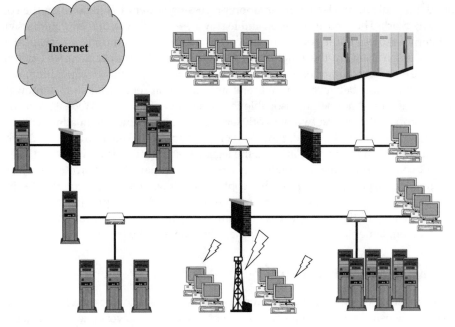

Figure 3.2 Example network segments.

dmz.tampa) or each of the physical components that compromise the network seg-ments may have to be individually itemized. As previously discussed, including only a portion of a network segment within the scope should be avoided because establish-ing the security of only a portion of a segment is of little value unless the remaining portion has already been (or will be) tested by another testing effort.

Once the network segments that comprise the scope of the testing effort have been defined, the scope can be further annotated to specify the hardware devices that make up these network segments, the physical facilities that are used to house this hardware, and any system software or application software that resides on this hardware, and finally any business processes (such as an intruder response process) that are intended to protect the security of the devices.

Scoping Examples

The specific approach used to identify the scope of the testing effort is very dependent on the size of the task and the culture of the organization, as the following scenarios illustrate.

Hotel Chain

A small hotel chain has decided to place its Web site (the originally stated target of the testing effort) on a handful of servers, which they own and administer, at an off-site facility owned and managed by their ISP. On occasion, the Web application running at this site needs to upload new reservations and download revised pricing structures from the organization's legacy reservation processing system that resides on the cor-porate network. The Web application and legacy reservation system communicates via the Internet. Access to the corporate network is via the same firewall-protected Inter-net connection used by the hotel chain for several other Internet services (such as employee emails and Internet browsing). Figure 3.3 illustrates this configuration.

Communication between the Web site and corporate network is via a firewall. Therefore, it would not be unreasonable to restrict the scope of the Web site security-testing effort to that of the two network segments that the hotel chain administers at the ISP facility (a demilitarized zone [DMZ] and back-end Web application). On the other hand, had the communication to the legacy system been via an unfiltered direct network connection to the corporate network, it would have been hard to justify not including the corporate network in the scope (unless it was covered by another testing project). A security breach at the corporate network could easily provide a back-door method of entry to the Web site, circumventing any front-door precautions that may have been implemented between the Web application and the Internet.

Furniture Manufacturer

A medium-sized furniture manufacturer has decided to develop its own Web applica-tion in house using contracted resources. Its entire Web site, however, will be hosted at

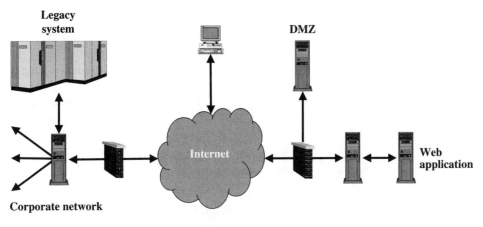

Figure 3.3 Hotel chain configuration.

an ISP's facility that offers low-cost Web hosting—so low cost that parts of the Web application (specifically the database) will be installed on a server shared with several other clients of the ISP. Assume that the ISP is unwilling (or perhaps unable) to provide the furniture manufacturer with the schematic of its network infrastructure and that it would not appreciate any of its clients conducting their own, unsolicited security assessments. The furniture manufacturer should restrict its security-testing activities to testing the in-house-developed Web application using its own test lab. The risk of the production version being attacked physically or via a system software vulnerability would be mitigated by requiring the ISP to produce evidence that it has already tested its infrastructure to ensure that it is well defended. Ideally, some form of guarantee or insurance policy should back up this assurance.

Accounting Firm

A small accounting firm, whose senior partner doubles as the firm's system administrator, has hosted its Web site on the partnership's one-and-only *file and print server*. (This is a questionable decision that the security assessment process should highlight.) This server is accessible indirectly from the Internet via a cheap firewall appliance and directly from any one of the dozen PCs used by the firm's employees. Figure 3.4 illustrates this configuration.

Because of the lack of any interior firewall or other devices to prohibit accessing the Web site from a desktop machine, the Web site is only as safe as the least secure PC. (Such a PC would be one that, unbeknownst to the rest of the firm, has a remote-access software package installed upon it, so the PC's owner can transfer files back and forth from his or her home over the weekend.) Such a situation would merit including all the PCs in the scope of the security assessment or suspending the security testing until an alternate network configuration is devised.

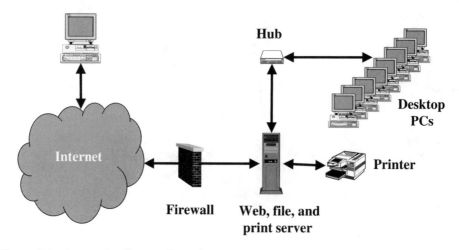

Figure 3.4 Accounting firm configuration.

Search Engine

A large Internet search engine Web site uses several identical clusters of servers scattered across multiple geographic locations in order to provide its visitors with comprehensive and fast search results. The Web site's LAN administrator is able to provide the testing team with a list of all the network segments used by the distributed Web site, and the devices connect to these different segments.

Because of the size of this security assessment, the testing team may decide to break the assessment up into two projects. The first project would concentrate on testing a single cluster of servers for vulnerabilities. Once any vulnerabilities identified by the first project have been fixed, the second phase focuses on ensuring that this previously assessed configuration has now been implemented identically on all the other clusters.

The Test Lab

An area that is often overlooked when deciding upon what should be covered by a security-testing effort is the devices and network segment(s) used by the testing team itself to test a nonproduction version of the system. Typically, these environments are referred to as *test labs*. If they are connected to the production environment or to the outside world (for instance, via the Internet), they might pose a potential security threat to the organization unless they are included in the security assessment.

Test labs are notorious for having weak security. They are therefore often the target of attackers trying to gain access to another network segment using the testing lab as a *stepping stone* to their ultimate goal. The following are just two of the scenarios that have contributed to this reputation. Test lab machines are often reconfigured or reinstalled so frequently that normal security policies and access controls are often disregarded for the sake of convenience. For example, very simple or even blank administrator passwords might be used because the machines are constantly being reformatted, or protective software such as antivirus programs are not installed because they generate too many false alarms during functional testing and potentially skew the test results obtained during performance testing. Secondly, minimum access controls are used in order to make automated test scripts more robust and less likely to fail midway through a test because the testing tool did not have sufficient privileges.

The scope of the security assessment should therefore always explicitly state whether or not a system's associated test lab is included in the testing effort and, if not, why it has been excluded. All too often, these test labs' only line of defense is the assumption that no attacker knows of their existence; solely relying on a *security-by-obscurity* strategy is a dangerous thing to do.

Suspension Criteria

If, during the scoping of a security assessment, clearly defining a testing scope proves to be completely impossible, then it might be wise to temporarily suspend the testing effort until this issue can be resolved. Such a situation could have come about because the information needed to make an informed decision about the network topology could not be obtained. This could also occur because the topology that has actually been implemented appears to allow such liberal access between multiple network segments that the size of security assessment needed to ensure the security of the network would become too vast, or if it is restricted to a single segment, it could not ensure the security of the segment because of the uncertainly associated with other adjacent segments.

Alternatively, a huge disclaimer could be added to the security assessment report stating that someone else has presumably already thoroughly tested (or will soon test) these adjacent segments using the same stringent security policies that this testing project uses. This so-called solution ultimately presents a lot of opportunity for miscommunication and potential finger-pointing at a later date, but may also provide the impetus for convincing management to devote more time and energy toward remedying the situation.

Device Inventory

Once the network segments that will form the subject of the security assessment have been identified, the next step is to identify the devices that are connected to these segments. A *device inventory* is a collection of network devices, together with some pertinent information about each device, that are recorded in a document.

A device can be referenced in a number of ways, such as its physical location or by any one of several different network protocol addresses (such as its hostname, IP address, or Ethernet media access control [MAC] address). Therefore, the inventory should be comprehensive enough to record these different means of identification. The security-testing team will need this information later in order to verify that the network has been constructed as designed. In addition, if a test lab is to be built, much of this information will be needed in order to make the test lab as realistic as possible.

Table 3.1   Example Layout Structure for a Device Inventory

DEVICE ID	DEVICE DESCRIPTION	PHYSICAL LOCATION	NETWORK ACCESSIBILITY	HOSTNAME(S)	IP ADDRESS(ES)	MAC ADDRESS(ES)
1	ISP router	ISP facility			123.456.789.123	
2	Internal router	Telecom room			123.456.789.124	
3	Perimeter firewall	Telecom room			123.456.789.130	
4	Web server #1	Main server room		web1.dmz.miami	123.456.789.131	aa.bb.cc.dd.bb.aa
5	Web server #2	Main server room		web2.dmz.miami	123.456.789.132	aa.bb.cc.dd.bb.bb
6	FTP server	Main server room		ftp1.dmz.miami	123.456.789.133	aa.bb.cc.dd.bb.cc
7	Load balancer	Main server room			123.456.789.134	
8	DMZ firewall	Main server room			123.456.789.135	
9	Internal switch	Main server room			123.456.789.136	
10	Application server	Main server room		weblogic1.main.miami	123.456.789.140	aa.bb.cc.dd.cc.aa
11	Database server	Main server room		sybase1.main.miami	123.456.789.141	aa.bb.cc.dd.cc.bb
12	Computer room PC #1	Main server room		joshua.main.miami	123.456.789.150	aa.bb.cc.dd.aa.aa
13	Computer room PC #2	Main server room		david.main.miami	123.456.789.151	aa.bb.cc.dd.aa.bb
14	Computer room PC #3	Main server room		matthew.main.miami	123.456.789.152	aa.bb.cc.dd.aa.cc

Note that instead of assigning a new inventory ID to each device, the testing team may find it more convenient to use the original equipment manufacturer (OEM) serial number or the inventory tracking number (sometimes represented as a barcode) internally assigned by the owning organization.

Table 3.1 depicts the pertinent information that the testing team should consider acquiring for each of the devices in the device inventory. Appendix A provides background information on the differences between these different network protocol addresses.

An organization's LAN administrator should be able to provide the testing team with all the information needed to construct a device inventory by either automatically running an already-installed network auditing tool (such as those listed in Table 3.6) or by referencing the network specification used to construct the network (or if it is not already built, the network design that will be used to build the network). If such documentation is not immediately available or if it can't be recreated in a timely manner, this may be a symptom of an unmanaged network and/or LAN administrators who are too busy administrating the network to keep track of its structure. Either way, such an undesirable scenario is likely to be indicative of a system prone to security vulnerabilities due to an undocumented structure and overtaxed administrators.

If the information needed to build a device inventory cannot be provided to the testing team, the testing team must decide whether the testing effort should be suspended until the situation can be remedied or attempt to acquire the raw information needed to construct the device inventory themselves (possible using one or more of the techniques described later in the verifying device inventory section of this chapter). Table 3.2 provides a checklist for building a device inventory.

Table 3.2 Network Device Inventory Checklist

YES	NO	DESCRIPTION
☐	☐	Has a list been acquired of all the network devices (servers, routers, switches, hubs, and so on) attached to any of the network segments that form the scope of the security assessment?
☐	☐	Has the physical location of each network device been identified?
☐	☐	Have the network addresses used to reference each network device been identified?

WIRELESS SEGMENTS

When documenting a network that utilizes wireless communications (such as Bluetooth or IEEE 802.11), the desired effective range of the communication should also be recorded and the method of encryption (if any) that will be used.

Although a wireless standard may stipulate that the broadcasting device only have a short range, in practice this range may be significantly larger, giving potential intruders the opportunity to attach their wireless-enabled laptops to a network by parking their cars across the road from the targeted organizations.

Network Topology

For simplicity, the LAN administrator may have connected (or if the network is yet to be built, may be intending to connect) all the devices that comprise the network under test to a single network hub, switch, or router, enabling any device to directly communicate to any other device on the network. A more compartmentalized approach would be to break the network up into several separate network segments. Such an approach should, if configured properly, improve security (and possibly network performance) by keeping network traffic localized at the cost of increased network complexity. If a compartmentalized approach is adopted, the network's intended topological configuration should be documented and subsequently verified to ensure that the network has actually been configured as desired. That would be advisable because an improper implementation may provide not only suboptimal performance, but it also may give attackers more options for circumventing network security precautions.

For a small network, this information can be displayed in a neat, concise diagram, which is similar to the ones depicted in Figures 3.3 and 3.4. This illustration might look nice on the LAN administrator's office wall, but unfortunately it would also pose a security leak.

For larger networks, a two-dimensional matrix may prove to be a more appropriate method of documenting links. Either way, this information should be kept under lock and key and only distributed to authorized personnel as an up-to-date network map would save an intruder an awful lot of time and effort.

Device Accessibility

By restricting the number of devices that can be *seen* (directly communicated to) by a machine located outside of the organization network, the network offers an external intruder fewer potential targets. Anyone looking for security vulnerabilities would be thwarted; hence, the network as a whole would be made more secure. The same is true when considering the visibility of a device to other internal networks: The fewer devices that can be accessed from other internal networks, the fewer opportunities an internal attacker has to compromise the network.

Device accessibility (or visibility) is an additional attribute that can be added to the device inventory. This attribute can be documented in detail, explaining under what specific circumstances a device may be accessed (for example, the database server should only be accessible to the application server and the network's management and backup devices) or may be defined in more general terms. For example, each device can be characterized in three ways: as (1) a *public* device that is visible to the outside world (for instance, the Internet), (2) a *protected* device that can be seen from other internal networks but not externally, or (3) a *private* device that can only be accessed by devices on the same network segment.

Once the network designers have specified under what circumstances a device may be accessed by another device (and subsequently documented as a network security policy), network traffic-filtering devices such as firewalls and routers can be added to the network design to restrict any undesired communication. Barman (2001), Peltier (2001), and Wood (2001) provide additional information on the process of defining

---

EXAMPLE NETWORK SECURITY POLICIES

Network security polices can be as straightforward as "only permit access to IP address 123.456.789.123 via port 80" or as smart as "don't permit any incoming network traffic that has a source IP address that matches the IP address of an internal machine." Such a scenario should not occur in the legitimate world, but an external attacker might alter (*spoof*) his or her originating IP address in an effort to fool an internal machine into thinking that it was communicating to another friendly internal machine.

BLOCK AND THEN OPEN VERSUS OPEN AND THEN BLOCK

Some LAN administrators first deploy a filtering device with all accesses permitted and then selectively block/filter potentially harmful ones. A more secure strategy is to block all accesses and then only open up the required ones, as an implementation error using the second approach is likely to eventually be spotted by a legitimate user being denied access to a resource. However, an implementation error in the former approach may go undetected until an intruder has successfully breached the filter device, been detected, and subsequently been traced back to his or her entry point, which is a much more dire scenario and one that should therefore be checked when inspecting the network filtering rules used by a filtering device.

---

security policies. The lack of a documented network security policy (and a process for updating this document) is often an indicator that different policies are likely to have been implemented on different filtering devices and can cause a potential process issue when the existing staff leaves.

Documenting the conditions (or rules) under which a device may be accessed in an organization's network security policy is one thing; however, implementing these rules is more difficult because each network security policy must be converted into an access-control rule that can be programmed into the appropriate network-filtering device. Zwicky, et al. (2000) provide information on how to implement network-filtering rules using a firewall.

Table 3.3 summarizes the network topology decisions that should ideally be documented before a network design (proposed or implemented) can be validated effectively.

Validating Network Design

Once the network's proposed design (if the network is yet to be built) or implemented design (if the assessment is occurring after the network has been built) has been accurately documented, it is possible to review the design to ascertain how prone the design is to a security breach. Often the goals of security run counter to the goals of easy maintenance. (A network that is easy for a LAN administrator to administer may also be easy for an intruder to navigate.) In some cases, stricter security may improve network

Table 3.3   Network Topology Checklist

YES	NO	DESCRIPTION
☐	☐	Has a diagram (or alternate documentation) depicting the network's topology been acquired?
☐	☐	Have the effective ranges of any wireless network segments been defined?
☐	☐	Has the network accessibility of each device been defined?
☐	☐	Have the network security polices needed to restrict undesired network traffic been defined?
☐	☐	Is there a documented policy in place that describes how these network security policies will be updated?

performance; in others, it may reduce the capacity of the network. For these reasons, it's unlikely that a network design can be categorized simply as right or wrong (blatant errors aside); instead, it can be said to have been optimized for one of the following attributes: performance, capacity, security, availability, robustness/fault tolerance, scalability, maintainability, cost, or, more likely, a balancing act among all of these attributes. Therefore, before starting any design review, the respective priorities of each of these design attributes should be determined and approved by the network's owner.

Network Design Reviews

Application developers commonly get together to review application code, but much less commonly does this technique actually get applied to network designs. Perhaps this happens because the number of people within an organization qualified to conduct a network review is smaller than the number able to review an application. Maybe it's because the prerequisite of documenting and circulating the item to be discussed is much easier when the object of the review is a standalone application program rather than a (as of yet undocumented) network design. Or maybe it's simply a question of the organization's culture: "We've never done one before, so why start now?" Whatever the reason for not doing them, reviews have been found by those organizations that do perform them to be one of the most cost-effective methods of identifying defects. A network design review should therefore always be considered for incorporation into a network's construction or, if already built, its assessment.

The first step in conducting a network design review is to identify the potential participants. Obviously, the LAN administrator, the network designer, and a representative of the security-testing team should always be included, if possible. Other candidates include the network's owner, internal or external peers of the LAN administrator, network security consultants, and end users. (At times, a knowledgeable end user can assist with giving the user's perspective on network design priorities as they are the ones that will primarily be using the network.)

Once the participants have been identified, they should be sent a copy of the network topology and device inventory in advance of the review plus any networking require-

Table 3.4   Network Design Security Inspection Checklist

YES	NO	DESCRIPTION
☐	☐	Is the number of network segments appropriate? For example, should a network be segmented or an existing network segment further divided? or should one or more segments be merged?
☐	☐	Is each network device connected to the most appropriate network segment(s)?
☐	☐	Are the most appropriate types of equipment being used to connect the devices on a network segment together, such as switches, hubs, direct connections, and so on?
☐	☐	Are the most appropriate types of equipment being used to connect different segments together such as bridges, routers, gateways, and so on?
☐	☐	Is each connection between the network segments absolutely necessary?
☐	☐	Does each network device have an appropriate number of network connections (network interface cards [NICs] and IP addresses)?
☐	☐	Has each device been made accessible/visible to only the appropriate network segments?
☐	☐	Will the network security policies that have been defined ensure that only the appropriate devices are accessible?

ments that have been explicitly specified. (It goes without saying that these review packages should be treated with the same confidentiality as the master network documentation because an intruder would find these copies as useful as the originals.) Once the participants have had a chance to review the network design, a meeting can be scheduled for everybody to discuss their findings. Oppenheimer (1999) and Dimarzio (2001) provide information on network design concepts and implementations.

Network Design Inspections

An inspection differs from a review in that an inspection compares the network design against a predefined checklist. The checklist could be based on anything from an industry standard defined by an external organization to a homegrown set of best-practice guidelines. Table 3.4 lists some questions that may be used as part of a network design inspection when evaluating the network from a security perspective.

Verifying Device Inventory

Once the network design has been reviewed and any changes have been agreed upon and implemented, the testing team can use the revised device inventory to verify that any changes that were identified as part of the network review process have been implemented by the networking team correctly.

Physical Location

For small networks, the task of confirming the precise physical location of each network device inventory may be as simple as going into the server room and counting two boxes. For larger, more complex network infrastructures, this process is not as straightforward and the answers are not as obvious. For instance, the device inventory may have specified that the router that connects an organization's Web site to its ISP be housed in the secure server room, but in reality this device is located in the telephone switching room and protected by a door that is rarely locked.

Even if a room's *head count* matches the number of devices that were expected to be found at this location (and the OEM serial numbers or internal inventory tracking numbers are not available), it is not guaranteed that two or more entries in the device inventory were not transposed. For instance, according to the device inventory, Web server 1 (with a hostname of web1.corp) is supposed to be located at the downtown facility, whereas Web server 5 (with a hostname of web5.corp) is at the midtown facility. However, in reality, web1 is at the midtown facility and web2 is at the downtown facility.

Verifying that devices that have a built-in user interface (such as a general-purpose server) are physically located where they are expected to be can be as simple as logging into each device in a room and confirming that its hostname matches the one specified in the device inventory. For example, on a Windows-based machine, this could be done via the control panel, or on a Unix system, via the hostname command. For devices such as printers and network routers that don't necessarily have built-in user interfaces, their true identity will need to be ascertained by probing it from a more user-friendly device directly attached to it.

The physical inventory is intended to do two things: confirm that all of the devices listed in the device inventory area are where they are supposed to be and identify any extra devices that are currently residing in a restricted area such as a server room. For instance, an old powered-down server residing in the back corner of a server room still poses a security risk. It should be either added to the device inventory (and hence added to the scope of the testing effort) or removed from the secure area because an intruder who was able to gain physical access to such a device could easily load a set

---

STICKY LABELS

Adding an easily viewable sticky label to the outside of each device, indicating its inventory identifier, should help speed up the process of confirming the physical location of each network device should this task need to be repeated in the near future.

If sticky labels are used, care should be taken to ensure that the selected identifier does not provide a potential attacker with any useful information. For example, using an organization's internal inventory tracking number (possibly in the form of a barcode) would be more secure than displaying a device's IP address(es) in plain view.

of hacking tools on to the machine and temporarily add it to the network via a spare port on a nearby network device.

Unauthorized Devices

Aside from physically walking around looking for devices that should not be connected to the network, another approach to discovering unwanted network devices is to perform an *IP address sweep* on each network segment included in the security-testing efforts scope.

The network protocol of choice for conducting an IP address sweep is the Internet Control Message Protocol (ICMP). (Appendix A provides more details on network protocols commonly used by Web applications.) ICMP is also known as *ping*; hence, the term *ping sweep* is often used to describe the activity of identifying all the IP addresses active on a given network segment. In the following Windows command-line example, the IP address 123.456.789.123 successfully acknowledges the ping request four times, taking on average 130 milliseconds:

```
C:\>ping 123.456.789.123

Pinging 123.456.789.123 with 32 bytes of data:

Reply from 123.456.789.123: bytes=32 time=97ms TTL=110
Reply from 123.456.789.123: bytes=32 time=82ms TTL=110
Reply from 123.456.789.123: bytes=32 time=151ms TTL=110
Reply from 123.456.789.123: bytes=32 time=193ms TTL=110

Ping statistics for 123.456.789.123:
    Packets: Sent = 4, Received = 4, Lost = 0 (0% loss),
Approximate round trip times in milliseconds:
    Minimum = 82ms, Maximum = 193ms, Average = 130ms
```

Unfortunately (from an IP address sweeping perspective), some LAN administrators may have configured one or more of the network devices not to respond to an ICMP (ping) protocol request. If this is the case, it may still be possible to conduct an IP address sweep using another network protocol such as TCP or the User Datagram Protocol (UDP).

IP ADDRESS SWEEP

One way to determine what devices are active on the network is to direct a "Hello is anyone there?" message at every IP address that might be used by a device connected to the network. A "Yes, I'm here" reply would indicate that the IP address is being used by a device. Since any active device needs an IP address to communicate to other network devices (a few passive devices may not use an IP address), the sum total of positive replies should comprise all of the powered-up devices connected to the network segment being swept.

These sweeps may prove to be quite time consuming if the entire range of potential IP addresses needs to be scanned manually. Fortunately, numerous IP-address-sweeping tools exist that can be used to automate this often tedious task (see Table 3.5). Klevinsky (2002) and Scambray (2001) both provide more information on how to conduct a ping sweep.

An IP address sweep is often the first indication of an intruder sniffing around, as an external intruder typically does not know what IP addresses are valid and active, and is therefore often forced to grope in the dark hoping to illuminate (or enumerate) IP addresses that the LAN administrator has not restricted access to. The testing team should therefore make sure that it informs any interested parties before it conducts their (often blatant) IP address sweeps, so as not to be confused with a real attack, especially if an organization has an intruder detection system that is sensitive to this kind of reconnaissance work.

Network Addresses

Several different techniques can be used to verify that the networking team has assigned each network device the network addresses specified by the device inventory. In addition, these techniques can also be used to confirm that no unauthorized network addresses have been assigned to legitimate (or unauthorize) devices. Appendix A provides additional information on network addresses and on some of the network-addressing scenarios that a testing team may encounter (and that could possibly cause them confusion) while trying to verify or build an inventory of network addresses used by a Web site.

Table 3.5   Sample List of IP-Address-Sweeping Tools and Services

NAME	ASSOCIATED WEB SITE
Fping	www.deter.com
Hping	www.kyuzz.org/antirez
Icmpenum & Pinger	www.nmrc.org
NetScanTools	www.nwpsw.com
Nmap	www.insecure.org
NmapNT	www.eeye.com
Ping	www.procheckup.com and www.trulan.com
Ping Sweep/SolarWinds	www.solarwinds.net
WS_Ping Pro Pack	www.ipswitch.com

Commercial Tools

The organization may have already invested in a commercial network-auditing or management tool (such as those listed in Table 3.6) that has the capability to produce a report documenting all the network addresses that each network device currently has assigned. Because some of these tools may require a software component to be installed on each network device, some of these tools may not be particularly capable of detecting devices that are not supposed to be attached to the network. Care should also be taken to make sure than when these tools are used, all the devices that are to be audited are powered up, as powered-down machines could easily be omitted.

Domain Name System (DNS) Zone Transfers

An extremely convenient way of obtaining information on all the network addresses used by a network is to request the common device used by the network to resolve network address translations to transfer en masse these details to the device making the request. A request that can be accomplished using a technique called a *domain name system (DNS) zone transfer*. DNS transfers have legitimate uses, such as when a LAN administrator is setting up a new LAN at a branch location and does not want to manually reenter all the network addresses used by the corporate network. Unfortunately,

Table 3.6 Sample List of Network-Auditing Tools

NAME	ASSOCIATED WEB SITE
Discovery	www.centennial.co.uk
LANauditor	www.lanauditor.com
Lan-Inspector	www.vislogic.org
Network Software Audit	www.mfxr.com
OpenManage	www.dell.com
PC Audit Plus	www.eurotek.co.uk
Systems Management Server (SMS)	ww.microsoft.com
Tivoli	www.ibm.com
Toptools and OpenView	www.hp.com
TrackBird	www.trackbird.com
Unicenter	www.ca.com
ZAC Suite	www.nai.com/magicsolutions.com

this capability is open to abuse and if it is made available locally, it may still be blocked by any network-filtering device such as a perimeter firewall.

A DNS zone transfer can either be initiated from a built-in operating system command such as nslookup or via a tool such as the ones listed in Table 3.7. Scambray (2001) and Skoudis (2001) both provide more information on how to attempt a DNS zone transfer.

Manual

If an automated approach cannot be used because of powered-down machines or suspicions that stealthy hidden devices have been connected to the network, then while confirming the physical location of each network device, the testing team may also want to manually confirm the network addresses assigned to each device. For Windows- or Unix-based devices, the network addresses can be determined using one or more of the commands (such as those listed in Table 3.8) that are built into the operating system. Network devices that do not offer built-in commands to support these kind of inquires (such as a network printer) may require probing from a more user-friendly device directly connected to it.

Table 3.9 summarizes the checks that can be used to verify that each device implementation matches its corresponding device inventory entry.

Table 3.7 Sample List of DNS Zone Transfer Tools and Services

NAME	ASSOCIATED WEB SITE
Dig	ftp.cerias.purdue.edu
DNS Audit/Solarwinds	solarwinds.net
Dnscan	ftp.technotronic.com
Dnswalk	visi.com/~barr
Domtools	domtools.com
Host	ftp.uu.net/networking/ip/dns
Sam Spade	samspade.org

Table 3.8 Sample List of Built-In Operating System Commands

OPERATING SYSTEM	COMMANDS
Unix	hostname, ifconfig, or nslookup
Windows	arp, ipconfig, net, nslookup, route, winipcfg, or wntipcfg

Note that not all commands have been implemented on every version of the operating system.

Table 3.9   Verifying Network Device Inventory Implementation Checklist

YES	NO	DESCRIPTION
☐	☐	Are all of the devices listed in the device inventory physically located where they should be?
☐	☐	Have unauthorized devices been checked for?
☐	☐	Have all of the devices listed in the device inventory been assigned their appropriate network addresses?

Verifying Network Topology

Once the testing team has verified that each individual device has been configured correctly, the next step is to confirm that the physical connections between these devices have been implemented exactly as specified and that any network-filtering rules have been applied correctly.

Network Connections

For most small networks, a visual inspection may be all that is needed to confirm that each device has been physically connected to its network peers. For larger, more complicated and/or dispersed networks, verifying that all of the network connections have been implemented correctly and no unneeded connections established is probably most productively done electronically.

The network's topological map (or matrix) can be manually verified by logging into each device on the network and using built-in operating system commands such as *tracert* (Windows) or *traceroute* (Unix). These commands show the path taken by an ICMP request as it traverses the network (hopping from device to device) to its ultimate destination. In the following Windows command-line example, it appears that the initiating device (IP address 123.456.789.123) is directly connected to the device with IP address 123.456.789.124 and indirectly connected to the target of the request (IP address 123.456.789.125).

```
C:>tracert web1.tampa
Tracing route to web1.tampa [123.456.789.125]
over a maximum of 30 hops:

1    69 ms      27 ms      14 ms      bigboy.tampa [123.456.789.123]
2    28 ms      <10 ms     14 ms      123.456.789.124
3    41 ms      27 ms      14 ms      web1.tampa [123.456.789.125]

Trace complete.
```

Table 3.10 lists some tools and services that provide more advanced and user-friendly versions of these trace route commands. In addition, some of the network auditng tools listed in Table 3.6 provide features for constructing a topological map of the network they are managing.

Device Accessibility

Contrary to popular belief, once a network-traffic-filtering device such as a firewall is connected to a network, it will not immediately start protecting a network; rather, the filtering device must first be configured to permit only the network traffic to pass through that is appropriate for the specific network it has just been attached to. Although the manufacturer's default configuration may be a good starting point, relying on default settings is a risky business. For instance, default outgoing network traffic policies are often too liberal, perhaps due to the mindset of an external intruder who does not consider the possibility of an attack being initiated from within an organization or that of an external intruder wanting to send confidential information out of an organization.

Therefore, each traffic-filtering device should be checked to make sure that it has been configured according to the filtering rules defined by the network's security policies and that only the network devices that should be visible to devices on other network segments are actually accessible. These network security policies are often implemented as a series of rules in a firewall's access control list (ACL). These rules can either be manually inspected via a peer-level review and/or checked by executing a series of tests designed to confirm that each rule has indeed been implemented correctly.

A filtering device can be tested by using a device directly connected to the outward-facing side of a network-filtering device. The testing should try to communicate to each of the devices located on the network segment(s) that the filtering device is

Table 3.10   Sample List of Trace Route Tools and Services

NAME	ASSOCIATED WEB SITE
Cheops	www.marko.net
NeoTrace	www.mcafee.com/neoworx.com
Qcheck	www.netiq.com
SolarWinds	www.solarwinds.net
Trace	www.network-tools.com
TraceRoute	www.procheckup.com
Tracert	www.trulan.com
TracerX	www.packetfactory.net
VisualRoute	www.visualroute.com

intended to protect. Although many organizations may test their network-filtering defenses by trying to break into a network, fewer organizations run tests designed to make sure that unauthorized network traffic cannot break out of their network. The testing team should therefore consider reversing the testing situation and attempt to communicate to devices located in the outside world from each device located on the network segment(s) being protected by the filtering device. Allen (2001) and Nguyen (2000) both provide additional information on how to test a firewall.

Testing Network-Filtering Devices

Although in many cases filtering implementations are too lax, in others a filter may be too strict, which restricts legitimate traffic. Therefore, tests should also be considered to make sure that all approved traffic can pass unfettered by the filter.

If multiple filters are to be used—such as a DMZ configuration that uses two fire-walls (a scenario expended upon in Appendix A)—each filter should be tested to ensure that it has been correctly configured. This procedure is recommended as it is unwise to only check a network's perimeter firewall and assume that just because it is configured correctly (and hence blocks all inappropriate traffic that it sees) every other filter is also configured correctly. This is particularly true when internal firewalls that block communication between two internal network segments are considered. The most restrictive perimeter firewall does nothing to prohibit a network intrusion initi-ated from within an organization (which is a more common scenario than an externally launched attack).

If some of the filter's rules are dependent not only on the destination address of the network traffic, but also on the source address, then in addition to requesting access to permitted and restricted devices, it may also be necessary to vary (*spoof*) the source address in order to create authorized and unauthorized network traffic data for inbound and outbound tests.

Firewalls often have the capability to log inbound and/or outbound requests. This feature can be useful if evidence is needed to prosecute an offender or the network security team is interested in receiving an early warning that someone is attempting to

SPOOFING

Spoofing refers to the technique of changing the original network address of a network message, typically from an untrusted address to one that is trusted by a firewall (such as the address of the firewall itself). Of course, one of the side effects of changing the origination address is that the target machine will now reply to the spoofed address and not the original address. Although it might be possible for an intruder to alter a network's configuration to set up bidirectional communication (or *source routing*), spoofing will typically result in the intruder only having unidirectional communication (or *blind spoofing*). Unfortunately, unidirectional communication is all an intruder needs if he or she is only interested in executing system commands (such as creating a new user account) and is not interested in (or does not need to be) receiving any confirmation responses.

Table 3.11   Network Topology Verification Checklist

YES	NO	DESCRIPTION
☐	☐	Does the implemented network topology match the topology specified by the approved network topology design?
☐	☐	Have default configuration settings for each network-traffic-filtering device been reviewed and, if necessary, changed (for example, assigning new and different user IDs and passwords)?
☐	☐	Have all the inbound network-traffic-filtering rules been implemented correctly on every filtering device?
☐	☐	Have all the outbound network-traffic-filtering rules been implemented correctly on every filtering device?
☐	☐	Do all of the filtering devices still work correctly when exposed to heavy network loads?
☐	☐	If network-traffic-filtering logs are being used, are the logs being monitored for signs of an intruder at work, lack of free disk space, or other noteworthy events?

gain unauthorized entry. If logging is enabled and unmonitored, aside from slowing down a firewall (another case of a performance optimization conflicting with a security consideration) and unmonitored, the logs may grow to a point where the firewall's functionality integrity is compromised. Endurance tests should therefore be considered to make sure that any logging activity does not interfere with the firewall's filtering capabilities over time.

Some filtering devices (such as proxy servers) have a harder time deciding what should and should not be filtered as the load placed on them increases. At high load levels, the device may be so stressed that it starts to miss data packets that it should be blocking. Running stress tests against the filtering device should be considered to ascertain whether or not they exhibit this behavior. If they do, consider inserting a network load governor to ensure that such a heavy load will not be placed on the susceptible device in a production environment.

A firewall only works if it's enabled. Forgetting to change or disable any default user IDs and passwords or removing any remote login capability that might have been enabled by the manufacturer may allow an intruder to disable the firewall or selectively remove a pesky filtering rule that is preventing him or her from accessing the network behind the firewall. Therefore, checks should be considered to make sure that neither of these potential oversights makes it into production (see Table 3.11).

Supplemental Network Security

In addition to the basic security measures described in the preceding sections, some organizations implement additional network security measures to make it harder for any attacker to compromise the security of the network. Unfortunately, these measures come at a price, typically one of additional network complexity, which in turn means additional network administration—an overhead that may not be justified for every network. However, if such additional measures are deemed desirable, then the security-testing team should consider running tests to check that these extra precautions have indeed been implemented correctly.

Network Address Corruption

To facilitate more compatible networks, most network protocols utilize several different network addresses (for instance, the Web sites typically use three addresses: a host/domain name, an IP address, and a MAC address). Each time a data packet is passed from one network device to another, the sending device typically must convert an address from one address format to another (for example, the domain name wiley.com must first be converted to the IP address 123.456.789.123 before the data can be passed across the Internet). Ordinarily, this translation process occurs without incident, each device remembering (*caching*) the translations that it repeatedly has to perform and occasionally refreshing this information or requesting a new network address mapping for a network address it has not had to translate before (or recently) from a network controller.

Unfortunately, if intruders are able to gain access to one or more devices on a network, they may be able to corrupt these mappings (a technique often referred to as *spoofing* or *poisoning*). They may misdirect network traffic to alternate devices (often a device that is being used by an intruder to eavesdrop on the misdirected network traffic). To reduce the possibility of this form of subversion, some LAN administrators permanently set critical network address mappings on some devices (such as the network address of the Web server on a firewall), making these network address translations static. Permanent (static) entries are much less prone to manipulation than entries that are dynamically resolved (and may even improve network performance ever so slightly, as fewer translation lookups need to be performed). However, manually setting network address mappings can be time consuming and is therefore not typically implemented for every probable translation.

Hostname-to-IP-Address Corruption

A device needing to resolve a hostname-to-IP-address translation typically calls a local DNS server on an as-needed basis (dynamically). To make sure that erroneous or unauthorized entries are not present, DNS mappings can be checked using a built-in operating system command such as nslookup or using a tool such as the ones listed in Table 3.7 . Alternatively, a LAN administrator may have hardcoded some critical DNS mappings using a device's hosts file (note that this file has no file-type extension), thereby removing the need for the device to use a DNS server and mitigating the possibility of this lookup being corrupted (improving network performance ever so slightly). The following is a sample layout of a hosts file that might be found on a Windows-based device:

```
# This is a HOSTS file used by Microsoft TCP/IP for Windows.
# This file contains the mappings of IP addresses to host names. Each
# entry should be kept on an individual line. The IP address should
# be placed in the first column followed by the corresponding host name.
# The IP address and the host name should be separated by at least one
# space.
# Additionally, comments (such as these) may be inserted on individual
# lines or following the machine name denoted by a '#' symbol.

127.0.0.1       localhost

123.456.789.123 wiley.com
```

The static hostname-to-IP-address mappings on each device can be tested by either a visual inspection of the hosts file in which the static mappings contained in this file can be viewed (or edited) using a simple text-based editor such as Notepad (Windows) or vi (Unix), or by using a simple networking utility that must resolve the mapping before it is able to perform its designated task. (For example, entering ping wiley.com from a command-line prompt requires the host device to convert wiley.com to an IP address before being able to ping its intended target.)

IP Address Forwarding Corruption

Instead of corrupting a network address mapping, an intruder may attempt to misdirect network traffic by modifying the routing tables used by network devices to forward network traffic to their ultimate destination. To confirm that a network device such as a router has not had its IP routing tables misconfigured or altered by an intruder, these tables can either be manually inspected (typically using the utility originally used to configure these routing tables) or verified by sending network traffic destined for all probable network destinations via the device being tested and then monitoring the IP address that the device actually forwards the test network traffic to.

IP-Address-to-MAC-Address Corruption

The Address Resolution Protocol (ARP) is the protocol used to convert IP addresses to physical network addresses. For Ethernet-based LANs, the physical network address is known as a MAC address.

As with hostname-to-IP-address mappings, a LAN administrator may choose to selectively use static mappings for IP-address-to-MAC-address mappings. If static ARP entries are supposed to have been implemented, each device should be checked to see which ARP entries are static and which are dynamic. This can be done by using a tool such as arpwatch (www.ee.lbl.gov) or manually visiting every device and using a built-in operating system command such as arp. In the following Windows command-line example, only one of the ARP entries has been set permanently (statically):

```
C:\>arp -a
Interface: 123.456.789.123 on Interface 0x2
    Internet Address      Physical Address       Type
```

```
123.456.789.124      aa.bb.cc.dd.ee.ff    static
123.456.789.125      aa.bb.cc.dd.ee.aa    dynamic
```

Table 3.12 provides a checklist for verifying that static network addresses have been implemented correctly.

Secure LAN Communications

Unless encrypted, any data transmitted across a LAN can potentially be eavesdropped (*sniffed*) by either installing a sniffer application onto a compromised device or attaching a sniffing appliance to the cabling that makes up the LAN (an exercise that is made a lot easier if the network uses wireless connections).

To protect against internal sniffing, sensitive data (such as application user IDs and passwords) transmitted between these internal devices should be encrypted and/or transmitted only over physically secured cabling. For example, a direct connection between two servers locked behind a secure door would require an intruder to first compromise one of the servers before he or she could listen to any of the communications.

To check for sensitive data being transmitted across a LAN in cleartext (unencrypted), a network- or host-based network-sniffing device (such as one of the tools listed in Table 3.13) can be placed on different network segments and devices to sniff for insecure data transmissions. Due to the large amount of background traffic (for example, ARP requests) that typically occurs on larger LANs, the sniffing tool should be configured to filter out this noise, making the analysis of the data communication much easier.

A more rigorous test would be to input selectively sniffed data into a decryption tool (such as the ones listed in Table 4.16) to ascertain whether or not the data was sufficiently encrypted and not easily decipherable. Table 3.14 is a sample checklist for testing the safety of LAN network communications.

Wireless Segments

It is generally considered good practice to encrypt any nonpublic network traffic that may be transmitted via wireless communications. However, due to the performance degradation caused by using strong encryption and the possibility of a vulnerability existing within the encryption protocol itself, it would be prudent not to broadcast

Table 3.12   Network Address Corruption Checklist

YES	NO	DESCRIPTION
☐	☐	Is there a documented policy in place that describes which devices are to use static network addresses and which specific addresses are to be statically defined?
☐	☐	Are all of the devices that should be using static network addresses actually using static addressing?

Table 3.13 Sample List of Network-Sniffing Tools

NAME	ASSOCIATED WEB SITE
Agilent Advisor	www.onenetworks.comms.agilent.com
Dragonware (Carnivore)	www.fbi.gov
CommView	www.tamos.com
Distinct Network Monitor	www.distinct.com
Esniff/Linsniff/Solsniff	www.rootshell.com
Ethereal	www.zing.org
Ethertest	www.fte.com
Iris	www.eeye.com
NetBoy	www.ndgssoftware.com
NetMon & Windows Network Monitor	www.microsoft.com
Sniff'em	www.sniff-em.com
Sniffer	www.sniffer.com
TCPDump	www.ee.lbl.gov and www.tcpdump.org
WinDump	www.netgroup-serv.polito.it

Note that some of the functional testing tools listed in Table 6.12 can also be used to sniff network traffic entering or leaving the device they are installed on.

Table 3.14 Secure LAN Communication Checklist

YES	NO	DESCRIPTION
☐	☐	Is there a documented policy in place that describes how sensitive data should be transmitted within a LAN?
☐	☐	When using a sniffer application on each network segment (or device), is sensitive data being transmitted or received by any service running on the network in cleartext or in a format that can be easily deciphered?
☐	☐	Are the physical cables and sockets used to connect each of the components on the network protected from an inside intruder directly attaching a network-sniffing device to the network?

any wireless communication further than it absolutely needs to be. If wireless communications will be used anywhere on the network under test, then the network's supporting documentation should specify the maximum distance that these signals should be receivable. The larger the distance, the more mobile-friendly the network will be, but the greater the risk that an eavesdropper may also be able to listen to any communications.

Although the wireless standard may specify certain distances that wireless devices should be effective over, each individual implementation varies in the actual reception coverage. The reasons why this coverage varies from network to network include the following:

Transmitter.   The more power a transmitter devotes to broadcasting its signal, the farther the signal is propagated.

Receiver.   By using specialized (gain-enhancing and/or directional) antennas, a receiving device can extend its effective range.

Height.   The higher the broadcasting (and receiving) device, the farther the signal can travel. For example, a wireless router located on the third floor has a larger radius of coverage than one located in the basement.

Building composition.   The construction materials and building design used to build the facility where the broadcasting device is located will impede the signal's strength to varying degrees. For example, steel girders can create a dead zone in one direction, while at the same time enhancing the signal in another direction. In addition, a building's electrical wiring may inadvertently carrier a signal into other adjacent buildings.

Background noise.   Electrical transmission pylons or other wireless networks located in the neighborhood generate background noise and thereby reduce the effective range of the broadcasting device.

Weather.   Rain droplets on a facility's windows or moisture in the air can reduce the effective range of a broadcasting device.

The actual effective wireless range of wireless network segments should therefore be checked to ensure that a particular wireless network implementation is not significantly greater than the coverage called for by the network's design.

Denial-of-Service (DoS) Attacks

Technically speaking, a denial-of-service (DoS) attack means the loss of any critical resource. Some examples of this attack include putting superglue into the server room's door lock, uploading to a Web server a Common Gateway Interface (CGI) script that's designed to run forever seeking the absolute value of π (slowing down the CPU), blocking access to the Web site's credit-card service bureau (blocking new orders), or by creating huge dummy data files (denying system log files free disk space, causing the system to hang). However, the most common DoS attack is an attempt to deny legitimate clients access to a Web site by soaking up all the Web site's available network bandwidth or network connections, typically by creating an inordinate number of phony Web site requests. Kelvinsky (2002) provides an extensive review of some of the most common techniques and tools used to launch DoS attacks.

A variation of a DoS attack is a distributed denial-of-service (DDoS) attack. Unlike a DoS attack, which is originated from a single source, a DDoS attack is launched from multiple sources (although it may still be orchestrated from a single point). This enables the amount of network traffic focused at the target network to be many times greater.

Machiavellian DoS Attacks

An attacker might choose to employ a DoS attack for other less obvious reasons. DoS attacks are therefore not always what they seem. Here are some examples:

- An attacker could launch a small-scale DoS attack, but instead of using a bogus source network address, he or she could use the network address of an important router/server on the Web site that is being attacked. A Web site that has already been attacked in a similar fashion may have installed an automated defense mechanism that blocks all communication from the source of a DoS attack. Of course, if the network address is the Web site's upstream router, the Web site may inadvertently cut itself off from the rest of the world!

- Depending upon how a Web site is configured, a large DoS attack might actually cause a device to pause or starve to death some (or all) of the background processes that are supposed to monitor and/or block intruder attacks. For instance, under normal loads, a network-based intrusion detection system (IDS) may be able to detect emails containing viruses, but at higher network loads, the IDS may be unable to monitor a sufficient number of network data packets to correctly match the virus against its virus signature database, enabling a virus to slip through unnoticed.

- An intruder may even use a DoS attack as a diversion measure, launching an obvious attack against one entry point while quietly (and hopefully unnoticed) attacking another entry point. Even if it is detected by an IDS, the IDS's warnings/alarms may be ignored or lost due to the chaos being caused by the blatant DoS attack that is occurring simultaneously.

- An intruder that has successfully accessed a server may need to reboot the server before he or she can gain higher privileges. One way to trick a LAN administrator into rebooting the server (which is what the intruder wants) is to launch a DoS attack against the compromised server. (Therefore, it always pays to check that a server's startup procedures have not been altered before rebooting a server, especially when recovering from a DoS attack.)

DoS Attack Countermeasures

Unfortunately, many organizations are completely unprepared for a DoS attack, relying on the get-lucky defense strategy. It may be infeasible to design a network to withstand every possible form of DoS attack. However, because many forms of DoS attack do have corresponding countermeasures that can be put in place to avoid or reduce the severity of a DoS attack, it may therefore make sense to ensure that a network and its critical services are able to withstand the most common DoS attacks that intruders are currently using.

DoS Attack Detection

A DoS countermeasure may only work if the DoS attack can actually be detected. Some attackers may try to disguise their initial onslaught (for instance, by using multiple

---

EXAMPLE DOS COUNTERMEASURE

An example of a countermeasure that can be employed against an ICMP (*ping*) DoS attack on a Web site is to have the Web site's ISP(s) throttle back the level of ICMP requests, reducing the amount of phony traffic that actually reaches the target Web server(s). Many high-end routers have throttling capabilities built into them. Therefore, an organization may want to check with its ISP to see if the provider has this capability. If so, the organization should find out what the procedures are for deploying this feature should a Web site become the subject of an ICMP DoS attack.

---

source network addresses) so that the DoS attack either goes completely unnoticed by the on-duty security staff or the deployment of any countermeasure is delayed.

To help detect unusual rises in system utilizations (which are often the first observable signs of a DoS attack), some organizations create a resource utilization baseline during a period of normal activity. Significant deviations from this norm (baseline) can be used to alert the system's support staff that a DoS attack may be occurring.

Whatever DoS attack detection mechanisms have been deployed, they should be tested to ensure that they are effective and that the on-duty security staff is promptly alerted when a DoS attack is initiated, especially a stealthy one.

DoS Attack Emulation

Although small-scale DoS attacks can be mimicked by simply running a DoS program from a single machine connected to the target network, larger-scale tests that seek to mimic a DDoS attack may need to utilize many machines and large amounts of network bandwidth, and may therefore prove to be quite time consuming and resource intensive to set up and run. As an alternative to using many generic servers to generate a DDoS attack, hardware appliances such as those listed in Table 3.15 can be used to create huge volumes of network traffic (more than tens of thousands of network connection requests per second and millions of concurrent network connections) and even come with attack modules (which are updateable) designed to emulate the most common DoS attacks.

Rather than having to set up an expensive test environment for only a few short DDoS attack tests (that will hopefully not have to be repeatable), another option is to use an online service. (Table 3.15 lists some sample vendors that offer this service.) For a relatively small fee, these online vendors use their own site to generate the huge volumes of network traffic that typically characterize a DDoS attack and direct this network traffic over the Internet to the target network—an approach that can be much more cost effective than an organization trying to build its own large-scale load generators.

In addition, some of the traditional load-testing tools listed in Table 3.16 can also be utilized to simulate DoS attacks that necessitate creating large volumes of Web site requests.

Table 3.17 summarizes the checks that the testing team can perform to help evaluate how prepared an organization is against a DoS (or DDoS) attack.

Table 3.15   Sample List of DoS Emulation Tools and Services

NAME	ASSOCIATED WEB SITE
FirewallStressor	www.antara.net
Exodus	www.exodus.com
Mercury Interactive	www.mercuryinteractive.com
SmartBits	www.spirentcom.com
WebAvalanche	www.caw.com

Table 3.16   Sample List of Traditional Load-Testing Tools

NAME	ASSOCIATED WEB SITE
Astra LoadTest and LoadRunner	www.mercuryinteractive.com
e-Load	www.empirix.com
OpenSTA	www.sourceforge.net
Portent	www.loadtesting.com
QALoad	www.compuware.com
RemoteCog	www.fiveninesolutions.com
SilkPerformer	www.segue.com
TestStudio	www.rational.com
VeloMeter	www.velometer.com
Web Application Stress Tool (WAST—"Homer") and Web Capacity Analysis Tool (WCAT)	www.microsoft.com
WebLoad	www.radview.com
Web Performance Trainer	www.webperfcenter.com
WebSizr	www.technovations.com
WebSpray	www.redhillnetworks.com

Table 3.17 DoS Attack Checklist

YES	NO	DESCRIPTION
☐	☐	Has a documented strategy been developed to defend against DoS attacks?
☐	☐	Is there a documented inventory of the specific DoS attacks for which countermeasures have been put in place?
☐	☐	Have the procedures that the on-duty security staff should follow when the network is under a DoS attack been documented?
☐	☐	When emulating each of the defended DoS attacks, are the attacks detected by the on-duty security staff?
☐	☐	Does the on-duty security staff always follow the procedures documented in the DoS policy documentation?
☐	☐	Is the degradation suffered by the network and/or the services running on the network still acceptable while the network is experiencing a DoS attack that has an implemented countermeasure?

Summary

The network infrastructure that each network application resides on represents the electronic foundation of the application. No matter how good an application's security procedures are, the application can be undermined by vulnerabilities in the underlying network that the application depends on for its network connectivity. This chapter has outlined a series of steps and techniques (summarized in Figure 3.5) that a security-testing team can follow (or customize to their unique situation) to first define the scope and then conduct a network security-testing effort.

One final point is worth emphasizing: In order for the testing effort to be as comprehensive and systematic as possible, the security-testing team must be granted access to highly sensitive documentation such as a diagram depicting the network's topology. It goes without saying that the testing team should take every feasible precaution to prevent this sensitive information from being leaked to a potential attacker (external or internal) and that any test results (regardless of whether or not they

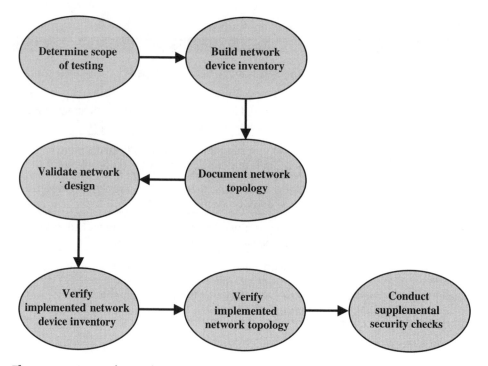

Figure 3.5   Network security-testing approach summary.

demonstrate the existence of a security vulnerability) must be kept under lock and key and only distributed on a need-to-know basis. Finding any of these artifacts could save an intruder a considerable amount of time and effort, and increase the possibility of a successful penetration. Additionally, the testing team should be careful to clean up after themselves, making sure that once the testing is complete, any testing tools that could be utilized by an attacker are removed from all of the devices they were installed upon.

System Software Security

This book uses the term *system software* to refer to the group of commercial and open-source software products that are developed and distributed by an external organization. These include operating systems, database management systems, Java 2 Platform Enterprise Edition (J2EE) implementations, file-sharing utilities, and communication tools. Table 4.1 lists some specific examples of such products.

Typically, whatever Web application that an organization has deployed or will want to deploy will depend upon a group of system software products. Before developing any application software, an organization would be well advised to evaluate any system software that the application is expected to utilize. Such an evaluation would ensure that the planned system software and the specific installation configuration do

Table 4.1 Sample List of System Software Products

NAME	ASSOCIATED WEB SITE
Apache	www.apache.org
Linux	www.redhat.com
Notes	www.lotus.com
MS SQL Server	www.microsoft.com
pcAnywhere	www.symantec.com
WebLogic	www.bea.com

not have any significant security issues. Determining security flaws or weaknesses early is important, as trying to retrofit a set of patches or workarounds to mitigate these system software security vulnerabilities can cause significant reworking. For example, applications might have to be reconfigured, as the original ones were developed using different, often default, system software configurations. Or perhaps, worse still, the applications would need to be ported to a new platform, because the original platform was found to be inherently unsafe.

This chapter looks at the tests that should be considered to ensure that any system software that is going to be deployed has been configured to remove or minimize any security vulnerabilities associated with this group of software products and thereby provide a firm foundation on which Web applications can be built.

Security Certifications

Although virtually every system software vendor will claim its product is secure, some products are designed to be more secure than others. For instance, some products differentiate the tasks that need to be performed by an administrator from those that are typically only needed by a user of the system, thereby denying most users of the system access to the more security-sensitive administrative functions. This is just one of the ways Windows NT/2000 is architected differently than Windows 9.x.

When evaluating system software products for use on a Web site, an organization would ideally want to review each proposed product's architecture to ensure that it has been sufficiently secure. Unfortunately, for all but the largest organizations (typically governments), such an undertaking is likely to be cost prohibitive. To mitigate this problem, the security industry has developed a *common criteria* for evaluating the inherent security of software products. The goal of the common criteria is to allow certified testing labs to independently evaluate, or certify, software products against an industry-standard criteria, thereby allowing potential users of the software to deter-

---

SECURITY CERTIFICATION HISTORY

Circa 1985, the U.S. Department of Defense (www.defenselink.mil) defined seven levels of system software security, A1, B1, B2, B3, C1, C2, and D1 (A1 being the highest level of security), for the purpose of providing a common set of guidelines for evaluating the security of software products from different vendors. The exact criteria used to assign products to different levels were spelled out in a document commonly referred to as the *Orange book*. During the early 1990s several European governments jointly developed a European equivalent of the Orange book. These guidelines were called the European Information Technology Security Evaluation and Certification Scheme, or ITsec (see www.cesg.gov.uk/assurance/iacs/itsec/).

Both sets of guidelines have been superseded by a new set of general concepts and principles developed under the auspices of the International Organization for Standardization (www.iso.ch). This new standard (ISO 15408) is being referred to as the Common Criteria for Information Technology Security Evaluation, or Common Criteria (CC) for short.

mine the level of security a product provides, without each user having to individually evaluate each tool.

Although comparatively few products have currently completed the evaluation process, the common criteria is becoming more widely recognized, which in turn should lead to more products being submitted for testing. Additional information about the common criteria and the status of the products that have been or are in the process of being evaluated can be found at www.commoncriteria.org.

Patching

The early versions of system software products used to support Web sites often contained obscure security holes that could potentially be exploited by a knowledgeable attacker. Thanks to an army of testers that knowingly (or unknowingly) tested each new version of software before and after its release, the later releases of these products have become much more secure. Unfortunately, *more* is a relative term; many of these products still have well-documented security vulnerabilities that, if not patched, could be exploited by attackers who have done their homework.

If a security issue with a particular version of a system software product exists, typically the product's end-users can't do much about it until the developers of the product (vendor or open-source collaborators/distributor) are able to develop a patch or workaround. Fortunately, most high-profile system software vendors are particularly sensitive to any potential security hole that their software might contain and typically develop a fix (patch) or workaround very quickly.

System software patches are only useful if they are actually installed. Therefore, rather than actually testing the product itself for as-yet-undiscovered security holes, the security-testing team would be much better advised to review the work of others to determine what known security issues relate to the products used on the Web site under testing. A common, manual approach to researching known security issues is to view entries on online bug-tracking forums or incident response centers such as those listed in Table 4.2. In addition, many vendors also post up-to-date information on the status of known security defects (sometimes referred to by vendors as *features*) and what the appropriate fix or workaround is on their own Web site.

In addition, many vendors also post up-to-date information on the status of known security defects (sometimes referred to by vendors as *features*) and what the appropriate fix or workaround is on their Web site.

OPEN-SOURCE VERSUS CLOSED-SOURCE DEBATE

A debate still exists as to whether a proprietary (*closed-source*) product such as Windows is more or less secure than an *open-source* product such as Linux or OpenBSD. Open-source advocates claim that a product is much less likely to contain security holes when the source code is tested and reviewed by hundreds of individuals from diverse backgrounds. However, proponents of the proprietary approach reason that an attacker is much less likely to find any security holes that might exist if they do not have access to the product's source code.

HOT FIXES, PATCHES, SERVICE PACKS, POINT RELEASES, AND BETA VERSIONS

Different vendors use different terms to describe their software upgrades. Often these names are used to infer that different degrees of regression testing have been performed prior to the upgrade being released. The situation isn't helped when the vendor offers such generic advice as "this upgrade should only be installed if necessary." Therefore, before installing any upgrade, try to determine what level of regression testing the vendor has performed. An organization should consider running its own tests to verify that upgrading the latest version will not cause more problems than it fixes. For example, an upgrade fixes a minor security hole, but it impacts an application's performance and functionality.

Table 4.2   Web Sites of Bug- and Incident-Tracking Centers

WEB SITE NAME	WEB ADDRESS
CERT® Coordination Center	www.cert.org
Computer Incident Advisory Capability (CIAC)	www.ciac.org
Computer Security Resource Center (CSRC)	http://csrc.nist.gov
Common Vulnerabilities and Exposures (CVE)	www.cve.mitre.org
Federal Computer Incident Response Center (FedCIRC)	www.fedcirc.gov
Information System Security	www.infosyssec.com
Internet Security Systems™ (ISS)	www.iss.net
National Infrastructure Protection Center (NIPC)	www.nipc.gov
NTBugtraq	www.ntbugtraq.com
Packet Storm	http://packetstorm.decepticons.org
System Administration, Networking, and Security (SANS)	www.sans.org
Security Bugware	www.securitybugware.org
SecurityFocus (bugtraq)	www.securityfocus.com
SecurityTracker	www.securitytracker.com
Vmyths.com	www.vmyths.com
Whitehats	www.whitehats.com
Windows and .NET Magazine Network	www.ntsecurity.net

Table 4.3 Sample List of System Software Assessment Tools

NAME	ASSOCIATED WEB SITE
HFNetChk and Personal Security Advisor	www.microsoft.com
Hotfix Reporter	www.maximized.com
Internet Scanner	www.iss.net
Nessus	www.nessus.org
QuickInspector	www.shavlik.com
Security Analyzer	www.netiq.com
Titan	www.fish.com

Instead of manually researching all the security holes and nuances of a system soft-ware product, the security-testing team could utilize an automated security assess-ment tool or online service. Such a tool or service can be used to probe an individual machine or group of machines to determine what known security issues are present and remain unpatched. Table 4.3 lists some of the tools available for this task.

Whichever approach is used, the goal is typically not to find new system software defects, but to ascertain what (if any) security patches or workarounds need to be implemented in order to mitigate existing problems.

For some organizations, installing patches every couple of weeks on every machine in the organization may consume an unacceptable amount of resources. For instance, a risk-adverse organization may want to run a full set of regression tests to ensure that the functionality of any existing application isn't altered by the workaround, or that the Web site's performance isn't noticeably degraded by a new patch. In some instances, a patch may even turn on features that have previously been disabled or removed, or it may alter existing security settings. Security policies should therefore be reviewed to ensure that they describe under what circumstances a patch or workaround should be implemented and what regression tests should be performed to ensure that any newly installed patch has not unknowingly changed any security con-figuration setting or otherwise depreciated the capabilities of the Web site.

Table 4.4 lists a series of checks that could be utilized to evaluate how well security patches are being implemented.

Hardening

Hardening is a term used to describe a series of software configuration customizations that typically remove functionality and/or reduce privileges, thereby making it harder for an intruder to compromise the security of a system. Unfortunately, the default

Table 4.4   System Software Patching Checklist

YES	NO	DESCRIPTION
☐	☐	Is there a documented policy in place that describes under what circumstances and how a security patch should be implemented? (This is especially important when multiple patches are to be applied, as the installation order may be critical.)
☐	☐	Have all the known security issues for each system software product that is or will be used by the Web site been researched and documented? (The research should include evaluating any consequences of installing the patch.)
☐	☐	Have all the security patches deemed necessary by the documented policy been obtained from a legitimate source? (It's not unheard of for a supposed security patch to actually contain a Trojan horse.)
☐	☐	Have tests been designed that can demonstrate the existence of the security hole(s) that needs to be patched? (This is necessary if confirmation is needed that the security hole has indeed been fixed by the correct application of the patch.)
☐	☐	Have all the security patches and workarounds deemed necessary by the policy been implemented on every affected machine?
☐	☐	In the event an issue is discovered with a newly installed patch, is a process in place that would enable the patch to be rolled back (uninstalled)?
☐	☐	Is the person(s) responsible for monitoring new security issues aware of his or her responsibility and does he or she have the resources to accomplish this task?

ROCKING THE BOAT

One of reasons that system administrators delay (or do not) apply system software patches is because they are afraid of "rocking the boat." Because a system administrator may not have time to thoroughly regression test a new patch, he or she probably fears that the new patch may destabilize the system. Holding off implementing the new patch until the next scheduled system upgrade (when the system will be rigorously tested) will allow an organization to find any unexpected consequences of installing the patch. Unfortunately, during this period of time, the organization may be vulnerable to an attack through any of the security holes that could have been filled by the uninstalled patch.

LOCKING DOWN THE OPERATING SYSTEM

Rather than requiring a system administrator to manually harden an operating system, organizations now offer products such as those listed in Table 4.5 that attempt to provide an extra level of protection to the operating system. These products often work by disabling or *locking down* all administrative-level services, which can then only be accessed using a secure password administered by the protecting product.

Table 4.5 Sample List of Operating System Protection Tools

NAME	ASSOCIATED WEB SITE
Bastille Linux	www.bastille-linux.org
EnGarde	www.engardelinux.org
IISLockdown	www.microsoft.com
Immunix	www.immunix.org
ServerLock	www.watchguard.com

installation options for many system software products are usually not selected based on security considerations, but rather on ease of use, thus necessitating *hardening* customizations. Therefore, in addition to checking for known security holes, it also makes sense to simultaneously check for known features that, if left unaltered, could be exploited by an intruder.

Table 4.6 is a generic list of tests that can be used to form the basis of a system software-hardening checklist, while Allen (2001) outlines processes for hardening several different platforms.

Table 4.6 System Software Hardening Checklist

YES	NO	DESCRIPTION
☐	☐	Have vendor- and industry-recommended hardening customizations been researched and documented for each system software product that is or will be used by the Web site?
☐	☐	Have all the procedures used to harden each system software product been documented?
☐	☐	Have all the documented system software hardening procedures been implemented on every affected machine?

Masking

The more information an intruder can obtain about the brand, version, and installation options of any system software product installed upon the Web site (such as what brand and version of operating system is being used by the Web server), the easier it will be for the intruder to exploit any known security holes for this particular version of the product.

For instance, buffer overflow attacks (discussed in more detail in Chapter 6) are typically operating system and architecture specific (for example, a buffer overflow attack that works on an NT/Alpha platform is unlikely to work on a NT/Intel or UNIX/Alpha platform). Therefore, to exploit this kind of attack, the operating system and hardware platform must first be deduced or guessed. Additionally, when designing new exploits, authors often need to recreate an equivalent system software and hardware architecture environment in order to compile and/or test their newly discovered exploit(s).

Given the usefulness of knowing this kind of information, it makes sense that an organization would want to minimize this knowledge. Unfortunately, many products give up this kind of information all too easily. For instance, much of this information can be obtained via hello (banner) or error messages that the product sends by default when somebody tries to initiate a connection with it. Intruders trying to deduce the brand and version of a product will often use a technique called *banner grabbing* to trick a machine into sending information that uniquely identifies the brand and version of the products being used by the Web site. To reduce this information leakage, many organizations choose to mask their Web sites, replacing these helpful default messages with legal warnings, blank or uninformative messages, or false banners that match the default response from a completely different brand of system software and therefore hopefully cause an intruder to waste his time using an ineffective set of exploits.

A security tester shouldn't have to rely on manual efforts (such as the ones illustrated in the "Banner Grabbing" sidebar). Rather, several tools now exist that will attempt to identify (*fingerprint*) a target by running a series of probes. Some even offer features designed to make this activity less likely to be noticed by any intrusion-detection system (IDS) that might be installed on the target Web site and tip off an organization that its Web site was being fingerprinted (also known as enumerated). Table 4.7 lists some sample fingerprinting tools and services, while Scambray 2001 provides more detailed information on the techniques used by intruders to fingerprint a target, and Klevinsky (2002) provides guidance on how to use many of the fingerprinting tools used by penetration testers and intruders alike.

Unfortunately, it's not always possible to completely mask the identify of an operating system due to the Transmission Control Protocol/Internet Protocol (TCP/IP) being implemented slightly differently by various operating system vendors. For example, TCP features and packet sequence numbering may differ among vendors. However, many novice attackers and some fingerprinting tools may still be fooled or at least delayed by a false banner.

If an organization has decided to use a nondescriptive legal warning or false banners on some or all of their machines, then these machines should be checked to ensure that this requirement has been implemented correctly. In the case of false banners

BANNER GRABBING

It is very easy to identify the version of system software being used by a Web site and thereby hone in on known bugs or features with this specific product version. For example, the following error messages were generated when an attempt was made to start a Telnet session to two different Web sites using a port number not normally used by the Telnet application (if installed, the Telnet application is normally configured to communicate on port 23).

From a command-line prompt, enter telnet www.wiley.com 80 (80 is the port number used by HTTP) or telnet www.wileyeurope.com 25 (25 is the port number used by SMTP).

```
Example 1
C:\telnet www.wiley.com 80

HTTP/1.1 400 Bad Request
Server: Netscape Enterprize/3.6 SP3

Your browser sent a message this server could not understand.

Example 2
C:\telnet www.wileyeurope.com 25

220 xysw31.hosting.wileyeurope.com ESMTP server (Post.Office v3.5.3
release 223 ID# 0-83542U500L100S0V35) ready Tue, 16 Jan 2002 17:58:18 -
0500
```

Both Telnet connections should subsequently fail (it may be necessary to hit Enter a few times), because Telnet is not configured to work on either of the requested port numbers, but not before the target machine sends an error message that identifies the brand and version of system software that is currently running.

Table 4.7 Sample List of Fingerprinting Tools and Services

NAME	ASSOCIATED WEB SITE
Cerberus Internet Scanner	www.cerberus-infosec.co.uk
Cheops	www.marko.net
HackerShield	www.bindview.com
Netcat	www.atstake.com
Nmap	www.insecure.org
Super Scan/Fscan	www.foundstone.com
What's That Site Running?	www.netcraft.com

Table 4.8   System Software Masking Checklist

YES	NO	DESCRIPTION
☐	☐	Is there a documented policy in place that describes under what circumstances a default banner should be replaced with a blank legal warning or false banner?
☐	☐	If a legal warning is to be used, has it been approved by the legal department?
☐	☐	Have all the banner modifications deemed necessary by the policy been implemented on every affected machine?
☐	☐	If false banners are to be used, are they deceptive enough to trick a significant number of automated probing tools?

designed to deceive an intruder's fingerprinting effort, an assessment of the effectiveness of the deception can be made by using several of the automated probing tools to see if they can successfully see through this ploy. Table 4.8 summarizes these checks.

Services

This book will use the term *service* to describe all the system software services, processes, or *daemons* (in UNIX terminology) installed on a machine that can communicate with the network it is attached to. Before a service can communicate over the network, it must first be bound to one or more network interface cards (NICs) and communication channels (ports).

Whenever a service is started on a machine, the operating system will typically grant the service the same security privileges the user account that initiated the service had. Unfortunately, if a service were to be tricked into executing malicious commands, these undesirable instructions would be executed using the same privileges that the service inherited from the account that *owns* this service. For example, if the Web server service was running with administrative (or in UNIX lingo, *root*) privileges, an intruder could be able to trick the Web server into emailing the intruder the operating system's password file (a file that normally only the administrator can access). Had the Web server service been running with a lower privileged account, then chances are that the Web server service itself would have been refused access to this system file by the operating system. It is therefore important to check that any service running on a machine is only granted the minimum privileges needed to perform its legitimate functions and any unneeded services are disabled (or ideally uninstalled).

Generally speaking, common network services such as the Hypertext Transfer Protocol (HTTP), Finger, or the Simple Mail Transfer Protocol (SMTP) use predefined (or *well-known*) port numbers. These numbers are assigned by the Internet Assigned Numbers Authority (IANA, www.iana.org), an independent organization with the aim of minimizing network conflicts among different products and vendors. Table 4.9 lists some sample services and the port numbers that the IANA has reserved for them.

Table 4.9 Sample IP Services and Their Assigned Port Numbers

PORT NUMBER	SERVICE
7	Echo
13	DayTime
17	Quote of the Day (QOTD)
20 and 21	File Transfer Protocol (FTP)
22	Secure Socket Shell (SSH)
23	Telnet
25	SMTP
53	Domain Name System (DNS)
63	Whois
66	SQL*net (Oracle)
70	Gopher
79	Finger
80	HTTP
88	Kerberos
101	Host Name Server
109	Post Office Protocol 2 (POP2)
110	Post Office Protocol 3 (POP3)
113	IDENT
115	Simple File Transfer Protocol (SFTP)
137, 138, and 139	NetBIOS
143	Internet Message Access Protocol (IMAP)
161 and 162	Simple Network Management Protocol (SNMP)
194	Internet Relay Chat (IRC)
443	Hypertext Transfer Protocol over Secure Socket Layer (HTTPS)

For an intruder to communicate with and/or try to compromise a machine via a network connection, the intruder must utilize at least one port. Obviously, the fewer ports that are made available to an intruder, the more likely it is that the intruder is going to be detected. In just the same way, the fewer the number of doors and windows a bank has, the easier it is for the bank to monitor all of its entrances and the less likely it is that

---

PORT NUMBER ASSIGNMENTS

Port numbers 0 through 1023 are typically only available to network services started by a user with administrator-level privileges, and are therefore sometimes referred to as privileged ports. An intruder who has only been able to acquire a nonadministrator account on a machine may therefore be forced to utilize a nonprivileged port (1024 or higher) when trying to communicate to the compromised machine.

The set of nonprivileged port numbers (1024 to 65535) has been divided into two groups: the *registered* group (1024 to 49151) and the *private* (*dynamic*) group (49152 to 65535). The registered ports differ from the well-known ports in that they are typically used by network services that are being executed using nonadministrator level accounts. The private group of ports is unassigned and is often used by a network service that does not have a registered (or well-known) port assigned to it, or by a registered network service that temporarily needs additional ports to improve communication. In such circumstances the network service must first listen on the candidate private port and determine if it is already in use by another network service. If the port is free, then the network service will temporally acquire (dynamically assign) this port.

---

an intruder would be able to enter the bank unnoticed. Unfortunately, a single NIC could have up to 131,072 different ports for a single IP address, 65,536 for TCP/IP, and another 65,536 for User Datagram Protocol (UDP)/IP. (Appendix A describes IP, TCP, and UDP in more detail.)

Once a port is closed, any request made to a machine via the closed port will result in a "this port is closed" acknowledgment from the machine. A better defensive strategy is to make the *closed* port a *stealth* port; a request to a stealth port will not generate any kind of acknowledgement from the target machine. This lack of acknowledgement will typically cause the requesting (attacker's) machine to have to wait until its own internal time-out mechanism gives up waiting for a reply. The advantage of a *stealth* port over a *closed* port is that the intruder's probing efforts are going to be slowed, possibly generating frustration, and potentially causing the intruder to go and look elsewhere for more accommodating targets.

While checking to see whether ports are open can be performed manually by logging on to each machine and reviewing the services running (as depicted in Figure 4.1), it's not always clear what some of the services are or which ports (if any) they are using, especially if more than one NIC is installed.

Fortunately, a number of easy-to-use tools can automate this test; these tools are referred to as port scanners and often come as part of a suite of security-testing tools. Chirillo (2001) goes into considerable depth on securing some of the most commonly used ports and services, while Klevinsky (2002) provides an overview of many of the tools that can be used to automated a port scan.

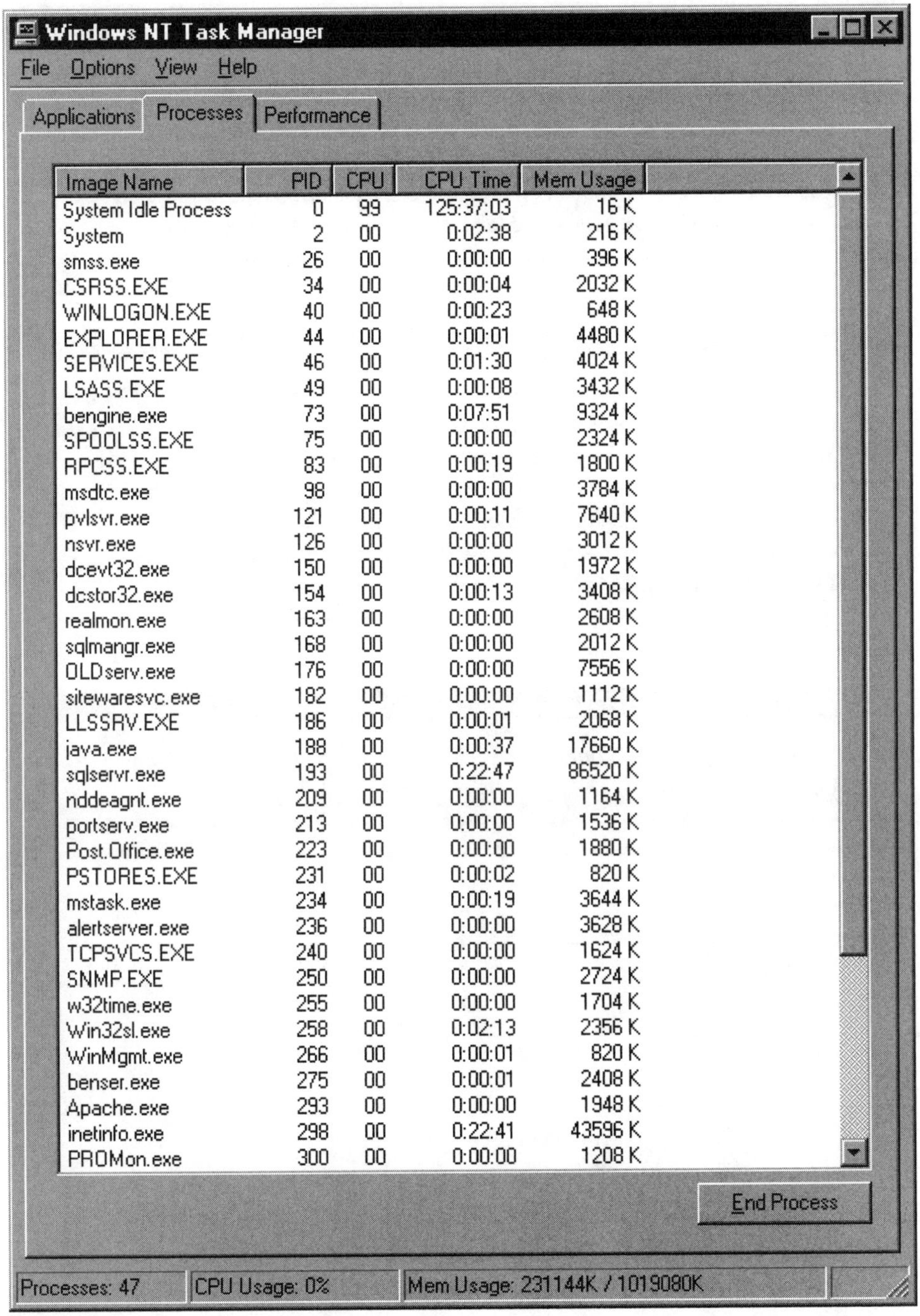

Image Name	PID	CPU	CPU Time	Mem Usage
System Idle Process	0	99	125:37:03	16 K
System	2	00	0:02:38	216 K
smss.exe	26	00	0:00:00	396 K
CSRSS.EXE	34	00	0:00:04	2032 K
WINLOGON.EXE	40	00	0:00:23	648 K
EXPLORER.EXE	44	00	0:00:01	4480 K
SERVICES.EXE	46	00	0:01:30	4024 K
LSASS.EXE	49	00	0:00:08	3432 K
bengine.exe	73	00	0:07:51	9324 K
SPOOLSS.EXE	75	00	0:00:00	2324 K
RPCSS.EXE	83	00	0:00:19	1800 K
msdtc.exe	98	00	0:00:00	3784 K
pvlsvr.exe	121	00	0:00:11	7640 K
nsvr.exe	126	00	0:00:00	3012 K
dcevt32.exe	150	00	0:00:00	1972 K
dcstor32.exe	154	00	0:00:13	3408 K
realmon.exe	163	00	0:00:00	2608 K
sqlmangr.exe	168	00	0:00:00	2012 K
OLDserv.exe	176	00	0:00:00	7556 K
sitewaresvc.exe	182	00	0:00:00	1112 K
LLSSRV.EXE	186	00	0:00:01	2068 K
java.exe	188	00	0:00:37	17660 K
sqlservr.exe	193	00	0:22:47	86520 K
nddeagnt.exe	209	00	0:00:00	1164 K
portserv.exe	213	00	0:00:00	1536 K
Post.Office.exe	223	00	0:00:00	1880 K
PSTORES.EXE	231	00	0:00:02	820 K
mstask.exe	234	00	0:00:19	3644 K
alertserver.exe	236	00	0:00:00	3628 K
TCPSVCS.EXE	240	00	0:00:00	1624 K
SNMP.EXE	250	00	0:00:00	2724 K
w32time.exe	255	00	0:00:00	1704 K
Win32sl.exe	258	00	0:02:13	2356 K
WinMgmt.exe	266	00	0:00:01	820 K
benser.exe	275	00	0:00:01	2408 K
Apache.exe	293	00	0:00:00	1948 K
inetinfo.exe	298	00	0:22:41	43596 K
PROMon.exe	300	00	0:00:00	1208 K

Figure 4.1 List of active processes running.

Note: Foundstone (www.foundstone.com) provides a utility Fport, which can be used to map running services to the ports that they are actually using.

REMAPPING SERVICES

If a potentially dangerous service such as Telnet (port 23) *absolutely* needs to be made available to external sources, the local area network (LAN) administrator may decide to try and hide the service by remapping it to a nonprivileged port (that is a port number above 1023), where it is less likely (but still possible) for an intruder to discover this useful service. If the LAN administrator is using such a technique, make sure that any port-scanning tool used for testing is able to detect these remapped services.

DUAL NICS

A machine that has two NICs can potentially have different services running on each card. For instance, a LAN administrator may have enabled the NetBIOS service on the *inward-facing* side of a Web server to make file uploads easier for the Webmaster, but disabled it on the *outward-facing* side to stop intruders from uploading their graffiti or hacking tool of choice. Although increasing the complexity of a network (which increases the risk of human error), using multiple NICs for some of the servers can potentially improve security and performance, and add additional configuration flexibility.

EXAMPLE PORT SCAN

It appears from the following sample nmapNT port scan report that this machine is running quite a few services, several of which could potentially be used to compromise this machine. nmap is a UNIX-based tool originally written by *Fyodor.* nmapNT is a version of nmap that was ported to the Windows platform by eEye Digital Security (www.eeye.com).

```
Interesting ports on www.wiley.com (123.456.789.123):
(The 1508 ports scanned but not shown below are in state: closed)
Port State       Service
21/tcp     open       ftp
25/tcp     open       smtp
79/tcp     open       finger
80/tcp     open       http
81/tcp     open       hosts2-ns
106/tcp    open       pop3pw
110/tcp    open       pop-3
135/tcp    open       loc-srv
280/tcp    open       http-mgmt
443/tcp    open       https
1058/tcp   open       nim
1083/tcp   open       ansoft-lm-1
1433/tcp   open       ms-sql-s
4444/tcp   open       krb524
5631/tcp   open       pcanywheredata
```

Tables 4.10 and 4.11 list some sample port-scanning tools and services.

Table 4.10   Sample List of Port-Scanning Tools

NAME	ASSOCIATED WEB SITE
Cerberus Internet Scanner (formally NTInfoScan or NTIS)	www.cerberus-infosec.co.uk
CyperCop Scanner	www.nai.com
Firewalk	www.packetfactory.net
HackerShield	www.bindview.com
Hostscan	www.savant-software.com
Internet Scanner	www.iss.net
IpEye/WUPS	www.ntsecurity.nu
Nessus	www.nessus.org
Netcat	www.atstake.com
Netcop	www.cotse.com
NetScan Tools	www.nwpsw.com
Nmap	www.insecure.org
NmapNT	www.eeye.com
SAINT/SATAN	www.wwdsi.com
SARA	www.www-arc.com
Scanport	www.dataset.fr
Strobe	www.freebsd.org
Super Scan/Fscan	www.foundstone.com
Twwwscan	www.search.iland.co.kr
Whisker	www.wiretrip.net
Winscan	www.prosolve.com

Table 4.11   Sample List of Port-Scanning Services

NAME	ASSOCIATED WEB SITE
Shields Up	www.grc.com
MIS CDS	www.mis-cds.com
SecurityMetrics	www.securitymetrics.com
Symantec	www.norton.com

A port scan should be performed against each machine that forms part of the Web site. Ideally, this scan should be initiated from a machine on the *inside* of any installed firewall, since an external port scan won't be able to tell if a service is disabled or if an intermediate firewall is blocking the request. The results of the port scan should be compared to the services that are absolutely required to be running on this machine and any additional/unexpected services should be either disabled (and, if possible, uninstalled) or justified.

A more stringent check would be to ensure that any unused ports were not only closed, but also configured to be *stealthy* and not provide any information on their status. Unfortunately, stealthy ports, while potentially slowing down an attacker's scan, may also slow down the testing team as they attempt to scan the machine for unnecessary services. Table 4.12 summarizes these checks.

Table 4.12   System Software Services Checklist

YES	NO	DESCRIPTION
☐	☐	Has each machine been reviewed and have any unnecessary services been stopped and, if possible, uninstalled?
☐	☐	Are the services that are active run under the lowest privileged account possible?
☐	☐	Has each machine been configured to respond in a stealthy manner to requests directed at a closed port?

REMOTE-ACCESS SERVICES

Perhaps one of the most popular side-entry doors available to attackers, remote-access utilities (such as Symantec's PCAnywhere, Windows's RAS, or UNIX's SSL/RSH) provide legitimate users with easy access to corporate resources from geographically remote locations. (The system administrator no longer has to make 3 A.M. trips into the office to reboot a server.)

Unfortunately, these convenient applications have two fundamental vulnerabilities. The first risk is that the client machine (for instance, a traveling salesperson's laptop) could be stolen, depending upon how the client is authenticated. The theft could potentially use this stolen machine to gain direct access to the corporate network by simply turning the machine on and double-clicking an icon on the desktop. The second risk is that the server-side component of the service running on the corporate network does a poor job of authenticating the client. Here the requester of the service is wrongly identified as a legitimate user and not an intruder trying to gain unauthorized access, especially when access is via an unsanctioned modem installed on a machine *behind* the corporate firewall.

Directories and Files

Each individual directory (or *folder* in Windows terminology) and file on a machine can have different access privileges assigned to different user accounts. In theory, this means each user can be assigned the minimum access privileges they need in order to perform their legitimate tasks. Unfortunately, because maintaining Draconian directory and file privileges is often labor intensive, many machines typically enable users (and the services that they have spawned) more generous access than they actually need.

To reduce the likelihood of human error when assigning directory and file access privileges, some LAN administrators will group files together based on their access privilege needs. For example, programs or scripts that only need to be granted execute access could be placed in a directory that restricts write access, thereby inhibiting an intruder's ability to upload a file into a directory with execute privileges.

Many products will by default install files that are not absolutely necessary; vendor demos and training examples are typical. Since some of these unneeded files may contain capabilities or security holes that could be exploited by an intruder, the safest approach is to either not install them or promptly remove them after the installation is complete.

Intruders are particularly interested in directories that can be written to. Gaining write and/or execute access to a directory on a target machine, even a temp directory that does not contain any sensitive data, can be extremely useful. An intruder looking to escalate his or her limited privileges will often need such a resource to upload hacking tools (rootkits, Trojan horses, or backdoors) on to the target machine and then execute them.

For an intruder to gain access to a directory, two things must happen. First, the intruder must determine the name and directory path of a legitimate directory, and second, the intruder must determine the password used to protect the directory (the topic of the next section of this chapter). In order to reference the target directory, the intruder must figure out or guess the name and directory path of a candidate directory. This is an easy step if default directory names and structures are used, or the intruder is able to run a *find* utility against the target machine.

In an effort to supplement the built-in file security offered by an operating system, several products now provide an additional level of authorization security. Typically, these products provide directory and file access using their own proprietary access

---

FILE-SEARCHING TECHNIQUE EXAMPLE

A complete listing of all the files present in a Web server's directory can be easily obtained if the webmaster has not disabled a Web server's automatic directory service or redirected such requests to a default resource (such as a Web page named index.html). Simply adding a trailing forward slash (/) to the end of a URL entered via a browser's URL entry line (such as http://www.wiley.com/cgi-bin/) would display the entire contents of the directory.

DIRECTORY-MAPPING TECHNIQUE EXAMPLE

The following is a simple exploit intended to show how easy it could be for an intruder to map out a directory structure. A feature with early versions of Microsoft IIS can display the directory structure of a Web site as part of an error message. Entering www.wiley.com/index.idc from a browser's URL entry line would result in a response such as this one:

```
Error Performing Query
The query file F:\wwwroot\primary\wiley\index.idc could not be opened.
The file may not exist or you may have insufficient permission to open
the file.
```

---

mechanisms, thereby potentially mitigating any security hole or omission that could be exploited in the underlying operating system. Table 4.13 lists some of these products.

Regardless of any third-party access control products that an organization may have deployed, the directory and file permissions for critical machines should still be checked to ensure that the permissions are no more liberal than they have to be. Fortunately, this potentially tedious manual task can to a large degree be automated using either commercial tools designed to find permission omissions or tools originally designed for attackers with other intentions. Table 4.14 lists some sample file-share-checking tools and Table 4.15 offers a checklist for checking the security of directories and files.

Table 4.13 Sample List of Directory and File Access Control Tools

NAME	ASSOCIATED WEB SITE
ArmoredServer	www.armoredserver.com
AppLock	www.watchguard.com
AppShield	www.sanctuminc.com
Authoriszor 2000	www.authoriszor.com
Entercept	www.entercept.com
InterDo	www.kavado.com
PitBull LX	www.argus-systems.com
SecureEXE/SecureStack	www.securewave.com
StormWatch	www.okena.com
Virtualvault	www.hp.com

Table 4.14   Sample List of File-Share-Scanning Tools

NAME	ASSOCIATED WEB SITE
Legion	www.hackersclub.com
Nbtdump	www.atstake.com
NetBIOS Auditing Tool (NAT)	www.nmrc.org
IP Network Browser	www.solarwinds.net
Winfo	www.ntsecurity.nu

Table 4.15   System Software Directories and Files Checklist

YES	NO	DESCRIPTION
☐	☐	Is there a documented policy in place that describes how directory and file privileges are assigned?
☐	☐	Is the directory structure on each machine appropriate? For example, are so many directories being used that administrative human errors are likely? Have read-only files been separated from execute-only files?
☐	☐	Have only the minimum access privileges been assigned to each user account?
☐	☐	Have services running on each machine been reviewed to make sure that any features that might give away information on the machine's directory structure have been disabled? An example would be a Web server's automatic directory service.
☐	☐	Using a file share scanner located *inside* the firewall, can any inappropriate file shares be detected?

UserIDs and Passwords

In most organizations, the assets on a network that could be of any use to an intruder are typically protected using combinations of userIDs and passwords. An intruder is therefore going to be forced to try and guess or deduce a useful combination. However, not all userID/password combinations are created equal; some are more useful than others. An intruder would ideally like to capture the account of an administrator, allowing him or her to do pretty much anything he or she wants on any machine that the captured account has administrative rights on. If the administrator's account proves to be unobtainable but a lower privileged account is susceptible, an experienced attacker may still be able to manipulate an improperly configured operating system into granting administrative privileges, a technique often referred to as *account*

WEAK PASSWORD PROTECTION EXAMPLE

Some Web servers provide the Webmaster with the ability to require client authentication (such as the .htaccess and .htgroup files that can be placed inside an Apache Web server directory) before displaying the contents of a directory. Upon requesting a protected directory, the Web server sends a request to the browser, which results in the browser displaying a simple userID/password pop-up window. Unfortunately, the data sent back to the server using this method isn't encrypted (it uses a base 64 conversion algorithm to encode the data) and is therefore extremely easy for an eavesdropper to decode. Web server client authentication should therefore not be relied upon to protect the contents of a directory.

escalation. Care should therefore be taken to ensure that not only are the administrators' userIDs and passwords sufficiently protected, but also any lower-level accounts.

Some system software products use weak or no encryption to store and/or transmit their userIDs and passwords from the client to the server component of the product, affording an eavesdropper with the chance to capture unencrypted or easily decipherable passwords. If the same password used for this service is the same as the password used for an administrative-level account, learning these weak passwords may not only allow an intruder to manipulate the service, but also compromise additional resources.

Although an attacker would like to compromise a single machine, compromising several machines is definitely more desirable. This can happen relatively quickly if other machines (or even entire networks) have previously been configured to *trust* the compromised administrator account. Alternatively, the LAN administrator may have used the same password for several administrative accounts, thereby making network administration easier, but also increasing the probability that if the password on one machine is deduced, the entire network may be compromised.

Even if different userIDs and passwords are used for each local administrative account and these accounts are granted limited trusts, an entire network may still be compromised if an intruder can get past the security of the machine used by the network for network security authentication, that is, the network controller. Capturing the network controller (or backup controller) allows an intruder complete access to the entire network and possibly any other network that trusts any of the accounts on the compromised network. Given the risk attached with compromising an administrator account on a network controller, many LAN administrators choose to use exceptionally long userIDs and passwords for these critical accounts.

One of the leading causes of network compromises is the use of easily guessable or decipherable passwords. It is therefore extremely important that an organization defines and (where possible) enforces a password policy. When defining such a policy, an organization should consider the trade-off between the relative increase in security of using a hard-to-crack password with the probable increase in inconvenience. Policies that are difficult to follow can actually end up reducing security. For example, requiring users to use a long, cryptic password may result in users writing down their passwords (sometimes even putting it on a post-it note on their monitor), making it

---

SINGLE SIGN-ON

Single sign-on (SSO) is a user authentication technique that permits a user to access multiple resources using only one name and password. Although SSO is certainly more user-friendly than requiring users to remember multiple userID's and passwords, from a security perspective it is a double-edged sword. Requiring users to only remember one userID and password should mean that they are more willing to use a stronger and hence more secure (albeit harder to remember) password, but on the other hand, should this single password be cracked, an intruder would have complete access to all the resources available to the compromised user account, a potentially disastrous scenario for a highly privileged account.

---

readily available to a potential attacker walking by. Requiring users to frequently change their password may result in some users using unimaginative (and therefore easily predictable) password sequences, such as password1, password2, and password3. Even if the access control system is smart enough to deduce blatant sequences, users may still be able to craft a sequence that is easy for them to remember but still acceptable to the access control system, such as passjanword, passfebword, and passmarword. As the following sections demonstrate, an intruder could acquire a userID/password combination in several distinct ways.

Manual Guessing of UserIDs and Passwords

Typically easy to attempt, attackers simply guess at userID/password combinations until they either get lucky or give up. This approach can be made much more successful if the intruder is able to first deduce a legitimate userID.

Obtaining a legitimate userID may not be as hard as you might think. When constructing a userID, many organizations use a variation of an employee's first name and last name. A sample userID format can be obtained, for example, by viewing an email address posted on the organization's Web site. Discovering the real name of a LAN administrator may be all that is needed to construct a valid userID, and that information is easily obtained by acquiring a copy of the organization's internal telephone directory. Or perhaps an intruder could look up the technical support contact posted by a domain name registrar to find a domain name owned by the organization.

Many system software products are initially configured with default userIDs and passwords; it goes without saying that these commonly known combinations should be changed immediately (www.securityparadigm.com even maintains a database of such accounts). What is less well known is that some vendors include userIDs and passwords designed to enable the vendor to log in remotely in order to perform routine maintenance, or in some cases the organization's own testing team may have created *test* accounts intended to help diagnose problems remotely. If any of the products installed at an organization, such as firewalls, payroll packages, customer relationship management systems, and so on, use this feature, the organization should consider

---

EXAMPLE PASSWORD POLICY GUIDELINES

Enforceable Guidelines
- Minimum length of x characters
- Must not contain any part of userID or user's name
- Must contain at least one character from at least four of the following categories:
  - Uppercase
  - Lowercase
  - Numeral
  - Nonalphanumeric, such as !@#$%^&*()
  - Nonvisual, such as control characters like carriage return <CR>
- Must be changed every X number of weeks
- Must not be the same as a password used in the last X generations
- Account is locked out for X minutes after Y failed password attempts within Z period of time

Hard-to-Enforce Guidelines

- Do not use words found in an English (or another language) dictionary
- Do not use names of family, friends, or pets (information often known by coworkers)
- Do not use easy-to-obtain personal information such as parts of a
  - Mailing address
  - Social security number
  - Telephone number
  - Driving license number
  - Car license plate number
  - Cubical number

USERID ADVERTISEMENTS

In an effort to improve customer relations, many organizations have started to advertise the email address of a senior employee, such as "Please email the branch manager, Jon Medlin, at jmedlin@wiley.com with any complaints or suggestions for improvement." Although providing direct access to senior management may help improve customer communications, if the format used for the email address is the same as the format used for the user's ID, the organization may also be inadvertently providing a potential attacker with userIDs for accounts with significant privileges.

---

whether or not this remote access feature should be disabled, or at the very least the remote access password changed.

If an intruder is truly just guessing at passwords, then perhaps the easiest way to thwart this approach is to configure the system to *lock out* the account under attack after a small number of failed login attempts. Typically, lockout periods range from 30 minutes to several hours, or in some cases even require the password to be reset.

THE NULL PASSWORD

Some organizations have adopted an easy-to-administer policy of not assigning a password to a user account until the first time it is used, the password being assigned by the first person to log in to the account.

Obviously, accounts that have no (or null) password are going to be extremely easy for an attacker to guess and should therefore be discouraged.

Automated Guessing of UserIDs and Passwords

Several tools now exist that can be used to systematically guess passwords; these tools typically employ one (or both) of two basic guessing strategies. The quickest strategy is to simply try a list of commonly used passwords. Most of the tools come with lists that can be added to or replaced (particularly useful if the passwords are expected to be non-English words). Hackersclub (www.hackersclub.com) maintains a directory of alternative wordlists.

The second approach is to use a brute-force strategy. As the name implies, a brute-force approach does not try to *get lucky* by only trying a comparative handful of passwords; instead, it attempts every single possible combination of permissible characters until it cracks the password. The biggest drawback with a brute-force approach is time. The better the password, the longer it will take a brute-force algorithm to crack the password. Table 4.16 lists some sample password-cracking tools.

Suppose the intruder intends to use an automated password tool remotely—and this approach is thwarted by locking out the account after a small number of failed attempts. To get in, the intruder would need to obtain a copy of the password file. But once that was in hand, the intruder could then run a brute-force attack against the file. Using only modest hardware resources, some tools can crack weak passwords within a few hours, while stronger passwords will take much longer. Skoudis (2001) provides additional details on how to attack password files for the purpose of determining just how secure sets of passwords are.

In theory, no matter how strong a password is, if the file that contains the password can be acquired, it can eventually be cracked by a brute-force attack. However, in practice, using long passwords that utilize a wide variety of characters can require an intruder to spend several weeks (or even months) trying to crack a file, a fruitless effort, if the passwords are routinely changed every week.

One approach to evaluating the effectiveness of the passwords being selected is to ask the LAN administrator to provide you with legitimate copies of all the password files being used on the production system. From a standalone PC (that is not left unattended), an attempt is made to crack each of these passwords using a password-guessing tool that uses as input a list of commonly used words (this file is obviously language specific). Any accounts that are guessed should be immediately changed.

A second time-consuming test would be to run a brute-force attack against each of these files, since in theory any password could be deciphered given enough time; this

Table 4.16   Sample List of Password-Deciphering/Guessing/Assessment Tools

NAME	ASSOCIATED WEB SITE
Brutus	www.antifork.org/hoobie.net
Cerberus Internet Scanner	www.cerberus-infosec.co.uk
Crack	www.users.dircon.co.uk/~crypto
CyberCop Scanner*	www.nai.com
(dot)Security	www.bindview.com
Inactive Account Scanner	www.waveset.com
Legion and NetBIOS Auditing Tool (NAT)	www.hackersclub.com
L0phtcrack	www.securitysoftwaretech.com
John the Ripper, SAMDump, PWDump, PWDump2, PWDump3	www.nmrc.org
SecurityAnalyst	www.intrusion.com
TeeNet	www.phenoelit.de
WebCrack	www.packetstorm.decepticons.org

*Effective July 1, 2002, Network Associates has transitioned the CyberCop product line into maintenance mode.

PASSWORD FILE NAMES

Password files on UNIX systems are generally named after some variation of the word *password*, such as *passwd*. The Windows NT/2000 family of systems name their password files *SAM* (short for Service Account Manager).

test should be time-boxed. For example, any password that can be cracked within 24 hours using modest hardware resources should be deemed unacceptable.

Particular care should be taken to destroy all traces of the copied password files, temporary files, and generated reports once the testing is complete, least these files fall into the wrong hands.

Even if only strong passwords are used, it still makes sense to try and ensure that these password files are not readily available to an intruder. An organization should therefore consider designing a test to see if an unauthorized person can acquire a copy of these files. Although security may be quite tight on the production version of these files, it's quite possible that backup files either located on the machine itself or offsite are quite easily accessible. For example, the file used by Windows NT/2000 to store its passwords is protected by the operating system while it is running. However, the operating system also automatically creates a backup copy of this file, which may be accessible. A simple search of a machine's hard drive using *sam*.* should locate the production and backup version(s) of this file.

A less obvious place to find clues to valid passwords is in the log files that some system software products use to store failed login attempts. For example, knowing that user Tim Walker failed to login with a password of *margarey* may be all an intruder needs to know in order to deduce the valid password is *margaret*. Such log files, if used, should therefore be checked to ensure that the failed password is also encrypted to stop an intruder from viewing these useful clues.

Gaining Information via Social Engineering

Covered in more detail in Chapter 7, social engineering refers to techniques used by intruders to trick unsuspecting individuals into divulging useful information. A classic example is that of an intruder calling an organization's help desk and asking them to reset the password of the employee the intruder is pretending to be.

Disgruntled Employees Committing Illicit Acts

Although many organizations seriously consider the risk of a trusted employee taking advantage of his or her privileged position to commit (or attempt to commit) an illicit act (a topic covered in more detail in Chapter 7), others chose to ignore this possibility. Obvious precautions include ensuring that employees are only granted access to resources they absolutely need, and accounts used by former employees are deactivated as soon as (or before) they leave.

Table 4.17 summarizes some of the checks that should be considered when evaluating the protection afforded to a system's userIDs and passwords.

User Groups

Most system software products support the concept of user groups. Instead of (or in addition to) assigning individual user accounts system privileges, privileges are assigned to user groups; each user account is then made a member of one (or more)

SHADOWED PASSWORD FILES

Some operating systems store their passwords in files that are hidden from all but administrative-level accounts; such files are typically referred as shadowed password files and obviously afford greater protection than leaving the password file(s) in plain sight of an attack with nonadministrative privileges.

Table 4.17   System Software UserIDs and Passwords Checklist

YES	NO	DESCRIPTION
☐	☐	Is there a documented policy in place that describes how userIDs and passwords are assigned, maintained, and removed?
☐	☐	When an employee leaves (voluntarily or involuntarily), are his or her personal user accounts deactivated and are the passwords changed in a timely manner for any shared accounts that he or she had knowledge of?
☐	☐	Are the procedures for handling forgotten and compromised passwords always followed?
☐	☐	Are security access logs monitored for failed logins? For instance, how long or how many tries does it take before someone responds to a legitimate account using invalid passwords?
☐	☐	Does the system lock out an account for X minutes after Y failed password attempts within Z period of time?
☐	☐	Are different administrative userIDs and/or passwords used for each machine?
☐	☐	Have all default accounts been removed, disabled, or renamed, especially any *guest* accounts?
☐	☐	Have all remote access accounts been disabled? Or at least have their passwords been changed?
☐	☐	Are variations of people's names *not* used when assigning userIDs?
☐	☐	Do none of the critical accounts use common (and therefore easily guessable) words for passwords?
☐	☐	Are hard-to-guess or decipher passwords (as defined by the organization's password policy) used for all critical accounts?
☐	☐	Are the details of any failed login attempts sufficiently protected from unauthorized access?

user groups and thereby inherits all the privileges that have been bestowed upon the user group. Using user groups can make security administration much easier, as a whole group of user accounts can be granted a new permission by simply adding the new privilege to a user group that they are already a member of.

The danger with user groups is that sometimes, rather than creating a new user group, a system administrator will add a user account to an existing user group that has all the needed privileges, plus a few unneeded ones. Thus, the system administrator grants the user account (and any services running under this account) greater powers than it actually needs. Of course, creating user groups that are so well defined that each user group only has a single member defeats the whole purpose of defining security privileges by groups instead of individual accounts.

SEPARATION OF DUTIES

A common practice for system administrators who need to access a machine as an administrator but would also like to access the machine (or initiate services) with nonadministrative privileges is to create two accounts. The administrator would thus only log into the administrator-level account to perform administrative-level tasks and use the less privileged account for all other work, reducing the possibility that he or she inadvertently initiates a service with administrative privileges.

Table 4.18   System Software User-Group Checklist

YES	NO	DESCRIPTION
☐	☐	Is there a documented policy in place that describes how user groups are created, maintained, and removed?
☐	☐	Do the user groups appear to have privileges that are too general, resulting in some user accounts being granted excessive privileges?
☐	☐	Do the user groups appear to have privileges that are too specific, resulting in so many user groups that the system administrator is more likely to make an error while assigning privileges?
☐	☐	Has each user account be assigned to the appropriate user group(s)?

Table 4.18 summarizes some of the checks that should be considered when evaluating the appropriateness of user-group memberships.

Summary

It is not enough to review and test a Web site's network topology and configuration (the subject of Chapter 3), since a poorly configured or unplugged security hole in a system software product installed upon the Web site could provide an attacker with an easy entry point.

Although few organizations have the resources to test another company's system software products for new vulnerabilities, it's not particularly desirable to discover that a known security patch or workaround in a system software product has not been applied until *after* the Web applications that will utilize this system software have been written, possibly necessitating an unscheduled enhancement to the Web application. System software products should therefore always be evaluated from a security perspective before being pressed into service.

Client-Side
Application Security

Think how convenient it would be if, once the security of the underlying infrastructure of a Web site—the network devices and system software—had been tested and found to be secure, anyone could host any Web application on this site and be confident that it would also be secure. Unfortunately, this is an unrealistic scenario, as each Web application brings with it the potential to introduce a whole new set of security vulnerabilities. For example, the seemingly most secure of Web servers, with a perfectly configured firewall, would provide no protection from an attacker who had been able to capture the userID and password of a legitimate user of a Web application, possibly by simply sneaking a look at a cookie stored on the user's hard drive (see the *Cookies* section that follows for a more detailed explanation of this potential vulnerability). Therefore, in addition to any testing done to ensure that a Web site's infrastructure is secure (the subject of Chapters 3 and 4), each and every Web application that is to be deployed on this infrastructure also needs to be checked to make sure that the Web application does not contain any security vulnerabilities.

Application Attack Points

Most Web applications are built on a variation of the multitier client-server model depicted in Figure 5.1. Unlike a standalone PC application, which runs entirely on a single machine, a Web application is typically composed of numerous *chunks* of code (HTML, JavaScript, active server page [ASP], stored procedures, and so on) that are distributed to many machines for execution.

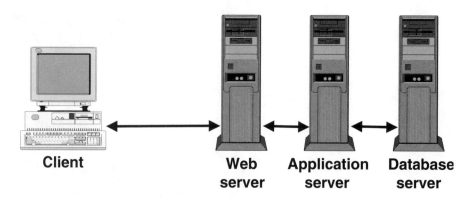

Figure 5.1   Multitier client/server design.

Essentially, an attacker can try to compromise a Web application from three distinct entry points. This chapter will focus on the first two potential attack points: the machine used to run the client component of the application, and the communication that takes place between the client-side component of the application and its associated server-side component(s). The next chapter will focus on the third potential entry point, the server-side portion of a Web application (for example, the application and database tiers of the application). Ghosh (1998) discusses numerous e-commerce vulnerabilities, which he groups into client, transmission, and server attack categories.

Client Identification and Authentication

For many Web applications, users are first required to identify themselves before being allowed to use some (or any) of the features available via the application. For some systems, this identification may be as simple as asking for an email address or a pseudonym by which the user wishes to be known. In such circumstances, the Web application may make no attempt to verify the identity of the user. For many Web applications, however, this laissez-faire level of identification is unacceptable, such applications may not only ask users to identify themselves, but also to *authenticate* that the individuals are who they claim to be.

Perhaps one of the most challenging aspects of a Web application's design is devising a user authentication mechanism that yields a high degree of accuracy while at the same time not significantly impacting the usability of the application or its performance. Given that in the case of an Internet-based Web application, users could be thousands of miles away in foreign jurisdictions and using all manner of client-side hardware and system software, this is far from a trivial task. Consequently, this is an area that will warrant comprehensive testing.

Most Web applications rely on one of three different techniques for establishing the authenticity of a user: relying upon something users know (such as passwords), something they have (like physical keys), or some physical attribute of themselves (for instance, fingerprints). These three strategies can all be implemented in a number of different ways, each with a different trade-off between cost, ease of use, and accuracy. Whichever approach is selected by the application's designers, it should be tested to ensure that the approach provides the anticipated level of accuracy.

The accuracy of an authentication mechanism can be measured in two ways: (1) the percentage of legitimate users who attempt to authenticate themselves but are rejected by the system (sometimes referred to as the *false rejection rate*) and (2) the percentage of unauthorized users who are able to dupe the system into wrongly thinking they are authorized to use the system (sometimes referred to as the *false acceptance rate*). Unfortunately, obtaining a low false acceptance rate (bad guys have a hard time getting in) typically results in a high false rejection rate (good guys are frequently turned away). For example, increasing the number of characters that users must use for their passwords may make it harder for an attacker to guess (or crack) any, but it may also increase the frequency with which legitimate users forget this information.

The risks associated with a false acceptance, compared to a false rejection, are quite different. A false acceptance may allow intruders to run amok, exploiting whatever application privileges the system had mistakenly granted them. Although a single false rejection may not be very significant, over time a large volume of false rejections can have a noticeable effect on an application. For instance, a bank that requires multiple, hard-to-remember passwords may make its Web application so user-unfriendly that its adoption rate among its clients is much lower than its competitor's. This would result in a larger percentage of its clients visiting physical branches of the bank or using its telephone banking system (both of which are more costly services to provide) and consequently giving its competitor a cost-saving advantage.

From a testing perspective, the testing team should attempt to determine if a Web application's false acceptance and false rejection rates are within the limits originally envisaged by the application's designers (and users). Additionally, because there is no guarantee that a particular authentication technique has been implemented correctly, the method by which the authentication takes place should be evaluated to ensure the authentication process itself can't be compromised (such as an attacker eavesdropping on an unencrypted application password being sent over the network). To this end, the following sections outline some of the techniques that might be implemented in order to authenticate a user of a Web application. Krutz (2001) and Smith (2001) provide additional information on user authentication strategies.

Relying upon What the User Knows: The Knows-Something Approach

The authenticity of the user is established by asking the user to provide some item of information that only the real user would be expected to know. The classic userID and password combination is by far the most common implementation of this authentication strategy. Variations of this method of authentication include asking the user to answer a *secret* question (such as "What's your mother's maiden name?") or provide a valid credit card number, together with corresponding billing address information.

Although the issues associated with application-level userIDs and passwords are similar to those affecting system software userIDs and passwords (see Chapter 4 for a discussion on this topic), an organization that has developed its own applications may have more flexibility in its userID and password implementations. Specifically, the organization may choose to enforce more or less rigorous standards than those implemented in the products developed by outside vendors. For instance, the organization may check that any new password selected by a user is not to be found in a dictionary, or the organization may enforce a one-user, one-machine policy (that is, no user can be logged on to more than one machine, and no machine can simultaneously support more than one user).

Therefore, in addition to the userID checklist in Table 4.17, the testing team may also want to consider including some or all of the checks in Table 5.1, depending upon what was specified in the applications security specifications.

Relying upon What the User Has: The Has-Something Approach

Instead of relying on a user's memory, the Web application could require that users actually have in their possession some artifact or token that is not easily reproducible.

Table 5.1 Application UserID and Password Checklist

YES	NO	DESCRIPTION
☐	☐	Does the application prohibit users from choosing common (and therefore easily guessable) words for passwords?
☐	☐	Does the application prohibit users from choosing *weak* (and therefore easily deciphered) passwords, such as ones that are only four characters long?
☐	☐	If users are required to change their passwords every X number of weeks, does the application enforce this rule?
☐	☐	If users are required to use different passwords for Y generations of passwords, does the application enforce this rule?
☐	☐	Is the application capable of allowing more than one user on the same client machine to access the server-side component of the application at the same time?
☐	☐	Is the application capable of allowing one user to access the server-side component of the application from two or more client machines at the same time?
☐	☐	Is the authentication method's false rejection rate acceptable? Is it measured by the number of calls made to the help desk for forgotten passwords?
☐	☐	Is the authentication method's false acceptance rate acceptable? For example, assuming no additional information, an attacker has a 1 in 10,000 chance of correctly guessing a 4-digit numerical password.

The token could be physical (such as a key or smart card), software based (a personal certificate), or assigned to a piece of hardware by software (for instance, a media access control [MAC] address could be assigned to an Ethernet card, a telephone number to a telephone, or an IP address to a network device).

If this *has-something approach* is used to authenticate a user to a Web application, the testing team will need to test the enforcement of the technique. For instance, if the authorized user Lee Copeland has a home telephone number of (123) 456-7890, then the organization may decide to allow any device to access the organization's intranet applications if accessed from this number. The testing team could verify that this authentication method has been implemented correctly by first attempting to gain access to the applications from Lee's home and then attempting access from an unauthorized telephone number such as Lee's next-door neighbor's.

Sole reliance on an authentication method such as the telephone number or network address of the requesting machine may not make for a very secure defense. For instance, Lee's kids could access the organization's application while watching TV, or a knowledgeable intruder may be able to trick a system into thinking he is using an authorized network address when in fact he isn't (a technique commonly referred to as *spoofing*). Scenarios such as these illustrate why many of these has-something authentication methods are used in conjunction with a *knows-something* method. Two independent authentication methods provide more security (but perhaps less usability) than one. So in addition to the telephone number requirement, Lee would still need to authenticate himself with his userID and password combination.

The following section describes some of the most common has-something authentication techniques.

Personal Certificates

A personal certificate is a small data file, typically obtained from an independent certification authority (CA) for a fee; however, organizations or individuals can manufacture their own certificates using a third-party product. (For more information on the use of open-source products to generate certificates, go to www.openca.org.) This data file, once loaded into a machine, uses an encrypted ID embedded in the data file to allow the owner of the certificate to send encrypted and digitally signed information over a network. Therefore, the recipient of the information is assured that the message has not been forged or tampered with en route.

Personal certificates can potentially be a more secure form of user authentication than the usual userID and password combination. However, personal certificates to date have not proven to be popular with the general public (perhaps because of privacy issues and their associated costs). So keep in mind that any Web application aimed at this group of users and requiring the use of a personal certificate may find few people willing to participate. In the case of an extranet and intranet application, where an organization may have more political leverage with the application's intended user base, personal certificates may be an acceptable method of authentication. Table 5.2 lists some firms that offer personal certificates and related services (and therefore provide more detailed information on how personal certificates work).

Brands (2000), Feghhi (1998), and Tiwana (1999) provide additional information on digital certificates.

Table 5.2 Sample Providers of Personal Certificates and Related Services

NAME	ASSOCIATED WEB SITE
BT Ignite	www.btignite.com
Entrust	www.entrust.com
GlobalSign	www.globalsign.net
SCM Microsystems	www.scmmicro.com
Thawte Consulting	www.thawte.com
VeriSign	www.verisign.com

Smart Cards

Smart cards are physical devices that contain a unique ID embedded within them. With this device and its personal identification number (PIN), the identity of the person using the device can be inferred (although not all cards require a PIN).

A *SecurID* smart card is an advanced smart card that provides continuous authentication by using encryption technology to randomly generate new passwords every minute. It provides an extremely robust authorization mechanism between the smart card and synchronized server. Table 5.3 lists some firms that offer smart cards and related services. Hendry (2001), Rankl (2001), and Wilson (2001) provide additional information on smart cards.

MAC Addresses

The MAC address is intended to be a globally unique, 48-bit serial number (for instance, 2A-53-04-5C-00-7C) and is embedded into every Ethernet network interface card (NIC) that has ever been made. An Ethernet NIC used by a machine to connect it to a network can be probed by another machine connected to the network directly or indirectly (for example, via the Internet) to discover this unique number. It is therefore possible for a Web server to identify the MAC address of any visitor using an Ethernet card to connect to the Web site. For example, the Windows commands winipcfg and ipconfig, or the UNIX command ifconfig can be used to locally view an Ethernet card's MAC address.

Privacy concerns aside, the MAC address can be used to help authenticate the physical computer being used to communicate to a Web server. But because some Ethernet cards enable their MAC addresses to be altered, this authentication technique cannot be guaranteed to uniquely identify a client machine. Therefore, it should not be relied upon as the sole means of authentication.

Table 5.3   Sample Providers of Smart Cards and Related Services

NAME	ASSOCIATED WEB SITE
Activcard	www.activcard.com
Dallas Semiconductor Corporation	www.ibutton.com
Datakey	www.datakey.com
Labcal Technologies	www.labcal.com
Motus Technologies	www.motus.com
RSA Security	www.rsasecurity.com
Signify Solutions	www.signify.net
VASCO	www.vasco.com

IP Addresses

Every data packet that travels the Internet carries with it the IP network address of the machine that originated the request. By examining this network source address, a receiver should be able (in theory) to authenticate the sender of the data. Unfortunately, this form of authentication suffers from two major problems; proxy servers hide the network address of the sender, replacing the original sender's network address with their own. This means that when proxy servers are involved, IP address verification is typically only going to be able to verify the organization or the Internet service provider (ISP) that owns the proxy server, not the individual machine that originated the request. The second problem with IP address authentication is that the source IP address is relatively easy to alter, or spoof, and it therefore should not be relied upon as the sole means of identifying a client.

Telephone Numbers

Using a telephone number for authentication is a technique used by many credit card issuers to confirm delivery of a credit card to the card's legitimate owner. The credit card is activated once a confirmation call has been received from the owner's home telephone number.

Requiring users to access an organization's remote access server (RAS) from a specific telephone number (often authenticated via a callback mechanism) is a common way of restricting access to applications on an intranet or extranet. Unfortunately, an attacker can subvert a callback mechanism by using *call forwarding* to forward the callback to an unintended destination. This would make this form of authentication undependable, if used as the sole method of authentication.

Table 5.4   Secure Token Checklist

YES	NO	DESCRIPTION
☐	☐	Is there a documented policy in place that describes how application security tokens are assigned and removed from circulation?
☐	☐	Are the procedures for handling lost tokens adequate and always followed?
☐	☐	Can the token be counterfeited? If technically feasible, how likely is it that this would actually take place?
☐	☐	Does the application enable the same token to be simultaneously used more than once?
☐	☐	Is the authentication method's false rejection rate acceptable?
☐	☐	Is the authentication method's false acceptance rate acceptable?

Table 5.4 lists some tests that should be considered if the application uses some form of token to determine who a user is.

Relying upon What the User Is: The Biometrics Approach

Undoubtedly the most secure of the three authentication approaches, a biometric device measures some unique physical property of a user that cannot easily be forged or altered, thereby providing an extremely accurate method of identifying an individual user. Biometric authentication methods include fingerprints, hand geometry, face geometry, eye patterns (iris and/or retina), signature dynamics (speed, pressure, and outline), keyboard typing patterns, and voice. Ideally, a combination of two or more of these methods should be used, as advances in technology have made some of these measurements easier to fake.

This approach also has the most resistance to adoption by the general population. However, in situations where the use of a biometric device can be deployed without adoption concerns (such as in the military), it is often the method of choice for Web applications that need unequivocal confirmation of who the user is. One drawback of a biometric measurement is what happens after an ID has been compromised. For example, suppose the input data sent from the scanner has been compromised because of eavesdropping or with the assistance of an infamous *evil twin*. Unfortunately, there is typically no way to issue the user a new identifying characteristic. (Eye surgery would seem a little drastic.) An additional drawback is the fact that some of the measurements are more susceptible than others to false acceptances and rejections. Nanavati et al. (2002) provide additional information on biometrics.

Table 5.5 lists some firms that offer biometric devices and related services. (For more detailed information on how they work, go to the individual Web sites listed.)

Table 5.6 lists some tests that should be considered if the application is to use a biometric device to authenticate a user's identity.

Table 5.5 Sample Providers of Biometric Devices and Related Services

NAME	ASSOCIATED WEB SITE
ActivCard	www.activcard.com
Cyber-SIGN	www.cybersign.com
DigitalPersona	www.digitalpersona.com
Identix	www.identix.com
Interlink Electronics	www.interlinkelec.com
Iridian Technologies	www.iridiantech.com
Keyware	www.keyware.com
SAFLINK	www.saflink.com
SecuGen	www.secugen.com
Visionics	www.visionics.com

Table 5.6 Biometric Device Checklist

YES	NO	DESCRIPTION
☐	☐	Is there a documented policy in place that describes how biometric measurements are originally captured and authenticated?
☐	☐	Are the procedures for handling compromised measurements adequate and always followed?
☐	☐	Can the biometric measurement be faked? If technically feasible, how likely is it that this would actually take place?
☐	☐	Is the false rejection rate too high? For example, the measuring device could be too sensitive.
☐	☐	Is the false acceptance rate too high? For example, the measuring device could not be sensitive enough.

User Permissions

It would be convenient if all legitimate users of an application were granted the same permissions. Alas, this situation rarely occurs. (For example, many Web-based applications offer more extensive information to subscription-paying members than they do to nonpayers.) Permissions can be allocated to users in many ways, but generally speaking, restrictions to privileges take one of three forms: functional restrictions, data restrictions, and cross-related restrictions. Barman (2001), Peltier (2001), and Wood (2001) all provide guidance on developing user security permissions.

Functional Restrictions

Users can be granted or denied access to an application's various functional capabilities. For example, any registered user of a stock-trading Web application may get a free 15-minute-delayed stock quote, but only users who have opened a trading account with the stockbroker are granted access to the real-time stock quotes.

One of the usability decisions a Web application designer has to make is to decide whether or not features that a user is restricted from using should be displayed on any Web page the user can access. For instance, in the previous example, should an ineligible user be able to see the real-time stock quote menu option, selecting this option will result in some sort of "Access denied" message being displayed. The following are some of the arguments for displaying restricted features:

- Seeing that the feature exists, users may be enticed into upgrading their status (through legitimate methods).

- In the case of an intranet application, when an employee is promoted to a more privileged position, the amount of additional training that he or she needs in order to use these new privileges may be reduced. The employee would already have a great degree of familiarity with the additional capabilities that he or she has just been granted.

- Having only one version of a user interface should reduce the effort needed to build an online or paper-based user manual. The manual would certainly be easy to follow, as any screen captures or directions in the manual should exactly match the screens that each user will see, regardless of any restrictions.

- Having only one version of a user interface will probably reduce the amount and complexity of coding needed to build the application.

Some drawbacks also exist, however, among which are the following:

- One of the simplest forms of security is based on the *need-to-know* principal. Users are only granted access to the minimum amount of information they need to know in order to perform their expected tasks. Merely knowing the existence of additional features may be more information than they need, as it could entice them into trying to acquire this capability through illegal channels.

- Some legitimate users may find the error messages generated when they try to access forbidden areas frustrating. They might think, "If I can't access this feature, why offer me the option?" or even assume the application is broken.

- Too many inaccessible options may overcomplicate a user interface, thereby increasing a user's learning curve and generating additional work for the help desk.

Whichever approach is taken, the application's user interface should be tested to ensure that the same style of interface is used consistently across the entire application, reducing the probability of errors while at the same time improving usability.

One recurring problem with function-only restrictions is that these controls may be circumvented if the user is able to get direct access to the data files or database. (Unfortunately, this is an all-too-common occurrence with the advent of easy-to-use reporting tools.) The database and data files should be checked to ensure that a knowledgeable insider couldn't circumvent an application's functional security measures by accessing the data directly. For instance, via an Open Database Connectivity (ODBC) connection from an Excel spreadsheet.

Data Restrictions

Instead of restricting access to data indirectly by denying a user access to some of an application's functionality, the application could directly block access to any data the user is not authorized to manipulate or even view. For example, sales representatives may be allowed to view any of the orders for their territory but not the orders for their peers. Correspondingly, a regional sales manager may be able to run reports on any or all of the reps that report to him or her, but not for any other rep.

Functional and Data Cross-Related Restrictions

Many applications use a combination of functional and data restrictions. For instance, in addition to only being able to see orders in their own territory, a rep may not be allowed to close out a sales quarter, an action that can only be performed by the vice president of sales or the CFO.

Less common are situations in which access to a particular function is based on the data that the user is trying to manipulate with the function. For example, reps may be allowed to alter the details of an order up until it is shipped, after which they are denied this ability, a privilege that is only available to regional managers. A more complicated example would be a financial analyst who is restricted from trading in a stock for 72 hours after another analyst at the same firm changes their buy/sell recommendation.

Each of these three forms of restrictions (functional, data, or a hybrid of both) can be enforced using one or more different implementations (for example, via application code, stored procedures, triggers, or database views). Regardless of the approach used to implement the restrictions, the application should be tested to ensure that each category of user is not granted too many or too few application permissions. Table 5.7 summaries these checks.

Table 5.7   User Permissions Checklist

YES	NO	DESCRIPTION
☐	☐	Is there a documented policy in place that describes under what circumstances users will be granted access to the application's functional capabilities and data?
☐	☐	Is there a documented policy in place that describes how user application privileges may be altered or removed?
☐	☐	Does the application's user interface take a consistent approach to displaying (or hiding) functions that the user is currently not authorized to use?
☐	☐	Can any of the users access a function that should be restricted?
☐	☐	Can all the users access every function that they should be permitted to use?
☐	☐	Can all the users access data that they should be permitted to use?

Testing for Illicit Navigation

One of the features of the Internet is that users are able to *jump around* a Web application from page to page in potentially any order. Browser options such as Go, History, Favorites, Bookmarks, Back, Forward, and Save pages only add to the flexibility. In an attempt to ensure that a user deliberately attempting to access Web pages in an inappropriate sequence (such as trying to go to the *ship to* Web page without first going through the *payment collection* page) cannot compromise a site's navigational integrity and security, designers may have to utilize one or more techniques to curtail illicit activities. If such precautions have been built into the application, they should be tested to ensure that they have been implemented correctly.

HTTP Header Analysis

Some Web sites will use the information contained in a Hypertext Transfer Protocol (HTTP) header (the Referer field) to ascertain the Web page that the client has just viewed and thereby determine if the client is making a valid navigational request. Although an attacker *could* easily alter this field, many attackers may not suspect that this defense is being employed and therefore will not consider altering this field.

HTTP Header Expiration

To reduce the ease with which an attacker can try to navigate to a previously viewed page (instead of being forced to download a fresh copy), the HTTP header information for a Web page can be manipulated via HTTP-EQUIV meta tags Cache-control, Expires, or Pragma to force the page to be promptly flushed from the requesting browser's memory.

Unfortunately, only novice attackers are likely to be thwarted by this approach (as previous viewed Web pages can always be saved to disk). However, if this defense has been designed into the application, it should still be checked to ensure that it has been implemented.

Client-Side Application Code

Some Web applications rely on client-side mobile code to restrict access to sensitive pages (mobile code is discussed in more detail later in this chapter). For instance, *before* entering a restricted Web page, a client-side script could be used to launch a login pop-up window. If the Web application uses such a mechanism, it should be tested to ensure that a user turning off scripting, Java applets, or ActiveX controls in his or her browser before attempting to access the restricted page does not allow the user to circumvent this restriction.

Session IDs

By placing an item of unique data on the client (discussed in more detail in the *Client-Side Data* section), a Web application can uniquely identify each visitor. Using this planted identifier (sometimes referred to as *session ID*), a Web application can keep track of where a user has been and thereby deduce where he or she may be permitted to go.

The effectiveness of this approach to a large degree depends on how and where this identifier is stored on the client machine (as will be described in the *Client-Side Data* section), with some methods being safer than others.

Navigational Tools

If access to a large number of Web pages needs to be checked using several different user privileges, it may make sense to create a test script using one of the link-checking

---

HIDING CLIENT-SIDE CODE

Storing code in a separate file (for instance, *hiddencode.js*) is a technique used by some developers to avoid a user casually viewing client-side source code that controls security functions. The Web page that needs this code then references this file, thereby avoiding the need to embed the code in the HTML used to construct the Web page (which would allow a viewer to easily view the code alongside the HTML code). Here's an example:

```
<script language="JavaScript1.2" src="hiddencode.js"
type="text/javascript"></script>
```

Unfortunately, even novice attackers are likely to realize that they could review the script by searching the browser's cache on their hard drive and opening the supposedly hidden file with their favorite text editor.

> ### THE ANONYMOUS USER
>
> One illicit navigation strategy that some Web application designers fail to consider defending against (and therefore should be tested for) is the attacker who, after logging on legitimately, saves a restricted Web page to his or her hard drive and then logs off. The attacker then opens this file (probably from an untraceable client), and using the links and client-side scripts on this saved page (which may have been edited with the use of a Web page authoring tool), he or she attempts to reenter the restricted portion of the Web application without going through a login procedure, thereby gaining complete anonymity.

tools listed in Table 5.8. The script can then be played back via different userIDs. One can also produce a report of all the Web pages that were previously accessible (when the test script was created using a userID with full privileges) but have since become unobtainable due to the reduced security privileges assigned to each of the userIDs.

Table 5.9 lists some of the scenarios that should be considered when trying to ensure that a user cannot inappropriately access any portion of the Web application.

Client-Side Data

Too often, sensitive application information (such as userIDs, passwords, authorization levels, credit card numbers, and social security numbers) is stored in unencrypted or weakly encrypted formats on the client machine. Given the frequency with which employees *share* their hard drives with one another (for instance, via Windows file-sharing capabilities), snooping colleagues could view this information without even leaving their desks. Alternatively, users could review and alter the information stored on their own machines and thereby attempt to gain access to a portion of the Web application they are not authorized to view. For example, after a successful login attempt, the user's security level is stored on the client machine and this level is then re-sent with every subsequent transmission back to the Web site as a means of authenticating the user. The user could then escalate his or her application privileges by simply editing the field used to store their level. Possible values to try might include Admin, Anonymous, DBA, Dummy, Guest, Master, Primary, QA, Root, Superuser, and, of course, *Test*.

Ideally, sensitive information about the client should be sent and stored in an encrypted format. This endeavor will require a little extra central processing unit (CPU) effort and a little more network bandwidth, as encrypted data is typically longer than its unencrypted equivalent. But any information that must reside on the client machine, if only temporarily, is vulnerable to an intruder who could potentially use it to cause mischief. So, protection is in order through encryption or at least reformatting (*hashing*). An intruder who collects unencrypted client-side data files (possible from several different machines) and then compares the data looking for a pattern may be able to crack any *security-by-obscurity* approach designed to protect the data.

If a Web application is going to store data on the client side, a designer may choose among several different places to locate this information. Although each location has

Table 5.8 Sample Link-Checking Tools

NAME	ASSOCIATED WEB SITE
Astra SiteManager	www.mercuryinteractive.com
e-Test Suite	www.empirix.com
Linkbot	www.watchfire.com
Site Check	www.rational.com
SiteMapper	www.trellian.com
WebMaster	www.coast.com

Table 5.9 Illicit Navigation Checklist

YES	NO	DESCRIPTION
☐	☐	Is there a documented policy in place that describes how clients will be prohibited from accessing the Web application illegally?
☐	☐	Can disabling client-side scripts or mobile code circumvent critical Web pages or pop-up windows?
☐	☐	By using a browser's Go, History, Favorites, or Bookmark features, can a restricted portion of the Web application be navigated to without first gaining authorization?
☐	☐	By using a browser's Go, History, Favorites, Bookmark, Forward, or Backward features, can a restricted portion of the Web application be navigated to illegally?
☐	☐	Is any HTTP header analysis or expiration option recommended by the designers implemented correctly?
☐	☐	Can a Web page previously saved to a local hard drive be used to navigate to a restricted portion of a Web application and circumvent any login process?

its pros and cons, whichever approach is implemented, the testing team should check that the data has been sufficiently protected from a malicious user trying to take advantage of the accessibility of this client-side data.

Cookies

A cookie is a little nugget of information that is sent to a browser from a Web server. This block of data can be anything: a unique session ID generated by the Web server, the current date and time, the network address of where the browser is accessing the Internet from, or any other chunk of data that might be useful to the Web application.

Dustin et al. (2001) and St. Laurent (1998) provide additional information on cookie security issues.

Browsers manage cookies automatically. After receiving a cookie, they will by default send this information back to the Web server that originated it every time the browser makes a request to that Web site (unless disabled by the browser's user). Basically, two types of cookies exist: persistent cookies and session cookies.

Persistent Cookies

Persistent cookies continue to be stored on the client machine after the browser has been closed and the machine has powered down. This is accomplished by physically storing the cookie on the user's hard drive. (Microsoft's Internet Explorer uses a directory called Cookies to store its persistent cookies, while Netscape uses a single file called Cookies.txt.) Ordinarily, a Web site will only use a single persistence cookie. Nevertheless, cookie implementations do enable each individual Web page to have its own cookie.

The option exists for persistent cookies to be flagged to expire after a specified period of time. This feature often is used if the cookie is being used to store the client's userID, thereby forcing users to periodically reidentify themselves.

Web applications can sometimes be tricked into giving away additional information by deleting just some of the information contained in a persistent cookie. Rather than completely rejecting or resetting a corrupted cookie, a Web application may replace the missing information with application defaults, which may enable the user to deduce more useful values to try in this field and thereby gain access to resources they should have been restricted from.

To reduce the possibility of cookie tampering (also known as cookie poisoning), some Web applications include a parity check in the cookie, rejecting the contents of any cookie that conflicts with its parity tag. In addition, some Web applications will embed the network address of the client machine into a cookie in an effort to hinder cookie-stealing (or counterfeiting) activities.

Session Cookies

Session cookies reside in the browser's memory and only *live* as long as that instance of the browser remains open. Each open browser instance will have its own session cookie for a Web site. However, if the client's machine is short of memory, a session (memory resident) cookie may be swapped out to the client's hard drive (virtual memory). If the browser were to be terminated abnormally (crash), it would most likely not clean up its virtual memory, and the session cookie would subsequently be visible to anyone interested in viewing the hard drive.

MAGIC COOKIES

The name *cookie* was originally derived from the UNIX term *magic cookies*, which referred to objects that could be attached to a user or program, and change depending on the areas entered by the user or program.

Hidden Fields

As an alternative to cookies, some Web applications use *hidden fields* on an HTML form, or an Extensible Markup Language (XML) file, to store information on the client-side component of the application. One of the advantages of this approach is that it works on browsers that have had their cookie capabilities disabled (or simply don't support cookies in the first place). Unfortunately, these hidden fields are not hidden very well. All a user has to do to view and alter the contents is to edit the Web page via a browser's built-in capabilities, or save it to a disk, and then edit it with his or her HTML or XML authoring tool of choice.

For example, suppose after a successful login, instead of storing the actual client userID in a hidden field on an HTML form, the Web site designer decided to use a single character to indicate the appropriate level of user privileges (for example, *A* for administrator, *R* for read-only, and *W* for read-write access). The theory behind this is that this information would never be displayed by the browser, and even if users reviewed the source code used to build the Web page, they would be unlikely to figure out that this single character was being used to control their security level. Although this may have been a reasonable assumption for some clients, it is certainly not true for members of the development and testing teams who are aware of this design and could therefore easily exploit this design should they chose to do so at a later date. Dustin et al. (2001) provides additional information on security issues related to hidden fields.

URLs

Some Web applications embed userIDs and other sensitive information into a URL, typically as parameters in the Query component of the URL (the fields that occur after the ? symbol in a URL). Unfortunately, this information is easily viewed by a passerby and also recorded in a Web site's log, where a corrupt Webmaster may view it at leisure.

Local Data Files

Depending upon the privileges assigned by the client to download mobile code (mobile code is discussed in the *Mobile Application Code* section), the mobile code may have free reign to create temporary or permanent data files on the machine it is being executed on or any network drive that the client is authorized to access.

An area of particular concern is what happens if execution of the mobile code is abruptly terminated. Under such conditions, any temporary files might not be cleaned up as the developer intended and may leave sensitive data lingering on the client's hard drive.

Windows Registry

In the case of mobile code such as an ActiveX control, the designer may choose to store application data in the client's registry. If unencrypted, this information could be viewed (and optionally modified) by simply running the built-in Windows utility *regedit*.

Table 5.10   Client-Side Data Checklist

YES	NO	DESCRIPTION
☐	☐	Is there a documented policy in place that describes what (if anything) will be stored permanently or temporarily on a client machine? Where will it be stored? What precautions will be used to protect the information from being tampered with?
☐	☐	Is any sensitive client-side data not protected by encryption?
☐	☐	Are there checks in place to prevent a client from tampering with client-side data?
☐	☐	Are there checks in place to detect tampered client-side data?
☐	☐	Is the client-side data easily visible to a casual passerby or via a network share? If so, could this information be utilized from another machine?
☐	☐	Do any memory-resident data files contain any information, which, if temporarily written to a hard drive (possible as the result of low memory), might pose a potential security risk?

Table 5.10 lists some of the checks that should be considered when trying to ensure that any data stored on a client machine is protected from abuse.

Secure Client Transmissions

Sensitive data transmitted over the Internet should always be encrypted to avoid potential intruders from eavesdropping on the communication anywhere along the route the data takes between the two machines. Wireless connections are particularly prone to this activity, as the eavesdropper does not even need to acquire a physical connection to the network being sniffed. Stories abound of would-be eavesdroppers driving around towns searching for unprotected wireless communications.

To protect against eavesdropping on Internet traffic being eavesdropped, the industry has developed several different encryption schemes. Examples include Secure-HTTP (S-HTTP), Secure Sockets Layer (SSL), and Internet Protocol Security (IPsec), each of which are described in more detail in Appendix A. In addition, several new encryption schemes are emerging, such as WAP's Wireless Transport Layer Security (WTLS) protocol, for securing the wireless hop(s) made by an Internet message. Burnett (2001), Feghhi et al. (1998), and Stallings (1998) provide additional information on secure network transmissions.

Digital Certificates

To allow two parties to communicate with each other via encrypted messages, at least one of the parties must have a digital certificate installed. (Typically, this certificate is referred to as a *server certificate* if installed on a Web server, or a *personal certificate* if installed in a browser.) The digital certificate contains a key that enables the sender to encrypt the data in a way that ensures that only the intended receiver is able to decipher the data and also proves to the recipient that it was really the alleged sender who actually sent the message.

Certificates are transported from issuer to user by means of a certificate file. Typically, these files are themselves encrypted and protected by a user-selected (ideally strong) password. If an attacker is able to guess the password used to protect the certificate, he or she may be able to transfer the certificate to another machine (inside or outside of the owning organization). Then the attacker uses this second machine to try and trick another Internet user into thinking that he or she is communicating with the legitimate owner.

To reduce the threat of a certificate file being copied, thereby allowing an attacker to try and crack the password protecting the certificate at his or her leisure, the file should be removed from any easily accessible location that an attacker may be able to get to. For example, a floppy disk in a bank's safe deposit box makes for a much more secure home for the file than the hard drive of the Web server on which the certificate was installed. (Note that, once installed, the certificate file does not need to be stored on the machine that is using it.)

Encryption Strength

When using SSL to encrypt a Web page, the URL displayed by a browser is typically preceded by https (as opposed to http). Some browsers also use a visual cue to indicate whether the communication is encrypted or not (with broken keys and padlock icons). What the visual cue, or https prefix, does not indicate is the type of encryption being used for the communication. A number of different encryption algorithms exist (such as RC4, DES, and MAC), as do different encryption keys lengths (40, 56, 128, and 168 are currently the most common key-length implementations).

The ease with which a message can be deciphered using a *brute-force* attack (brute-force attacks are described in more detail in Chapter 4) is dependent upon the key size used to encrypt the message. (The larger the key, the longer it will take to break it.) So, a larger key size will make the data being transmitted more secure. Unfortunately, a larger-sized key will also make the encrypted data file larger, thereby utilizing additional network bandwidth, and it will place an additional strain on the CPU doing the encryption and deciphering. Therefore, a trade-off exists between improved security

---

CERTIFICATE CLASSES

Certificates come in several different classes, the class reflecting the ease with which the certificate can be obtained from its issuer, and therefore the implied authenticity of its user. Class 1 certificates are typically easy to obtain; a valid credit card number may be all that is needed. Class 3 certificates typically require thorough background checks before they are released and therefore infer a higher level of trust that the person or organization purchasing the certificate is really the entity that they claim to be.

and improved performance. For marginally confidential information, such as a financial analyst's report that only paid subscribers are supposed to have access to, perhaps a weak and speedy encryption strategy would work best. On the other hand, super-sensitive data, such as a Swiss numbered bank account, ought to be encrypted using the strongest strategy available.

Whatever method of encryption an organization deems appropriate, the encryption method actually implemented by a Web site should be checked to ensure that it complies with the strength of encryption specified by the Web application's designers. One way to test this is to communicate with the target Web site using a browser that can be configured to work with different encryption settings, varying the settings to ensure that the data is not being under- or overencrypted. For instance, Opera 6.0 and Netscape 6.2 enable users to select which SSL encryption algorithms and key lengths may be utilized by the browser. In addition, some browsers provide the user with the opportunity to view the details of a downloaded certificate, such as its key length.

Mixing Encrypted and Nonencrypted Content

Because typically not every Web page on a Web site needs to be encrypted, most Web servers enable each page to be individually selected (or omitted) for encryption, thereby reducing the amount of data that actually needs to be encrypted. For instance, unlike the *confirm trade* page, it's unlikely that the *help* page on a stockbroker's Web site would need to be encrypted.

This concept can be taken to a more granular level, with individual Web page components being selectively encrypted or left unencrypted. For instance, typically most of the time spent downloading a Web page is in fact spent waiting for the images (as opposed to the text) on the Web page to be downloaded. Frequently, there is nothing confidential about these images and consequently little point in encrypting these network bandwidth-intense graphic files. (Once downloaded, the user could always save the unencrypted image to disk anyway.)

Mixing encrypted and unencrypted components on the same Web page has a drawback, as does, to a lesser extent, using encrypted and unencrypted Web pages on the same Web site. This is that some browsers will generate numerous (well-intentioned, but still annoying) messages, warning users that some of the components that make up the Web page are unencrypted, thereby creating a potential usability issue.

Just because a Web page has been downloaded in an encrypted format does not necessarily mean that the reply will be encrypted (or vice versa). For instance, a Web site's login page may be sent from the Web server to the browser unencrypted; there's no

---

COOKIE ENCRYPTION

A Web site can use the HTTP *Secure Cookie* option to ensure that a cookie is only transmitted back to it if the cookie is first encrypted. This is a useful option if the Web site contains a mixture of encrypted and unencrypted Web pages.

security risk in an eavesdropper viewing an empty login form. But the corresponding reply from the user, with the associated userID and password, should be encrypted. Unfortunately, this approach also has usability issues, as a user may incorrectly assume their reply (containing their userID and password) will not be encrypted and therefore be hesitant to use. That deduction would be made because the download empty login form had not been encrypted, causing the browser to display the unencrypted visual cue: an open padlock or broken key.

If a *mix-and-match* approach to encryption is adopted, the testing team should check that all the Web pages (or page components) that should be encrypted are indeed encrypted, and any that should not be, aren't. This test can be accomplished by manipulating browser security settings or by performing source code inspections.

Avoiding Encryption Bottlenecks

For many secure Web applications, encryption may be the first scalability bottleneck. Due to the heavy requirements of encryption, even a small number of simultaneous clients can saturate a Web server. To mitigate this problem, Web sites have adopted a number of different strategies, which are discussed in the following sections.

Directing Traffic to Dedicated Security Servers

By directing all encrypted network traffic to a dedicated Web server(s), the impact of a sudden surge in encrypted traffic can be localized to the secure portion of the Web application, and not the entire Web site. In addition, the Web server's operating system and services can be tuned (and hardened) to better handle copious amounts of encrypted traffic.

Using Encryption Cards

Because encryption is so CPU intensive, the CPU is often the first component of a Web server to suffer from an increase in encrypted traffic. For this reason, many companies manufacture encryption accelerator cards to help alleviate the stress placed on a general-purpose CPU by large amounts of encryption and decryption. This is analogous to the way video cards are used to offload graphic manipulation from the CPU. For a list of companies manufacturing such cards, see Table 5.11.

If encryption is going to be used to any great extent on the Web site, the testing team should consider running performance tests to ensure that a surge in encrypted traffic will not bring the Web site to its knees. If another group is doing some performance testing, the team should ensure that the load profiles used by the other group adequately reflect the degree to which encryption will be used.

Evaluating the security of client transmissions is unfortunately not simply a case of determining whether or not the Webmaster has enabled SSL on the Web server. It also includes checks to make sure that not too much, or too little, is being encrypted, that the level of encryption is appropriate, and that the safety of any digital certificate files is ensured. Table 5.12 lists some tests that should be considered when evaluating the

Table 5.11 Sample Providers of Encryption Accelerators

NAME	ASSOCIATED WEB SITE
Accelerated Encryption Processing	www.aep-crypto.com
Andes Networks	www.andesnetworks.com
Cryptographic Appliances	www.cryptoapps.com
Global Technologies Group	www.powercrypt.com
IBM	www.ibm.com
nCipher	www.ncipher.co
Rainbow Technologies	www.rainbow.com
SafeNet	www.safenet-inc.com
SonicWall	www.sonicwall.com

Table 5.12 Secure Client Transmission Checklist

YES	NO	DESCRIPTION
☐	☐	Is there a documented policy in place that describes what level of data encryption should be used between the client-side and server-side components of a Web application?
☐	☐	Are the administrative records maintained by the certification authority (such as contact name, owner, and domain name) and kept up-to-date for each digital certificate used by the Web site?
☐	☐	Are digital certificates renewed ahead of expiration? (Many certificates must be renewed annually.)
☐	☐	Are strong passwords used to protect each certificate file? With no two files using the same password?
☐	☐	Are the certificate files stored under *lock and key*, away from the production Web site?
☐	☐	Is the design of the Web application sufficiently robust to handle clients who may not wish to install a client-side (personal) certificate?
☐	☐	Is the encryption algorithm and strength used by the Web site supported by all the Web site's potential visitors? If not, is there a strategy for handling those visitors that cannot communicate using the preferred form of encryption?
☐	☐	Is the encryption strength used by the Web site too strong (and resource intensive) or too weak (and potentially crackable)?

(continues)

Table 5.12   Secure Client Transmission Checklist (*continued*)

YES	NO	DESCRIPTION
☐	☐	Have all the Web site's servers been set to use the same strength of encryption? Using different strengths on the same Web site may optimize performance but may also cause additional compatibility problems at the client.
☐	☐	Have only the Web pages that need to be encrypted been encrypted?
☐	☐	If only portions of a Web page are to be encrypted, are only the appropriate components encrypted? For example, there is little benefit in encrypting a Web banner advertisement.
☐	☐	Is the Web site able to handle the expected volume of encrypted network traffic now and in the foreseeable future?

security of sensitive data being transmitted from or to the client-side component of a Web application.

Mobile Application Code

Mobile code refers to the chunks of code that are downloaded for execution from one machine to another; in the Web world, this typically occurs as the result of a browser requesting the mobile code from a Web server.

Currently, the majority of Web applications use one of two competing standards for downloading executables over the Internet: Sun Microsystems's Java applets and Microsoft's ActiveX controls. Unfortunately, these two technologies are currently incompatible, which means that most Web applications that use downloadable executables tend to standardize on one or the other of the technologies. Both standards offer similar functionality but differ in their run-time environments; ActiveX controls can potentially be written in any programming language, but once compiled, they are primarily intended to be used only on Windows 32-bit platforms. In contrast, Java applets need to be written in Java but may be executed on any platform that has an associated Java Virtual Machine (JVM) (described later in this section). In addition to executables, a browser may also download interpretive code written in one (or more) scripting languages (such as EMCAScript, JavaScript, Jscript, or VBScript).

Whichever technology a Web application implements, the organization needs to be conscious of the fact that it is using its Web site to distribute and install code to potentially all the visitors that frequent its Web site. An organization should therefore take every reasonable precaution to ensure that the code it is distributing is free of any unauthorized features that could perform malicious activities or be subverted by another piece of code with ill intentions.

ActiveX Controls

Two closely related security considerations only apply to ActiveX controls. At the developer's discretion, ActiveX controls can be marked as *safe for scripting*, which means that the developer believes that the ActiveX control is safe for any possible use of its properties, methods, and events by any other program that might wish to utilize its functionality. For example, an ActiveX control downloaded from a *bookkeeping* Web site could be instructed by a piece of JavaScript code downloaded by the browser from a *tax preparation* Web site to upload all of this tax year's income and expense records to the tax preparation Web site.

The second security consideration relates to the capability of an ActiveX control to be initialized with local or remotely supplied data. The developer can optionally permit the input parameters of an ActiveX control to be reset (or initialized), thereby allowing a third party to not only control execution of the ActiveX control but also modify the data used by the control to perform the requested operation. For example, an ActiveX control downloaded from a computer manufacturer's Web site in order to install updates to the client machine's operating system could be utilized by a rogue script (inadvertently downloaded from a malicious Web site) to install a Trojan horse variant of an operating system file on the client machine.

Since developers typically do not know where or how their ActiveX controls will be used, it is normally prudent to disable the scripting and initialization options for the control. If a control really does need to be made available in an unprotected form, extensive testing should be performed to ensure that an ill-intentioned script (possibly from another Web site) could not cause the ActiveX control to do anything undesirable. This would include deleting files or emailing confidential information to another Web site.

Control safety is ultimately a subjective judgment. However, Table 5.13 lists some Microsoft recommendations for determining whether an ActiveX control can be marked as *safe for scripting* or *initialization*. As a general rule, none of the following undesirable effects should be possible from any conceivable use of the control.

Java Applets

Java was defined by Sun Microsystems and originally aimed at the *set-top* boxes that cable operators use (Java was also called *Oak* back then). When the Web started to take off, Sun decided to redeploy the language for use over the Internet. Unlike many computer languages, Java is not defined by a standards committee but is still *owned* by Sun. One advantage to this model is that new features, or extensions, can be added to the language comparatively quickly. Of course, from a testing perspective, this can make the testing harder; as the number of versions increases, so does the number of potential Java versions that will need to be tested.

One of Java's most touted benefits "write once, run anywhere" is accomplished by using a JVM installed on the machine where the program is to be run. Each platform needs a separate JVM customized and optimized for the underlying platform. Each JVM converts the Java code into platform-specific machine code that, although different, appears to the user to execute identically on any of the JVM-supported platforms (as depicted in Figure 5.2). Unfortunately, because the various JVMs are written by different organizations, and the underlying operating systems and hardware architecture

Table 5.13 ActiveX Control Safety Checklist

YES	NO	DESCRIPTION
☐	☐	Does the control access information about the local computer or user?
☐	☐	Does the control expose private information on the local computer or network?
☐	☐	Does the control modify or destroy information on the local computer or network?
☐	☐	Can faulting the control (causing it to have an error) potentially cause the browser to crash?
☐	☐	Does the control consume excessive time or resources such as memory?
☐	☐	Does the control make potentially damaging system calls, such as executing another program?
☐	☐	Can the control be used in a deceptive manner and thereby cause unexpected results?

Source: http://msdn.microsoft.com/workshop/components/activex/security.asp

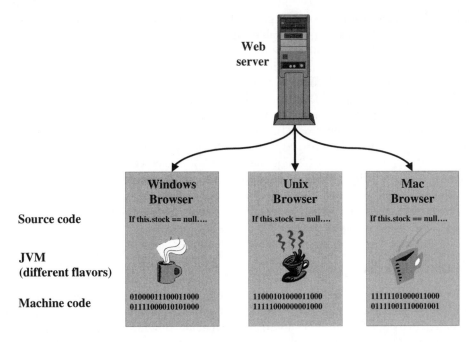

Figure 5.2 JVM implementation.

have different capabilities, each JVM implementation may behave slightly differently and may therefore necessitate testing with multiple JVMs.

The early versions of Java (circa 1.0) used a security mechanism called *sandboxing*. Sandboxing makes untrusted code (such as a Java applet downloaded from a Web site of unknown trustworthiness) run inside a secure area, and it limits the applet's capability to access any resource outside of the secure area. This sandbox principle is enforced on the machine executing the code by three components built into most browsers: the byte code verifier, the class loader, and the security manager.

Byte Code Verifier

The verifier performs a number of static checks before the code is executed. Checks include making sure that all variables are initialized before being used and that arguments use correctly typed parameters.

Class Loader

The loader ensures that all classes needed by the applet are loaded and it remembers where each class was loaded from. Downloaded classes are typically regarded as untrusted, while classes loaded from the local system are trusted. In addition, the class loader keeps classes from different applets separated.

Security Manager

The security manager provides run-time verification that the resource requests being made by an applet are acceptable. Together, these three components restrict an applet's access to local data files and executables, network services, and a browser's internal services. One particular challenge with testing Java applets is that the applet being tested may not be able to print to a file on the host machine. Instead, this information must be sent back to a Web server for later analysis and review.

In hindsight, the original Java 1.0 sandbox implementation proved to be too restrictive for many application environments (such as an intranet application where the applet could be completely trusted). With the release of Java 1.1, the sandbox became porous. Java 1.1 enabled code to be marked as *trusted* and subsequently allowed to run outside of the sandbox. Java 1.2 took the concept of trusted code a step further, using more granular security policies established by the user or system administrator, a more flexible solution but one that has the disadvantage of making security administration more complex to administer. McGraw (1999) provides additional information on security issues related to mobile Java code.

Client-Side Scripts

Client-side scripts are used by many Web applications to perform simply client-side processing, such as recalculating a shopping cart after the method of shipping has been changed. In theory, the browser should ensure that any downloaded client-side scripts cannot do anything malicious to the machine that the browser is installed upon. Unfortunately, security vulnerabilities have been discovered in numerous browsers.

Typically, the vulnerability allows a script downloaded from a rogue Web site to read some private information on the client machine (such as cached URLs, specific files stored on a hard drive, cookies, or keystrokes). This information is then relayed back to the script's author for him or her to digest and exploit. In addition to the client-side script advisors posted on the Web sites listed in Table 4.2, Georgi Guninski maintains a Web site (www.guninski.com) that demonstrates many of these vulnerabilities.

Detecting Trojan Horse Mobile Code

Because most Web site visitors will unknowingly automatically download any mobile code attached to the Web page they are viewing, an organization should consider protecting itself against a supposedly *trusted* employee embedding a small piece of rouge code inside a legitimate program, thereby creating a Trojan horse out of the organization's legitimate mobile code (Trojan horses are discussed in more detail in Chapter 8).

How can an organization ensure that a disgruntled employee (contractor or permanent) is not building a Trojan horse or other form of rogue code into the mobile code hosted on its Web site? Possible solutions are discussed in the following sections.

Inspections and Reviews

Assuming a conspiracy does not exist within an entire team of developers, standard manual code review and inspection practices may detect undesirable code. Even if the possibility of rogue code slipping through a review exists, the likelihood of it being detected may be sufficient to deter all but the most determined of mischief-makers. Craig (2002), Myers (1979), and Perry (2000) provide additional information on the technique of conducting software inspections and reviews.

Unfortunately, a loophole to this process exists. If configuration management practices allow the developer to rework their own code after the review or inspection has taken place (a common practice), it would be quite easy for the disgruntled developer to insert the malicious code into his or her work *after* the source code approval process has been completed.

THE DISGRUNTLED DEVELOPER

Imagine a contract developer being told that his contract is being terminated early due to corporate cutbacks. The developer, being upset at this development, decides to seek revenge by adding a couple of lines of code to the ActiveX control he is currently working on. This additional code is designed to delete as many files as possible on the client machine's hard drive, but only if the system date is at least three months later than today. The developer then recompiles the code and forwards the binary file to the testing team for functional testing. The control passes and is then uploaded to the production Web site. Several weeks after the developer leaves, the organization's customer support desk is hit with a tidal wave of confused and angry customers.

Code Coverage

Using a code coverage tool such as McCabe and Associate's IQ product (www.mccabe .com), functional testing can be evaluated to determine what percentage of the source code has been exercised with the current set of tests. Code that for some reason had not been exercised may then be scrutinized to ensure that the reason the code was excluded was justifiable, and not part of a ploy by the code's author to prevent the undesirable code from being detected during testing.

Of course, if the testing effort were only able to exercise a small portion of the code (often the case in large projects, which are short on time), the amount of code that would need a manual review would be so large as to be prohibitively resource intense.

Scanning Mobile Code

Mobile code-scanning tools (such as those listed in Table 8.10) can be used to exercise the code in a monitored environment. The testing tools look for suspicious behavior that might be indicative of rogue code being present.

An organization may also wish to ensure that its *good* code does not give off false positives when scanned by any commonly deployed firewall, intrusion detection systems (IDS), application security server, or antivirus program (Chapter 8 discusses these products in more detail). It's quite possible that many of their clients have installed such products and would discard any mobile code that the tool flagged as being potentially harmful (regardless of whether the code is harmful or just appears to be).

Code Signing

Assuming the ActiveX controls and Java applets originally loaded on the production Web site were found to be clear of malicious code, how can an organization ensure that this *good* code is not subsequently modified and *Trojanized* either on the hosting Web site or in transit from the Web site to the requesting client?

Code signing is a technique that seeks to ensure that any program (ActiveX control, Java applet, or other downloaded executable) has not been altered since the original developer compiled and packaged it, a process that is outlined in Table 5.14.

Unfortunately, code-signing techniques such as Microsoft's Authenticode or Netscape's Object Signing do not provide any assurance that the code will not perform an undesirable action; they only ensure that the code has not been tampered with since it was packaged by the certificate's owner. It goes without saying that any code-signing certificate file should be closely guarded, in order to ensure that an unauthorized person can't trick viewers into downloading malicious code onto their machines, because it appears that the code was written by a trusted organization.

Configuration Management

Rather than embedding malicious functionality in their own code, employees with less desire to be caught would probably try to plant their Trojan horse code into somebody else's work. The best defense against such attempts is good configuration management

Table 5.14   Code-Signing Process

STEP	DESCRIPTION
1.	The developer writes the code.
2.	The developer *signs* the code using a digital certificate obtained from a certification authority.
3.	The code is uploaded to the Web site.
4.	The viewer requests the Web page containing the code and thereby downloads the code.
5.	The viewer is then prompted to decide whether or not to trust the downloaded code (based upon how trustworthy the viewer regards the owner of the digital certificate). Note that depending upon the viewer's browser setting, the browser may not prompt the viewer, automatically accepting or rejecting the code instead.
6.	If the viewer decides to trust the code, then the code is allowed to execute; otherwise, the code is discarded.

procedures, typically employing some form of configuration management or code comparison tool (such as those listed in Table 2.2 and Table 8.7). Dart (2000), Haug (1999), and Leon (2000) provide additional information on configuration management practices.

Table 5.15 summarizes the *checks and balances* that an organization could consider implementing to reduce the possibility of a rogue employee (or someone else who has access to the Web application's source code) inserting some malicious lines of code into the mobile code portion of a Web application.

Client Security

After a user has been identified and authenticated as legitimate, the Web application runs the risk that this (now-trusted) client machine will be successfully compromised by an attacker, allowing the assailant to access the application using the privileges intended to be bestowed upon a legitimate user.

Although the onus may be upon the users (or their technical support personnel) to ensure that any session that they initiate with a Web application is not *hijacked* via an intruder gaining access to their client machine, the precautions that users may seek to employ in order to protect their machines can have a direct impact on the functionality of a Web application. A Web application should therefore be tested to ensure that it is still usable, even when accessed by clients with reasonable client-side security measures in place. For example, an application that is completely dependent upon a user granting a Java applet (downloaded from the application's Web site) unfettered access to the client machine, may find that a significant proportion of their users refuse to grant this code such access, and are consequently unable to use the Web application.

Table 5.15 Detecting Trojan Horse Mobile Code Checklist

YES	NO	DESCRIPTION
☐	☐	Is there a documented policy in place that describes the security procedures that should be used to ensure that any mobile code used by the Web site is free of any malicious code?
☐	☐	Are any of the ActiveX controls used on the Web site marked *safe for scripting* or *initialization*? If so, are they safe?
☐	☐	Are any of the Java applets used on the Web site able to function in a sandbox environment? If not, are the permissions that they need reasonable and likely to be granted by potential users of the applet?
☐	☐	Has the mobile code been reviewed and inspected for malicious code (perhaps focusing on portions of the code that were not executed during normal functional testing)?
☐	☐	Is the mobile code flagged as suspicious when scrutinized by any commonly used mobile code-scanning product?
☐	☐	Has the mobile code been signed with an authorized digital certificate?
☐	☐	Are processes in place to ensure that any digital certificates used to sign mobile code are renewed with the certification authority before it expires?
☐	☐	Are any digital certificate files used by the Web application stored in a safe place?
☐	☐	Have configuration management procedures been implemented that would inhibit a rogue employee tampering with another employee's code?

The following sections look at some of the precautions a user could be expected to take and therefore what client-side environments the testing team may wish to consider emulating in order to ensure that the Web application functions with these fortified-minded clients.

Firewalls

Many organizations use proxy servers to manage their employees' Internet access, improve performance, and also provide their employees with a degree of anonymity. Unfortunately, this level of anonymity can prove problematic to Web applications trying to authenticate a user based on some piece of information that the proxy server is masking. An example of this would be the proxy server replacing the network address of the client machine it serves with its own. Allen (2001), Rubin (2001), and Zwicky et al. (2000) provide additional information on securing firewalls.

Another consideration is the filtering that a network or personnel firewall may perform. An organization's perimeter firewall is typically used to provide some level of protection from an attack originating outside the organization. A PC-based (or personal) firewall (often used in conjunction with an antivirus program) is often deployed to stop internal colleagues (or, in the case of home users with cable modems, their neighbors) from attempting to compromise machines via local network connections. Either way, communication between the client-side and server-side components of a Web application may be inhibited by the firewall if the Web application is designed to use unusual methods of communication (such as via a port other than port 80 or 443 or using a network protocol other than HTTP or HTTPS). Table 5.16 lists some sample personal firewalls, and Table A.3 lists some sample network firewalls and proxy servers.

Browser Security Settings

A number of browser-based technologies have the potential to do harm to a client machine using a browser to access a Web application. Recognizing the concerns of their users, most browser manufactures allow users of their products to disable some or all of these potentially dangerous capabilities (although it should be noted that these options vary from browser to browser).

Having a Web application that works fine on a developer's desktop where liberal security settings have been used (thereby making it easier for the developer to get the software to work) does not guarantee that the application will function correctly for all

Table 5.16 Sample List of Personal Firewalls

NAME	ASSOCIATED WEB SITE
BlackICE	www.networkice.com
CyberGatekeeper	www.infoexpress.com
CyberwallPLUS	www.network-1.com
eSafe Desktop	www.esafe.com/ealaddin.com
FireWall	www.mcafee.com
F-Secure Distributed Firewall	www.f-secure.com
Internet Connection Firewall (ICF)	www.microsoft.com
NeoWatch	www.neoworx.com
Netfilter/iptables	www.netfilter.samba.org
Norton Personal Firewall	www.symantec.com
Seattle Firewall (ipchains)	www.seawall.sourceforge.net
ZoneAlarm	www.zonelabs.com

the clients. This is due to users disabling or limiting some of their browser's capabilities for security or privacy reasons.

In the case of an intranet or extranet, users may not have any control over their choice of browser or browser security settings. This makes for a homogenous set of client machines that can be easily replicated by the testing team to ensure that the Web application being tested will work correctly in this tightly controlled environment. However, this does not take into account the issue of what happens when the organization decides to upgrade their version of browser or operating system.

Unfortunately, the same is not true for Internet-based Web applications. Although the vast majority of Internet users never change any of their browser's (typically liberal) default security settings, the larger the number of these *suspect* technologies that a Web application uses, the more likely it is that one or more of these technologies will be (rightly or wrongly) disabled by a cautious user. For instance, suppose 5 percent of a Web site's potential audience rejects cookies, 15 percent won't let ActiveX controls run, and 20 percent don't have a browser with strong encryption capabilities. Combined, these groups could represent a sizable portion of a Web site's client base, large enough that a marketing department might be rather disconcerted to hear that such a large percentage of its potential customers won't be able to fully utilize the Web application.

Even if a particular technology is specified in the Web application's requirements (and any corresponding end-user agreement), a user-friendly Web application should degrade gracefully (if only to issue a warning message), rather than simply not function and thereby confuse and frustrate the user.

Whichever technology is used, the Web application should be tested using different combinations of browsers and operating systems with varying client-side security settings. Techniques such as *orthogonal arrays* (or *all-pairs*) can be used to help mitigate the possible combinatory explosion that such exhaustive compatibility testing may cause. Hedayat (1999) and Kaner et al. (2001) provides more information on orthogonal arrays. Table 5.17 lists some tools that can be used to help pair down the number of possible environmental permutations.

The following are some of the most common client-side security settings that should be considered when evaluating whether or not a Web application will function correctly on a client machine due to a user's security concerns. The higher (or more restrictive) the security settings that the Web application is able to still functional correctly with, the more likely the application will actually be used by its intended audience. At a minimum, consider checking that the Web application can still provide expectable functionality with the default security settings of the most commonly used versions of browsers.

Table 5.17 Sample List of Orthogonal Array Manipulation Tools

NAME	ASSOCIATED WEB SITE
AETGWEB	www.argreenhouse.com
RdExpert	www.phadkeassociates.com
StatLib (oa.c and owen)	www.lib.stat.cmu.edu

Cookies

Primarily because of privacy concerns, many Internet users choose to block cookie use partially or completely. This could be a problem if the Web application's security depends upon this feature being enabled.

Encryption Capabilities

Unfortunately, not all Web servers and browsers support the same encryption algorithms and key lengths, in some cases because of legal considerations (for example, for many years the U.S. government restricted the export of software able to support 128 or higher key lengths) while other versions of Web servers and browsers support different encryption algorithms and key lengths due to software vendors choosing to charge different prices for their products based on the level of encryption supported by the tool. Therefore, a highly secure encryption setting may result in a substantial number of potential clients being unable to utilize the encrypted portion of a Web application.

Client-Side Mobile Code

As previously discussed in this chapter, a great many security issues are associated with running client-side mobile code, which is one of the reasons why some browsers offer quite elaborate options for deciding when and with what restrictions (if any) a piece of mobile code will be allowed to execute. Although the default settings of most browsers are quite liberal, many organizations have instigated corporate policies that limit or completely prohibit the use of mobile code from an *untrusted* source.

Tiny Windows

Because very small windows or floating frames (HTML *IFRAME* tags) have been used to hide illicit activities, some browsers either prohibit them completely or enable a user to disable them.

Multiple Domains and Redirection

In order to improve performance and/or make content configuration management easier, many Web sites actually distribute their content over multiple domain names and/or redirect a request for one domain to another. For instance, a national newspaper may host a news article that forms the main component of a page on their own site, but they use Web banner advertisements from a separate online advertiser's site (such as www.aol.com or www.doubleclick.net). Unfortunately, because exploits have been developed that can allow an intruder to trick a user into unknowingly communicating with a secondary Web site using redirection, some browsers enable a user to prohibit a Web page from downloading any page component that does not reside on the same Web site that the original resource request was made to.

Automatic Updates

Technologies such as Netscape's SmartUpdate and MS-IE's Install on Demand enable browsers to download and install missing or more up-to-date software without any user involvement. Although such technologies may be very user friendly, they also have the potential to be abused by a rogue Web site that would like to download a Trojaned version of the software. Therefore, most browsers enable this feature to be disabled by the client.

Client Adaptive Code

Rather than trying to develop a single instance of a Web application that will work in every perceivable client environment, some organizations choose to develop multiple variations of the same application, or a portion of an application. An example would be one version of the application being designed for presentation by a Netscape browser (using proprietary extensions only supported by Netscape) and another especially for MS-IE (perhaps using features only found in MS-IE). The Web application then uses information freely supplied by the client (typically as part of the client's HTTP header request) to identify what platform the user is using and then serves up the most appropriate variant of the application.

Taking this concept a step further, instead of basing the adaptive code on the brand and version of the browser installed on the client, the Web application could base its decision on which technologies have been enabled (or disabled) by the user. For example, the login page of a Web site may be used to send a cookie to the client. Upon receiving the corresponding reply, the Web application can check for the existence of a returned cookie. The absence of a returned cookie would imply that the user has either disabled this technology or that the browser simply does not support it. Either way, the Web application will now have to employ a noncookie method of communicating with the user or issue a warning to the effect that access has been denied due to this capability being disabled.

If a Web application uses client adaptive code that is dependent on any client-side security setting or is used to implement any client-side security measure, then the testing team should ensure that all the client environments that have been specifically targeted by the adaptive components of the Web application are represented in the test configurations used to test the application.

JAVA FALLBACK

One approach to handling Java being disabled on the client is to place an HTML-based warning message between the <Applet> tags on a Web page. The message explains to the user why the Java applet's functionality is not available; this HTML will be ignored if Java is enabled in the browser but is executed if it is turned off.

Client Sniffing

Unwilling to trust that a client has taken reasonable security measures to protect their machine from intruders, some extremely cautious Web sites will download mobile code to reconnoiter (or sniff) a prospective client machine. For example, the mobile code may check for the existence of the latest operating system security patch or the most recent antivirus signature file (.dat file).

Once sniffed and assessed, the mobile code reports back to the Web application (and optionally the user as well) what it has found. Aside from the huge privacy issues involved with such an approach, this proactive defensive measure runs the risk that a knowledgeable attacker could either prohibit the mobile code from being executed or even modify the code to report back incorrect information.

Table 5.18   Client Security Checklist

YES	NO	DESCRIPTION
☐	☐	Is there a documented policy in place that describes which client-side technologies are necessary for the Web application security to function correctly? And is there a policy for how the Web application should handle a client that does not support or permit one of these required technologies?
☐	☐	Is the design of the Web application sufficiently robust to handle some clients accessing the Web site from behind a proxy server?
☐	☐	Is the design of the Web application sufficiently robust to handle some clients accessing the Web site from behind a network and/or personal firewall?
☐	☐	Is the design of the Web application sufficiently robust to handle some clients disabling cookies?
☐	☐	Is the design of the Web application sufficiently robust to handle some clients who do not have encryption capabilities or only have a browser capable of weak encryption?
☐	☐	Is the design of the Web application sufficiently robust to handle some clients disabling mobile code?
☐	☐	Is the design of the Web application sufficiently robust to handle some clients disabling tiny windows or floating frames?
☐	☐	Is the design of the Web application sufficiently robust to handle some clients not wanting to work across multiple domains or enable redirects?
☐	☐	Is the design of the Web application sufficiently robust to handle some clients not wanting to allow automatic software updates?

(continues)

Table 5.18   Client Security Checklist (*continued*)

YES	NO	DESCRIPTION
☐	☐	If client-adaptive code is used by the Web application, do the application's security capabilities still work with all client-side environments?
☐	☐	If client-sniffing is used by the Web application for any security precautions, can the application's security be compromised by disabling or restricting mobile code execution on the client?
☐	☐	If client-sniffing is used by the Web application for any security precautions, can the mobile code be easily reverse engineered or modified in such a way as to send bogus security information back to the server-side component of the application?

If mobile code is used by a Web application for any security-related reconnaissance or enforcement, then the mobile code should be tested using as many of the client environments as it may be expected to be executed in. At a minimum, the mobile code should be tested with browsers that have had their mobile code execution capability disabled or highly restricted, or tested with a browser that simply does not support that particular technology.

Table 5.18 summarizes the checks that a testing team may wish to consider performing to ensure that a Web application will function acceptably and that its security will not be compromised when used by clients with widely varying security settings.

If the Web application is found to frequently only work in an extremely liberal security environment, then the organization may wish to reconsider deploying the application in its current state, potentially reworking the application to make it work with less demanding client-side environmental requirements.

Summary

At a simplistic level, the client-side application security tests described in this chapter can be grouped into two categories. The first consists of those that are designed to ensure that the Web application's security capabilities function correctly for the *good guys*, providing acceptable usability, performance, and compatibility. The second set of tests (that are often not as frequently employed) attempt to establish that the application's security implementation is robust enough to stop the *bad guys* from trying to gain unauthorized access to the application's resources (data, functionality, or connectivity).

What percentage of its resources the testing team should spend on *positive* testing (making sure it works) for the good guys, versus *negative* testing (making sure it can't be broken) for the bad guys, will vary from project to project. To a large degree, it will be influenced by how important it is to try and keep the good guys happy, versus keeping the bad guys unhappy.

# CHAPTER 6

Server-Side
Application Security

Wouldn't it be nice if a Web site's perimeter defenses completely protected it from all external intruders? And wouldn't we all rest easier if we knew that a Web application's client-side components would always ensure that users only submit nonmalicious input to the application's server-side components? The reality, of course, is not quite as idyllic. Unfortunately, a supposedly well-configured perimeter firewall may have an as-yet-undiscovered hole or be completely circumvented by an employee attacking the Web site from a machine located behind the perimeter firewall. And since few organizations have any control over the machines that Internet users will use to access the Web application, there can be no guarantee that any client-side checks have actually taken place or been done the way they were intended to be performed. For these reasons alone, a Web application designer would be well advised to include additional security precautions on the server-side as well. These precautions should be checked by the testing team to make sure that they have been implemented correctly.

Breaking through a multilayer defense that employs safeguards at each and every juncture is much tougher than breaking through a single layer (such as a Web site that solely relies upon a perimeter firewall). The previous chapter focused on testing the security of the client-side component of a Web application. This chapter will focus on what needs to be checked on the server side by looking at the different technologies that may have been used. It will then examine the vulnerabilities associated with each technology and consequently what features the testing team should check to determine if a specific implementation is vulnerable.

The sections in this chapter can be conceptually grouped into three topics. The first group focuses on the vulnerabilities associated with programming technologies that are specific to Web implementations, such as Common Gateway Interfaces (CGI), Server Side Includes (SSI), Active Server Pages (ASPs), and Java Server Pages (JSP), and then general vulnerabilities that are applicable to all server-side application code. The second grouping looks at what can be done to guard against invalid input data being received by the Web application and then subsequently what defenses can be put in place to protect legitimated data stored on the Web site. Finally, the last section in this chapter looks at the controversial topic of using client behavioral patterns to detect compromised application security.

Common Gateway Interface (CGI)

CGI is a protocol (not a programming language). Many Web applications use the CGI protocol to enable a Web server to communicate (pass data) with other programs running on the Web server or another server such as an application or database server. Figure 6.1 depicts this situation.

Unfortunately, many known security vulnerabilities are associated with CGI implementations, and therefore vulnerabilities that the testing team should check for, should the Web application's designers decide to use CGI in their architecture.

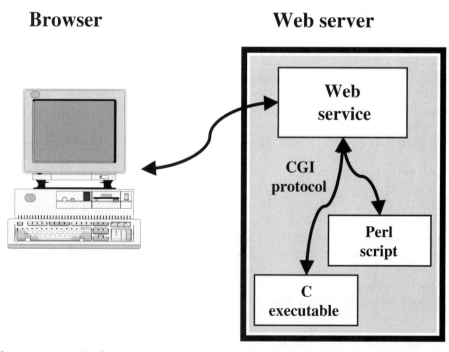

Figure 6.1   CGI implementation example.

Language Options

A CGI implementation may be written in a scripting language such as Perl or less commonly in a compiled language such as C. Table 6.1 lists some of the languages that may be used to write CGI applications.

The following points seek to compare and contrast some of the typical differences between compiled CGI implementations and interpretive ones:

- A compiled version is likely to execute faster and consume fewer resources than an equivalent script being parsed and then executed by an interpreter.

- A script must have a resource-consuming interpreter installed on the server that is going to execute it, with each interpreter requiring additional resources.

- The object code (binary executable) of a compiled application provides an attacker with fewer opportunities (even using a code reverse-engineering tool) to understand a program's logic and thereby discover a security hole than the source code of an equivalent script. Note that this assumes that the source code used by the compiler to generate the executable is removed from any machine to which the attacker might be able to gain access.

- Running a program through a compiler will result in the entire program's source code being syntax-checked before being executed, as opposed to interpreters that typically perform their syntax checks on-the-fly as the script is

Table 6.1 Possible CGI Application Languages

SCRIPTING	COMPILED/PSUEDOCOMPILED
AppleScript	C
AWK	C++
JavaScript	C#
Perl	COBOL
PHP	Java
Python	J++
Ruby	J#
Tcl	PowerBuilder
VBScript	Visual Basic
Various shells*	

*Shells are a group of operating-system-interpretive languages (such as bash, bourne, csh, sh, and DOS) that give a user the ability to invoke basic operating system utilities from a command line or via a batch script file.

being executed (which is one of the reasons why compiled code normally runs faster than interpretive code). Although some interpreters have the capability to parse a script ahead of time, the optionality of this check leads some developers to skip this step when deploying interpretative scripts, possibly allowing errors that would have been caught by a compiler to make their way into production.

- The strict data-typing syntax often used by compiled languages may make it harder for an attacker to pass off malicious input (such as system commands) as legitimate user input.

- The syntax of a scripting language is often simpler and easier to learn than a compileable language.

- A script need not first be compiled and linked before it is ready to run, potentially reducing development time.

- Configuration management is simpler for scripting code because only one version of the code exists, as opposed to compiled code where two versions are used (object code and source code).

- Once a program is compiled, it becomes platform dependent; the resulting executable only runs on the platform for which it was compiled. In contrast, a script should (in theory) be easily portable from one platform to another with few or no modifications.

From a security perspective, an inherent advantage exists in standardizing on a single language when implementing a Web application's CGI needs. For example, the more CGI interpreters that are loaded on to a Web server (an interpreter is needed in order to execute a script), the greater the chance for misconfiguration and the subsequent possibility of an attacker exploiting this installation error. Also, standardizing on a single language improves the probability that a CGI programming error will be caught during a program review (as all the developers speak the same language). It also increases the usefulness of *safe* common routines (which have been extensively examined and tested for any security vulnerability).

Input Data

A CGI program can receive input from a Web server through a variety of channels (for instance, via command-line arguments, by requesting environmental information such as the date and time, or being *piped* information from another program). Unfortunately, CGI programs are all too often not set up to handle input error conditions very well.

Bad input to a CGI program is a particular problem when the input data is used as a parameter in a subsequent CGI system call, the CGI program misinterpreting the input data as a *system command* and subsequently executing the command instead of treating it as *data*. Therefore, before being used, the input data should always be scanned to ensure that it only contains legitimate characters (easier in some languages than others) and, if possible, that it is never actually used as a parameter in a subsequent CGI system command.

To mitigate the potential problem of a CGI program inadvertently treating input data as a system command, an organization may wish to consider using a combination

TAINTED DATA

Perl interpreters come with a useful data *tainting* option for making sure that any user input data is first inspected before being used in a potentially dangerous situation. When this environmental variable is set, the interpreter will not enable the tainted data to be used as a parameter for any high-risk system command (such as a *path name*, *file name*, or *directory name* parameter). To confirm that this feature is being used, inspect the beginning of the script file to look for the line that invokes the Perl interpreter. The -T parameter must be present in order to force the interpreter to use its tainted data functionality. An example would be `#!/usr/bin/perl -T`.

of code inspections and destructive testing to ensure each CGI program is robust enough to handle data input errors correctly. (These techniques are described in more detail later in the *Input Data* section of this chapter.) The Web Design Group (www.htmlhelp.com) provides a CGI test harness (cg-eye) that can be used to assist the destructive testing.

Permissions and Directories

A CGI program inherits the security permissions of the process that invokes it, because of an attacker's potential to trick a CGI program into executing a malicious command; the owning process should be assigned a minimal set of privileges, thereby limiting the potential impact of an attack. Since the privileges that the owning process is granted are determined by the user account it is run under, this process should be assigned to a *lowly* user account (and definitely not a system administrator account such as *root*, *superuser*, or *administrator*).

Under normal circumstances, there should be no reason to permit a Web application's user to upload (or download) a CGI program over the Internet (and should therefore be blocked). If, by chance, this capability were to be unintentionally available (for instance, because the FTP service was unintentionally left running on the Web server), an intruder could use this capability to upload a rogue CGI program (possibly

HTTP HEADERS

Examining the HTTP *Referrer* field in a CGI request is one method that some Web sites use to detect suspicious CGI invocation attempts, as this environmental variable can be used to check that the CGI program in question was requested from a legitimate Web page (and not an attacker's editor). Although not foolproof (due to the ease with which the HTTP Referrer field can be faked), this technique does add one more layer of protection for the Web application.

If employed, simply *cutting and pasting* a legitimate invocation into a test harness Web page and then attempting to invoke the CGI script from this illegitimate starting point can verify the correct implementation of this defense.

designed to email the attacker sensitive data files). Then, once installed into an appropriately privileged directory, the rogue CGI program could be executed by simply requesting it from a browser. Allowing a CGI program to be downloaded would make it easier for an intruder to examine the code and potentially find a security hole (such as unscreened input data being directly used in a system call). Running the tests outlined in Table 4.12 should detect the presence of any such potentially ruinous service running on the Web server, and thereby deny an intruder the opportunity to commit this easy exploit.

Some Web servers can be configured to use multiple directories to store their CGI programs, while others require files with an extension of .cgi to be placed in a directory called cgi-bin. Since it is much easier to administer a single directory than a distributed set, the chances of a system administrator making the mistake of assigning the wrong security privilege to a directory is much lower, thereby making a single directory the preferred choice of most webmasters. Of course, keeping all the CGI programs in a single directory can also make it easier for an attacker to find these scripts, especially if the directory name is cgi-bin. Either way, the security permissions should be checked to ensure that the CGI programs are granted minimum access privileges.

If an interpreter has been installed on the Web server, installing the interpreter into its own directory and not the directory containing the CGI programs that it will execute permits a Webmaster to grant different (and thereby more restrictive) directory and execution permissions to the interpreter and its programs.

One way to test the collection of CGI programs to see if the security permissions that they have inherited are too generous is to create a short CGI program (for example, called testcase.cgi) and upload it to the Web server to be tested. The CGI program should contain one or more commands (written in the appropriate language for the Web site) that attempt to perform an operation that (in theory) should be blocked by the server's security settings. For example, adding a new subdirectory to the root directory of the Web server's operating system.

If, after requesting this CGI program via a browser (for instance, by entering the URL www.wiley.com/cgi-bin/testcase.cgi), the program is successfully executed and the new directory is created, then a further inspection of the Web server's security settings would be warranted.

Scalability

Typically, each time a legitimate user requests a CGI program to be run, a unique copy of the script is loaded into the Web server's memory. Because of the additional resources used by each CGI invocation, CGI programs have been known to have scalability issues and are therefore potential candidates for denial-of-service attacks. A CGI-enabled Web server should therefore be performance tested to ensure that it has sufficient resources to handle (in an acceptable manner) an unexpectedly large number of CGI requests. FastCGI is a more advanced implementation that reduces some of CGI's inherent scalability issues. For more information on how FastCGI works, visit www.fastcgi.com.

Table 6.2 lists the checks that a testing team may wish to consider utilizing if the Web site they are testing supports CGI. Traxler (2001) provides additional information on CGI security issues.

CGI ALTERNATIVES

As an alternative to CGI, Microsoft has developed the Internet Server Application Programming Interface (ISAPI). In contrast to a CGI implementation, an ISAPI application is only loaded once. This is possible because ISAPI is designed to enable multiple threads to run within a single instance of the application and therefore does not have the same scalability issues that CGI programs have. The Netscape Server API (NSAPI) and Apache API provide similar alternatives to CGI on Netscape/iPlanet and Apache Web servers.

Table 6.2 CGI Checklist

YES	NO	DESCRIPTION
☐	☐	Is there a documented policy in place that describes when and how a CGI program may be used?
☐	☐	If compiled CGI programs are used, are the original source code (often located in the cgi-src directory) and any backup copies removed from the production Web server?
☐	☐	Are old CGI programs from previous releases removed from the production Web server as soon as they are no longer needed?
☐	☐	Are all CGI inputs first scanned for inappropriate input characters?
☐	☐	If programming standards call for HTTP header analysis, is it always implemented?
☐	☐	Have only the bare minimum of system privileges been assigned to the process that will run the CGI programs?
☐	☐	Does the Web site degrade gracefully when an exceptionally large number of CGI program invocations are requested?

Third-Party CGI Scripts

Some CGI programs that come with third-party software (such as Web servers) have been found to contain security holes. For example, the PHF script was a standard CGI script that came with some early versions of the NCSA, Apache, and Netscape Web servers (and has since been fixed). Unfortunately, this script did not parse its input data thoroughly (permitting the *line feed* control character to remain in any input data). Once this exploit became known, attackers were then able to exploit this feature by tagging an operating system command to the end of a request to the phf.cgi script. For example, if the PHF script were located in the cgi-bin directory, the following string would instruct the operating system to send the contains of the password file back to the requester:

```
http://wiley.com/cgi-bin/phf?Qalais=x%0A/bin/cat%20/etc/passwd
```

```
Note: The space character is represented as 20 In Hexadecimal ASCII
And line feed is represented as 0A
```

PHF has become such a classic exploit that tools have been specifically designed to scan for it (such as *phfscan*), and drop-in replacements act as *tripwires* for intruder detection systems to detect when it's requested (tripwires and intrusion detection systems are discussed in Chapter 8).

Rather than searching for a single CGI program, CGI scanners can specifically scan for the presence of numerous flawed CGI programs. The attacker can then subsequently customize his or her attack based on the CGI vulnerability detected at the target Web site. Klevinsky et al. (2002) and Skoudis (2001) provide additional information on how to use CGI scanners. Table 6.3 lists some sample CGI scanners.

Because of known and (as yet) undiscovered security defects with third-party CGI programs, it's generally considered a good idea to remove (or, better still, not install) any vendor demo scripts, training scripts, or utility scripts that the Web application does not *absolutely* need. If third-party CGI programs are to be used, each CGI program found as the result of a *wildcard* file search on each Web server should be thoroughly researched to ensure that it doesn't have any known vulnerabilities. An example would be searching for cgi files from a server's root directory through all subdirectories with the wildcard string *.cgi. (Table 4.2 provides a list of alert centers that track such vulnerabilities.) In addition, the testing team should consider running at least one CGI scanner against each Web server to ensure that no vulnerable CGI program inadvertently got installed.

Adding a custom HTTP 404 error page (resource not found) to a Web site can cause many of the simple CGI scanning tools to return false positives for all of their probes, as these scanners typically determine the presence of a flawed CGI program based on receiving any positive response (such as a custom "Requested resource does not exist" Web page) from the Web server. The scanning tool's report is effectively made useless,

Table 6.3   Sample List of CGI Scanners

NAME	ASSOCIATED WEB SITE
Advanced Administrative Tools	www.glocksoft.com
Cgicheck	http://packetstorm.decepticons.org
Cgichk	www.sourceforge.net
Cgiscan	www.nebunu.home.ro
Nessus	www.nessus.org
Webscan	www.atstake.com
Whisker	www.wiretrap.net
Zcgiscan	www.point2click.de

Note that many of the security assessment tools listed in Table 9.4 include a CGI scan in their assessment.

HELPFUL SEARCH ENGINES

One technique that attackers have used to locate Web sites with vulnerable CGI programs installed is to use the services on a regular Internet search engine. These search engines sometimes come across these CGI programs as they index (*spider*) the Web site, and they may provide a list of these identified sites if the CGI program is used as the input query to the search engine.

Table 6.4 Third-Party CGI Script Checklist

YES	NO	DESCRIPTION
☐	☐	Is a documented policy in place that describes which third-party scripts (if any) may be installed on a Web server?
☐	☐	Have all third-party CGI scripts that will be installed been researched to make sure that no known security issues exist with the CGI script?
☐	☐	Can any of the widely available CGI scanners detect the presence of a flawed CGI script? Note: This may involve temporally disabling any custom error pages used by the Web site.

as every possible exploit will be falsely reported as being present. Table 6.4 summaries the third-party CGI checks that should be considered.

Server Side Includes (SSIs)

Server Side Includes (SSI) are placeholders (or markers) in an HTML document that the Web server will dynamically replace with data just before sending the requested document to a browser. Should viewers review the resulting HTML from their browsers, they will probably not be able to tell if the HTML was static (fixed) or had been dynamically built by the Web server as it parsed the HTML source code. This is because the SSI commands would have been replaced with the actual contents of the SSI placeholder.

HTML source code files containing SSI commands are often saved with the .shtml suffix instead of the usual .html (or .htm) suffix to ensure the Web server parses the HTML code with an SSI interpreter that looks for SSI commands and replaces these markers with the corresponding data referenced by these commands. Different Web servers support slightly different implementations of SSI. However, Table 6.5 lists six of the SSI commands that are typically available.

The Include command can be particularly useful to a developer wanting to reuse standard components in multiple Web pages; the common code is dynamically *cut and*

Table 6.5   Common SSI Commands

NAME	DESCRIPTION
Config	Specifies the format of data sent to the browser.
Echo	Retrieves the value of an environmental variable.
Exec	Executes a shell command or CGI application.
Flastmod	Retrieves the last modified date for a specified file.
Fsize	Retrieves the file size for a specified file.
Include	Includes the contents of another file into the current file.

pasted into the requested Web page at the point indicated by the Include statement. For example, let's say a copyright.inc file contains an organization's standard copyright notice that appears at the bottom of every page on its Web site. This enables the organization to change the wording of its copyright notice across every Web page on the site by simply updating this single file. Thus, the following HTML code

```
<HTML>
<HEAD><TITLE>Show SSI at work</TITLE></HEAD>
<BODY>
<P>Lots of really Interesting stuff to read</P>
<!--#Include file = "copywrite.Inc"-->
</BODY>
</HTML>
```

would be parsed by the Web server before it is sent to a requester and cause the following HTML to actually be sent to a requesting browser:

```
<HTML>
<HEAD><TITLE>Show SSI at work</TITLE></HEAD>
<BODY>
<P>Lots of really Interesting stuff to read</P>
<P>Copyright 2002 wiley.com all rights reservered</P>
</BODY>
</HTML>
```

The danger with an Include command comes when an intruder is able to manipulate a Web page into including a file that would otherwise not be available. For example, if an intruder is able to gain write access to a directory on a Unix Web server (possibly a .temp directory that didn't have any sensitive information stored in it and was therefore not *locked down*), the intruder could upload a .shtml Web page containing the following include statement:

```
<!--- #exec cmd="/bin/cat /etc/passwd" --->
```

By subsequently requesting the uploaded .shtml file from a browser, the intruder causes the Web server to parse the file and attempt to substitute the include statement with the password file using its authority to read the requested file.

Another security risk associated with the Include command occurs when executable code is placed inside a file that will be *included* in another file. An attacker could download the source code for an included file by directly entering its URL in a browser and then download the file without the source code first being parsed by the SSI interpreter. For example, the include file getHITcounter.inc on the wiley.com Web site could be downloaded by entering the following URL via a browser: www.wiley.com/common /getHITcounter.inc. Being able to review this source code may allow an attacker to discover some internal secret about the application that the developer thought no one would ever see. For example, a database connection string, together with userIDs and passwords, is a common use for include files (a problem expended on later in this chapter).

The Exec command has even more issues associated with it, instead of simply being used to surreptitiously download privileged information. The Exec command can be used to invoke existing (or covertly uploaded) CGI programs or any valid shell command. For example, DOS shell commands such as Ver (which displays the version of the operating system), Dir (which lists the contents of a directory), or Ipconfig (which displays network address information) would all provide useful information to an intruder.

If the SSI Exec command capability is enabled on a Web server, then the only challenge that an intruder faces is trying to figure out a way to trick the Web server into executing a malicious command. The following are two possible ways an intruder could accomplish this:

- Uploading an .shtml Web page containing the malicious Exec command to the Web server, and then requesting it via a regular browser (in the same way the Include command could be abused).

- Entering the SSI command into a regular data entry field on a legitimate Web page and hoping that the input from this Web page is reused in a subsequent Web page, thereby causing the command to be executed. An example would be the mailing address field on a *Ship to* Web page being redisplayed on the *Order Confirmation* Web page.

When programs referenced by an Exec command are executed, they run with the system privileges of the Web service. A Web site could incur significant damage if an intruder were able to install a virus, or Trojan, and then invoke it via an SSI Exec command running with administrative privileges. Therefore, if the Exec command is enabled, the Web service should be checked to make sure it is running with the fewest privileges possible (as described in the sidebar "SSI Configuration Test").

Because the security risks may outweigh the programming benefits of enabling SSI (especially the Exec command), many Web sites simply choose not to enable the SSI interpreter at all. If this is the case, then each Web server should be inspected to ensure that this feature has indeed been disabled. In the case of an Apache Web server, this can be achieved by using the *includesnoexec* option in the server's configuration file (httpd.conf). To block this feature on an IIS Web server, the SSIEnableCmdDirective entry must not be present in the Web server's Windows registry.

SSI CONFIGURATION TEST

To check if SSI has been disabled, create an HTML/SSI file called testssi.shtml (the .shtml suffix is used to ensure that the Web server knows the HTML file needs to be parsed by the SSI interpreter) with the following lines of code:

```
<HTML>
<HEAD><TITLE>Test SSI Configuration</TITLE></HEAD>
<BODY>

<H1>Test 1 - Is SSI Enabled?</H1>
<P>This file was last modified on
<!--#flastmod file = "testssi.shtml" --></P>

<H1>Test 2a - Is SSI Exec Command Enabled on an
Apache/Unix server?</H1>
<P>Today's date is <!--#exec cmd = "/bin/date" --></P>

<H1>Test 2b - Is SSI Exec Command Enabled on an
IIS/Windows server?</H1>
<P>Today's date is <!--#exec cmd = "c:\testssi.bat" --></P>

<!--Note: For the IIS test to be successful, the
testssi.bat file must contain a valid shell
command like "date /t" and the .bat and .cmd file
extensions must be mapped to the cmd.exe for this
Web server.
-->

</BODY>
</HTML>
```

If SSI is enabled, the Web server will attempt to parse any text that starts with <!--# (and ends with --->). The flastmod SSI command will retrieve the date when the specified file (in this case the test file itself) that was last modified can be used to determine if SSI is enabled.

The SSI Exec command will attempt to run the specified shell command (in this case the UNIX date function or the Windows .bat file) and can be used to determine if the Web server has been configured to permit SSI Exec commands:

- If SSI is disabled or is unavailable, both commands will fail.
- If SSI is enabled, but the Exec command has been selectively disabled, then only the flastmod command will work.
- If SSI is enabled and the Exec command has not been restricted, then both commands should work.

Table 6.6 summaries the SSI configuration checks that a testing team may wish to consider running.

Table 6.6 SSI Configuration Checklist

YES	NO	DESCRIPTION
☐	☐	Is there a documented policy in place that specifies which SSI commands (if any) will be enabled on the Web server?
☐	☐	If SSI is not to be enabled, has each Web server been checked to ensure that it has not actually been enabled?
☐	☐	If any SSI feature is to be enabled, has the Web service on each server been checked to ensure that it is running with minimal privileges? (This is a prudent measure to take even if SSI is not used.)
☐	☐	If only the SSI Exec command is to be disabled, has each Web server been checked to ensure that this feature has been disabled?

Dynamic Code

Instead of using an SSI statement to include a small section of code into a static Web page, dynamic code can be used to build an entire Web page *on the fly* (dynamically). Dynamic code can be crudely thought of as programming code used to dynamically construct other program code (such as using some VBScript on a server to create the HTML that will be sent to a browser for rendering).

Dynamic code is particularly useful for Web pages whose structure will change based upon user interactions or frequently changing content. For example, a shipping confirmation Web page may contain a line entry for each item the viewer has purchased. Using traditional static Web pages, a developer may have to code a separate Web page to handle a visitor purchasing one item, two items, three items, and so on, or have a single, fixed-length Web page long enough to handle the largest of orders. With dynamic code, the developer can simply write a template that loops around, building the shipping confirmation Web page by repeatedly inserting the HTML code for a single line item until the order is complete.

When a Web server receives a request for a resource that is marked as a dynamic code template (such as a file with a .jsp suffix), the Web server automatically knows to use the resource as a template for building the Web page that will ultimately be sent to the requestor (rather than actually sending the template itself). The Web server parses the template with the appropriate dynamic code interpreter, executing any dynamic code it finds, before sending the template's output to the requestor.

Although dynamic code makes developing Web sites with nonstatic content much more feasible, it does have some security issues. These issues are typically environment specific. For example, an ASP security issue is unlikely to be a problem in a PHP environment. Table 6.7 lists some common dynamic code environments.

The details of the most recent security issues that apply to a specific dynamic code environment can be identified by visiting the incident-tracking Web sites listed in Table 4.2. However, a large portion of these incidents can be considered to belong to one of the following general categories of vulnerability.

Table 6.7   Sample Dynamic Code Environments

NAME	ASSOCIATED WEB SITE
Active Server Pages (ASP) and ASP.NET (ASP+)	www.microsoft.com
ColdFusion	www.macromedia.com
ContentSuite	www.vignette.com
Instant ASP	www.halcyonsoft.com
Sun Chili!soft ASP	www.chilisoft.com/sun.com
Java Server Page (JSP)	www.sun.com
Personal Home Page (PHP)	www.php.net

Viewing the Template

Some of the dynamic code environments have been found to contain defects that, unless patched, allow an intruder to trick the Web server into not processing the template with the associated interpreter. This causes the template's source code to be downloaded, rather than the code that should have been generated by executing the template. For instance, early versions of IIS could be persuaded to cough up ASP source code by merely adding a period to the end of a URL (for example, wiley.com/resource.asp.). The danger with allowing intruders to view the source code is that they may be able to find sensitive information (such as in the following example ASP code) or a weakness in the template's design that they could then exploit:

```
<%
' Use this when you need to establish a connection to the
database.
data_source  = "primedb"
data_user    = "maintrader"
data_password      = "m15A384$G"

DSN = "Data Source=" & data_source & ";User ID=" & data_user
& ";Password=" & data_password & ";"
%>
```

Templates should therefore be checked to ensure that sensitive information that could be useful to an attacker is not being hard-coded into the templates (such as userIDs, passwords, directory and file structures, and database schemas) and could be potentially viewable to an intruder via an unpatched security hole.

Single Point of Failure

Unlike CGI programs that often run as separate processes, a dynamic code environment may have the template interpreter running as a single process. If the entire Web site is being processed by this single (multithreaded) process, then it may be possible

Table 6.8   Dynamic Code Checklist

YES	NO	DESCRIPTION
☐	☐	Is there a documented policy in place that specifies which dynamic code interpreters (if any) are to be installed on the Web server?
☐	☐	Have all the known security issues been researched and documented for the specific dynamic code environment that will be installed?
☐	☐	Have any security patches and workarounds necessitated by a known security issue been implemented on every Web server?
☐	☐	Have all templates been reviewed for the presence of hard-coded sensitive information?
☐	☐	Have all unneeded dynamic code scripts been removed from the production environment?
☐	☐	Has the dynamic code environment been checked to ensure that it does not provide too detailed information about the application, in the event that an application error occurs?

for an attacker to bring down the Web site by submitting input data that, when processed by the interpreter, causes the interpreter to crash, effectively creating a denial-of-service attack on the entire Web site. An example of this would be a sufficiently large input string that causes a buffer overflow error. Hence, the need exists to test any dynamic code to ensure that it is robust enough to handle any erroneous input that could possibly cause it to fail in a catastrophic manner (a topic discussed in detail in the *Input Data* section of this chapter).

System Commands

In the same way that an intruder could trick an SSI interpreter into executing SSI commands, so can dynamic code interpreters be tricked into executing the system commands that are passed to the Web site via a data input field on a legitimate Web page. Therefore, any input data received from the client should always be parsed to ensure that it does not contain any covert system commands that might be inadvertently executed by a dynamic code interpreter (a topic covered in more detail later in this chapter).

Demonstration Scripts

Vendors of dynamic code environments will often include example dynamic code in their default installations. Unfortunately, as mentioned previously in regard to CGI programs, some of these scripts may not have been exhaustively tested and may therefore contain features that an intruder could exploit. For this reason, many Web sites remove any nonessential demo, training, and utility dynamic code that may have been installed during installation.

Helpful Error Messages

Environments should be checked to ensure that if the dynamic code interpreter encounters an error, they don't give up too much detailed information about the internal workings of the system. For example, IIS/ASP can be configured by the Webmaster to provide different levels of error messages when it encounters an error, the most detailed of which is useful during development, but has a higher security exposure in a production environment. Table 6.8 summaries the dynamic code security checks that a testing team should consider conducting. Traxler (2001) provides additional information on testing some of the more common dynamic code environments.

Application Code

Client-side source code, such as HTML, can be expected to be seen by a Web site's visitors. Simply click View, Page Source (Netscape), or View, Source (MS-IE). However, often the amount of client-side code needed to build a Web page is so voluminous that a developer might doubt that anyone other than him- or herself could be bothered to read this source code. Unfortunately, this assumption can lull some developers into a false sense of security, allowing them to include sensitive information in the source code that they would not normally do, had they thought that an intruder would read this information.

The same is true for server-side interpretive code (CGI scripts, SSI includes, ASP code, and so on), where the developer assumes no one other than the webmaster would see this code. But as can be seen from some of the exploits previously discussed, it should not be assumed that any source code (client-side or server-side) will not be reviewed by an intruder. There are, however, a few precautions that can be practiced to minimize the amount of useful information an intruder can glean, should he or she gain access to an application's code base.

Compileable Source Code

Should a Web server become compromised, needlessly storing source code used to compile executables on the Web server may provide an intruder looking for sensitive information (such as userIDs and passwords), with the opportunity to review this code. Yet this opportunity can easily be denied by only storing the executable (object code) on the production server. Note that although code reengineering tools can reconstruct source code from object code, this computer-generated source code is often devoid of comments and meaningful naming conventions, typically making the code extremely hard to read and comprehend.

Noncompileable Source Code

Well-commented source code is often a sign of a quality-minded developer and an admirable characteristic, because these comments provide assistance to other developers (or even the original author) trying to understand how the code works. Unfortunately, comments left in the production version of any interpretive (noncompileable) code (client-side or server-side) may also prove useful to an intruder trying to figure out how an application works, and thereby deduce a potential flaw in the application that could be exploited.

Source code comments for interpretive code should ideally be removed before the code is placed into production. Removal could be done by hand or with the assistance of a tool (such as Imagiware's HTML Squisher (www.imagiware.com), which removes superfluous HTML). Table 6.9 lists some Web sites that have software tools that can be used to scan source code for specific character strings, such as a comment header. Note that removing comments should also have the beneficial side effect of slightly speeding up the download of any client-side code.

If testing occurs against nonfinal code (such as commented code that has yet to be stripped of its comments), then another iteration of testing against the final (comment-stripped) version would be recommended. Otherwise, the application runs the risk that an error will be accidentally introduced as a by-product of removing the comments (especially if the comments are deleted by hand).

In the case of client-side code, an intruder may not even need to compromise the Web site. Certain tools can enable an intruder to download and then search an entire Web site for such useful keywords as passwords or userIDs (see Table 6.10).

Copyrights

One exception to the *no production comments* rule is the inclusion of a copyright statement in the source code. Depending upon the jurisdiction, adding such protection may increase the number of offenses intruders would commit if they attempted to access a

Table 6.9 Sample Software Tool Libraries Web Sites

NAME	ASSOCIATED WEB SITE
ACME Laboratories	www.acme.com
CNET Networks	www.download.com/shareware.com/zdnet.com
Tucows	www.tucows.com
Ultimate Search	www.freeware32.com
VA Software	www.davecentral.com/osdn.com/sourceforge.net

Note that the Unix Grep command can also be used to search source code and the *strings* command can search object code.

Table 6.10 Sample Web Site Crawlers/Mirroring Tools

NAME	ASSOCIATED WEB SITE
Crawl	www.monkey.org
Sam Spade	www.samspade.org
Teleport Pro	www.tenmax.com
Wget	www.wget.sunsite.dk

Web site by altering the Web site's code, potentially increasing the penalty they would face should they be caught.

Helpful Error Messages

In the same way that dynamic code environment should be checked (described previously in this chapter), applications should also be checked to ensure that if an error occurs in the production environment the application doesn't give up too much detailed information about the internal workings of the application to an external user. For example, returning the source code of a failed SQL statement to the requesting browser may provide an intruder with information on the application's database schema, which he or she may be able to utilize, should the intruder gain limited access to the database server.

Another common error message that is often more helpful than it needs to be is that of the failed login attempt. Some applications will inadvertently let attackers know when they have guessed the right userID. For instance, if entering an invalid userID and password combination results in an "Invalid login attempt" error message, but guessing the right userID (while still using an invalid password) results in an "Invalid password" error message, observant attackers will notice the change in error messages. They will thus be able to deduce that they have stumbled across a valid userID and thereby focus their effort on cracking the password (a much easier task to accomplish now that a valid userID is known).

Old Versions

Any components of a Web application that are no longer needed or that have been superseded by a more recent version should be removed from the production server as soon as configuration management procedures permit. Should an intruder discover these components, they might be able to use these legacy components to interfere with (or crash) a legitimate process or even corrupt the application's database, in effect launching a form of a denial-of-service attack. Table 6.11 summarizes the application code security checks that should be considered. Viega (2001) provides additional information on auditing application source code for security vulnerabilities.

Input Data

A Web application can receive input data in a number of ways (for example, from visible and hidden HTML form fields, cookies, and HTTP headers/URLs). Because an attacker could disable or modify any client-side validation routine, none of this input data should be processed until it has first been reexamined by a server-side validation routine. There are several different data input scenarios that the server-side validators should be able to deal with, and should therefore be tested to ensure that they are indeed robust enough to handle these situations. Whittaker (2002) offers extensive guidance on the categorization and selection of test input data that may be used by a testing team to *break* software.

Table 6.11 Application Code Checklist

YES	NO	DESCRIPTION
☐	☐	Do the coding standards used to build the application include guidelines on the use/nonuse of comments, copyright notices, error messages, and hard-coding sensitive data into an application?
☐	☐	With the exception of a copyright notice, have all comments been removed from the production version of any noncompileable (interpretive) application code?
☐	☐	Have the application's error handlers been reviewed to ensure they do not divulge too much information to the client when invoked in the production environment?
☐	☐	Has all unneeded application code, compiled source code, old versions of code, test harnesses, and so on been removed from the production environment?

Invalid Data Types

Most programming languages do not take kindly to receiving input data in a data format different from the one specified by a program's input parameters. Such an occurrence may result in data truncation, incorrect conversations, or even the demise of the program itself. For example, a developer may have used a drop-down HTML control for a user to rate a new product, and expect to receive a rating between 1 and 10 (inclusive) from the resulting HTML form submittal. Unfortunately, a HTML-savvy attacker could quite easily edit the HTML form (or HTTP message) and replace the expected numeric input with a value such as *astalavistababy*. If this erroneous data is not caught by the data validation routine, the recipient application may do any number of things with the bogus input, none of which are likely to be desirable.

Each data validation routine should therefore be tested to ensure that it is able to appropriately handle input data of the wrong data type. This testing can be accomplished by editing the HTML used to build the data input Web page, writing a custom test harness, or using the scripting capabilities of a functional testing tool (such as one of those listed in Table 6.12).

Invalid Ranges

A Web developer may decide to use some of the built-in validation capabilities of a client-side language (such as HTML, JavaScript, or VBScript) to ensure that an input value is no longer (or shorter) than expected. For example, the developer may have used an HTML form field with a maxlength of 2, combined with some client-side JavaScript, to ensure that when the user is asked to "enter the month you were born," he or she enters a value between 1 and 12. However, if the user has disabled client-side scripting (perhaps as a security precaution of his or her own), the user would be able to enter values such as 0, 35, 58, or 93. If he or she were also willing to edit the HTML

Table 6.12 Sample Web-Testing-Based Scripting Tools

NAME	ASSOCIATED WEB SITE
AutoTester ONE	www.autotester.com
e-Test Suite	www.empirix.com
EValid	www.soft.com
Function Checker	www.atesto.com
SilkTest	www.segue.com
TeamTest and Test Studio	www.rational.com
TestPartner	www.compuware.com
WebART	www.oclc.org
WebFT	www.radview.com
WinRunner, XRunner, and Astra QuickTest	www.mercuryinteractive.com
WinTask	www.wintask.com

form itself, values such as 123, 4567, 89012, and so on, become possible. This would potentially cause problems for an unsuspecting server-side process.

Rather than relying on manual tests to input numerous combinations of test input data, scripting tools (such as those listed in Table 6.12) can be used to automate this often-tedious process and also potentially reduce the effort needed to run a regression test of these features in the future.

Instead of testing each input field with a random selection of input values or a large range of numbers traditional testing techniques such as *equivalence partitioning* and *boundary value analysis* can be used to help identify optimal test data for invalid range testing as it is typically impossible to test every conceivable input value, because the possible number of input values are often infinite.

Buffer Overflows

A variation on the invalid input attack is to submit huge volumes of data in the attempt to cause a *buffer overflow* (a technique described in great detail by *Aleph One* in his white paper; "Smashing the Stack for Fun and Profit," available from www.insecure.org/stf/smashstack.txt). A buffer overflow occurs when the size of the input data exceeds the room reserved for it in a program's memory, causing the program that was processing the data to fail. An attacker may use this type of attack to bring down the Web site, effectively creating a denial-of-service attack. He or she could also use a buffer overflow as a means of inserting a command into the portion of memory that the server uses to store the data and commands that it is currently processing (for instance, a *stack* or *heap*). This is done in the hope that the server will inadvertently execute this covert command, a sequence of events described in greater detail by Skoudis (2001) and Viega (2001). If the program that is compromised is running with administrator (or root) privileges, then the rogue command will be executed with this inherited power.

A CRASH COURSE IN TWO TESTING TECHNIQUES

Equivalence partitioning attempts to group the entire set of possible values for an input field into two classes: valid and invalid (a task that may necessitate gaining knowledge of how the application will process the data). A minimal set of test cases would necessitate using at least one value from each class.

Boundary value analysis (BVA) complements equivalence partitioning. Rather than selecting any element in an equivalence class, those values at the *edge* (or boundary) of the class are selected. The assumption being that errors tend to occur at the boundaries of valid input data, and using the values that are closest to the boundary will most likely expose any errors. Typically, this means selecting the boundary value, the boundary plus the smallest possible increment, and the boundary value minus the smallest possible increment.

For instance, let's perform a BVA using the month field example previously described in this section. An appropriate set of input values for the lower boundary would be 0, 1, and 2 (basically the boundary value plus and minus the next possible input value). For the upper boundary, the values 11, 12, and 13 would be appropriate.

Jorgensen (1995) and Kaner et al. (1999) provide much more detailed explanations of these two testing techniques, while Beizer (1995) explains an associated testing technique: domain testing.

All input data should therefore be bounds-checked to avoid buffer overflows (a technique expanded on later in this chapter).

Hatching an Egg

Application-level buffer overflow attacks are application, operating system, and hardware architecture specific; some platforms and programming languages enforce better memory management on their applications than others. Therefore, these attacks typically necessitate an intruder gaining access to the application's source code as well as an equivalent system software and hardware environment. This is done in order to construct an appropriately formatted input stream (sometimes referred to as an *egg*) that can result in one of the attacker's own system commands being executed.

Denying an attacker the knowledge to design an application-specific buffer overflow is just one reason why access to the application's source code, and knowledge of which system software and hardware is being used by the Web site, should be restricted. Without this information, an attacker trying to author a new exploit is forced to rely on a *brute-force* or *get-lucky* strategy, which can be quite time consuming and therefore less likely to be pursued.

Execution Denial

Although not foolproof, one method of preventing malicious system commands being executed via a buffer overflow is to configure the system software to prohibit command execution directly from memory. This is an option that (if supported by the system software) will defeat many buffer overflow attacks but may cause issues with some legitimate applications that require this functionality to be enabled in order to run correctly. For example, Sun Microsystems's Solaris operating system has a built-in option to disable stack execution, while similar protection can be added to other platforms using third-party plug-ins, such as SecureStack (www.securewave.com) for Windows NT/2000 or StackGuard (www.immunix.org) for Linux.

Code Reviews and Inspections

One of the most effective ways of detecting application-level buffer overflows is via peer-level code reviews and inspections (a technique described in more detail in Chapter 3). Unfortunately, this approach has at least two drawbacks: The sheer volume of code that needs to be reviewed may make it resource prohibitive for many organizations to conduct a peer review for every component of a Web application. In such circumstances, reviews may have to be restricted to components that have been identified as being particularly at risk (such as brand new code, code written by a novice programmer, or code responsible for bounds-checking data from an untrusted source like the client-side portion of a Web application).

The second issue that relates to an application code review is that the application code may be devoid of errors, but the system software or third-party utilities that the application depends on may contain a buffer overflow. Few organizations have the resources to review third-party source code before utilizing it in their own applications (assuming the source code for the third-party utility is even available for review; Chapter 4 discusses the pros and cons of closed-source versus open-source code). However, if an application fails because it uses a system utility that has a buffer overflow vulnerability and an attacker can compromise the application because of this, any Web site using this application may be vulnerable. This is despite the fact that no overflow exists in the lines of code written by the application's developer. Traxler (2001) provides additional information on reviewing a Web application for buffer overflows.

As an alternative to conducting manual reviews, several source-code-critiquing tools attempt to automatically detect problematic code, using proprietary heuristics to look for suspicious code, calls to specific utilities known to have vulnerability issues, or a combination of both (see Table 6.13). For example, Illuma from Reasoning Solutions (www.reasoning.com) is designed to check for memory management issues, uninitialized variables, and poor pointer management, while ITS4 from Cigital (www.cigital.com) examines function calls, specifically looking for security issues, such as potential buffer overflows.

Buffer Overflow Testing

If application source code reviews and inspections are not an option, or nonfailure of the application is so critical that additional testing is warranted, then an application (together with any third-party and system utilities that it utilizes) can be further tested. This can be done by executing destructive tests intentionally designed to detect the existence of a buffer overflow vulnerability. Dustin et al. (2001) and Whit-

Table 6.13 Sample Source-Code-Scanning Tools

NAME	ASSOCIATED WEB SITE
CodeWizard	www.parasoft.com
Illuma	www.reasoning.com
ITS4	www.cigital.com
LDRA Testbed	www.ldra.co.uk
PC-lint	www.gimpel.com
QA C/C++	www.programmingresearch.com
RATS	www.securesw.com
Splint	www.splint.cs.virginia.edu
WebInspect	www.spidynamics.com

taker (2002) provide additional information on testing applications for buffer over-flow vulnerabilities.

Unlike an attacker trying to create a new exploit, a tester should not have to refine an application crash (or any observable weird behavior) to the point where he or she would insert a malicious system command into memory to prove that the application is vulnerable to a buffer overflow. Any application crash or uncontrolled behavior is a potential denial-of-service issue.

Testing Tools

A number of tools could be used to create and submit the huge volumes of data typi-cally needed to simulate a buffer overflow attack to the target application:

- Programs specifically built for sending large amounts of input data, such as NTOMax at www.foundstone.com or Hailstrom (www.cenzic.com).

- Network packet manipulation tools such as SendIP (www.earth.li /projectpurple).

- HTML authoring tools, which can be used to edit an application's Web pages to permit huge data inputs via a regular browser, such as FrontPage (www.microsoft.com.)

- Scripting languages, such as Perl (www.perl.com)

- Testing tools which record and play back HTTP transactions at the network layer, such as Webload (www.radview.com).

- Testing tools that record and play back browser interactions at the browser layer, such as e-Test Suite (www.empirix.com).

Whichever data submission tool is used, it should be evaluated with the rest of the test environment to ensure that it does not prematurely truncate the test data that it is being asked to submit to the target application.

Calibrating the Test Environment

Before being able to test any application for a buffer overflow, the testing environment must first be checked out to determine the maximum size of test input data that will be permitted by the test environment. This is due to the fact that many system software products will truncate extremely long input data. This truncation not only protects any recipient of the data, but also ironically inhibits tests designed to probe an application beyond this system limitation. Unfortunately, these system software truncations can't always be counted on to protect an application, as the point at which a truncation may occur may vary from module to module. For example, the system software code used to handle an HTTP Get command may have a different limitation than that used to process an HTTP Post request.

In an ideal test environment, it should be possible for the testing team to use input data of an infinite size. Unfortunately, sooner or later the test environment itself will truncate the data, thereby prohibiting further testing. Since a truncation could occur at any system software layer, the fewer layers that the test input data has to pass through, the more likely it is that it will make it to the intended target application without being curtailed. At a minimum, the test environment should permit an input string of 64K characters to be passed to the target application without being truncated. Figure 6.2 illustrates these different layers.

Test Logs

Using an automated tool makes data submission a lot easier (no need to hit the X key several thousand times). Unless the tool generates some sort of test log, however (recording the input used for each test and the associated test results), identifying the input stream that first caused an application to fail is likely to necessitate several reruns and prove rather tedious.

Identifying the specific input field that caused the failure, together with the length of data being used at the time, should prove invaluable for the developer charged with diagnosing the application's overflow problem.

Test-Entry Criteria

If not already done as part of functional testing, the initial series of tests should establish the positive functionality of the application (for example, does the application process valid input sizes correctly, never mind invalid lengths), effectively creating an *entry criteria* for the destructive testing that will be performed to search for the exis-

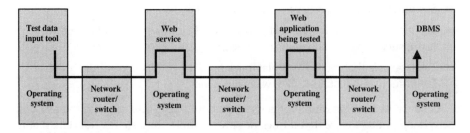

Figure 6.2   Test environment layers.

tence of a buffer overflow. The exact size of the input data should be the maximum size allowed by application's user interface, program specification, application requirements, or the size of the database field used to store the data (which theoretically should all be the same).

A supplemental functional check would involve reviewing the final destination of the input data (typically a database field) to ensure that the largest permissible input has not been inadvertently truncated somewhere on its way through the application. This is useful when conducting internationalization testing using non-Latin character sets that utilize double-character byte encodings.

Small-Scale Overflows

The next set of tests should focus on testing the functional boundary of the application. By using input values just a few characters larger than those used in the previous set of tests, the application can be tested to make sure that the input data does not solely rely on any client-side checks (which can be easily circumvented) to prohibit invalid data from being submitted to the server-side component of the application.

A small-scale test may be easier to monitor if the final destination of the input data can be modified to accommodate input data slightly larger than what it would normally be expected to receive. For example, if the final destination were a database field defined as 256 characters, temporally expanding the field to accommodate 300 characters would facilitate the testing team by demonstrating whether or not any truncation took place. If the input data is not truncated, then a high probability exists that the input field is not being bounds-checked correctly and is therefore a good candidate for a buffer overflow scenario. Unfortunately, an appropriately truncated file being deposited in the corresponding database file does not necessarily mean the input field is immune from a buffer overflow attack. At this point, there is no telling where the truncation took place, and a buffer overflow could occur before the point at which the data is truncated.

Large-Scale Overflows

If a small-scale overflow has not resulted in any noticeable impact on the application, then it's time for the testing team to *pump up the volume*. Progressively increase the size of the input data until the application starts to behave abnormally, or completely fails.

Rather than repeating the test time after time by incrementing the input stream by a single character, the testing team may wish to focus on the input sizes that are more prone to buffer overflows. Designers, developers, and database administrators (DBAs) often select (implicitly or explicitly) the size of a data field based on its data type declaration (such as integer, varchar, smallint, or text). Therefore, selecting input stream lengths that are clustered around the common maximum lengths for data types is likely to drastically reduce the number of tests used, without significantly reducing the quality of the testing. (This is an example of *boundary value analysis* at work.)

For example, for a text-based input field, increasing the data input size in the increments of 256, 512, 1K, 2K, 4K, 8K, 16K, 32K, 64K, and so on, is likely to be a much more efficient testing strategy than each time simply incrementing the input data by single character. The latter would result in 65,536 tests before reaching a test that uses a data input stream of 64K characters.

Since some languages or platforms add or subtract a few characters from the logical length of a data declaration (for instance, a varchar(256) declaration may actually consume 258 bytes), unless the testing team completely understands the inner workings of the platform being used, it may pay to simply add a few additional characters to each input stream. An example would be using data sizes of 264 (256 + 8) and 520 (512 + 8), instead of 256 and 512.

Test Optimization

Assuming no observable failure occurs, sooner or later the input steam will reach the maximum size that the test environment can handle without the input data being truncated. If, based on previous experience, the application should be able to handle the maximum input that the test environment can punish it with, a quicker way to prove this hypothesis is to start with the maximum input size that the test environment can submit. If the application can withstand this worst-case scenario, then there is no need to perform the smaller-sized tests. If, on the other hand, this extreme test fails, additional smaller tests will probably be needed to assist with diagnosing the approximate location of the problem.

The Return Leg

If a database field has been defined to be larger than what would normally be needed to store input data from a legitimate source (for example, a varchar(256) field that under normal circumstances never exceeds 50 characters), the testing team may want to consider inserting data directly into the database to fill up such fields. Once populated, these fields can be requested via the application, causing these unexpectedly long values to travel back through the application to the clients, thereby allowing the testing team to check for buffer overflows on the *return leg* of an application.

Test Observations

One of the challenges of testing an application for buffer overflows is that in many instances a small buffer overflow does not produce any observable symptoms. For example, a 257-character input stream may actually cause a buffer overflow to occur, but if the application does not crash because the extra character overflowed into a portion of memory that by chance isn't referenced, the defect may be indistinguishable from an application that correctly truncates the input string to 256 characters.

Even if a buffer overflow has occurred, a significantly larger input may be required before the situation can be detected, and then the event may not be as dramatic as a program crash but much more subtle. Examples would be a degradation in system performance or the gradual loss of allocated memory (a memory leak). These are symptoms that may not have much of an impact on the system under light processing loads but could prove disastrous under higher loads.

The ease with which a buffer overflow can be observed is also dependent upon the resources available to the testing team. For example, testing teams that have access to memory monitors which can dynamically report on an application's memory allocation, are at a distinct advantage to those who have to rely on symptoms observable to the naked eye.

Diagnostics

Once a program crashes, or some sort of weird behavior is detected, the testing team may be able to refine their input data to determine the approximate point of the failure, thereby speeding up debugging. Although executing additional destructive tests may identify the exact circumstances that cause a program to fail, it is likely that a code review will prove to be the most efficient way of identifying the exact program location of the defect that results in the buffer overflow.

Since all input data should first be bounds-checked before being processed by any other component of the application, the first candidate for a code review is likely to be the server-side routine that initially receives the input data (and therefore theoretically performs the bounds check). Often the cause can be as simple as a developer forgetting to bounds-check just one of the input fields, or using logic that only permits bounds-checking the data for *reasonable* out-of-bounds values.

Escape Characters

Some operating systems will execute system-level commands if they are embedded in an application's data input stream. This can occur when the system command is hidden in input data that is prefixed by special control (*escape*) characters, such as $$. The application may then permit the command to *escape* up to the process that is currently running the application. The receiving process then attempts to execute the system command using its own system privileges.

Data input streams should therefore always be scanned for suspicious characters as soon as they arrive. Although the specific escape sequence will vary from platform to platform, it's generally considered a safer programming practice to check for the inclusion of only legal characters than to check for and attempt to discard illegal ones. A Justification for this viewpoint includes the possibility that a developer might have inadvertently forgotten to check for one illegal character (not checking for one legal character would not pose a security risk). Another possibility is that the application was being ported to a platform the developer had not considered (thereby offering the opportunity for a new set of escape characters).

One *temporal* usability problem with having extremely tight input data validation rules is that some legitimate input may get rejected, stripped, or replaced, because it was wrongly identified as illegal input. For example, a validation routine that checks the input data for the *surname* field may only permit characters A through Z (lower- and uppercase) and *space*. Unfortunately, this routine fails to consider the situation of a double-barreled name (Baxter Smith-Crow), stripping the hyphen and offending a small number of individuals. This problem is usually temporal in nature, because it is typically identified and fixed relatively quickly.

Whichever route is taken, excluding illegal characters or only including the legal ones, each input data stream should be checked to ensure the code has been implemented according to the application's design specification. If the specification doesn't document exactly what is acceptable and what is not (and assuming the specification is unlikely to be clarified before testing), then it would be prudent for the security-testing team to assume that any input other than a through z, A through Z, or 0

POISONING DATABASE INPUT DATA

One technique that attackers may use to execute illicit commands against a database is to insert a database expression where the developer was expecting to receive a single input parameter. For instance, suppose a login Web page consistent of two input fields (userID and password). In addition to entering a bogus userID and password, an attacker might append to each input field the following string:

```
" or "123" <> "1234"
```

If the input fields are fed directly into a database request, then it's possible that a database might not treat this input string as a single parameter, but instead attempt to evaluate the expression and then find that 123 is indeed not equal to 1234, and thereby permit the attacker to successfully log in. Of course the probability of such an attack being successful is increased if the attacker is first able to view the source code that he or she intends to manipulate (or poison).

through 9, including spaces, is suspicious. The team should thus report on any input fields that do not discard this input. For convenience, Table 6.14 lists all possible 128 (7-bit) ASCII input characters. Ideally, the application's specification should explicitly document which of these characters are acceptable (and consequently which ones are not).

Unfortunately, writing individual, customized data validation routines for each data input stream may result in more coding errors making it into production than if a common (and therefore probably slightly more liberal) set of well-tested data valuation routines were reused. Therefore, a trade-off exists between using a large collection of *tight* validation routines and using a small set of more *liberal* validation routines.

While certainly not a replacement for good data input (and output) validation routines, there are some tools (examples of which are listed in Table 6.15) that attempt to validate all the input data sent to a Web site, intercepting and discarding any suspicious input data before it is able to do any harm.

Whichever approach is used, all data input options should be tested to ensure that their corresponding data input validation routines (third-party or otherwise) are robust enough to withstand the worst possible scenarios. Table 6.16 summarizes these scenarios.

Server-Side Data

If an organization's firewall(s) were to be breached or circumvented, sensitive information stored in obviously named files or database tables (as depicted in Figure 6.3 as a means of improving design readability) may allow an intruder to locate desirable information much more easily. This is especially true if the information is conveniently located on a Web server (a practice not recommended).

To mitigate this threat, many organizations have been known to implement one or more datacentric defenses, such as the examples in the following sections.

Table 6.14 ASCII Data Input Characters

CHARACTER	ASCII HEXDEC CODE	CHARACTER	ASCII HEXDEC CODE
Null	00	File separator	1C
Start of heading	01	Group separator	1D
Start of text	02	Record separator	1E
End of text	03	Unit separator	1F
End of transmission	04	Space	20
Enquiry	05	Exclamation	21
Acknowledge	06	Quote	22
Bell	07	Number sign	23
Backspace	08	Dollar sign	24
Character tabulation	09	Percent sign	25
Line fed	0A	Ampersand	26
Line tabulation	0B	Apostrophe	27
Form fed	0C	Left parenthesis	28
Carriage return	0D	Right parenthesis	29
Shift out	0E	Asterisk	2A
Shift in	0F	Plus sign	2B
Datalink escape	10	Comma	2C
Device control 1	11	Hyphen/minus sign	2D
Device control 2	12	Full stop	2E
Device control 3	13	Forward slash	2F
Device control 4	14	Digits 0 through 9	30-39
Negative acknowledgement	15	Colon	3A
Synchronous idle	16	Semicolon	3B
End of transmission block	17	Less than sign	3C
Cancel	18	Equals sign	3D
End of medium	19	Greater than sign	3E
Substitute	1A	Question mark	3F
Escape	1B	@	40

(continues)

Table 6.14 ASCII Data Input Characters (*continued*)

CHARACTER	ASCII HEXDEC CODE	CHARACTER	ASCII HEXDEC CODE
Uppercase A through Z	41-5A	Lowercase a through z	61-7A
Left square bracket	5B	Left curly bracket	7B
Backslash	5C	Vertical line	7C
Right square bracket	5D	Right curly bracket	7D
Circumflex	5E	Tilde	7E
Low line	5F	Delete	7F
Grave	60		

Source: www.ansi.org.

Table 6.15 Input Data Validation Tools

NAME	ASSOCIATED WEB SITE
APS	www.stratum8.com
G-Server	www.gilian.com
iBroker SecureWeb	www.elitesecureweb.com
URLScan	www.microsoft.com

Table 6.16 Valuation Routine Checklist

YES	NO	DESCRIPTION
☐	☐	Do the coding standards used to build the application include guidelines on the use of input data validation routines?
☐	☐	Have all data input validation routines been inspected and/or tested to ensure they are able to handle invalid data types?
☐	☐	Have all data input validation routines been inspected and/or tested to ensure they are able to handle invalid data ranges?
☐	☐	Have all data input validation routines been inspected and/or tested to ensure they are able to handle buffer overflow attempts?
☐	☐	Have all data input validation routines been inspected and/or tested to ensure they are able to detect system command escape characters?

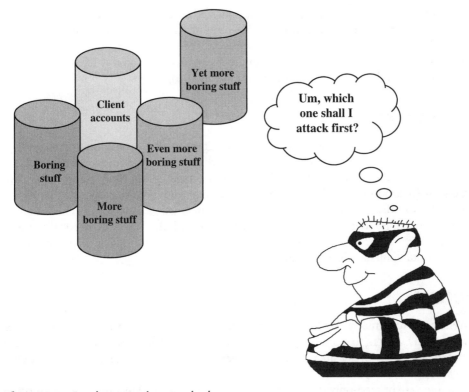

Figure 6.3 Database naming standards.

Data Filenames

If sensitive application data (such as userIDs and passwords) is to be stored in a database accessible via the Web site, the database design may have called for such fields and files to be named in a manner that does not give away their true usage. If such a strategy is employed, the database design should be reviewed at an early stage to ensure that sensitive information is not stored in such obviously named files as *users*, *userIDs*, *passwords*, *security*, *accounts*, and so on.

Unfortunately, if blatantly obvious names do make it into production, the cost of reworking (and testing) the application code just to use alternate filenames may be unjustifiably expensive, hence the need to decide early on in the application's design whether or not this security by obscurity approach should be adopted by the application's developers.

Data Tripwires

An exception to this security by obscurity rule would be when these easily identifiable files are used to store *bogus* userIDs and passwords. An attempt to log in with a userID from one of these bogus files may then be used as a *tripwire* to alert support staff to the fact that someone has already gained unauthorized access to the application's database and is attempting to penetrate further. (Tripwires are discussed in more detail in Chapter 8.) Unfortunately, tripwires are generally only effective if someone takes notice of their alerts. Therefore, if a database tripwire is deployed, when it is triggered, the on-duty staff should monitor and react appropriately if triggered.

Data Vaults

Vulnerable data may be placed inside a *data vault* for further protection. A data vault is a database (or data repository) that has had additional security measures applied to it to ensure that the data is protected from unauthorized access. Such controls improve the security around the data but add to the administrative workload and may impact data I/O speeds. If a data vault is implemented, the testing team should check that all the sensitive data that should be placed inside the vault does actually reside there, and that no performance-enhancing copies have been replicated outside the vault. Examples of data vaults are listed in Table 6.17.

WORMs

Write-once read-many (WORM) devices may impact performance, but using devices such as CD writers to store transaction logs or network audit trails would most likely thwart any attempt by an intruder to cover their tracks by deleting or modifying these logs.

In the case of read-only data files and executables, fast CD readers (with no writing capabilities) and ample memory may make for a more secure storage solution than storing these files on hard drives that could be compromised. The amount of memory needed should be sufficient to keep the read-only files in memory long enough to avoid the considerable performance hit that repeatedly reading this data from the CD would cause.

If a Web application's design calls for hardware-based write restrictions, a quick visual inspection of the hardware may not be able to detect the difference between a write-once CD writer and a CD writer with rewriting capabilities. In such cases, a software-based test may be warranted to see if files on the CD can be altered or deleted. To ensure that any restriction is due to the hardware device, as opposed to a security setting, the file access request should be done with an administrative account, which is not limited by any software-based security restriction.

Table 6.17 Sample Data Vaults

NAME	ASSOCIATED WEB SITE
BorderWare	www.borderware.com
Cyber-Ark	www.cyber-ark.com

Data Encryption

Although stringent precautions may be taken to protect data files used to permanently store data, less attention may be paid to transient data files such as temporary files, Web logs, database logs, application logs, third-party data files, .ini files, and obscure storage locations such as Window's registry entries. Unfortunately, these files are often used to temporarily store sensitive data (credit card numbers, social security numbers, and so on). They should therefore be checked to ensure that if such data is stored, it is only stored in an encrypted format, lest an intruder stumble across these forgotten nuggets of information.

In addition, or as an alternative to any file encryption capabilities that the host operating system may provide (for instance, Windows 2000's Encrypting File System [EFS]), products such as those listed in Table 6.18 can be used to encrypt data stored on a server.

Data Deception

Since even the most strongly encrypted files can theoretically be cracked given enough time and resources, deception may be a more viable alternative to using heavy encryption. In other words, by making encrypted data not look like it's actually encrypted, an intruder may never suspect that the data has been encrypted and therefore not even attempt to decipher it, thereby protecting the data *ad infinitum*. For example, instead of encrypting a client's PIN into a 128-bit binary format (which would make the resulting

Table 6.18   Sample File Encryption Tools

NAME	ASSOCIATED WEB SITE
AgProtect	www.hallogram.com
Blowfish and Crypto	www.gregorybraun.com
CipherPack	www.cipherpack.com
Data Vault	www.reflex-magnetics.com
DataSAFE	www.data-encryption.com
EasyCrypt	www.easycrypt.co.uk
Encryption Plus	www.pcguardian.com
FileCrypto	www.f-secure.com
GNU Privacy Guard	www.gnupg.org
Kryptel	www.bestcrypto.com
RSA BSAFE	www.rsasecurity.com
Steganos Security Suite	www.steganos.com

data longer), a hashing algorithm could be used that creates in another value that is the same length. Unsuspecting intruders may never figure out that the data is actually encrypted, and when they try using these values, they'll become frustrated because none of these stolen numbers work.

A fundamental weakness of a deception strategy is that for it to be effective, the deception must be kept secret. If such a strategy is to be employed, knowledge of its use should be restricted to a *need-to-know* basis, and certainly not documented in a requirements specification that any employee of the organization could easily gain access to. (Chapter 8 discusses the implications of testing defenses based on deception in more detail.)

Data Islands

Many organizations choose not to expose their master database to the Internet. One strategy for doing so is to replicate the master data on a database server that is part of the Web application and then to remove all physical network connections between the Web application and this master database, effectively creating a *data island*.

If a Web application's design calls for a data island implementation, then the testing team should determine if the implementation has left open any network path from the Web site to the master database. For instance, via an internal firewall that has not been tested, or via a temporary unsecured network connection that only exists while the two databases are being synchronized.

Distributed Copies

In an effort to improve scalability, some Web sites use a distributed database design to store data across multiple servers. In addition to any capacity flexibility that this design enables, such an approach may make a Web application harder for an intruder to corrupt, as the intruder would need to gain access to several servers before being able to corrupt every single copy of a data file.

Where feasible, these distributed copies should ideally have different security permissions, meaning that if an intruder is able to crack a userID and password protecting one copy, the same combination could not be used to access the others. Therefore, the testing team should check that as few accounts as possible are granted access to more than one copy of the data.

Fragmented Data

In contrast to storing multiple copies of the same data, extremely sensitive data may be broken up and distributed across multiple geographic locations, making the information useless unless the intruder is able to compromise all the storage sites and reassemble this fragmented data. For instance, some credit-card-processing Web sites store a client's userID, password, and account information in three separate databases, each residing at a different physical location.

One danger with this approach is that in order to improve database performance, a developer may reassemble the fragmented data into a single temporary file, which, if discovered by an intruder, would circumvent the need to attack all the dispersed locations. This situation is more likely to be discovered via design reviews than through test execution.

Database Management System (DBMS) Enforced Constraints

Most Database Management Systems (DBMSs) offer several different ways in which the data inside a DBMS can be protected from unauthorized access. The following are some of the more common approaches:

User groups.   Rather than assigning security privileges to individual userIDs, most DBMSs enable the DBA to assign users to user groups, and then grant access to the group, which in turn is passed on to all the members of the group. Because user groups typically make security administration easier and therefore less prone to human error, they are generally considered a more secure approach than assigning privileges directly to individual users.

Views.   Instead of assigning access directly to the data, many DBAs create an intermediate database object—a *view*. Instead of accessing a table (or group of tables) directly, users reference the data indirectly via a view. This extra level of indirection can allow a DBA to hide some of the database's physical attributes, such as the table's real name and location, or limit the user to only viewing some of the table's columns and/or rows.

Stored procedures.   Rather than actually assigning read and write access to users (or user groups), some DBAs will only grant direct access to a database's tables (or views) to a program stored within the database itself (a stored procedure). Users are then limited to executing these predefined programs, thereby removing the data manipulation flexibility intruders would have if they were able to gain direct access to the tables (or even views) themselves.

Referential integrity (RI).   Features such as foreign keys, triggers, user-defined data types, rules, and constraints that are intended to ensure that the data stored within the database remains consistent may also frustrate an intruder that is trying to insert, update, or delete illicit data in an ad hoc fashion. For instance, trying to delete a customer account may first necessitate purging all the client's transactions, which in itself may require tampering with the application's audit trail. Or as another example, trying to add a fictitious stock purchase transaction could require the intruder to simultaneously add an associated stock sale transaction. However, many DBAs disable RI on production databases in order to improve database performance (if no RI exists for the DBMS to enforce, then these resource-consuming operations will not be performed). Therefore, a trade-off takes place between performance and security/data integrity priorities.

Whichever approach the database design calls for, the database schema that has actually been created in the production environment should be reviewed to ensure that all the intended methods of protection have been implemented correctly. In addition, tools such as AppDetective from Application Security (www.appsecinc.com) and

Database Scanner from Internet Security Systems (www.iss.net) can be used to scan database implementations looking for DBMS-specific security vulnerabilities. Castano et al. (1994), Dustin et al. (2001), and Heney et al. (1998) provide additional information on database security measures.

Filtered Indexes

Internal search engines can be useful to legitimate users trying to locate hard-to-find content. Unfortunately, a malicious user could also use this common Web site feature to locate confidential information using search words such as password, security, fraud, secret, or even the name of a competitor. To mitigate this possibility, some internal search engines enable a Webmaster to list words that should not be indexed. Either way, the internal search engine should be tested to ensure that it doesn't provide any sensitive information.

The defenses designed to protect an application's data are often an application's last line of defense. They should therefore be thoroughly exercised by the testing team, especially when you consider that unlike some defenses that are under constant attack (such as a perimeter firewall), an organization may never have had this final line of defense put to the test by a real attacker. Table 6.19 summarizes the checks that a test-

Table 6.19 Server-Side Data Checklist

YES	NO	DESCRIPTION
☐	☐	Does the Web application's design specify which defensives should be put in place to protect data stored on the server side (with the possible exception of a deception-based defense)?
☐	☐	Have sensitive data files been given names that do not indicate their true purpose?
☐	☐	If the application has a database tripwire, does the on-duty support staff react to an alert appropriately, or are the alerts ignored?
☐	☐	Are any devices (or media) that are intended to be read-only or write-once actually write inhibited?
☐	☐	Are all data files protected from being corrupted, altered, or prematurely destroyed by an intruder using data vaults, WORM devices, data islands, distributed copies, DBMS-enforced constraints, and so on?
☐	☐	Are all sensitive data files protected from being read by an intruder using data vaults, encryption, deception, fragmented copies, and so on?
☐	☐	Has the desired database schema been implemented correctly in the production environment?
☐	☐	Has any internal search engine been checked to ensure that it does not return any confidential information?

ing team may want to consider performing as a means of determining if the data residing on the server-side portion of a Web application is adequately protected.

Application-Level Intruder Detection

Financial institutions such as credit card issuers have long used a client's behavior to help detect when another person has gained unauthorized access to a client's account. For instance, many jewelers expect a credit card's verification department to want to talk to the purchaser. This is to verify that their client is the one who is actually performing this unusually large transaction, not someone who has stolen a card and is using it before the rightful owner has noticed that it is being used inappropriately. Another sign that some credit card issuers use to indicate a potential problem is the sudden use of the card at several locations that do not require signature confirmation (such as gas station pumps). Thieves will often use these low-risk purchases to determine whether a card is still active before attempting a higher-risk transaction.

If a Web application attempts to identify unauthorized transactions based on a client's past behavior, then the testing team should consider including tests to determine how sensitive the monitoring is. For example, let's look at a buy-and-hold investor, who normally buys shares in blocks of $500 once a month and generally holds on to them for several years. This client would probably appreciate a phone call to confirm that the 20 daytrades that were placed yesterday were actually done by him or her and not an unauthorized person (such as an intruder or one of the client's own children). On the other hand, the organization's customer service department may not be able to handle calling 1 percent of their customer base every day, just because the behavioral model being used is too sensitive (and additionally notifying their customers that behavior data on them is being collected and analyzed, possibly generating privacy concerns amongst them). Table 6.20 summarizes these scenarios. Garfinkel (2002) and Ghosh (2001) provide additional information on the topic of Web privacy.

Table 6.20   Application Intruder Detection Checklist

YES	NO	DESCRIPTION
☐	☐	Does the application's specification document under which user behavioral circumstances an alert should be raised?
☐	☐	Are the detection rules too sensitive, resulting in too many false alarms?
☐	☐	Are the detection rules too lax, allowing blatant changes in user behavioral patterns to go unnoticed?
☐	☐	If an application-level intruder detection system is used, does the on-duty support staff react to an alert appropriately, or are the alerts ignored?

Summary

As can be seen from the preceding sections, having the most perfectly secured Web site network and system software infrastructure is little protection if the Web application being hosted on the site is not designed and developed with security in mind. By thoroughly testing both the client-side and server-side components of a Web application, an organization can endeavor to make the Web application as secure as the infrastructure that the application itself depends upon.

Sneak Attacks: Guarding against the Less-Thought-of Security Threats

Although many people imagine attackers slaving away over a hot keyboard hundreds of miles away from their intended target, assailants could use any of several alternative approaches to meet their objectives. This chapter looks at several of these sneaky attacks and offers suggestions on how the security policies that an organization has decided to adopt can be tested to ensure that they provide an acceptable level of protection from these often overlooked security risks. Harris (2001), Krutz et al. (2001), Parker (1998), and Peltier (2002) provide additional information on this problem domain.

Combating Social Engineers

The term *social engineering* is used to describe the various tricks used to fool innocent people (employees, business partners, or customers) into voluntarily giving away information that would not normally be known to the general public. These techniques were expanded upon by Winkler (1999). Examples include names and contact information for key personnel, system userIDs and passwords, or proprietary operating procedures. Armed with this newfound knowledge, the attacker may then be able to penetrate even the securest of Web sites.

As the following scenarios seek to demonstrate, an attacker could seek to employ an almost infinite number of tricks, using any one of several different communication channels.

Tricks by Telephone

An attacker could call an organization's help desk and try any one of the following plausible stories:

- *"Hi, this is David, the VP of sales. I'm at the Chicago branch today and I can't remember my password. The machine in my home office has that 'Remember password' set, so it's been months since I actually had to enter it. Can you tell me what it is, or reset it or something? I really need to access this month's sales reports ASAP."*

- *"Hi, this is Melissa at the Salt Lake City branch. I'm the new LAN administrator and my boss wants this done before he gets back from Chicago. Do you know how I can:*
  - *Configure our firewall to have the same policies as corporate?*
  - *Download the latest DNS entries from the corporate DNS server to our local server?*
  - *Run a transaction on a remote file and print server using a Shell command?*
  - *Back up the database to our off-site disaster recovery location?*
  - *Locate the IP address of the main DNS server?*
  - *Set up a backup dial-up connection to the corporate LAN?*
  - *Connect this new network segment to the corporate intranet?"*

Tricks by Email

Alternatively, attackers could utilize emails to communicate to their victims:

> *To: An unsuspecting employee*
> *Hi Shawn,*
> *This is Brian from network support. We are currently testing our new corporate Web application at testwiley.com and are having intermittent problems getting anyone from your location signed in correctly. As soon as you read this, can you please try to log into the main application using your existing userID and password?*
> *ThX*

Of course, the wiley.com Web site doesn't contain a real application, but rather a single HyperText Markup Language (HTML) form designed to capture and relay to the attacker any login attempts after it has informed the user that the login has failed.

> *To: The registrar for the organization's domain name*
> *Hi Registrar,*
> *I'm Rajan, the admin contact for the wiley.com Web site. We're moving to a cheaper ISP, effective immediately. Can you please set the IP address for our Web site to 123.456.789.123?*
> *Thanks, Rajan*

If the only security precaution the registrar requires is that the From: field of the email match the email address on file (which may be obtainable from the registrar's own Web site), then the Web site's traffic could be redirected to a new (less friendly) machine.

> *To: The ISP hosting the organization's Web site*
> *Hi tech support,*
> *I'm Carrie, the new contact point for the wiley.com Web site. The old guy Sundari quit last week to go work for some dot.com startup and didn't stick around to do any kind of handover, so can you update your contact records to show me as the new contact point for our Web site?*
> *Thanks, Carrie*

A couple of days later, after the contact records have been altered, the original email is followed up with a second email:

> *Hi tech support,*
> *I'm Carrie, the contact point for the wiley.com Web site. Can you set up a subnet (test.wiley.com) on the same Web server that wiley.com is hosted on and email me the FTP userID and password so we can upload and test the new version of our Web application?*
> *Thanks, Carrie*

Of course, instead of uploading a new application, the attacker uploads a toolkit (otherwise known as a *rootkit*) for compromising the server's system administrator account.

Tricks by Traditional Mail

An attacker could even use a mass-mailing strategy, sending letters in the mail to hundreds of organizations, in the hope that several of them will fall for the scam. Here's an example:

> *Attn: Network Engineer*
> *Congratulations, you've been preapproved for a 1-year free subscription to NetworkMag. To claim your gift, please complete the enclosed circulation survey and return it to us at Bogus Publishing.*
> *STOP PRESS.*
> *If you accept this offer by <insert date two weeks from today>, we will also send you a complementary round of golf at <insert name of exclusive local golf course>.*

Of course, in addition to asking for personal information such as one's first name, last name, mailing address, work telephone number, and email address, the survey also asks what type of hardware and system software the Web site uses.

> *Attn <insert name of product with a detected security vulnerability>*
> *Engineer*
> *Bogus Training Corporation would like to offer you a complimentary wall chart graphically depicting all of <insert product name's> most common*

commands. To receive this free gift, please fill out the attached coupon and return it to us here at . . .

Needless to say, there is no wall chart; all the attacker is trying to do is find potential candidates who may not have gotten around to installing the latest security patch for a vulnerable product.

Tricks in Person

Depending upon how confident attackers are and how much they are willing to risk being caught to acquire the information they seek, they may attempt to gain entry to a secure facility by blatantly walking in through the front door and utilizing stories like the following:

- At the IT nightshift leader's office:

  "Hi, I'm Thomas Copeland. I'm with the external auditors Arthur Waterhouse. We've been told by corporate to do a surprise inspection of your disaster recovery procedures. Your department has 10 minutes to show me how you would recover from a Web site crash."

- At an ISP Web-hosting facility:

  "Hi I'm Cathleen, I'm a sales rep out of the New York office. I know this is short notice, but I have a group of perspective clients out in the car that I've been trying for months to get to outsource their Web-hosting needs to us. They're located just a few miles away and I think that if I can give them a quick tour of our facilities, it should be enough to push them over the edge and get them to sign up. Oh yeah, they are particularly interested in what security precautions we've adopted. Seems someone hacked into their Web site a while back, which is one of the reasons they're considering the outsourcing route."

  In reality, the sales rep and clients are a group of intruders who in addition to learning more information about their next potential target, hope to outnumber the facility staff giving the tour, thereby allowing at least one member of the group to, unnoticed, grab a backup tape or even try to gain access to a server long enough to download a password file onto a floppy disk.

- Dressed in appropriate *engineerial* attire (complete with clipboard):

  "Hi, I'm with Cooler and Sons Air Conditioning. We received a call that the computer room was getting too warm and need to check your HVAC system." Using professional-sounding terms like HVAC (Heating, Ventilation, and Air Conditioning) may add just enough credibility to an intruder's masquerade to allow him or her to gain access to the targeted secured resource.

Due to the sheer number of imaginative stories an attacker could come up with, it's not practical to describe every possible scenario in an organization's security policies, although documenting the techniques used (together with preventive countermeasures) for some of the most common methods might merit inclusion. Instead, the best defense against the myriad social engineering attacks is employee awareness. To this end, an organization should have a training scheme in place to ensure that employees

Table 7.1   Social Engineering Checklist

YES	NO	DESCRIPTION
☐	☐	Does the organization have security policies in place that provide guidance (preventive measures and procedures for confirming the legitimacy of a request) on the most common forms of social engineering? For example, how can a member of the help desk differentiate between a legitimate user who has forgotten his or her password and an imposter trying to work the system?
☐	☐	Has personal contact information for critical individuals such as the webmaster, LAN administrator, and database administrator (DBA) been removed from publicly available documentation? Examples would be domain name registrations and corporate phone directories.
☐	☐	Does the new employee orientation process teach employees the organization's security procedures, and, in particular, social engineering awareness?
☐	☐	Are employees continually reminded to be vigilant against social engineering? For example, are they required to reread the organization's security policies on a regular basis?
☐	☐	Are all social engineering attempts made by the security assessment team thwarted by observant employees?

(and any temporary staff) are able to recognize a con artist at work and promptly notify the appropriate security personal. A training scheme could be evaluated by the security-testing team attempting some of the most common social engineering exploits on unsuspecting employees who have been through the training program and should therefore know better. Table 7.1 summarizes these social engineering checks.

Twarting Dumpster Divers

The term *dumpster diving* is used to describe searching disposal areas for information that has not been properly destroyed. Since this information may be stored on a number of different mediums and vary in degrees of its sensitivity, an organization may use a number of alternate methods to dispose of this information. The security-testing team may therefore need to evaluate whether the appropriate disposal methods are actually being employed for all an organization's *waste items*.

Proper Disposal of Paper

An organization should ensure that any paper-based report, audit trail, transaction log, fax, letter, or post-it note containing confidential information is destroyed beyond

CLASSIFYING A DOCUMENT

Many organizations use multiple categories for specifying how sensitive a particular document is. Terms such as *public, unclassified, sensitive, secret, company confidential, top secret, internal use only, private,* and *for your eyes only* are just some of the names used to categorize different levels of sensitivity. Security policies should therefore clearly state the differences between each category, process, or criteria for assigning a document to the most appropriate category and the procedures utilized to handle these documents.

recognition before it is discarded. For the most sensitive documents, regular shredding may not be enough; instead, crosscutting shredders or furnaces may be required.

Cleaning Up Brainstorms

Many organizations utilize hotel conference rooms or other unsecured facilities (internal or off-site) to conduct *brainstorming* sessions. Unfortunately, it is often the case that once the session is complete, no one considers wiping down the whiteboard(s) used to record the output of the meeting, potentially leaving sensitive information (such as a network topology) up on the whiteboard for days, weeks, or basically until somebody else needs to use the whiteboard.

A quick tour of an organization's meeting rooms should provide the security-testing team with an indication of how adept the organization's culture is at cleaning up sensitive information after group meetings.

Proper Disposal of Electronic Hardware

Old hard drives (especially if leased machines are to be returned to a leasing company), tapes, Zip and Jaz disks, floppy disks, and CDs that at one time were either used in the production environment or to back up production data should (where possible) be *degaussed* (a process described in the sidebar "Degaussers"), or overwritten multiple times with dummy data files before being recycled and then physically crushed before being disposed of.

Contrary to popular opinion, overwriting the data once may still leave a magnetic residue that could be used to recreate the erased data. In the case of a reformatted disk, the operating system may not even delete the data files but simply mark the sectors on the disk used to store this information as free space, again making it possible to recover the data that had appeared to have been destroyed.

If, instead of being destroyed on-site, media are transported to a secondary site for disposal while still in a readable format, adequate precautions should be taken to ensure that an attacker cannot intercept these items en route and acquire this information before it reaches its final destination. Table 7.3 summaries these checks.

DEGAUSSERS

Degaussing is the process of passing magnetic media (such as tapes and floppy disks) through a powerful magnet field to rearrange the polarity of the particles used to store electronic data, thereby completely removing any trace of the previously recorded data.

Degaussers are sometimes referred to as *bulk erasers* because whole packs of media (such as a carton of 100 floppy disks) can be erased in one operation. Table 7.2 lists some sample vendors who manufacture or sell these devices.

Table 7.2   Sample List of Vendors Who Manufacture or Sell Degaussing Devices

NAME	ASSOCIATED WEB SITE
Benjamin	www.benjaminsweb.com
Data Devices International	www.Datadev.com/degausser.com
Data-Link Associates	www.datalinksales.com
Data Security	www.datasecurityinc.com
Garner Products	www.garner-products.com
Proton Engineering	www.proton-eng.com
Verity Systems	www.veritysystems.com/degaussers.net
Weircliffe	www.weircliffe.co.uk

Table 7.3   Data Disposal Checklist

YES	NO	DESCRIPTION
☐	☐	Do the organization security policies define what sensitive data is, and if multiple categories are used, do they explain how a particular item of data would be assigned to the most appropriate category?
☐	☐	Does the organization have security policies in place that provide guidance on how media that contains (or previously contained) sensitive data should be recycled or destroyed?
☐	☐	Does the policy include all mediums used to store sensitive data such as tapes, floppy disks, hard drives, and paper?
☐	☐	Does the policy provide guidance on what constitutes an acceptable location for the storage or disposal of sensitive data? For example, are DBAs allowed to take database backups home, and are computer room wastepaper bins acceptable receptacles for the disposal of network management reports?
☐	☐	Does the policy include protection measures for the transportation of sensitive data to remote locations?
☐	☐	Does the policy include protection measures for sensitive data at off-site/backup locations or disposal destinations (including third parties)?
☐	☐	Do all employees adhere to these data disposal policies?

Defending against Inside Accomplices

Life is a lot easier for external attackers if someone on the inside is willing to help them (or if the attackers are insiders themselves). This help could take any number of different forms:

- A developer building a *Trojan horse* or *time bomb* into a Web application (especially if the developer is a short-term consultant)

- A DBA adding some attacker-friendly stored procedures to the production database

- A Webmaster installing a *backdoor* or *rootkit* on the Web server

- A network engineer making an illicit copy on a production server's entire hard drive

- A system administrator forgetting to install an operating system security patch

- A value-added retailer (VAR) installing a firewall and leaving the manufacturer's default maintenance account active

- An engineer from the local utility company attaching a network sniffer to a LAN

- A member of the cleaning crew retrieving any useful-looking post-its from the computer room's wastepaper bin

Fortunately, many techniques are available for an organization to protect itself against someone on the inside abusing his or her privileged position. These techniques generally fall in one (or more) of the categories mentioned in the following section.

Preventative Measures and Deterrents

The following sample security measures can either actually prevent an insider from committing a breach of confidence or, by acting as a deterrent, result in the insider deciding not to attempt the act:

- Establishing a *continuous* security awareness program.

- Locating critical servers in a secure room with the doors locked at all times (not just when the last person leaves at night).

- Ensuring authorized personnel supervise any janitorial staff while they clean a secured area.

- If local employment practices permit, running preemployment (and/or ongoing) background checks on employees to detect employees who may be predisposed to committing a network intrusion. Such checks might include calling references, confirming resume details, checking for criminal records, testing for drug use, and running a credit check.

- Appropriately using authorization badges and "Authorized Personnel Only" signs. For example, authorized employees should be clearly identifiable and all unauthorized personnel (especially visitors) should be escorted at all times when they are present inside a secure area.

- Training employees to appropriately challenge someone who does not appear to be authorized for the area they are in.

- Configuring each machine to use a different BIOS password.

- Configuring each machine to use a password-protected screensaver.

- Mounting video cameras in clearly visible locations.

- Monitoring all electronic media that is brought into or out of secure areas. An example would be checking to see that only blank floppies are brought into a secure area and only crushed floppies are removed.

- Establishing revolving duties. For example, each week reassigning the machines that each LAN administrator is responsible for. Unless there is a conspiracy, corrupt LAN administrators will know that they run the risk that a vigilant peer will detect one or more of their wrongdoings.

- Defining procedures that separate duties or require dual controls and consequently prevent any single employee from accomplishing anything significant without the help of a second employee. An example would be only allowing the librarian to promote new protection code into the staging area and then restricting the webmaster from uploading files on to a production Web server from anywhere else other than the staging area. Or perhaps network administrators would be required to get a supervisor's approval before creating a new user account.

- Requiring all employees who are leaving the organization (both voluntarily and involuntarily) to return all hardware owned by the organization, changing any passwords that the employees might have known and disabling their personal login IDs (especially any dial-up accounts).
  From a security perspective, requesting the return of software may be a moot point, due to the ease with which software can be duplicated (CD burners have become extremely inexpensive). However, an organization may still want to explicitly request the return of software, so that any software licenses can be recycled and to prohibit a former employee from legally using the software.

- Using objective third parties to regularly perform security assessments.

Detective Measures

Detective measures are intended to alert an organization to the fact that a security breach has, is, or will take place (discussed further in Chapter 8). Some examples of measures that can be used to detect an inside accomplice include the following:

- Installing anomaly-based intrusion detection systems that monitor for unusual behavior

- Using tripwires that check for any activity on theoretically static files

- Placing motion detectors in supposedly uninhabited rooms

- Monitoring outbound emails for suspicious content (assuming local emplacement practices permit this activity)

- Installing keyboard-logging devices (such as the ones listed in Table 7.4) on critical consoles (assuming local emplacement practices permit this activity)

Corrective and Prosecutive Measures

Once a wrongdoing has been detected, an organization will need to attempt to recover from this disturbance (a topic discussed in more detail in Chapter 8). The corrective actions will obviously be heavily dependent on what and how much damage has been done. An organization is also likely to want to identify beyond repudiation which individual(s) was responsible for the security breach and take some form of action to ensure that the event does not happen again. If formal disciplinary actions or criminal prosecutions are sought, then the organization will need evidence indicating the suspected employee's guilt. Such evidence is typically much easier to collect if the systems and computer facilities have been designed with this requirement in mind. Examples of such measures include the following:

- Creating transaction logs, network audit trails, file access (including read) logs, and Web logs

- Logging keyboard stokes from critical terminals

- Videotaping everyone entering and leaving a restricted area

As can be seen from these preceding scenarios, an insider could consciously assist an external attacker or commit an intrusion him- or herself in many different ways. Although trying to protect against every conceivable scenario is unlikely to be feasible, it's not unreasonable to attempt to ensure that at least one preventive, detective, and corrective measure exists for each category of employee that has access to some critical or sensitive resource. (Table 7.5 summarizes these checks.) This may

Table 7.4   Sample List of Keyboard-Logging and Screen-Recording Tools

NAME	ASSOCIATED WEB SITE
Black Box	www.enfiltrator.com
Computer Spy	www.computerspy.com
eBlaster/Spector	www.spectorsoft.com
KEYKatcher	www.keykatcher.com
Online Recorder	www.internet-monitoring-software.com
Snapshot Spy	www.snapshotspy.com
WinGuardian	www.webroot.com

not be as hard to implement as it might first appear, as some security measures may actually fulfill the needs of more than one category. For example, a monitored video camera in plain sight that is backed up to tape may act as a deterrent, allow an on-duty guard to detect unauthorized access, and also provide evidence that can be used in a prosecution.

An organization may wish to internally publicize an attack initiated from the inside, helping to raise employee awareness (and perhaps act as a deterrent). Alternatively, an organization may wish to keep knowledge of such an attack confidential, possibly because criminal charges may be brought, or to reduce the likelihood that news of the attack makes it into the public domain and subsequently causes the organization to lose credibility. Either way, the organization should clearly document what its standing policy is toward this matter.

Table 7.5   Inside Accomplice Checklist

YES	NO	DESCRIPTION
☐	☐	Has the organization clearly defined the unacceptable activities, and are employees made aware of these activities and the ramifications should they pursue them?
☐	☐	Does the organization have security policies in place that include measures to protect against an inside (as well as an outside) assailant? Note that some of these measures may be more effective if left undisclosed to anyone not involved in implementing the policy, while other policies should be published if they are intended to act as a deterrent.
☐	☐	Specifically, are there preventive measures in place to dissuade any employee with access to sensitive data or a critical component of the Web site not to behave inappropriately?
☐	☐	Specifically, are there detective measures in place that should detect inappropriate employee behavior?
☐	☐	Are any inappropriate actions performed by the security assessment team as part of the security assessment detected?
☐	☐	Once an internal security breach has been detected, are procedures in place that would allow the organization to correct this situation?
☐	☐	If the organization would like to have the option of prosecuting or taking formal disciplinary action against an employee suspected of inappropriate behavior, is the system designed to collect sufficient evidence to allow this to happen?

Preventing Physical Attacks

Even the best firewalls provide no protection against an unauthorized person gaining physical access to a machine. Intruders don't have to be able to pick up a machine and walk out of the building. Typically, all they need is an unguarded console or an easily guessed screensaver password and a few minutes to change a few security settings, or to be able to copy all important password files to a floppy disk. For example, even if nobody is logged in or the screensaver password is unguessable, an intruder could potentially circumvent this precaution. This could be achieved by simply turning the power off, restarting the machine by booting to DOS (via a floppy disk or CD), and then copying the file onto the floppy before finally executing a normal reboot.

No security assessment is complete without addressing the physical security used to protect the hardware that the Web site will utilize and the facility that it is to be housed in. Disregarding this topic is analogous to only crash-testing the front half of a car, ignoring the less frequent but potentially more dangerous side and rear impacts. Therefore, tests should be designed to ensure that each component of a Web site (the servers, the cabling, the medium used to store software and data, and the facilities) is adequately protected from an intruder willing to employ some form of physical attack.

Securing a Facility

A great many precautions can be implemented when trying to ensure that no one is able to gain unauthorized physical access to a secure area, such as the computer room used to store the servers that host the Web site being assessed. The best form of defense is a layer approach, requiring an intruder to successfully breach several security measures before being able to access a target machine.

Shielding Knowledge of a Facility's Proximity

Put simply, if attackers don't know where the physical location of the Web site is, they are not going to be able to break into it. Therefore, to hinder any attempt by an attacker to acquire this information, all nonessential references to a secure location should be removed. For example, corporate telephone and mailing directories should be scrutinized to determine if the location of a secure site could be deduced. Removing driving directions from the organization's Web site and road signs from private roads may not only frustrate and delay a FedEx delivery guy, but also a potential intruder trying to reconnoiter a target facility.

Protecting the Facility Perimeter

Many secure sites use a fence or wall as an outer perimeter, creating a buffer zone that an intruder must cross before reaching a building's exterior. Ideally, some form of detection mechanism such as monitored video cameras, motion detectors, or even guard dogs should be used to detect entry into this buffer zone. With the possible

LOCATION DECEPTION

During the Cold War, the Soviet Union was particularly adept at naming sensitive facilities after towns located hundreds of kilometers away and ensuring that these facilities (and even their supporting townships) never showed up on any maps. Although it's probably a little James Bond-esque to use a functioning bakery as a facade for a secure computer room, trying to pass the room off as a document archive might not be unreasonable.

exception of guard dogs, the security-testing team may want to consider running unannounced mock intrusions at different times of the day to ascertain whether or not an intruder might be able to evade detection while traversing this outer defense. Having an accomplice create a diversion such as delivering pizza to the guards charged with monitoring the buffer zone may provide a more strenuous variation of the test.

In the case of video surveillance, also check that tapes are not recycled too quickly. In the event of an attempted break-in, tapes may need to be reviewed to help determine when the event occurred and identify who the assailant was. This task can be made near impossible if the tape has already been overwritten with more recent surveillance footage.

Protecting Facility Entrances

It goes without saying that all external entry points such as doors and windows should be checked to ensure that they are always locked and that any attempt to break in through any of these openings would result in an alarm (silent or otherwise) being raised. Less obvious is checking that the means by which the alarm is to be raised is functional and tamper-resistant. This would include ensuring that any telephone line used by an alarm has not been disconnected by the telephone company due to no one paying the standing charge for the line (yes, this happens). Another example would be making sure an intruder can't nullify the alarm by simply cutting the wire running from the alarm box to the telephone poll (to mitigate this threat, some alarms employ a *line supervision* technique to protect their connection to the outside world from being cut without anyone being notified).

Although safety considerations may necessitate multiple exits from a secure facility, from an ideal security perspective, there should only be one entryway into the facility (and no windows present). This entrance should be tested to ensure that it has a reliable method of ensuring that only authorized personal are allowed in. Traditional methods of restricting entry to a facility include smart cards, photo badges, and good old-fashioned keys.

Making Rooms Secure

The entrance to the room(s) storing the computers themselves may be protected by another authentication method, ideally different in nature from the one used to gain access to the building. The method could be a biometric device such as a fingerprint scanner or a voice recognition unit. Once again, whatever form of authentication is used, it should be checked to ensure that it cannot easily be fooled or circumvented. For example, many computer rooms are housed in facilities that make use of artificial ceiling or raised floors. If used, these structures should be checked to ensure that an intruder can't circumvent a locked door by simply crawling under or over the door.

If video surveillance is used within a computer room, the positioning of the cameras should allow a computer's keyboard and/or screen to be clearly viewable or angled so that these details can definitely not be captured. If the former placement is adopted, then precautions should be taken to ensure that userIDs, passwords, and other sensitive information are not inadvertently leaked by an unauthorized person gaining access to the surveillance videos.

Protecting Cabling

Although locked doors protect many computer rooms, the cables and telephone wires that enter and leave these rooms are often left unprotected. Access to cable and telephone wiring closets or local exchanges should be as secure as access to the computer room. Otherwise, an eavesdropper armed with a network sniffer may be able to obtain all the information he or she needs without ever setting foot inside the computer room itself.

Securing Hardware

If an intruder is able to gain physical access to the inner sanctum, all may not be lost. If the intruder is interested in acquiring some piece of data on one (or more) of the servers, as opposed to destroying or stealing the hardware, then hardening the server may either thwart or at least delay intruders long enough for their illicit activity to hopefully be detected. Server-hardening options include the following:

- Enabling screensaver password protection.
- Locking down any network-accessible tape unit or CD jukebox.
- Removing all floppy drives and CD (or other external media) drives. Note: This measure may be circumvented if external ports are available for an intruder to plug his or her own media devices into and the operating system is able to auto detect the device (plug-and-play style).
- Removing all nonessential external ports: serial, parallel, IDE, SCSI, USB, and firewire. Note: This measure may be circumvented if an intruder is able to gain physical access to the machine's motherboard and is able to install his or her own interface cards.
- Using a locked shield to restrict access to the server's on/off switch or reset button (and thereby inhibiting an intruder from rebooting the machine). Note: This measure may be circumvented if the power cable is easily accessible.
- Configuring machines to boot from their hard drive first (just in case intruders try to boot from their own floppies or CDs). Note: This measure may be circumvented if an intruder is able reset the machines' BIOS configuration.

- Enabling BIOS-level password protection.
- Automatically sending an alert to the LAN administrator every time the machine is rebooted.

Securing Software

Often-overlooked physical assets that should be secured against thieves are CDs and other media used to store the system software, third-party software, and application software used by the Web site. Although it may prove easy to obtain the most recent version of an operating system, it may be much more troublesome to try and locate an older version that is not being distributed by the vendor but is still being used by the Web site. In some instances, the vendor may have stopped supporting the product or even gone out of business. Conversely, the challenge with application software is making sure that the version used for a restoration is up-to-date with the most recent fixes. No one wants to restore a server back to a previous version and then have to manually reapply the last 20 fixes before it can go back into production.

SAMPLE SECURE ROOM AND SERVER ACCESS TESTS

To test the physical security of a Web site, consider asking an unauthorized fellow employee to attempt to gain physical access to a target machine located within a supposedly secure room. Then once inside, attempt to copy the machine's password file (such as the SAM file on a Windows NT/2000 system or the passwd file on many UNIX systems) to a floppy disk. Once captured, this file could be cracked at leisure by a real attacker. Some tactics that the unauthorized employee could use include the following:

- Working late and attempting to follow the cleaning crew into the locked computer room
- Standing by the locked computer room door with two very full cups of coffee, waiting for somebody to open the door
- Taking advantage of a scheduled fire alarm drill to slip unnoticed into an unlocked computer room (Even if an alarm were to go off, who would hear it?)
- Adding the words "IT Auditor" (ideally in big red letters) to a standard identification badge and calmly following someone else into the secure area
- Carrying a large box that appears to contain a new server and waiting for somebody to open a locked door
- Carrying a clipboard and toolbag with a utility company's name on it and then requesting to be allowed access to the utilities junction box
- Offering to pick up lunch (pizzas, sandwiches, and so on) for someone in the computer room or even pretending to be the pizza delivery guy

If the fellow employee is successful, consider repeating the test, but this time using the assistance of a contractor or somebody off the street.

Software libraries (ideally located off-site) and configuration management systems should also be audited to ensure that in the event of a disaster this software vault contains a copy of all the software needed to recreate the Web site and its associated application(s). In addition, the mechanism for checking out any physical copies should be checked to ensure that an intruder could not easily pilfer a critical disk or review an application's source code to look for an as-yet-undiscovered vulnerability.

Securing Data

Many organizations offload historical data from production servers onto backup/ archival mediums such as tapes, Zip disks, and CDs. For a Web site that does so, the storage of these tapes and disks should be checked to ensure that they are stored as securely as the current production data. For instance, a DBA backing up the production database onto tape and then storing it in a home office may sound like a cheap off-site backup strategy, but it may also be easily exploitable by an intruder knowledgeable about this practice and willing to break into a residence while no one is home. That's much easier than having to deal with those pesky guard dogs and heavyset guards protecting the facility housing the Web site.

In addition to checking the security of any off-site location, the transportation of any sensitive data to or from the site should also be considered, especially if a predictable pattern is used to transfer this information. Although carjacking is perhaps a little far-fetched, walking off with the floppies sitting in the network engineer's briefcase is not. Table 7.6 summarizes this list of physical security checks.

Table 7.6   Physical Security Checklist

YES	NO	DESCRIPTION
☐	☐	Does the organization have security policies in place that provide guidance on what physical security measures should be implemented at each secure facility?
☐	☐	Are all recommendations on obscuring the actual location of a facility followed?
☐	☐	Are all recommendations on securing the facility's perimeter followed?
☐	☐	Are all recommendations on securing the entrance to a facility followed?
☐	☐	Are all recommendations on securing the room(s) used to house the Web site's hardware infrastructure followed?
☐	☐	Are all recommendations on securing any cabling that the Web site depends on followed?
☐	☐	Are all recommendations on securing each server used by the Web site followed?

(continues)

Table 7.6 Physical Security Checklist (*continued*)

YES	NO	DESCRIPTION
☐	☐	Are all recommendations on protecting the media that stores software used by the Web site followed?
☐	☐	Are all recommendations on protecting the media that stores current or archived data used by the Web site followed?
☐	☐	Are all unannounced attempts by the security assessment team to gain physical access to the hardware, cabling, or media used to store software or data thwarted?

Planning against Mother Nature

Planning against and recovering from natural disasters is in itself an entire discipline and, as such, developing a disaster recovery plan and an associated business continuity plan is in all probability outside the scope of any security-testing effort. That said, during a security assessment, it would be prudent to check that these plans do indeed exist and cover such major eventualities as hurricanes, tornadoes, floods, earthquakes, subsidence, and lightning strikes. Maiwald et al. (2002) and Toigo et al. (1999) provide additional information on disaster recovery.

One area that may not be covered by a disaster recovery plan is that of environmental degradation caused by nature. Examples include dust, mold, bacteria, condensation, humidity, ultraviolet light, cosmic radiation, and static electricity slowly corroding away hardware components. Fortunately, such slow-acting deteriorations should ensure that only one hardware component will fail at a time and should therefore not seriously impact the Web site. Two exceptions do exist, however; if the failing component is a single point of failure, or if the failure of one component can cause a chain reaction that results in additional components failing, then the entire Web site may be affected. Hopefully, any single points of failure and potential chain reactions were evaluated as part of the Web site's reliability and availability test plan, and they can therefore be regarded as outside the scope of the security-testing effort. Of course, this assumption should be confirmed. Table 7.7 summarizes this list of checks.

Guarding against Sabotage

What if an attacker is not interested in stealing data or hardware, but instead wants to launch a denial-of-service (DoS) attack using physical means? This attack could be as obvious as putting a shovel through the telecommunication lines connecting the Web site to its ISP or swinging a sledgehammer in a computer room. Or it could be as subtle as placing powerful magnets next to unshielded cables or removing nearly all the memory cards from the Web server—attacks that might not completely bring down the Web site but could significantly impact its capacity.

Table 7.7 Protection from Nature Checklist

YES	NO	DESCRIPTION
☐	☐	Has a disaster recovery and business continuity plan been developed for the Web site?
☐	☐	Do these plans cover all conceivable natural disasters that could in any way affect the Web site?
☐	☐	Has the Web site's design been reviewed and tested to determine if any single point of failure exists?
☐	☐	If one or more single points of failure exist, is the organization willing to accept the risk associated with these critical components failing?
☐	☐	Has the Web site's design been reviewed and tested to determine if a failure by a single component could result in a chain reaction that could significantly impact the Web site?
☐	☐	If a chain reaction could occur, is the organization willing to accept the risk associated with this event occurring?
☐	☐	Have the disaster recovery and business continuity plans been fully tested?
☐	☐	Has environmental compliance been covered by another testing effort?

Some attacks don't even require the assailant to be present. Telephoning in a bomb threat or sending hazardous material in the mail can cause disruption not only to the computer room, but also to the entire facility for an extended period of time.

Ideally, the plans and procedures put in place to handle natural disasters should also provide equivalent protection against these human-made disasters as well. However, it would be a wise precaution to review these plans to ascertain whether or not they do indeed cover an attacker deliberately sabotaging any of the critical components on which the Web site depends.

Summary

As can be seen from the topics covered in this chapter, ensuring the security of a Web site encompasses much more than simply testing software for security holes. Failing to consider these other potential exposures during a security assessment is likely to leave an organization open to some form of alternate attack, especially when the physical security of a Web site is distributed across several departments that operate independently. For example, building security may monitor video cameras, while the IT department keeps track of who has a key to the computer room. But who keeps an eye on those critical utility junction boxes?

# CHAPTER 8

Intruder Confusion, Detection, and Response

This chapter looks at the defenses and processes an organization may have put in place to respond to attacks by accomplished intruders. The first section, *Intruder Confusion*, focuses on tactics that an organization may have adopted to confuse and distract intruders, thereby frustrating them to the point that it is hoped they voluntarily give up their pursuit, or at the very least hinder them long enough for the organization to detect them at work. Testing defenses that rely upon confusion differs from testing traditional security precautions in that actually knowing the desired outcome (a state of confusion) may influence the testing and consequently affect the validity of the test results. Consequently, orchestrating a test of a confusion-based defense typically necessitates a more unorthodox testing strategy, an approach expanded upon by this chapter.

Of course, slowing down a dedicated intruder isn't likely to help much unless intrusion-detection mechanisms are in place to detect the intruder's activities. The second section of this chapter, *Intrusion Detection*, reviews the various methods an organization could employ to detect an intruder and how these methods could be tested to ensure their effectiveness.

The final section, *Intrusion Response*, discusses the need for an organization to plan ahead of time how they might react to an intruder probing a system looking for an exploitable security hole or, the *unthinkable*, an intruder being detected in an unauthorized area. Once documented, this plan can be reviewed to ensure its comprehensiveness and be exercised to ensure that, when needed, the on-duty staff will implement it correctly.

Intruder Confusion

Some people in the security industry believe that, given enough time and resources, any Web site can be cracked. This belief appears to be born out with the seemingly ever-growing list of high-profile (and therefore assumed to be well-fortified) Web sites that have been successfully compromised. The theory behind this belief is that dedicated attackers will eventually always find a way through or around a fixed, or static, defense. It is merely a matter of time before they find some little crack that they can then exploit into something more threatening. Applying this theory to American football, even the worst offense in the league will sooner or later figure out a way to beat any defense that never changes its formation or strategy.

So how can an organization avoid this apparent inevitability? By implementing better and more up-to-date static defenses an organization can certainly make the task much more difficult and therefore delay the attackers, perhaps long enough that they give up trying. However, there is an alternate strategy that could be deployed and, if successful, might thwart an attacker indefinitely. If techniques designed to confuse an attacker are used, the attacker may never get a clear picture of the Web site being attacked and therefore never be able formulate a strategy that will ultimately lead to its demise.

Dynamic Defenses

One approach that can prove to be a formidable defense is that of a *moving target*. Even the most tenacious of attackers will become confused and frustrated if the target they are so painstakingly mapping out keeps changing before they are able to utilize any information they have been able to acquire. Options for varying a Web site's configuration include the following:

- Frequently changing all the system administrator userIDs and passwords.

- Regularly reassigning new IP addresses to each of the Web site's servers. This situation may already be occurring if the network uses a Dynamic Host Configuration Protocol (DHCP) to assign IP addresses to its servers.

- Installing and configuring multiple operating systems on a server and occasionally rebooting the machine into a different operating system. This strategy is much easier to implement for a relatively simple application like a Web server than a more complicated environment like an application server being used to support a Java 2 Platform Enterprise Edition (J2EE) environment. A side benefit of this approach is that if a new vulnerability is discovered in one of the operating systems, the other operating system can be utilized until a patch or workaround is developed for the newly discovered hole.

Unfortunately, continuously reconfiguring a Web site is likely to place too heavy a burden on all but the highest funded IT department. Also, the risk is run that one of these frequent changes will inadvertently introduce a security hole that might not be discovered by the organization until after an intruder has found and exploited it.

Deceptive Defenses

For thousands of years, military commanders have realized that often it is not necessarily the strongest army that wins a battle but rather the army that is best informed.

Consequently, a general attaches great value to discovering an opposing army's size, strength, location, and objectives. Also highly valued is a means to deceive the foe with as much disinformation as possible in order to hide the general's own true disposition and intentions.

In the IT security world, this strategy of deception is most easily implemented through the use of decoys (or red herrings), incorrect or useless information that has been purposely planted for attackers to find and thereby causes them to waste their time and energy on a completely useless endeavor. The following are some examples of decoys that could be used to frustrate and slow down an intruder who is able to compromise a network's outer defenses:

- Place some files called userids.txt and passwords.txt on a Web server, and populate these files with completely bogus account information.

- Add a table to the production database called *CreditCards* and then fill this table with invalid credit card numbers.

- Install the operating system and any other software packages in nondefault directories and then manually create empty directories using the names the default installation would have used. For example, install Windows 2000 into a directory called Acrobat and then create an empty Windows directory so that attackers waste time trying to figure out why they can't see any of these system files. Alternatively, instead of leaving this decoy directory empty, a second nonexecuting version of the operating system with different configuration settings could be copied into the directory.

- Some Unix environments support the *chroot* command, which may be used to limit the visibility of a system's real directories and files, and instead enable access to a bogus (decoy) file structure.

Of course, as with dynamic defenses, the added complexity of a deceptive defense may confuse not only a would-be intruder, but also the legitimate administrators of a Web site, potentially causing them to introduce more errors than they would under a more straightforward security strategy. An organization should therefore carefully weigh these pros and cons before deciding to implement supplemental defenses based on deception.

Honey Pots

A *honey pot* is a variation of the decoy theme. In this case, a resource is purposely left poorly defended. Unbeknownst to the attacker, this resource has no data or privileges that could be used against the Web site and has been set up with a tripwire to automatically set off an intruder alert as soon as the resource is accessed. The Honeynet Project et al. (2001) provides additional information on the concept and employment of honey pots.

One of the reasons honey pots should always have some sort of tripwire implemented is the risk that the easily compromiseable honey pot machine may be used as a staging point for not just an attack on the organization's Web site, but other people's sites as well (a potentially libelous situation).

The honey pot could be used passively, with the security personal simply watching the attackers at work and learning from their behavior the types and frequency of the exploits that might be employed against the real Web site. A more offensive strategy would be to gather information that could be used to identify and prosecute the attackers. Indeed, honey pots come in all shapes and sizes:

- A standalone Web server posted outside an organization's perimeter firewall could be used by an organization as an early warning system.

- In the case of Web sites that support extremely sensitive applications (such as the military), an entire network of honey pots may be deployed, complete with fictitious users requesting data and services just to make the network look real. In reality, the only real users are the security personnel watching and tracing the attackers who try to compromise the network of honey pots.

- Law enforcement agencies have been known to recreate fully functional e-commerce Web sites that appear to be storefronts for small naive businesses that, not too surprisingly, have not protected their clients' credit card information too well. Of course, these customer records contain bogus credit card numbers whose only useful purpose is to help expose the identity of the attackers, should they try to use these card numbers.

DECEPTION AT WORK

During World War II, the Allies spent considerable effort trying to convince the German army that their intended invasion of Western Europe would take place in the vicinity of Calais. By many accounts, when the invasion got underway in Normandy, Hitler refused to commit the main body of the German army to this landing, as he believed the Normandy invasion was a diversion for the *real* invasion, which he still expected to occur at Calais. By the time the German high command realized that there would be no Calais landing, the Allies had secured their beachheads and were making good progress into the French hinterland.

- Commercial organizations who market intrusion-detection systems and alert centers who report on the latest exploits may deploy numerous honey pots scattered around the world in order to discover what new tactics are being developed and refined by attackers. In effect, they are creating a *global intruder weather map*.

A more cost-effective approach to deploying an entire network of honey pots is to configure a single machine to appear as if it is several distinct servers, creating in effect a *virtual* honey pot network. This reduces the cost of the hardware and system software needed to recreate a network, making the honey pot more complex.

One more consideration when weighting whether or not to deploy a honey pot (or pots) is that adding an enticing, poorly defended resource to a Web site may actually draw attention to the site. It may also consequently attract more assailants than if no honey pot were deployed, which is hardly a desirable situation. Table 8.1 lists some sample honey pots.

Evaluating Intruder Confusion

For a confusion strategy to be effective, its very existence must be kept secret, meaning that this is one of the few features of a Web site that should not be documented in the Web site's standard requirements documentation. Instead this aspect of the Web site's design should be secretly documented elsewhere, and only made available on a need-to-know basis.

Assuming one or more confusion strategies have been employed, any serious evaluation of the deceptiveness (and hence effectiveness) of these strategies must be done by testers who are not *in the know*. Obvious choices are the firms that specialize in security testing and have had no prior knowledge of the Web site to be tested; if such firms are to be used, then their activities should be closely monitored to see if they can be misdirected or delayed by the site's confusion strategy. Even the most honest of security testing firms is unlikely to want to admit they were duped, and if it is mentioned at all in the firm's test summary report, it is likely to be underreported. It somehow just doesn't sound right to be telling a client that you wasted an extended amount of expensive time being sidetracked.

Table 8.1   Sample List of Honey Pots

NAME	ASSOCIATED WEB SITE
CyberCop Sting	www.nai.com
Dragnet	www.snetcorp.com
HoneyNet Project	www.project.honeynet.org
ManTrap	www.recourse.com
NetFacade	www.netsecureinfo.com

Table 8.2   Confusion Checklist

YES	NO	DESCRIPTION
☐	☐	Have dynamic defenses been considered for the Web site?
☐	☐	Have deception defenses been considered for the Web site?
☐	☐	Have honey-pot deployments been considered for the Web site?
☐	☐	Have all the specific details on the implementation of any deception defense been removed from the Web site standard requirements documentation and placed in a separate document with extremely restricted access?
☐	☐	Have any defenses that rely on confusion been evaluated to determine just how confusing they actually are to a would-be intruder (and optionally for a system administrator to manage)?

Of course, the acid test for a confusion strategy is not determining if consultants at a security-testing firm can be fooled, but whether real-life attackers can be tricked. In this sense, the best way to gauge the effectiveness of these diversions is to monitor their use in a production environment. Compare how many attackers are *suckered* into spending at least some measurable amount of time on the decoys, as opposed to the attackers that do not stumble across the decoys or seem to ignore their existence (perhaps because they can see them for what they really are).

Unfortunately (from a test metric's perspective), if the decoys are deployed within an organization's perimeter defenses and (as yet) no known intruder has compromised this line of defense, the test sample is going to consist of zero occurrences, hardly an effective means of measuring decoy effectiveness. In such circumstances, an organization may wish to create a bogus Web site with sufficiently weak perimeter defenses to permit a statistically significant number of attackers (test samples) to encounter the decoys. This is a rather expensive exercise but ultimately is the only realistic way of testing this deceptive line of defense. Table 8.2 summarizes these confusion strategies in the form of a checklist.

Intrusion Detection

Having an intruder compromise your Web site is a situation that's not supposed to happen because "the perimeter firewall will protect us." But what if the unthinkable happens and an intruder makes it past a Web site's perimeter defenses, perhaps because the intrusion is initiated from the inside? It would be nice to know that there is still a chance that the intruder will be detected and stopped before he or she has a chance to do any significant damage, a topic expanded upon by Allen (2001), Northcutt (2000), and Proctor (2000). Security personnel monitoring a Web site may be alerted to the presence of an unwanted guest in many ways.

The following are example tale-tale signs of an intruder at work:

- Shrinking log files
- Changes to file attributes of supposedly static files (date, size, user, and so on) or directories (possibly caused by an intruder planting a toolkit for later use)
- Unexplained performance degradation
- The creation of unauthorized new user accounts

Intrusion Detection Systems (IDSs)

Relying on the vigilance of an overworked LAN administrator to continuously monitor raw Web logs and other eyeball-unfriendly files is likely to result in the administrator missing the tell-tale signs of an intruder at work. For this reason, several companies have developed tools that can be used to automate this tedious task and thereby detect an intruder rummaging around. These tools are commonly referred to as intrusion detection systems (IDSs). Table 8.3 lists some sample IDSs.

Table 8.3   Sample IDS List

NAME	ASSOCIATED WEB SITE
Attacker	www.foundstone.com
BlackICE and RealSecure	www.iss.net
Cisco IDS (NetRanger)	www.cisco.com
Dragon	www.enterasys.com
e-Sentinel	www.esecurityinc.com
Etrust	www.ca.com
IDS/9000	www.hp.com
INDESYS	www.infinity-its.com
Intruder Alert/NetProwler	www.symantec.com
ISA Server	www.microsoft.com
ManHunt/ManTrap	www.recourse.com
NFR HID/NID	www.nfr.com
OneSecure IDP	www.onesecure.com
Scanlogd	www.openwall.com
Snort	www.snort.org
STAT	www.statonline.com/harris.com
StormWatch	www.kena.com
TriSentry	www.psionic.com

IDSs can be crudely categorized into four groups, although some IDSs may exhibit properties of more than one group:

- Signature detection via network traffic
- Signature detection via host activities
- Anomaly detection via network traffic
- Anomaly detection via host activities

Signature detection works by matching the observed parameters of network traffic or host activities against a database of known attack characteristics (signatures). Unfortunately, this database must be updated regularly to keep up with newly developed attack methods and consequently is poor at detecting new types of attacks. In comparison, anomaly detection works by comparing current network traffic and/or host activities with a previously defined baseline of normal behavior, looking for suspicious deviations from this norm.

Of course, a network-based IDS will only scan network traffic that it is able to detect; a segmented network that does not broadcast network traffic to every device on the network is likely to need several network-based IDSs in order to listen to all of the traffic being sent across its network. In addition, skilled attackers have been known to deceive network-based IDSs by breaking up, or fragmenting, their attacks (thereby making their attack signatures hard to detect) as they are sent over the network to their intended target. Therefore, a host-based IDS solution may need to be considered as an alternative (or in addition), as it may prove to be more secure. The downside would be that it might necessitate installing and maintaining an IDS on every machine that needs to be protected.

It is important to understand that IDSs are often passive in nature. They attempt to detect attacks or attack preparations by passively monitoring network traffic or the activities of the host machines they are installed on in real time (or a delayed mode). Once an attack is detected, the IDS is typically configured to raise an alarm and enables the on-duty security personnel to decide what to do next. However, some IDSs can be configured to automatically react to a perceived attack, attempting to trace the source of the attack or shutting down external network connections. The most aggressive of these reacting IDSs are sometimes referred to as *intrusion detection and response systems* (IDRSs). Unfortunately, the possibility of false positives tends to limit the range of *reflex reactions* that an IDRS might be entrusted to perform.

IDSs can also provide information on what was attacked and how, thereby assisting damage assessment and hopefully assisting in the development of a patch to prevent the same thing from happening again. In addition, this forensic evidence may also prove useful in identifying and potentially prosecuting attackers.

An IDS may be the most likely way an organization learns that an intruder has successfully breached their perimeter defenses, and the information captured by an IDS could be used against an attacker at a later date. It is for these reasons that attackers often target IDSs, attempting to disable the IDS in the same way a burglar cuts the telephone wires running from a building's security alarm. Attempts to disable, isolate, or overwhelm an IDS should therefore be taken very seriously, as it may be the last thing that the IDS ever gets to report. Indeed, it may pay to install a secondary service that regularly checks the health of the IDS, immediately reporting if an IDS becomes

Table 8.4   IDS Sensitivity Checklist

YES	NO	DESCRIPTION
☐	☐	Does the IDS detect a blatant attack, such as sequentially port scanning all 65K ports in a matter of minutes from a single IP source address? Table 4.10 lists sample tools for conducting a port scan.
☐	☐	Does the IDS detect a stealthy attack, such as a partial scan of all possible 65K ports over a period of days (or even longer), randomly using different IP source addresses?
☐	☐	If network-based IDSs are to be used, are they located on the network such that all network traffic can be monitored?
☐	☐	If host-based IDSs are to be used, is an IDS loaded on to every critical server that needs to be monitored?
☐	☐	Do the on-duty security personnel notice and respond appropriately to a failed (or even successful) attempt to disable or isolate the IDS?
☐	☐	Do the on-duty security personnel notice and respond appropriately to every IDS alert, or have they become desensitized?

unavailable, either because the IDS itself is disabled, or because the means of communication from the IDS has been interrupted (perhaps by the attacker launching a denial of service attack against the mail server used to forward emails from the IDS alerting the organization of an attack).

Since most IDSs have sensitivity settings, the security testing team should check that the detection level is set appropriately. If an IDS is too sensitive, frequent false alarms may cause the security personal to ignore all alarms. Alternatively, if the IDS sensitivity is turned down too low, an attacker may be able to compromise a Web site without being noticed. To determine how sensitive an IDS is and whether anyone reacts to an IDS alert, the security testing team should consider running tests similar to those outlined in Table 8.4.

Audit Trails

Unless a Web site keeps audit trails (or system logs), an organization is less likely to be able to identify and successfully prosecute an attacker. Audit trails can therefore also act as a deterrent if their existence is known or suspected (a situation that is quite possibly the case for an internal assailant). Any organization that intends to prosecute an attacker should check with their legal counsel to make sure that the data being captured in the system's logs is sufficient to be legally useful, and that this information is being archived appropriately. There is no point collecting this information if it's deleted before it can be used. Retracing the work of an intruder who has been undetected for quite a while may necessitate conducting forensic work on log files several months old. The last thing a cybercrime prosecutor wants to hear is that the log files that were to be used as evidence have been purged during a routine tape-recycling process. Unfortunately, enabling auditing will slow down the system's performance. However, selective audits have less of a performance impact and may be an acceptable compromise.

Since more experienced attackers will often try to either purge an audit trail or manipulate it to hide their tracks, unauthorized attempts to access an audit trail are often an indication that an intruder is at work. Because system logs are so useful—acting as deterrents and providing prosecutorial evidence, assistance in detecting vulnerability, and recovery from an intrusion—these critical files should be protected with additional security measures to prohibit an intruder from tampering with them. One tactic that can be employed to reduce the possibility of tampering is to set the file attributes of the log files to *append only*, which is a potentially trivial defense to implement but one that an intruder may find troublesome to circumvent. Other options include writing the files to a heavily fortified server or even burning the logs onto a *write-once* CD.

Of course, if auditing isn't turned on, or nobody ever reviews the logs, then there's nothing for the attacker to worry about! This is why several companies now offer tools that will automatically create or review existing system logs, reporting on suspicious activities in a real or delayed timeframe. Table 8.5 provides a list of such tools.

To evaluate whether sufficient system logging is enabled and that someone takes notice of an attack, the security testing should consider running an unannounced test to see if anyone notices an obvious or a less obvious attack. Maybe no one is paying any attention to the logs, perhaps there are too many low-grade alarms occurring, or possibly the LAN administrator has forgotten to pull the logs because he or she has too many "more important" things to do first. If the logs are continually ignored, then an organization may want to consider whether or not creating these logs is worth the performance hit that the system is taking to create them. The organization may also need to determine whether the existing log reviewers need additional assistance, perhaps in the form of training, review automation, or a larger staff.

Table 8.5   Sample List of System Event Logging and Reviewing Tools

NAME	ASSOCIATED WEB SITE
Consul/eAudit	www.consul.com
ETrust Audit	www.ca.com
LANguard	www.gfisoftware.com
LogAlert	www.spidynamics.com
LT Auditor+	www.bluelance.com
netForensics	www.netforensics.com
Private I	www.opensystems.com

Table 8.6   Audit Trail Checklist

YES	NO	DESCRIPTION
☐	☐	Is there a documented policy in place that describes which events are to be recorded in an audit trail or system log?
☐	☐	Are all audit trails specified in the audit trail policy that has been implemented? Or have some or all of the trails been disabled to improve system performance?
☐	☐	If the organization desires to have the ability to prosecute intruders, has the documented audit trail policy been reviewed by the organization's legal counsel to ensure that the information being collected is sufficiently comprehensive to allow an organization to pursue a prosecution?
☐	☐	Are all audit trails protected to prevent them from being deleted or tampered with?
☐	☐	Are all auditing trails monitored vigilantly (manually or via an automated tool)?
☐	☐	Are all audit trails archived for a sufficiently long enough period of time?

If the simulated attack by the testing team is detected, the next phase of the evaluation would be to assess the data that could be collected by the forensics team (see the *Damage Assessment and Forensics* section later in this chapter). That data has to be sufficient to meet the organization's needs, which will to a large degree depend upon how aggressive an organization wants to be in the prosecution of an offender. Table 8.6 summarizes these auditing issues in a checklist.

Tripwires and Checksums

A tripwire is a mechanism that alerts a Web site to the presence of an intruder. A common implementation of a tripwire is to create *checksums* for directories and/or files that are supposed to be static. In the event that a static file is altered, deleted, or replaced by an intruder, the checksum should differ and thereby signal the presence of an intruder at work. This would happen, for example, after an intruder successfully uploads a toolkit into a system directory or replaces a legitimate system file with a Trojan horse variant. Table 8.7 lists some sample tripwire and checksum tools.

When used judiciously, checksums typically place only a small additional load on their host system. A factor that influences the load is how often the checksum algorithm runs. The more frequent the check, the more system resources will be consumed by this activity. However, the longer the period between checks, the longer an intruder has for mischief (such as trying to disable the tripwire) before potentially being detected. Additionally, the time it takes each iteration of the checksum to run is affected by the amount

Table 8.7 Sample List of Tripwire and Checksum Tools

NAME	ASSOCIATED WEB SITE
Intact	www.pedestalsoftware.com
Intergrit	www.sourceforge.net
MD5sum	www.redhat.com
Tripwire	www.tripwire.com/tripwire.org
ViperDB	www.resentment.org
WebAgain	www.lockstep.com

CONFIGURATION MANAGEMENT CHECKSUMS

Checksum tools have uses other than protecting a system against a malicious attacker. In the event that an organization has not invested in a full-blown configuration management system, these tools can be pressed into service to act as a lightweight configuration management tool for application source code, test scripts, and test data sets, detecting any unauthorized modifications to these files.

of directories and files included in the checksum, and the frequency with which these static files are altered (such as monthly updates, instead of hourly).

Checksum-scanning tools can even be enhanced to create a *self-healing* system. In the event that the checksum utility finds a system file has been modified, it automatically installs a fresh version of the file from a secure source (such as a read-only CD drive), an extremely annoying obstacle for an intruder.

As with any audit trail, a tripwire implementation should be tested to ensure that it has been implemented correctly, and that if a tripwire is triggered, somebody notices. Table 8.8 lists some of the checks that can be used to evaluate the implementation of a tripwire-style defense.

Malware

Not all intrusions are instigated manually. In addition to an attacker sitting at a remote terminal trying to compromise a Web site, a whole host of software programs can be utilized to attack Web sites. These programs are collectively known as *malware*. They have evolved over the years from slow-spreading programs that require a human to physically carry a floppy disk from one infected machine to a new victim into virulent forms that can spread themselves around the world in a matter of hours, causing billions of dollars' worth of damage.

Depending upon the method used to replicate them, each of these troublesome programs can be grouped into one of three different subcategories of malware: viruses, Trojan horses, and worms.

Table 8.8 Tripwire and Checksum Checklist

YES	NO	DESCRIPTION
☐	☐	Is there a documented policy in place that describes which machines, directories, and files should be protected by a tripwire?
☐	☐	Does the documented policy also specify the frequency with which the protected machines should be scanned?
☐	☐	Are all the resources that are supposed to be protected by a tripwire actually protected?
☐	☐	When modifying a directory that is protected by a checksum defense, do the on-duty security personnel take notice and react appropriately?

VIRUSES, TROJAN HORSES, AND WORMS

Symantec (www.symantec.com) defines these different flavors of malware in the following ways:

■ A computer *virus* is a computer program written by an ill-intentioned programmer. A computer can catch a virus from disks, a local network, or the Internet. Just as a cold virus attaches itself to a human host, a computer virus attaches itself to a program. And just like a cold, it is contagious.

■ A *Trojan horse*, while not technically a virus, has the potential to cause the same kinds of problems that viruses do. Many Trojan horses are designed to steal login IDs and passwords and then email them to someone else who can make use of the account. Other Trojan horses display obscene messages or delete the contents of hard drives. A Trojan horse is typically acquired by downloading a program that seems safe or promises something like free online time. Once it is downloaded and executed, the malicious code begins to work. The difference between Trojan horses and viruses is that Trojan horses do not replicate or spread on their own. They can only be transmitted intentionally via email, disk, or a download directly onto a computer.

■ Like viruses, *worms* replicate themselves. However, instead of spreading from file to file, they spread from computer to computer, infecting an entire network. Worms copy themselves from one computer to another over a network (using email, for example). Because worms don't require human interaction to replicate, they can spread much more rapidly than computer viruses.

To guard against this horde of malicious software that now wanders the electronic planet, many commercial organizations have developed software products that attempt to detect these malware programs before they have a chance to do any harm or replicate themselves. Commonly referred to as *antivirus software* (even through they are designed to search for more than just viruses), these software products should be used

Table 8.9 Sample List of Antivirus Products

NAME	ASSOCIATED WEB SITE
Command AntiVirus	www.commandcom.com
eTrust Antivirus	www.ca.com
F-Secure Anti-Virus	www.f-secure.com
InterScan/PC-cillin/ServerProtect	www.antivirus.com
LockDown	www.lockdowncorp.com
Norton AntiVirus	www.norton.com/symantec.com
PestPatrol	www.pestpatrol.com
Sophos Anti-Virus	www.sophos.com
Tauscan	www.agnitum.com
VirusScan	www.mcafee.com/nai.com/drsolomon.com

Note that www.vmyths.com maintains a list of computer virus hoaxes and myths.

to scan all incoming and outgoing mobile code, file downloads, and emails (including their attachments). In addition, regularly scheduled full scans of every machine directly connected to the Web site should also be conducted to ensure that any malware that escaped initial detection (perhaps with the aid of an inside accomplice) can still be caught before further damage can occur. Table 8.9 is a sample list of commercial antivirus software products.

According to several of the antivirus tool vendors, by the summer of 2002, there were over 60,000 malware programs in circulation. Fortunately, the majority of these programs are clones of existing programs or are built from standard virus-generation kits, making it easier for an antivirus-signature-based product to detect it due to common code usage. However, as with signature-based IDSs, antivirus programs that rely on signatures to detect a malware program must continuously update their signature databases in order to stay abreast of the most recent mutations. Unfortunately, even the most recent and extensive signature file still provides less than 100 percent protection. Therefore, some antivirus tools also provide functionality to monitor the machine they are installed on for suspicious or anomalous activities (such as writing to the boot sector of a hard drive) that do not typically occur under normal circumstances. Such monitoring would thereby indicate the potential presence of a malware program that would not be detected by the standard signature-detection algorithm.

To prevent malicious mobile code (such as a Java applet or ActiveX control attached to a Web page) from reaching its intended destination, some organizations scan all inbound (and optionally outbound) mobile code. The scan can take place at one or more of the following locations:

■ At the organization's perimeter firewall, using security policies defined in the firewall's network traffic filtering rules.

TESTING ANTIVIRUS PROTECTION

To ensure that an antivirus product has been installed correctly, a security testing team may be tempted to install a real live virus onto a machine or send an infected attachment over a network that is theoretically protected by the antivirus software.

Unfortunately, using a real virus for testing purposes (even if it is a comparatively harmless one) could result in the virus inadvertently escaping the controlled test environment and making it into the real world, contributing to the problem that the virus detection solution is trying to mitigate.

Fortunately, there exists an industry-standard dummy virus definition that, when detected by a virus detection product, will be reported as a virus and can be used to test that the antivirus product has been installed correctly. This inert test file (known as the eicar test file/string) and advice on how to use it can be obtained from www.eicar.org.

- En route across the organization's LAN via a network-based IDS.
- Via a special-purpose application server residing on the organization's LAN, which intercepts all mobile code requests and attempts to evaluate the potential for mischief by exercising the code in a contained environment. The server then forwards the mobile code only if it appears not to request any suspicious resources or performs any questionable activity. Table 8.10 provides a list of mobile code-scanning tools.
- At the client machine requesting the mobile code. Many desktop-based antivirus tools now also perform security checks on Java applets and ActiveX controls.

Table 8.11 summarizes the checks that may be performed to determine if an organization is taking reasonable precautions to prevent malicious code from infiltrating a Web site.

Monitoring

If any kind of automated intrusion detection mechanism is to be deployed, whether it's a tripwire, IDS, or log analyzer, someone needs to be alerted if a suspicious event occurs. Unfortunately, these alerts don't always indicate the presence of an intruder. The activity could be legitimate and just so happen to have a profile similar to that of a known security problem. Therefore, before any drastic response is initiated, the security personnel will typically evaluate the alert and decide if there really is an intruder at large.

Evaluating suspected threats requires a great deal of expertise. Rather than set up the intrusion detection mechanism to send alerts to different points of contact, many organizations choose to send these system alerts to the same person(s) or to a central monitoring system that filters and then relays all the alerts to a single point of contact.

Ensuring that any deployed central monitoring system has been configured correctly may necessitate emulating an attempted breach on every device and service that has

Table 8.10 Sample List of Mobile Code-Scanning Tools

NAME	ASSOCIATED WEB SITE
AppletTrap	www.trendmicro.com/antivirus.com
eSafe Enterprise	www.esafe.com
eTrust Content Inspection	www.ca.com
SurfinGate	www.finjan.com

Table 8.11 Malware Prevention Checklist

YES	NO	DESCRIPTION
☐	☐	Is a documented policy in place that describes how antivirus products are to be deployed?
☐	☐	Are all the resources that are supposed to be protected by antivirus software actually protected? Or have they been partially or completely disabled to improve performance or cut down on those annoying alerts that keep popping up onscreen?
☐	☐	If the deployed antivirus products use a signature database to detect viruses, is there a process in place that ensures that the signature database is regularly updated?
☐	☐	When an antivirus program detects what it believes to be a virus, are the on-duty security personnel notified? And if so, do they react appropriately?

been tied into the monitoring system. The central monitoring console would then need to be checked to ensure that each event was reported in a timely manner. Table 8.12 lists some of the tools that act as central clearinghouses for security alerts from other products such as network-based IDSs, host-based IDSs, honey pots, firewalls, and performance monitors (a performance degradation is often a sign that an intruder is at work).

For some organizations, having the single point of contact be an outsourced vendor, typically located at a remote location, would make more economic sense. Once the vendor installs one or more software agents on each system to be monitored, each agent then makes an initial assessment of any detected activity and reports back suspicious events to the vendor's control center for further assessment and potential escalation. The agent could also simply forward the raw log files to the vendor's control center where they are typically scanned by proprietary forensic tools. The results would then be manually reviewed to determine what, if any, action should then be pursued.

If a remote control center is implemented, then the response time of the control center should be evaluated to ensure that the control center can detect and report any attempted intrusion within the period of time specified in the accompanying service level agreement (SLA). If the SLA states that some activities will be immediately

Table 8.12   Sample List of Centralized Security-Monitoring Tools and Services

NAME	ASSOCIATED WEB SITE
1stWatch	www.redsiren.com
Affinity	www.mis-cds.com
Brinks	www.brinksinternetsecurity.com
e-Sentinel	www.esecurityinc.com
Etrust	www.ca.com
Exodus	www.exodus.net
Guardent	www.guardent.com
IntelliSecurity	www.verio.com
Isensor	www.secureworks.com
ISS	www.iss.net
Harvester	www.farm9.com
META Security	www.metases.com
Network Security Manager	www.itactics.com
NeuSECURE	www.guarded.net
NSEC	www.nsec.net
OnlineGuardian	www.ubizen.com
Riptech	www.riptech.com
SAVVISecure	www.savvis.com
Security Manager	www.netiq.com
Sentry	www.counterpane.com
Spectrum	www.aprisma.com
TruSecure	www.trusecure.com
VeriSign	www.verisign.com
Veritect	www.veritect.com
VigilEnt Security Manager	www.pentasafe.com
Vigilinx	www.vigilinx.com

reported and others which have been determined by the control center to be of no immediate threat will be logged and reported on a weekly (or other frequency) basis, an organization should confirm exactly what activities will not be immediately

Table 8.13 Intrusion-Monitoring Checklist

YES	NO	DESCRIPTION
☐	☐	Is there a documented policy in place that describes how each security defense will be monitored to detect attempted breaches?
☐	☐	If manual monitoring is to be used, is each and every defensive measure actually monitored with the frequency specified in the documented policy guidelines?
☐	☐	If automated monitoring is to be used, is each and every defensive measure connected to the central monitoring application?
☐	☐	If a remote control center is used, does the control center detect and report on each suspected intrusion attempt within the period defined by the control center's SLA?

reported and then assess whether or not this is acceptable. For example, every firewall that is *pinged* or each email that is stripped of its virus-infected attachment would probably not warrant a phone call from the central control center to the local security personal. It would instead be included on the regular status report, whereas the disappearance (or reduction in size) of a system log should warrant immediate notification. Table 8.13 summarizes some of the tests that could be run to determine if the security defenses that have been deployed are being monitored adequately.

Intrusion Response

Perhaps because so many organizations believe that being *hacked* is something that happens to other people, few of these organizations take sufficient time to plan their response to such an unpalatable event happening. For a CIO, being woken up at 3:00 A.M., to be told that an intruder may be at large on the organization's Web site is bad news, but then being asked, "What do we do now?" is truly a nightmare. To avoid making an undesirable situation worse than it already is, an organization should have a clearly defined procedure in place for handling the unenviable situation of an intruder successfully compromising some part of the organization's internal network.

The specific activities that each organization will want to undertake in response to the detection of an intruder will vary from organization to organization. For example, the laws governing what an organization can and cannot do vary significantly from country to country. If fact, within a single country, the laws may differ, depending upon whether the system being attacked is used for regular commerce or national security. Krutz et al. (2001), Lierley (2001), and Matsuura (2001) provide additional information on the legal aspects of computer crimes. An organization's response policy should therefore be reviewed to ensure that it is complete and appropriate within the legal and resource constraints that it will be utilized under. The following sections focus on the main components that typically make up an organization's intrusion response policy.

Confirmation of Intrusion

Depending upon the source and severity of the initial alert, it may be desirable to obtain a second independent assessment of the situation (assuming that this assessment can be done within an appropriate timeframe), thereby attempting to rule out any false alarms before excessive actions are implemented. For example, suppose a network-based IDS believes it has detected suspicious communications between two servers. The host-based IDSs installed on either of the servers in question could be reviewed to see if some event occurred that, although unusual, wasn't deemed odd enough for the host-based system to raise an alert.

Damage Containment

Once an organization has made the assessment that an intruder is or has recently been active in a restricted area, the organization then needs to decide whether to attempt to cut off the attack or to allow the intrusion to temporarily continue. Although a knee-jerk reaction might be to pull the plug on the Web site, if the method of entry has not yet been identified, monitoring the intruder's activities until his or her method of entry has been deduced may prove to be the most secure approach in the long term. Prematurely sealing the Web site may cause the site's outage to be longer, effectively creating a more severe denial-of-service (DoS) attack (even if this was not the intruder's intention). Of course, the longer that intruders have access to the Web site, the more opportunity they have to cause damage, and subsequently the more costly the cleanup. For example, if the intruder appears to be just moments away from downloading the swiss_number_bank_account file, then pulling the plug is quite probably the right thing to do.

Hopefully, the scenarios under which an intruder would be allowed to continue to roam or be cut off won't be a split-second decision made by a barely awake CIO at 3:00 A.M. or by the unfortunate LAN administrator who happened to be carrying the site pager that night. Instead, guidelines on how to manage some of the probable intrusion scenarios should have been thought out, documented, and tested ahead of time. For instance, one major consideration that affects whether an intruder should be put under surveillance is whether or not the organization has sufficient evidence to prosecute the offender. If the organization has decided that it has no intention of prosecuting an intruder (perhaps because of the adverse publicity it might attract), then allowing the intruder continued access to the compromised system while efforts are made to trace the attack back to its source may not be a particularly productive endeavor. Another consideration is whether or not the portion of the Web site that has been compromised can be isolated and quarantined, which is more likely if internal firewalls have been built into the site's design. If it can, the organization's immediate exposure can be limited.

Damage Assessment and Forensics

"So just how bad is it?" is possibly the first question the CIO is going to ask upon hearing that the organization's Web site has just been hacked. It's at this point that the site's designers start to wish that they had enabled the various logging features that had been turned off to improve the site's performance.

Ideally, the damage assessment will be able to recreate the exact movements and activities of the intruder(s) and thereby precisely deduce what has been compromised. Questions that this assessment will seek to answer include the following:

- Have any executables been added, altered, or deleted? This could possibly have happened as the intruder uploaded a rootkit, Trojan horse, backdoor, or some other kind of executable that could be used later to reenter the site.

- Has any sensitive data been compromised? For instance, a credit card file could have been viewed or downloaded.

- Has the systems environment been altered in any way? For example, new user accounts or directories could have been added.

The ease with which a damage assessment can be carried out will not only depend upon the amount of raw data available for examination, but also the tools available to automate this research. For instance, utilizing a Web log analyzer makes reviewing Web logs much easier than eyeballing the raw files. (The University of Uppsala in Sweden maintains an extensive listing of log analysis tools at www.uu.se/software/analyzers.)

Instead of trying to identify exactly which files were tampered with, it might be more expedient to simply assume that every file has been compromised and reinstall the operating system on a reformatted (or, better still, brand-new) hard drive on every suspected machine. In the case of sensitive data files, instead of trying to figure out which specific records may have been viewed or downloaded by an intruder, assume that all the records have been compromised and notify all the possibly affected data owners accordingly.

The primary purpose of doing damage assessment is to assist an organization in recovering from the intrusion and restoring normal service as quickly as possible. The closely related field of forensics is concerned with collecting evidence that can subsequently be used in legal proceedings. (Typically, this endeavor requires a much higher standard of data collection than would necessarily be needed by an organization for its own internal purposes.) Kruse et al. (2001), Marcella et al. (2002), and Vacca et al. (2002) provide additional information on computer forensics. Unfortunately, an expedient damage assessment may negatively impact forensic data collection. For example, a LAN administrator quickly reviewing a system directory to see if any files have recently been changed may inadvertently alter the *last accessed* information for the directory, potentially destroying evidence that the forensic team would like to have had the opportunity to collect.

DAMAGE ASSESSMENT FOLKLORE

A classic story is of a Webmaster stating that he would rather his Web site be completely purged by an attacker than have an attacker *deface* a single Web page and the Webmaster not find out about it for several hours. Why? Because the Webmaster could completely restore the purged site from backups, but the damage done to the company's credibility by the defaced page could take months or even years to restore.

Table 8.14 Sample List of Forensic Data Collection Tools

NAME	ASSOCIATED WEB SITE
DIBS Analyzer	www.dibsusa.com
EnCase	www.encase.com
Forensic Toolkit/NTLast	www.foundstone.com
FRED	www.digitalintel.com
FTK	www.accessdata.com
Ilook	www.ilook-forensics.org
Intelligent Computer Solutions	www.ics-iq.com
Various	www.dmares.com
Various	www.forensics-intl.com
Various	www.tucofs.com

Because the task of collecting evidence in a manner that permits it to be used in a court of law may delay or hinder the completion of an internal damage assessment, an organization should decide ahead of time whether formal forensics collection will be done. If so, the organization should ensure that all employees likely to be involved in a damage assessment are made aware of the precautions that they will need to follow in order to avoid contaminating forensic evidence. Since many manual data collection efforts, or the tools not specifically intended for the task of collecting forensic evidence, may inadvertently corrupt the very evidence being collected (breaking the *chain of evidence*), the forensics team may wish to use one or more tools especially designed for this task. Table 8.14 lists some tools designed to assist with forensic data collection.

It is perhaps the damage assessment and forensics phase of an intrusion response that could benefit the most from a simulated (or *mock*) intrusion. The intrusion may show just how hard it is to do dependable forensic research, especially when key system logs have been disabled, tampered with, or were never even implemented. Indeed, one of the action points that may come out of running the simulated intrusion is that the organization decides to evaluate and select a firm that specializes in computer forensics. The firm may even be placed on a retainer, so that if a real intrusion occurs, a team of preapproved experts can immediately be summoned to assist the local staff in conducting a damage assessment and forensic collection. Table 8.15 lists some firms that provide forensic consulting services.

Damage Control and Recovery

The damage control and recovery phase is concerned with minimizing the impact of the intrusion on the organization. For example, based on the findings of the initial damage assessment, an organization may not be comfortable with allowing the

Table 8.15   Sample List of Forensic Consulting Firms

NAME	ASSOCIATED WEB SITE
ASR Data	www.asrdata.com
Computer Forensics	www.forensics.com
CrypTEC Forensic	www.cryptec-forensic.com
DIBS USA	www.dibsusa.com
Fred Cohen and Associates	www.all.net
Lee and Allen	www.lee-and-allen.com
New Technologies	www.forensics-intl.com
Science.org	www.forensics.org

Note that the inclusion (or exclusion) of a specific firm in this list should not be construed as any form of recommendation by this book.

compromised components of a system to stay online, possibly even deciding to *lock down* the entire system. In the event that this outage is on a mission-critical system, the organization may not be able to postpone using this functionality until after this valuable resource has been thoroughly examined by forensic experts, cleaned up, and restored to a state that would prevent the same intrusion from occurring again. This would necessitate some sort of interterm recovery measure to control the amount of damage done to the business of the organization.

Rather than waiting for a system to be taken offline due to an intrusion before considering how to implement some temporary solution, an organization should develop damage control and recovery plans for their most critical system ahead of time. Maiwald et al. (2002) and Toigo et al. (1999) provide additional information on disaster-recovery planning. Example recovery strategies include the following:

- A Web site is distributed across multiple geographic locations and the damage assessment has concluded that only one site has been compromised. No evidence suggests that the remaining sites are susceptible to the same kind of attack that affected the infected location. (For example, it appears that the breach was a result of a local system administrator's password being mistakenly reset by the help desk, and this account does not have any privileges at the other geographic sites.) One possible recovery strategy would be to take the affected site offline. Temporarily disabling some of the resource-intensive (but less critical) components at the remaining uncontaminated locations would enable the Web site to return to an acceptable, albeit less than optimal level of performance until the compromised location can be safely brought back online.

- If the organization has invested in a backup site for protection against natural disasters, it may be possible to press this site into service to help the organization also recover from an unnatural disaster, such as an intruder compromising the primary site.

■ A Web site purely being used to process a small number of sales orders has been compromised. It may be feasible to replace the site's normal home page with a simple Web page, hosted on an uncompromised machine, explaining that the Web site is experiencing technical difficulties and anyone wishing to place an order should call the following toll-free telephone number.

Whatever damage control and recovery strategies an organization decides to adopt, once documented in the form of a plan, these strategies should be tested to make sure that these paper plans can actually be implemented within the desired timeframe. Unfortunately, all too often, what sounds like a perfectly easy procedure to follow on paper turns out to take significantly longer to implement than originally envisaged. Merely trying to document this process diagrammatically may indicate just how complex the process is and/or may identify holes in the perceived process.

By performing a test run of these recovery procedures, it should be possible to identify which steps need improvement, thereby placing an organization in better shape should the unthinkable happen and it actually have to utilize these plans for real.

System Salvage and Restoration

Once the damage has been controlled and a temporal fix put into place (or, if sufficient staff are available, to initiate in parallel with the damage-control effort), the organization can turn its attention to restoring the system back to full strength. The first step is for the organization to decide which parts of the system should be salvaged and which parts should be written off as a total loss.

Hardware and Software

With the exception of physical sabotage, it's rare for a piece of hardware to be so badly damaged from an intrusion that it can't be salvaged and returned to service. (An exception to this rule would be a microprocessor that is the victim of a DoS attack designed to overheat the CPU by performing excessive numerical calculations.) However, it may be more expedient to swap out compromised hardware devices such as hard drives rather than trying to recycle them, especially if the original hard drives are going to be needed by forensics.

In the case of system and application software, rather than trying to figure out exactly which services may have been compromised, it's probably safer to assume the worst and erase and reformat any hard drives (and possibly backup tapes and disks) that may have been accessed by the intruder. This would entail reinstalling the system and application software from a trusted medium such as a nonrewriteable CD. Unfortunately, all too often weak configuration management procedures may have allowed developers or Webmasters to make changes to the production Web site without updating the original source code or test environments, thereby resulting in recent fixes and optimizations being lost as the result of the restoration process. Restoration procedures should therefore be checked to ensure that they are comprehensive and can be implemented in a timely manner.

Data

Although restoring the system and application software that provides a Web site's functionality may be tedious, a much more challenging situation exists when a Web site's nonstatic data needs to be restored. Assuming the damage assessment is able to determine at what point in time an intruder gained unauthorized access to the data, it may be possible to restore the data to a precompromised state. Unfortunately, rolling the data forward from the last backup made before the intrusion may not be possible if transaction logs have not been kept (or cannot be trusted), leaving the organization with an unenviable dilemma of implementing a less-than-ideal recovery process, such as one of the following strategies:

- Restore the data back to its last known uncompromised state and then attempt to reenact all the transactions that are believed to have occurred after this point in time. For example, the first step would be to restore last week's version of a database used to support an intranet application that processes all the invoices a company receives. The database could then be brought up-to-date by rekeying all the paper invoices and resubmitting any electronic invoices that the company had received within the last week.

- Restore the database back to the last known uncompromised state and then void any transaction that occurred after that point in time. Such a course of action may be chosen because noncorrupted versions of the voided transaction cannot be found (or can't be trusted) or the business cost of reapplying these transactions outweighs the benefit of a full restoration. For example, the administrator for a fantasy football league Web site that did not maintain any transaction logs may decide to simply void all the games that took place after the Web site was defaced. He would do so rather than rely upon the recollections (and honesty) of the individual players to resubmit their game selections. Play would then be resumed for all future games.

- Attempt to patch the compromised data files or databases by trying to identify and fix the individual records that have been tampered with, typically using information from an independent trusted source. For example, suppose it appears that the only data that was tampered with was a few employees' salary records. It may be possible to fix these records by reconciling them with records held in a separate uncompromised system, such as the human resource department's paper files, or the payroll run that took place immediately before the intrusion occurred.

Recovering corrupted data becomes increasing more difficult the longer the corruption goes unnoticed. So, an organization wanting to test the capabilities of its data restoration procedures might wish to challenge the team responsible for recovery efforts. It could see how long the recovery team takes to salvage a tampered database that has subsequently had several days' (or weeks') worth of legitimate, nonvoidable transactions applied to it since the corruption occurred.

Once the primary system has been salvaged and restored, one additional step may need to take place before it can reenter service: synchronizing, or reapplying the transactions that have occurred on the temporal system while the primary system was offline. This task should be feasible if the temporal system has been maintaining adequate transaction logs; nevertheless, the synchronizing process should be tested to ensure that it can be completed in a timely manner.

Notification

One more item that should be specified in an organization's intrusion response policy is the people who should be notified of a successful (or unsuccessful) intrusion. The policy should also spell out when these parties should be informed. Possible candidates would include the following:

- An organization's legal counsel.
- Law enforcement agencies such as the FBI (www.fbi.gov).
- Coordination centers such as the Computer Emergency Response Team coordination center (www.cert.org) or the System Administration, Networking, and Security (SANS) institute (www.sans.org).
- The unwitting owners of the machines from which the attack was launched.
- Business partners who might be affected, such as credit card issuers, banks, customers, and suppliers.
- The media and general public. If the news of the attack is likely to make it into the public domain, an organization's public relations department may want to be the source that announces the incident, thereby being given the opportunity to put a more palatable spin on the event.
- If the organization has a cybercrime insurance policy, then the organization may need to put the insurance carrier on notice that the organization may be filing a claim. Table 9.2 provides a sample list of insurance carriers that offer cybercrime insurance policies.

Retaliation and Prosecution

One critical decision that should have been made long before any serious attack is detected is whether or not an organization, given the opportunity, would consider trying to prosecute an offender. This decision is critical, as the collection and preservation of evidence for use in a possible prosecution will most likely slow down the recovery effort and potentially increase the recovery cost. Possibly too, an organization may decide to adopt a different policy for internal attacks than for an externally launched attack.

Some organizations may choose to attempt to acquire information on the attacker by trying to trace the attack to the original source. Unfortunately, many sophisticated attackers choose not to launch an attack from their own machine but instead employ a previously compromised (or drone) machine to do their bidding. So, any counterattack launched by the organization that suffered from the original attack may only end up affecting another of the intruder's victims. Although attempting to trace the source of the attack may yield useful information (if only to inform another organization that their system has been commandeered by an intruder), more aggressive action is probably best left to local, nation, or international law enforcement.

In situations when successfully compromising the Web site under attack would be considered a breach of national security, the attack may be considered an act of *cyberwar*. It could therefore warrant much more aggressive action by the nation's government than actions likely to be taken by national or international law enforcement agencies.

Policy Review

Even when no successful intrusion attempt has been detected, the rapidly changing nature of Web security and the relative inexperience of some of those charged with protecting an organization's Web sites and applications can still make holding a regular policy review extremely beneficial. In addition, it is considered good practice to always review the current security policies and infrastructure after a successful break-in has occurred to make sure that a similar attack would not be successful in the future. Table 8.16 lists the questions to ask when creating an intrusion response policy.

Table 8.16   Intrusion Response Checklist

YES	NO	DESCRIPTION
☐	☐	Is there a documented policy in place that describes how the organization should respond to a concerted external attack that is in progress but appears not to have been successful so far?
☐	☐	Is there a documented policy in place that describes how the organization should respond to an external intruder who has (at least) breached the Web site's perimeter defense?
☐	☐	Is there a documented policy in place that describes how the organization should respond to an attack that appears to have been launched from within the organization?
☐	☐	If a policy does exist, does it adequately address all the following considerations: confirmation of intrusion, damage containment, damage assessment, forensic collection, damage control and recovery, system salvaging and restoration, notification, retaliation and prosecution, and policy review?
☐	☐	Under simulated intruder attacks, does the on-duty security staff follow the procedures documented in the policy? And if followed correctly, are they completed within the anticipated timeframe?

Summary

Testing the topics covered in this chapter has primarily two benefits. First, by testing the success of confusion tactics, the accuracy of detection devices, and the reliability of response procedures, it becomes possible to identify deficiencies and thereby improve the system's defenses. The second benefit is the experience the security staff gains by running through simulated attacks, training that should hopefully allow them to execute these procedures more efficiently when placed under the emotional stress of a real attack.

Test Implementation

# CHAPTER 9

Assessment and Penetration Options

Many different terms are used within the security industry to describe the tests associated with legitimate security testing. However, fundamentally these activities can be grouped into two categories of testing:

Security assessment or security audit.   The tester will endeavor to verify that no known security vulnerability is present on the target system. This type of testing is typically implemented by exercising the target system against an extensive proprietary checklist, in effect conducting a form of *software inspection*. This is a structured approach that lends itself to automation due to its high degree of predictability and need for repeatability. Myers (1979) and Perry (2001) provide additional information on the general concept of software inspections, while Allen (2001) and Skoudis (2001) describe security specific software inspections.

Penetration testing or ethical hacking.   In an attempt to recreate the trickery and creativity that a real-live attacker would seek to employ, the tester uses *creative* techniques, which are modified and honed as the tester learns more about the system being interrogated. In some respects, this resembles an exploratory testing approach. Kaner et al. (2001) provide additional information on the exploratory testing approach, while Klevinsky et al. (2002) describes the approach used in penetration testing.

Resources permitting, a security-testing project will include tests from both of these categories, with exploratory penetration tests complementing the structured testing of known security vulnerabilities. This chapter looks at the different ways these categories of security testing could be conducted, specifically focusing on who will conduct the tests and what tools they will use to accomplish these tasks.

Staffing Options

Perhaps one of the toughest decisions an information services (IS) director has to make is to decide who will actually carry out a security assessment or penetration test of the organization's Web site and associated applications. Fundamentally, the choice boils down to adopting a *do-it-yourself* (DIY) approach, outsourcing the work to a firm that specializes in this area, or some hybrid of the two. Obviously, the organization's size and potential exposure will be a significant input into this decision, a multinational telecommunications company, for example, having a far greater need for on-staff security testing personnel than that of a small-town newspaper. However, for many organizations, the choice is less clear, so the following sections examine the pros and cons to each of these approaches. Black (2002), Craig et al. (2002), and Kaner et al. (2001) provide additional guidance on the challenges of managing a team of testers (internal or external).

Do It Yourself (DIY)

If new staff are to be hired, a major consideration will be whether or not qualified individuals will be attracted to the compensation package that the organization can afford to offer. Perhaps this would not be a problem for a cash-rich bank located in New York, but not necessarily as easy for a financially strapped rural hospital. Conversely, if instead of hiring experienced staff, the organization makes a commitment to train some of its existing employees, this process could (depending upon the employees' starting point) take months or even years before the employees reach the required level of proficiency. In the meantime, the organization is left potentially exposed.

A DIY approach may well be the best path to follow if the IS director is able to obtain a budget to allow the organization to hire highly skilled security personal and/or retrain the existing staff in the knowledge needed to conduct rigorous security testing. The long-term benefit of having competent security professionals on staff may outweigh any short-term costs associated with bringing the organization *up to speed*. Bragg (2002), Endorf (2001), Harris (2001), Krutz et al. (2001, 2002), and Peltier (2002) provide additional information on the knowledge domain that a security tester needs to comprehend in order to pass the certified information systems security professional (CISSP) exam (www.cissp.com and www.isc2.org), the security industry's widely recognized security certification (not tied to a specific product).

One of the major variables that will affect the skill level and time needed to run a security assessment is the degree to which the testing will be automated (as the *Tools* section in this chapter describes in more detail). The increasing sophistication of these tools makes it easier for less knowledgeable individuals to actually perform an assessment. Also, the automation of many of the mundane tasks speeds up the work of even the most skilled consultant. Therefore, when trying to derive the total cost of a security implementation, the degree of test automation must be taken into account, as the extra cost of purchasing a tool, and the time needed to get up to speed with it, may in fact be less than the additional cost associated with a longer manual testing period, facilitated by more knowledgeable (and hence expensive) testers.

Outsourcing

Due to the complexity and depth of knowledge needed to thoroughly test the security of a Web site and its associated applications, many organizations are now outsourcing their security testing needs to firms that specialize in this service. Advantages to this approach include the following:

- Due to a faster implementation time, testing can potentially be scheduled and executed within hours.

- No need exists to purchase expensive security-testing tools, and no maintenance fees are needed to keep the tools up-to-date. Typically, the outsourcing firm's charges include any fees they may have to pay to the vendor whose tools they are using. Also, by not purchasing a tool, the organization removes the risk that it might buy an inappropriate or hard to use tool, which results in the tool becoming *shelfware*. Finally, from an accounting perspective, the entire fee can often be absorbed in the current tax year rather than having to depreciate an expensive tool over a number of years.

- Because these firms specialize in this activity, they can be expected to be up-to-date with the latest versions of tools and are aware of the most recent penetration strategies that are being employed by attackers.

- No need exists to hire expensive (and potentially hard to find) full-time security experts (although such staff may still be needed to fix any problems that the outsourced testing discovers). For smaller organizations that cannot justify full-time dedicated security personnel, this may be a particularly compelling consideration.

- The need to train internal staff to use the various security assessment tools (or their manual equivalents) is reduced.

- The organization may be able to explicitly establish that it has shown *due diligence* towards securing the assets it is responsible for, a standard that may be harder to prove if the testing is done internally. For many organizations, demonstrating due diligence is particularly important, as it may potentially reduce the liability an organization faces in the event of a successful intrusion occurring (assuming the organization showed due diligence in the selection process used to hire the firm that the security testing was outsourced to).

Leaving aside the issue of evaluating and selecting a competent testing firm for a moment, the main disadvantage with using an outsourced firm is the fee that the firm charges. A one-time fee may be more cost effective than building up the necessary skills in-house, but the costs associated with retesting several Web sites every few months, or having an outside firm continuously monitor a Web site, will soon add up. For some organizations, this may ultimately be a more expensive approach than conducting the same level of testing in-house.

Deciding upon a particular security-testing firm (or firms) is unlikely to be as easy as it might first appear. As can be seen from Table 9.1, which lists just a few of the firms offering this type of service, quite a few firms exist from which to choose.

Table 9.1 Sample List of Firms Offering Security Testing Services

NAME OF FIRM	ASSOCIATED WEB SITE
AlphaNet Solutions	www.alphanetsolutions.com
@Stake	www.atstake.com
Baltimore	www.baltimore.com
Boran Consulting	www.boran.com
Cigital	www.cigital.com
ConQWest	www.conqwest.com
Control Risks Group	www.crg.com
Cryptek	www.cryptek.com
Defcom	www.defcom.com
Emprise Technologies	www.emprisetech.com
eSMART	www.esmartcorp.com
Exodus	www.exodus.net
Ernst & Young	www.ey.com
Farm9	www.farm9.com
Foundstone	www.foundstone.com
Grayhat Security	www.grayhatsecurity.com
GRC International	www.grci.com
Guardent	www.guardent.com
Hyperon Consulting	www.hyperon.com
IBM	www.ibm.com
Infidel	www.infidel.net
InfoScreen	www.infoscreen.com
Internet Security Systems	www.iss.net
iXsecurity	www.ixsecurity.com
Maven Security Consulting	www.mavensecurity.com
META Security Group	www.metasecuritygroup.com
MIS Corporate Defence Solutions	www.mis-cds.com

(continues)

Table 9.1 Sample List of Firms Offering Security Testing Services (*continued*)

NAME OF FIRM	ASSOCIATED WEB SITE
Network Security	www.nsec.net
Predictive Systems	www.predictive.com
ProCheckUp	www.procheckup.com
RedSiren Technologies	www.redsiren.com
Riptech	www.riptech.com
SecureInfo	www.secureinfo.com
Security Automation	www.securityautomation.com
Sword & Shield Enterprise Security	www.sses.net
Sysinct	www.sysinct.com
System Experts	www.systemexperts.com
TesCom	www.tescom-usa.com
TestPros	www.testpros.com
Tiger Testing	www.tigertesting.com
Tritonic	www.tritonic.com
TruSecure	www.trusecure.com
TrustAsia	www.trustasia.com
VeriSign	www.verisign.com
Veritect	www.veritect.com
Vigilinx	www.vigilinx.com

Note: The inclusion (or exclusion) of a specific firm in this list should not be construed as any form of recommendation by this book.

Aside from the usual considerations associated with outsourcing work to another party (such as availability, consulting rates, and scheduling), security testing has some additional considerations that do not necessarily apply to the same degree to other outsourced activities. The following sections will expand upon these considerations.

Trustworthiness of Firms Doing Outsourced Work

By hiring another firm to attempt to break into one or more of its systems, an organization is implicitly trusting that the individuals doing the testing will not take advantage of this opportunity to do something untoward. For example, a tester could fail to report one or more detected security vulnerabilities that could be exploited at a later point in time. Another example would be uploading software (such as a *rootkit*) on to a client's machine that could be used later to enable the tester to anonymously take control of the machine for malicious purposes, such as a load generator for a distributed denial-of-service attack. After all, if the rootkit were to be detected, the tester could simply claim to have forgotten to remove it after the testing was complete.

Many testing firms that provide functional and performance-testing services also offer security testing, but due to the specialist nature of this form of testing they outsource any such work to a subcontractor with expertise in this area, a scenario that the end-client may or may not be aware of. Given the risk an organization assumes when it requests another party to attempt to penetrate or assess its defenses, care should be taken to ensure that any firm hired to undertake this task is reputable and will only delegate this work out to subcontractors that the client is comfortable with. Any security-testing contract should therefore state whether or not a subcontractor may be used, and if so, who they are or the criteria for selecting one (such as requiring x number of satisfactory third-party references).

Perhaps the most controversial debate surrounding the use of outsourcing security testing is the use or nonuse of reformed criminals. The basic premise is that only someone who has had *real* experience trying to illegally break into numerous systems would be able to think like a real intruder and thereby create a realistic probe of the client's defenses. Several problems exist with this reasoning, for instance, just because someone alleges that they were able to break into someone else's system does not necessarily mean that he or she is an expert. Many Web sites out there have negligible defenses, and trying to use a criminal conviction as a form of certification only proves that they were not devious enough to cover their own tracks. Another problem is how do you know they are really reformed? Even a positive reference from a probation or parole office can't guarantee that while testing a Web site the reformed criminal won't do a little *extracurricular* reconnaissance work.

Some firms actively advertise the fact that some of their staff are convicted criminals, while others make a specific point of telling their perspective clients that they run extensive background checks on all their employees in order to avoid such individuals. It appears that the *marketplace* has yet to decide which solution is the most desirable. It is therefore a good idea to explicitly ask a potential security-testing firm what viewpoint they prescribe to, and make sure that it does not run counter to the organization's own view on this subject.

Use of Insurance Underwriters

Many insurance companies offer policies designed to help compensate an organization that has been penetrated by an intruder, as part of a general business continuity policy, or as part of a special purpose cybercrime policy. Table 9.2 lists some examples of carriers that offer this type of insurance.

These insurance carriers will often require any organization applying for such a policy to first be audited by an approved security assessment firm. This is done in order to obtain a security certification that may be used as proof of due diligence and subsequently qualify the organization for the policy or a reduced insurance premium. Although passing such an assessment will not guarantee that the organization will not

Table 9.2   Sample List of Insurance Carriers Offering Cybercrime Policies

NAME	ASSOCIATED WEB SITE
INSUREtrust.com	www.insuretrust.com
Lloyds of London	www.lloydsoflondon.co.uk
Safeonline	www.safeonline.com

be successfully attacked, in the eyes of the insurance company's underwriter at least some level of minimum protection has been implemented. The possibility of an intrusion is therefore reduced to the point that the underwriter finds it acceptable to transfer the risk of such an event from the applicant to the insurance company.

If an organization intends to purchase insurance coverage to mitigate the ramifications of their Web site's security being compromised, then the number of firms from which they can choose to perform a security assessment may be limited to those firms that have been preapproved by the potential insurance carrier.

Explication of Terms of Engagement

Before an organization sanctions a penetration test against any of its production systems, it should ensure that the contract agreed upon with the security-testing firm explicitly states the terms of engagement (or terms of reference) under which the testing firm can interact with the target of the testing effort. Examples of such terms include questions like can social engineering be exploited, or can the testers attempt to overload an intrusion detection system by launching a denial-of-service attack (which may have the unpleasant side effect of denying legitimate users access to the target Web site)?

Offers of Compensation

Does the security-testing firm offer any kind of compensation (possibly specified in the form of a service level agreement [SLA]) should they inadvertently bring down or severely impact the system they are testing? What if an intruder compromises a Web site that has already been tested, using an exploit that the security-testing firm should have been expected to find, but the testing firm either failed to check for such an opening or wrongly interpreted their own test results?

Comprehensiveness of Coverage

Many companies offering security-testing services do not in fact offer a complete range of services. For example, some firms (particularly those that have performance testing as one of their many offerings) may offer to recreate one or more forms of denial-of-service attacks by generating huge volumes of network traffic (from the comfort of their own facilities), but do not know the first thing about testing an application for potential buffer overflows. Similarly, some firms are willing to perform an external port scan of a Web site remotely, but are unwilling to fly out to a client's site to conduct an internal port scan from inside of the client's perimeter firewall.

Another way to differentiate testing firms is whether or not they include recommendations on how to fix all the issues they detected or merely document the issues. Some may even go a step further and offer a consulting service that can be hired to actually implement these recommendations.

As with most things in life, you often get what you pay for. The cheapest firm may simply be the cheapest because it doesn't do much. This is perhaps an acceptable situation if the client doesn't have much of a budget, but it is an extremely dangerous situation if the client wrongly believes they are getting a more comprehensive checkup. Before signing on the dotted line, an organization should make sure that the contract documents exactly what types of tests will be covered (and not covered) and that they are comfortable with this level of test coverage. Beizer (1995) provides additional information on the concept of test coverage.

Which Tools Are Selected

Because some tool vendors charge security-testing firms a per-use fee, many firms opt to create their own tools or use freeware tools. A probing question to consider asking a candidate security-testing firm is what tools do they use. Although using an expensive commercial tool will not necessarily detect more holes than a bunch of freeware tools in the hands of an expert, a leading commercial tool can provide the client with a higher level of comfort that the testing will provide a minimum level of comprehensiveness.

Although far from a perfect measure, expensive commercial tools may also indirectly gauge the financial strength of the testing company. A fly-by-night or start-up testing firm is not as likely to have invested in top-notch, expensive security assessment tools as a well-funded firm that has been around for a while. Conversely, using tools developed by the firm's own staff may be indicative of highly skilled employees who don't necessarily need the help of expensive tools.

Starting Point of Testing

One consideration that will have an immediate effect on the effort needed (and hence cost) of running a penetration test is whether or not the security-testing team should be given a comprehensive set of network addresses to be tested. (Another consideration is specifying telephone numbers if remote access is included in the scope.) Providing these pseudoattackers with such a head start will save them a considerable amount of time (and hence expense) that they would otherwise have had to spend discovering this information themselves (a technique commonly referred to as enumerating the target). Of course, the onus is now on the client to make sure that this list is indeed complete and not missing some overlooked entry point, such as a recently configured test system for another testing group to use.

Providing a penetration-testing team with additional information such as the exact version of system software used by the target system will also speed up the testing, but it may provide the testers with an unrealistic advantage. The same goes for providing highly sensitive information, such as the network-filtering rules that were supposed to have been used to configure a perimeter firewall, or the names and userIDs of system administrators. Therefore, a trade-off must be made between helping the testing team conduct their test more quickly and making the testing environment more realistic by keeping them in the dark.

If the objective of the penetration effort is to find as many vulnerabilities as possible, providing the testing team with as much information as possible will help decloak any *security by obscurity* defense, possibly showing areas that were solely protected by this unreliable form of defense. On the other hand, if the purpose of the penetration test is to evaluate the effectiveness of the security defenses as a whole (including any confusion or obscurity defenses), then withholding this information will make the results more realistic. For some organizations, it may even make sense to perform the penetration test twice. The testing team conducting the first test would be provided the bare minimum of information needed to make sure the testing is applied to the right systems, while the second team (which may in fact be the same team that did the first test) is provided with as much information as the organization is comfortable providing.

Ending Point of Testing

One consideration that should be agreed upon before testing starts is under what conditions should the testing be considered completed or temporally suspended. This is an easy situation to define in the case of a straightforward scan by a commercial security assessment tool, but it is less obvious if a manual penetration test is being contemplated. In the case of a penetration team attempting to compromise a Web site by using creative means instead of merely running through a predefined list of checks, it may be more appropriate to time-box the testing effort to a maximum of X elapsed days for a team of Y, or alternatively Z person-hours of testing effort. The amount of time allocated would depend on the size of the task and the business risk that the organization faces should the Web site be compromised. For instance, the time needed to exhaustively test a single-server, *brochureware* Web site would be much less than that needed to sufficiently probe a large e-commerce Web site. As a rule of thumb, the effort expended on a penetration attempt should not be less than the amount of time a real intruder (or team of intruders) would be reasonably expected to expend trying to compromise the target Web site.

In the event that the Web site is easily cracked, it may be more prudent to suspend further testing until these obvious flaws have been fixed. To facilitate detecting this condition, some organizations will strategically plant *trophies* for the penetration-testing team to try and acquire (a variation on the *capture the flag* theme) and may even award bonuses for the successful capture of such trophies before the allotted testing time has expired.

Reconfirmation of Test Results

The longer the period of time taken to complete a security-testing effort, the higher the probability that a change to the testing environment will occur, resulting in the earlier

---

TEST EFFECTIVENESS

By deliberately adding known defects to the target of a penetration effort, some organizations hope to measure the effectiveness of the penetration-testing effort, in effect implementing a variation of a *defect-seeding* testing technique. Since defect seeding has become largely discredited in the broader testing community, using such a technique to form the basis for evaluating the effectiveness of the testing effort (or the effectiveness of a system's defenses) is likely to lead to an inaccurate assessment. A significant problem with this approach is the inability to plant vulnerabilities in exactly the same frequency and manner that real vulnerabilities will occur, not to mention the possibility of a planted vulnerability being *lost* or forgotten, and subsequently proving a real intruder with an additional opportunity. Craig et al. (2002) and Musa (1998) provide additional perspectives on the concept of defect seeding.

---

test results being called into question. For example, such a change could be a new, must-implement hotfix security patch that has been released for the operating system used by the majority of the system's servers.

This problem is not only related to changes brought about by external stimuli, but an early penetration test may have detected a serious misconfiguration in a perimeter firewall that warrants immediate attention. In such circumstances, tests may need to be rerun to confirm that any fix has indeed fixed the problem and has not created a new vulnerability somewhere else. Unfortunately, retesting takes time and is rarely free. Therefore, the organization should agree up front, with any testing team (outsourced or internal), under what circumstances a change may be made to the system being tested while testing is in progress, and if such an event should occur, how much retesting will be done. Possible strategies include rerunning only the high-priority tests, only rerunning tests that have previously failed, or performing a complete retest of the entire system.

Location Where the Testing Is Conducted

Some security-testing firms may only be willing to conduct their tests from an offsite or remote location, typically utilizing the Internet to reach the target Web site. Others may be willing to send their consultants to a client's site but may charge an additional fee that makes this scenario prohibitively expensive, especially if the consulting firm is based overseas. Although many may argue that testing over the Internet is a more realistic test environment, a well-configured perimeter firewall may mean that a remotely located testing team is only able to confirm that a Web site's outer network and Web application defenses are working correctly. The team may not be able to test any additional inner network defenses put in place to guard against an internal intruder or as a second line of defense in case an as-yet-undiscovered flaw exists with a perimeter firewall.

A possible solution includes opening up the firewall to provide the remote testing team with access to the inner workings of the Web site, a potentially risky endeavor since the firewall would be opened up for the rest of the world as well. Another option is to package up the Web application(s) and ship it to the testing firm for them to install in a testing lab that has been configured to closely match the client's own production environment. Of course, the accuracy of these test results will largely depend upon how close the test lab's configuration matches that of the clients. Table 9.3 attempts to summarize the points that should be considered when evaluating a perspective outside security-testing firm.

Table 9.3 Outside Security Testing Firm Consideration Checklist

YES	NO	DESCRIPTION
☐	☐	Has the testing firm taken reasonable precautions to ensure that its own employees or the staff of any subcontractor will not take advantage of the opportunity afforded them by the testing assignment to later initiate an unsanctioned attack against the client?
☐	☐	Is the testing firm acceptable to the organization's insurance underwriter (if any)?
☐	☐	Does the testing firm agree to be bound by clearly defined (and documented) terms of engagement?
☐	☐	Does the testing firm provide any kind of compensation if they, as a result of their testing activities, significantly disrupt the normal operation of the system being tested?
☐	☐	Does the testing firm provide any kind of compensation (or guarantee) if they fail to detect a security hole that is later successfully exploited by an intruder?
☐	☐	Does the contract with the testing firm specify what types of tests will be conducted? Examples would be ping sweeps, port scans, simulated distributed denial-of-service attacks, file share scans, application source code reviews, submitting system commands via application input data, and so on.
☐	☐	Does the contract with the testing firm specify whether the testing firm will include recommendations on how to fix any detected vulnerability?
☐	☐	Does the testing firm also offer a consulting service for implementing any recommendations they might make?
☐	☐	Is the testing firm willing to divulge what testing tools (and versions) they will use to conduct their tests?
☐	☐	Does the contract specify what head-start information (if any) will be provided to the testing firm prior to commencement of the assessment? Examples include a complete list of network addresses used by the target site, specific version numbers of the system software installed on the target site, or a list of services running on the servers located closest to the perimeter firewall.
☐	☐	Does the contract with the testing firm specify the duration of the testing effort and under what circumstances may testing be terminated, suspended, or extended?
☐	☐	If the testing is to be done remotely, have additional tests been scheduled that will test the security of the Web site from an internal attacker?

Combination of In-House and Outsourced Testing

Perhaps the most cost-effective approach to conducting a comprehensive security assessment and an associated penetration test of a system that is already built is to use a combination of in-house and outsourced testing. An in-house testing team using free or low-cost tools that require only a moderate degree of training might conduct an initial security assessment, finding obvious and easily detected vulnerabilities without the need for expensive outside consultants. Once all the detected holes have been plugged, one or more testing firms that specialize in penetration testing may be hired to attempt to compromise the system externally and, if resources permit, internally too. This approach not only provides a second set of eyes and thereby reduces the chance that an unplugged hole exists in the production environment, but also provides a crude means of gauging the effectiveness of the testing process used by the in-house team. This is a useful gauge to have when deciding whether or not future assessments or penetration tests should be outsourced or conducted by in-house staff.

In the case of a system being created, bringing in outside security experts early on may prove to be a cost-effective form of prevention. Not only would the system's design be more secure, but the in-house staff can incorporate the expert's recommendations into their security assessment checklists.

Tools for Testing

Although it would be possible to manually conduct the vast majority of the tests mentioned in the previous chapters of this book, it often makes sense to try and automate as many of these tests as feasibly possible. To this end, each section of this book has, where possible, included an accompanying list of sample tools that can be used to automate some or all of the tests discussed within its section. Since all these lists contain more than one tool, a recurring task is to evaluate each group of tools to determine which tool (or subset of tools) would be the most appropriate for a specific security-testing assignment. The following sections summarize some of the main differences between a predominately manual approach and a predominately automated approach to security testing. If an automated approach is desired, considerations for selecting the most appropriate tool are also included.

Manual Approach

A manual approach may be cheaper to initially implement than an automated approach, but the ongoing costs are likely to be higher. In addition, manual approaches typically do not scale as well as automated tests. For instance, a vulnerability assessment tool barely takes any longer to scan two Web sites than it does to scan one. In contrast, a manual effort may take considerably longer.

Highly creative security professionals performing a penetration test on a Web site may be able to figure out an ingenious way around a Web site's defenses and thereby reveal vulnerabilities that a less imaginative automated test might not have found. Unfortunately, unless these tests are well documented, such tactics may not prove to be as repeatable as an automated script. Such tests are more vulnerable to staff turnover, with the expertise literally walking out of the door, something that is not likely to happen to an assessment tool owned by the organization.

Automated Approach

Rather than relying on an army of security experts, many organizations and security-testing firms are now automating their Web site security assessments. In such a scenario, an organization acquires a security tool that is run against a target Web site in an attempt to replicate the attacks that intruders have been known to use. Based on the success or failure of these attacks, the tool attempts to assess and report which security vulnerabilities may be present. Although these systems are fast, easily repeatable, and a possibly cheaper way of probing a Web site, they do have several potential drawbacks:

- Because the tools rely upon developers to create probes that look for each specific security hole, the tool vendors are always running a little behind the latest tricks that attackers have discovered. Just like antivirus programs that rely on signature .dat files, it always takes a while before a new exploit is discovered by the good guys and subsequently added to the list of automated probes.

- Although quick, many automated tools are not as smart or as flexible as an experienced security professional. A situation that often results is the automated tool generating a test summary report that contains many false positives (the testing tool wrongly detecting nonexistent problems).

- Automated tools rarely do a good job of prioritizing the legitimate issues, potentially burying must-fix-immediately problems in a sea of trivial warnings. For example, installing a custom HTTP 404 error on a Web site will cause some security assessment tools to generate false positives for every Common Gateway Interface (CGI) script vulnerability it tests for. The security assessment tool mistakenly interprets the Web server returning the custom error page as an indication that the flawed CGI script it requested is present on the target Web server.

- If the tool has a high learning curve (possibly learning which automated warnings should be taken seriously and which ones are false positives), the tool may be vulnerable to staff turnover. Klevinsky et al. (2002) and Scambray et al. (2001) provide an introduction to using many of the tools commonly used for security testing (such as those listed in Table 9.4).

The pros and cons of manual versus automated testing are not restricted to security testing. Many of these same issues affect other types of testing such as functional and performance testing. Buwalda et al. (2001), Dustin et al. (1999), Graham et al. (1999), and Hayes (1995) provide additional information on test automation. Table 9.4 lists some security assessment tools that can be used to help automate a security-testing effort.

Table 9.4 Sample List of Security Assessment Tools

NAME	ASSOCIATED WEB SITE
AppScan	www.sanctuminc.com
bv-Control for Internet Security/HackerShield	www.bindview.com
Cerberus Internet Scanner	www.cerberus-infosec.co.uk
Cybercop Scanner*	www.nai.com
FoundScan	www.foundstone.com
Nessus	www.nessus.org
NetRecon	www.symantec.com
Retina	www.eeye.com
SAINT	www.wwdsi.com
SANS Top 20 Scanner	www.cisecurity.org
Scanner Database/Internet/System/Wireless	www.iss.net
SecureNet	www.intrusion.com
SecureScan	www.vigilante.com
Security Administrator Tool for Analyzing Networks (SATAN)	www.fish.com
Security Analyzer	www.netiq.com
Security Auditor's Research Assistant (SARA)	www.www-arc.com**
STAT Analyzer/Scanner	www.statonline.com/harris.com
Twwwscan	www.search.iland.co.kr
VigilEnt	www.pentasafe.com
WebInspect	www.spidynamics.com

*Effective July 1, 2002, Network Associates has transitioned the CyberCop product line into maintenance mode.
** This is not a typographical error—the Web site address is www.www-arc.com.

Tool Evaluation

Because the needs and resources of each organization and each project within a single organization will differ, it is not possible to specifically recommend a best tool (or set of tools) for each organization, especially when many of these tools are continually being upgraded and ported, making any judgment only valid for a snapshot in time and subsequently rapidly out-of-date. Instead, this section discusses the recurring criteria that should be considered when evaluating a group of similar tools.

Dustin et al. (2001), Graham et al. (1999), and Stottlemyer (2001) provide additional suggestions for evaluating testing tools.

Platform on Which Tools Will Be Used

The vast majority of security-testing tools available today were either initially intended to be executed from the Windows 9.x (95, 98, or ME), Windows NT (NT, 2000, or XP), or UNIX families of operating systems. Although some of the most popular tools have been ported from their original platform (such as eEye Digital Security's porting of the nmap fingerprinting tool from a UNIX to a Windows NT platform), many tools are still only available on one platform. Interestingly, some client/server security tools have been partially ported, typically the client-side being usable from many platforms, but the server-side being installable on a much smaller number of platforms—for example, Nessus (www.nessus.com).

The choice of tools available to a tester may therefore be immediately restricted based upon the platforms available from which to conduct the tests. Unfortunately, for some testers, their hardware budget may be nonexistent, restricting them to a single machine and consequently forcing them to either install a boot manager (Table 9.5 lists some example tools for managing multiple operating systems on the same machine) that enables them to boot into two or more operating systems (a solution that typically degrades the available disk space, virtual memory, and processing speed of the host machine) or restricting them to the tools from a single family. Although there typically exists a tool from each category that will run on the Windows NT and UNIX families of platforms, the Windows 9.x family is not supported as well.

Since no platform has a monopoly on the best tool for every category, many security testers regard having a sufficiently powered Windows NT family machine and a separate machine running some flavor of UNIX (often a Linux or BSD variant) as a bare minimum for conducting efficient testing. This, of course, assumes that the person(s) conducting the tests is familiar with both operating systems, a consideration that may play a significant factor in the selection of an appropriate set of tools. Ideally, an

Table 9.5 Multiple O/S Management Tools

NAME	ASSOCIATED WEB SITE
Boot Manager (System Selector)	www.bootmanager.com
OS/2 boot manager	www.ibm.com
PartitionMagic	www.powerquest.com
System Commander	www.v-com.com
Vmware	www.vmware.com
Windows NT/2000 boot manager	www.microsoft.com

Note: In contrast to the software-based solutions listed above, Romtec (www. romtecusa.com) offers a hardware product (TriOS) that can be used to run several operating systems via multiple hard drives.

organization may wish to invest in a small test lab that contains the various operating systems needed to support the tools used to not only probe the target site, but also to build a replica of the site. This reduces the number of tests that need to be actually executed in the production environment and consequently reduces the risk that one of these tests might inadvertently affect the production site. Extreme care should be taken to exactly replicate the production environment in the test lab, and even then, some testing would still be warranted in the production environment to confirm that it does indeed match the test lab and to execute tests against parts of the production environment known to differ from the test lab (for example, ensuring the passwords on the production environment are sufficiently encrypted, as presumably these passwords are likely to be different from the ones used in the test lab). An additional advantage of having an isolated testing lab is that the tools used to assess the replica environment do not themselves pose the same security risk. Having these tools installed on a machine that has direct access to the production environment could make life a lot easier for an attacker should they be able to compromise such a machine. Short of being given system administration userIDs and passwords on a silver platter, an attacker could not wish for a better find than to stumble across a *trusted* machine with all their favorite fingerprinting and cracking tools already installed, possibly along with test summary reports (saving the attacker the trouble of even having to run these tools). For this reason, if an isolated environment is not to be used, care should be taken to uninstall or disable any security-testing tool present on a machine that might become accessible to an attacker.

Cost

No matter how big or small an organization, cost will always be a factor when comparing two or more tools, frequently being the main factor. Something that is often not considered so readily is the *total cost of ownership*. This cost not only includes the purchase price of a tool (if any), but also the cost associated with training people to use the tool, any hardware and system software licenses needed to use the tool, and the cost of keeping the tool up-to-date (either in terms of a maintenance fee or the time spent by internal staff upgrading the tool). From a purchase cost perspective, tools can be grouped into one of the following categories.

Freeware

Upon manually discovering a new vulnerability, many exploit authors will invest some time converting their sequence of manual steps into an automated tool and then freely make it available to the population at large. This is sometimes done as a means of encouraging the owner of the compromised product to quickly bring out a patch or merely as a means of demonstrating the tester's own prowess.

Additionally, some security testers who are tired of running tedious and lengthy checks for known exploits have developed useful utilities that significantly reduce the amount of time needed to probe and potentially penetrate a target site. The net result is that a vast array of security tools are available that can be downloaded from numerous Web sites free of charge. Table 9.6 lists some sample Web sites that contain libraries of such tools.

Table 9.6 Sample List of Tool Libraries

NAME	ASSOCIATED WEB SITE
ACME Laboratories	www.acme.com
@stake	www.atstake.com
Church of the Swimming Elephant	www.cotse.com
CNET Networks	www.download.com
	www.shareware.com
	www.zdnet.com
DaveCentral	www.davecentral.com
HackingExposed	www.hackingexposed.com
Ideahamster Organization	www.ideahamster.org
Insecure	www.insecure.org
Nomad Mobile Research Centre (NMRC)	www.nmrc.org
Ntsecurity	www.ntsecurity.nu
SourceForge	www.sourceforge.net
Tucows	www.tucows.com
Ultimate Search	www.freeware32.com

When trying to locate and download testing tools via the Internet, it would be prudent to temporarily disable any mobile code capability (such as ActiveX controls or Java applets) that the browser uses. Unfortunately, some of the Web sites professing to offer free security-testing tools may have also placed a hidden surprise on their Web site—a piece of malicious mobile code that the visitor potentially downloads and executes (the promise of the free tool being used as bait to lure unsuspecting victims to the Web site).

An even safer strategy for downloading files would be to use the services of an anonymous Web server service (such as www.anonymizer.com), which hides personnel information (such as the network address being used by the browser) from a Web site of questionable integrity.

Some Trojan horses masquerade as security tools, performing their intended function as well as some undesirable activity. For example, a well-known and trusted security-scanning tool could be enhanced to send a copy of its output report to an email account located in a foreign country, from which the author of the Trojan horse could review this sensitive information at his or her convenience. Therefore, after downloading any tool over the Internet, the file should be thoroughly scanned for viruses and Trojan horses, and then only initially used in a safe, controlled environment where it can be monitored (such as via a network or a host-based intrusion detection system [IDS]).

Although a downloaded executable may be easier to initially get working, acquiring and reviewing the source code for an equivalent tool may allow the tool to be enhanced and customized (such as porting the tool to another platform). This also provides a developer a greater learning opportunity. Additionally, having access to a tool's source code affords the organization the opportunity to examine the algorithms used by the tool to ensure that no Trojan horses are present. The organization can also determine if the tool contains any bugs (or features) that might result in inaccurate test results being produced or misinterpreted.

Interestingly, many of the freeware tools intended to run on a Windows platform are typically distributed as binary files (exes, dlls, and so on). Tools destined for the UNIX environment are often made available as source code, requiring the perspective user to first install an appropriate compiler or interpreter before being able to execute the program. This trend is in part due to the relative homogeneity of the Windows platforms in comparison to the diversity of UNIX.

Unfortunately, many freeware tools come with minimum documentation, which may not be sufficient for anyone who is not highly conversant in the operating environment that the tool was originally intended to be deployed in or will be installed into. Nor are there likely to be very many training courses or books that provide detailed instructions on how to install, run, and interpret the tool's findings. This is not necessarily a huge concern for simple tools such as a basic ping-sweeping tool that comes with a near self-explanatory graphic user interface (GUI). However, it is more of an issue with a tool that uses cryptic attribute settings via a command-line interface and is only available as source code intended to be compiled with obscure compiler options.

Shareware

Shareware differs from freeware in that the tool may be downloaded free of charge, but the tool's author expects anyone who continues to use the product after an evaluation period to remit some sort of payment. What makes shareware different from other commercially available tools is that the payment is *requested,* not demanded by the author, relying on the *honor* of the user rather than some built-in, time-elapsed control that disables the tool after a short evaluation period.

Build It Yourself

Given the breadth of existing freeware security-testing tools currently available, it is unlikely that an organization developing its own set of testing tools from scratch will ever get a sufficient return on investment (ROI) to make this approach feasible. This situation may not be the case, however, if the organization intends to market its security-testing expertise to other firms or produces a tool with a unique feature not readily available anywhere else. An acceptable ROI may also be achieved if, instead of starting from scratch, a tool's existing source code is modified to provide additional functionality, such as the capability to read network addresses from an input file rather than a GUI. A tool's source code could also be customized to meet the precise needs of an organization; for instance, the tool could be ported to a new environment, such as a different flavor of UNIX.

Low-Cost/Budget Software

Many security-testing products can now be purchased for less than a few hundred dollars. Boutique software companies, often composed of only a handful of full-time developers, have created many of these products, while other products may have started life as a hobby before being turned into a part-time business by the product's author. Needless to say, product support, reliability, compatibility, and the frequency with which upgrades are made available vary greatly from product to product.

Some tools are dependent on the functionality provided by products from other software vendors (for example, many tools have been designed to reuse components of MS-IE). Although using services from another vendor may often save the tool vendor considerable expense and improve its time to market, dependency on another vendor's product can often cause compatibility issues. For example, tool X works fine with MS-IE v5.0, but not with v6.0, while the latest version of tool Y expects MS-IE 6.0 or higher to be installed. This causes an issue, because only one version of MS-IE can typically be installed on a single machine (boot managers and so on aside). The situation is further compounded if all the members of the testing team needs to install MS-IE 5.5 sp1, because this is the corporate standard that all the in-house-developed intranet applications have been designed for and therefore need to be tested with.

Freeware and shareware executables could also fall into this category if the product requires a large amount of effort to install. Due to the typical lack of comprehensive documentation and nonexistent customer support, it may take a significant amount of time, and time is rarely free.

High-End Software

Some of the best tools on the market cost thousands of dollars, so much that actually purchasing them might not be the most cost-effective way of acquiring them. Leasing an expensive tool for a short period of time or hiring another firm that already owns the software to test the target site might be a cheaper way of conducting a one-time security assessment. Of course, over the long run, a single purchase may prove to be cheaper than a recurring expense.

Typically, these tools are executed remotely from the tool vendor's location or are distributed as a platform-specific executable that is relatively easy to install. Thus, you have no need to worry about trying to build a new executable using dozens of source code files and a free compiler downloaded from a university's Web site.

The tool vendor may also offer a consulting service or be partnered with numerous value-added retailers (VARs) who, for an additional fee, will install, configure, run, and even interpret the tool's results. This provides a low-learning-curve entry into security testing, albeit an expensive one. If such services are not easily available, then before investing in the tool, an organization should weight the additional risk of not being able to find or train staff who can effectively use the tool, causing the tool to either be underutilized or, worse still, abandoned.

High-end products have the potential to generate sufficient revenue to support frequent product updates (something a low-cost tool vendor may not be able to cost-justify), an important consideration given the rate with which new exploits are being discovered. Before purchasing an expensive security-testing tool, an organization should determine how frequent the tool vendor releases updates and what the cost of obtaining these updates is expected to be (an expense that is often quoted as a percentage of the original purchase price).

Finally, before investing a considerable sum into acquiring and learning how to use a specific tool, the tool's vendor should be evaluated to gauge how likely it is that they will still be in business in the foreseeable future. This is especially true if the lion's share of the costs is to be expended up front. Table 9.7 lists the points to consider when evaluating different security-testing tools.

Table 9.7   Security-Testing Tool Selection Checklist

YES	NO	DESCRIPTION
☐	☐	Does the organization have the resources to create a test lab for security-testing purposes?
☐	☐	Have all the ancillary costs such as training, setup time, future software upgrades, consultant fees, and so on been included into the total cost of ownership of the tool?
☐	☐	Is the proposed tool affordable?
☐	☐	Are all tools downloaded from the Internet scanned for viruses and Trojan horses before being installed?
☐	☐	Are all recently installed tools initially monitored for suspicious behavior in a quarantined area before being deployed against the production environment?
☐	☐	Are all tools that potentially have access to the production environment uninstalled or disabled when not in use?
☐	☐	Will a proposed tool run on the organization's existing infrastructure?
☐	☐	Will a proposed tool require extensive training? This includes any time needed to learn a new operating system or set up a custom environment needed by the tool. An example would be installing a new interpreter.
☐	☐	Is the proposed tool available as an executable for the desired platform?
☐	☐	Can the proposed tool be used without any customization?
☐	☐	Is the proposed tool available as source code?
☐	☐	Can the proposed tool be used independently of any other product?
☐	☐	Is the proposed tool intuitive and easy to use, or does it come with comprehensive documentation?

Summary

Unless the organization has been the victim of a recent attack, the decision on who will conduct the testing and what tools they will use often comes down to how quickly and cheaply an initial assessment can be done in order to make it appear that the organization is being *duly diligent*.

Activities such as ongoing monitoring and reassessments may be given a lower priority than a single initial assessment and consequently be underfunded. An approach that may work well for accountants looking for a quantifiable one-time cost, as opposed to a recurring cost that will never go away, but may ultimately result in the organization being lulled into a false sense of security, and thereby exposed to any unknown exploit that may be present in an existing (or as-yet-unwritten) Web application or system software product installed on the Web site.

10

Risk Analysis

You may know what you are supposed to test, but you realize you don't have the time or resources to test everything. So which tests should you perform first (thereby ensuring that these tests are executed), and which tests should you leave to last (and thereby risk never getting to)? This chapter seeks to help the security-testing team answer these questions by looking at how a risk analysis can be used to help the team decide which tests will provide the best return on their testing investment and the order in which these tests should be run (test priority) just in case an unexpected event causes the testing effort to be curtailed after testing has commenced. For example, it might turn out that the testing schedule was overly optimistic or that the quality of the system being tested was much poorer than anticipated and thereby slow the testing effort.

It may well be the case that the original designers of the system conducted a security risk analysis prior to deciding upon what security measures would be incorporated into the system. Since it may be possible to reuse this analysis for the testing effort, the first portion of this chapter provides a brief overview of three different techniques that may have been performed. If no such analysis exists, then the second section of this

SOME DEFINITIONS

"A *risk* is a measure of a probability and consequence of some undesirable event or outcome." Gerrard et al. (2002)

  "*Risk analysis* is the process of identifying, estimating, and evaluating risk." Craig et al. (2002)

chapter should prove useful, as it describes a simple approach that can be used to quickly help a security-testing team decide where to focus their testing effort. The final section of this chapter outlines a more rigorous approach, that of a Failure Mode, Effects, and Criticality Analysis (FMECA), which some practitioners may wish to use for highly critical systems. Gerrard et al. (2002) and Peltier (2001) both provide additional information on security risk analysis.

Recycling

Ideally, the architects of the system being tested will have chosen the security measures to implement based upon a risk analysis of the security threats posed against the system. If this is the case and the results of the risk analysis are still available, one approach for determining what should be tested and in what order is to simply review the results of the original analysis. Then tests can be designed to specifically check that each safeguard specified by the design (as a means of mitigating each identified threat) has been implemented correctly or if it has been implemented at all.

Of course, the danger with recycling an earlier risk analysis is that any previous assumptions are no longer valid. For instance, at the time a new technology was selected to be used in the implementation of a Web site, there may not have been any known security issues associated with the technology. With the passage of time, problems may have surfaced, affecting the assumptions made during the original risk analysis. With the benefit of hindsight, it would be prudent for the security-testing team to review the original analysis before reusing it to make sure any previously made assumptions are still valid.

The following are brief explanations of three different techniques that may have been used by the system's architects to help them assess what safeguards to implement: asset audits, fault and attack trees, and gap analysis.

Asset Audit

One strategy used by some practitioners is that of an asset audit. This approach focuses on which assets (typically confidential information, but potentially including physical assets as well) the organization possesses and then attempts to determine if they are being sufficiently protected. Krutz et al. (2001) provides additional information on asset audits. The following is an outline of this approach:

- Identify all the data that the system being tested stores or has access to. Although customer records and bank accounts should obviously be included, less obvious candidates for inclusion are files containing program source code, photographic images, backup tapes, or other intellectual property. Care should therefore be taken to ensure that the list of identified assets is truly comprehensive.

- For each identified data asset, the means by which the data arrives and leaves the system should be determined (possibly using good old-fashioned dataflow diagramming techniques), because each entry and exit point also poses a security risk.

- Determine which mechanisms (threats) could be employed by an attacker to acquire this information as the data enters the system, is stored on the system, or leaves the system. For example, an intruder could walk into a computer room and steal a backup tape or use a service running on a server (such as a Telnet) to view data files stored on the machine.

- Once the threats have been identified, an approximation should be made of how likely it is that each threat will be realized.

- Assign a monetary value to the impact of data being destroyed, unavailable for a certain period of time, stolen, or corrupted. This may depend to a large extent on how long the organization could continue to operate with the problem.

- Develop a security policy (or modify an existing policy) that specifies the safe-guards that need to be implemented in order to protect all of the organization's critical data.

- Although not necessarily a step in the asset audit that developed the security policy, the measures specified in the policy should be checked to ensure that they have been implemented correctly.

One issue that this technique quickly raises is the additional security risks associated with distributing confidential information across multiple locations instead of in a heavily controlled central location. For example, when temporary copies of confidential data are cached on multiple hosts to improve performance, a speed-versus-security dilemma occurs, which the designer of a system must respond to by making trade-offs.

Fault Trees and Attack Trees

An asset audit takes the approach of focusing on what an organization needs to protect. An alternative approach, or one that can be used in combination with an asset audit, is to think about what a potential assailant would want to acquire and then consider all the ways in which the attacker could go about trying to obtain the sought-after information.

To help document the different tactics that an attacker could use, some practitioners have adopted the fault-tree analysis or failure-tree analysis (FTA) technique, which is commonly used by the manufacturing industry. FTA is a deductive, top-down method for analyzing a system's design. It involves specifying a root event to analyze (such as a physical break-in to a computer room), followed by identifying all the associated events (or second-tier events) that could cause the root event to occur.

Fault trees are generally depicted graphically using a logical structure that consists of *and/or* decision boxes. Sometimes more than one second-tier event needs to occur before the root event is triggered. In this case, these second-tier events would be arranged under an *and* box, meaning that all the second-tier events connected by the *and* would need to happen in order to cause the root event to occur. All single second-tier events that would trigger the root event on their own would be grouped under an *or* box. Leveson (1995) provides additional information on fault trees, while Relex Software (www.relexsoftware.com) offers a tool (Relex) designed to support a fault-tree analysis. Figure 10.1 shows a fault tree for an attacker trying to acquire a system administrator's password.

Attack trees are a variation of *fault trees*. An attack tree provides a formal, methodical way of describing who, when, why, how, and with what probability an intruder might attack a system. It thereby helps identify potential gaps in the current set of security policies.

Potential attacks against a system are represented using the same tree-like structure used to illustrate a fault tree. The root node of the tree represents the ultimate goal of the attacker, and the branch and leaf nodes illustrate the different ways of achieving that goal. The following steps outline how an attack tree can be built:

1. Identify all the different types of intruders that might want to attack the system. This would include script kiddies, accomplished attackers, dishonest employees, organized criminals, competitors, foreign governments, and so on.

2. For each type of adversary, consider what their ultimate goal(s) might be. Each goal will then be used as the root node for a separate attack tree. Although many of the attackers may share common goals, if their respective resources differ significantly, it may make more sense to model their respective capabilities using separate trees than to show a composite view of their combined capabilities in a single tree (although two or more trees may share common subtrees).

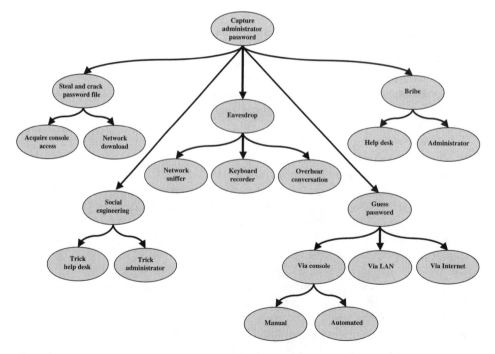

Figure 10.1   Fault tree example.

3. Identify all the possible ways in which an attacker could hope to achieve each goal; these tactics then become the second-tier goals that hang off the root node (goal).

4. For each second-tier goal, consider whether this sub-goal could be accomplished in several different ways. For each strategy that could be employed to obtain a subgoal, create a third-tier goal connected to the second-tier goal that it supports.

5. This process should be repeated until each of the leaf nodes on the tree are specified as a single, clearly defined approach.

6. Evaluate each attack path using criteria such as the likelihood of this approach being attempted, the impact to the business should the goal be reached, and the ease (cost) with which safeguards can be put in place to block the attack.

7. Modify the existing security policy (or if none exists, specify a new one) that specifies the safeguards that need to be implemented in order to block all the critical attack paths.

8. Once the measures specified in the policy have been applied, they should be checked to ensure that they have been implemented correctly.

One drawback with this approach is that it requires the analyst to be sufficiently educated in the ways of all the different types of attackers in order to accurately predict which strategies they may choose to use. For this reason, this approach is probably not an ideal technique for a novice security tester who may not have the insight needed to use this procedure (and may even prove challenging to a seasoned veteran). Schneier (2000), Viega et al. (2001), Cigital Labs (www.cigitallabs.com), and Counterpane Internet Security (www.counterpane.com) provide additional information on attack trees.

Gap Analysis

A gap analysis is another strategy that can be used to determine how complete a system's security measures are. The purpose of a gap analysis is to evaluate the discrepancies (or gaps) between an organization's vision of where it wants to be and its current reality. In the realm of security testing, the analysis is typically accomplished by establishing the extent to which the system meets the requirements of a specific internal or external standard (or checklist). Examples of external security standards include BS 7799 (for more information, go to www.bsi-global.com) and ISO 17799 and 15408 (for details, go to www.iso.ch). The analysis may also optionally make recommendations on which gaps should be plugged and how.

If the gap analysis is to be conducted by comparing the system undergoing a test against a standard list of items that need to be checked, the rigor of the analysis will depend to a large extent on the comprehensiveness and detail of the specified checks. A loosely worded checklist intended for a wide range of applications is more likely to be open to interpretation than a technology- and application-specific standard, and therefore less likely to provide the same degree of assurance. Of course, the downside to using a platform-specific standard is the time and skill needed to initially put one together and then keep it up-to-date as the technology evolves and as new weaknesses are discovered and subsequently patched. Greenbridge Management (www.green-bridge.com), the Praxiom Research Group (www.praxiom.com), and the Victoria Group (www.victoriagroup.com) provide additional information on the gap analysis technique.

Test Priority

The security-testing team's work is simplified if it is able to inherit and reuse a comprehensive risk analysis that has already been performed on the target of the testing effort. Unfortunately, this scenario seldom occurs. If the testing team is unable to inherit a previous risk analysis, the team would be well advised to conduct its own risk analysis for the purpose of deciding which tests should be given the highest priority, and test design and execution should be scheduled accordingly. Any testing team that does not perform some form of risk analysis runs the risk that some of the most critical risks to the system will not be tested. Such tests may be scheduled to be done at the end of the process, and due to a time crunch, they would quite probably be omitted, leaving the system dangerously exposed.

The following sections describe a risk analysis that can be done relatively quickly for the purpose of assisting the security-testing team as they try to decide which areas of the system should be tested first and most comprehensively. This process does not purport to be precise or necessarily the appropriate approach for selecting security defenses. It is merely a quick and simple way of systematically assigning priorities to the collection of tests that the testing team would ideally want to perform, but either know for certain or suspect that they will not have sufficient time to actually execute.

Device Inventory

The first step in the risk analysis process is to build an inventory of all the devices that are to be tested. Hopefully, this should already have been completed (at least at a high level) when the scope of the testing effort was defined (refer back to Chapter 3 on identifying the scope of the security-testing project). The amount of descriptive detail to include in the device inventory will depend upon how large and complicated the system to be tested is. For instance, for larger installations, using static IP addresses or

---

TECHNIQUE HISTORY

The approach outlined in this section is derived from a test-prioritizing technique that Rick Craig devised while conducting a risk analysis of U.S. military computer systems for the purpose of determining security-testing priorities. A more detailed explanation of the approach as it applies to testing all software features (usability, performance, functionality, and so on) can be found in his book, *Systematic Software Testing* (Craig et al. [2002]).

hostnames may be a more accurate way of identifying a specific hardware device than using generic role names, such as Web Server 1. Each of the identified devices may be further described by specifying the key software and data components that are present on the device. The software installed on a particular device will, to a large degree, determine which vulnerabilities may be present for that device, while the data stored on the device will influence the impact on the business should a particular threat be realized. Each entry in the device inventory (sometimes referred to as a test objective inventory) will subsequently be evaluated to determine what degree of testing (if any) will be applied to it. Table 10.1 depicts an example layout structure for a device inventory.

Threats

Once a device inventory has been compiled, the next step in this process is to list the different security threats (or failure modes) that each hardware device and software component faces. Table 10.2 illustrates a worksheet for recording the threats that a Web site could face.

The possible threats could be determined by identifying the specific exploits that could cause such threats to occur. "A group of drone servers infected with the Stacheldraht tool may be used to launch a tribal-flood network style denial-of-service attack." Although going into such detail may make designing a test case that can establish whether or not a system is susceptible to this sort of attack easier, for the purposes of assigning a testing priority it is probably overkill. Instead, describing in more generic terms groups of similar exploits that pose substantially the same threat should help to keep the list of exploits to a more manageable size. For example, "Exploitable third-party CGI scripts are present" may be more useful at this stage than listing each individual CGI script that's known to be exploitable.

Note a device, threat, and exploit ID column can be added to make referencing each of the device, threat, and exploit combinations easier. A common way by which a list of threats may be compiled is to host a *brainstorming workshop*. Ideally, the workshop candidates would have different skill sets and knowledge domains. For instance, candidates would include network administrators and engineers, application developers and testers, security officers and consultants, auditors, and so on.

To make the workshop more productive, the security-testing team may wish to put together an initial candidate list of threats to prompt the workshop discussions. This candidate list may be based on an inventory produced in a previous workshop or the team's own research and experiences. The participants in the workshop can then initially focus on adding threats that have not yet been identified, later removing threats that do not appear to be worth testing, and merging or splitting threats into more meaningful and manageable groupings.

Some threats may be removed during the course of the workshop because they are considered extremely unlikely, would have a negligible effect on the business if they were to happen, or are too impractical to reliably test for. Their removal and the associated rationale for their removal should be documented, thereby allowing future risk analysis to reexamine any assumptions made and subsequently reevaluate the threat's removal.

Table 10.1 Layout Structure Example for a Device Inventory

DEVICE ID	DEVICE DESCRIPTION	KEY SOFTWARE COMPONENTS	KEY DATA COMPONENTS
Internal			
1	Perimeter firewall	Embedded operating system	Firewall rules.
2	Web server 1	Windows 2000, IIS (HTTP only), ASP, SSI, CGI, host-based IDS, and Web-server-tier portion of the application	Web server and IDS logs. Non-sensitive data such as image files and source code for the portion of the application not requiring a user to login.
3	Web server 2	Windows 2000, IIS (HTTP and HTTPS), ASP, SSI, CGI, host-based IDS, and Web-server-tier portion of the application	Web server and IDS logs. Source code for the portion of the application requiring a user to login.
4	Web server 3	Windows 2000 and FTP	Publicly available reports.
5	Load balancer	Embedded operating system	Routing restrictions (if any).
6	Local area network (LAN)	TCP/IP and Ethernet	LAN data communication between different tiers of the application.
7	Demilitarized Zone (DMZ) firewall	Embedded operating system	Firewall rules.
8	Internal switch	Embedded operating system	Routing tables.
9	Network sniffer	Windows 2000 and Network-based IDS	IDS logs.
10	Application server	UNIX, application-server-tier portion of the application, and host-based IDS	IDS logs, lots of application .tmp files, and an application audit trail.
11	Database server	UNIX, Oracle DBMS, host-based IDS, and database-server-tier portion of the application being tested	DBMS and IDS logs, application data.

(continues)

Table 10.1 Layout Structure Example for a Device Inventory (*continued*)

DEVICE ID	DEVICE DESCRIPTION	KEY SOFTWARE COMPONENTS	KEY DATA COMPONENTS
12	Network controller and Domain Name System (DNS) server	Windows 2000	DNS lookup tables as well as network user IDs and passwords.
13	Backup network controller and DNS server	Windows 2000	DNS lookup tables as well as network user IDs and passwords.
14	Computer room desktop	Windows 2000	Local password file.
15	Gateway firewall (connection to legacy system)	Embedded operating system	Firewall rules.
16	Computer room printer	Embedded operating system	N/A
17	Physical security of all hosts in the computer room	N/A	All of the above.
18	Physical security of all cabling at the host site	N/A	LAN data communication component of the application and any system software communication.
19	And so on . . .		
External			
32	ISP router	Unknown	Routing restrictions (if any).
33	Internet	Unknown	WAN data communication component of the application.
34	Client machine	Any hardware, operating system, browser, and plug-in combination. Client-tier portion of the application	Browser cached files and Web site cookie.

Note: The Device ID column may be populated with an organization's existing inventory-tracking ID, vendor serial number, or with a new ID assigned by the security-testing team, whichever is easiest to implement.

Table 10.2 Example Worksheet for Recording Threats

DEVICE/ THREAT/ EXPLOIT ID	DEVICE DESCRIPTION	THREAT	POSSIBLE CAUSES (EXPLOITS)
1.1.1	Perimeter firewall	Legitimate network traffic is unable to pass through firewall.	Denial-of-service attack.
1.1.2			Physical thief or damage to the firewall.
1.1.3			An intruder changes the firewall's rules to block everything or more than it did before.
1.2.1		Unauthorized network traffic is permitted to pass through the firewall.	Wrongly configured firewall rules.
1.2.2			An intruder changes the firewall rules (possibly using vendor default user ID/password).
2.1.1	Web server 1	An unauthorized process may be run on the server using system-administrator-level privileges.	Exploitable third-party CGI scripts are present.
2.1.2			Easily guessable system administrator user ID and password.
2.2.1		Confidential information (source code, data files, system configuration information, and so on) stored on the server can be altered (appended, changed, or deleted).	File and directory shares are not adequately protected.
2.2.2			Unneeded services are left enabled on the Web server. An example would be NetBIOS on ports 135 through 139.

(continues)

Table 10.2 Example Worksheet for Recording Threats *(continued)*

DEVICE/ THREAT/ EXPLOIT ID	DEVICE DESCRIPTION	THREAT	POSSIBLE CAUSES (EXPLOITS)
2.3.1		Confidential information stored on the server can be deduced, viewed online, or downloaded.	Perimeter firewall does not block inappropriate communication. DNS zone transfers are an example.
2.3.2			User account with null password is present.
2.3.3			Unneeded services are left enabled on the Web server. FTP is an example.
2.4.1		An unauthorized process may be run on the server using limited privileges.	Canned buffer overflow exists for installed system software.
2.4.2			Server wrongly trusts an insecure server.
2.4.3			Server Side Include (SSI) options are misconfigured.
2.5.1		Access to the server's functionality is lost.	Denial-of-service attack.
2.5.2			Physical theft or damage to the server.
2.5.3			An intruder acquires control of the server and disables the functionality.
3.1	Web server 2	… and so on.	… and so on.

Note: A device, threat, and exploit ID column can be added to make referencing each of the device, threat, and exploit combinations easier.

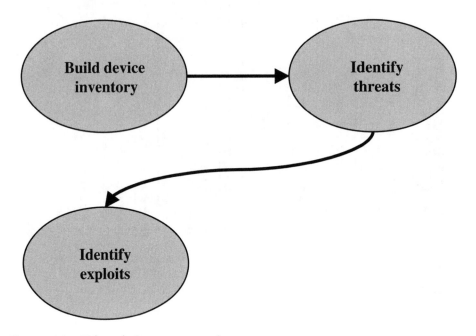

Figure 10.2 Risk analysis process overview.

The outcome of the workshop should be a worksheet that may not list every conceivable threat, but it should be comprehensive enough to have hopefully identified all the system's significant threats. If time permits, this threat list can be validated by researching the various exploit-tracking databases to ensure that the list is comprehensive and up-to-date (see Table 4.2 for a sample list of such databases.) Figure 10.2 summarizes the steps performed in this research process.

Business Impact

What would be the business impact on the organization if a threat were to be realized? Unfortunately, every security breach has the potential to escalate, so the typical gut reaction of a security tester is to rate the severity of every potential breach as critical. Although assigning a value of *critical* to each threat may help to stress the importance of security testing to senior management, it does not help a security-testing team prioritize their testing effort (not every test case can be run first). While technicians such as network engineers and security analysts are often best suited to determine the likelihood of a particular exploit occurring, the users or owners (or their proxies) of the system are usually in the best position to judge how great an impact each security failing might be on the business. Of course, these users may require the help of a knowledgeable security expert in order for them to convert a security threat into a business impact that they can comprehend and thereby accurately assess.

It would be nice to specify the business impact in terms of dollars (a quantitative assessment), but trying to put an exact monetary figure on the cost of an intruder being able to execute a shell command on a Web server is hard to do. Instead, it may prove easier to apply an approach that uses a qualitative assessment. For example, one can simply rank the threats that have been identified, placing the most undesirable threats near the top of the order and the threats that have the least relative impact at the bottom.

A relative severity can then be assigned to each threat. Although some risk analysis techniques identify many different degrees of severity, for the purposes of identifying test priority, three categories typically prove sufficient. The three levels of severity are as follows:

- **High.** Of all the threats identified for this system, these have the greatest potential impact on the business.

- **Medium.** These threats would still have a significant impact on the business, but in comparison to the ones listed in the high category, they would be relatively moderate.

- **Low.** These would have a small or negligible impact when compared to the previous threats.

Note that the key word here is *relative*. Because this process is trying to determine the testing priority, the ultimate goal is to determine which test to run first, which means that even the most trivial of systems will have some threats that are relatively high compared to other threats. Table 10.3 illustrates the relative business impact of some of the threats that were identified in Table 10.2.

From a test priority perspective, it would be convenient if a third of all the threats could be assigned to each of the three categories. In reality, the dividing point between a high impact and a medium impact may not happen exactly one-third of the way down the list, which is fine. But an analysis that results in 90 percent of the threats being assigned a relative severity of high will diminish the usefulness of the analysis for test priority purposes.

RATING VARIANCE

A rating system that is predominately subjective or judgmental in nature (such as assigning low, medium, or high values to the business impact in a risk analysis) and demonstrates a wide variation in the values assigned to a specific entry by the raters may indicate that the raters do not possess enough information to make a valid assessment. For example, if two of the four raters feel a particular threat is extremely improbable (low), but the other two feel that it very likely (high), then the average rating is going to be in the middle (medium), a rating that no one currently concurs with. Under such circumstances, the group would be well advised to postpone making a final assignment until they have had a chance to debate why they have such differing opinions and, if deemed necessary, to conduct further research on the topic.

Table 10.3 Assigning a Relative Business Impact to Threats

DEVICE/ THREAT ID	DEVICE DESCRIPTION	THREAT	RELATIVE BUSINESS IMPACT	COMMENT
1.1	Perimeter firewall	Legitimate network traffic is unable to pass through firewall.	M	Some loss of revenue and increased help desk calls. Impact to business would increase the longer the outage lasted.
1.2	Perimeter firewall	Unauthorized network traffic is permitted to pass through the firewall.	H	Failure of perimeter firewall would potentially allow intruders to try and compromise any (or all) of the machines in the DMZ. The interior firewall may still provide security to the internal LAN.
2.1	Web server 1	An unauthorized process may be run on the server using system-administrator-level privileges.	H	Gives intruder access to all confidential information stored on machine. A concern exists that the machine could be used as a drone in a distributed denial-of-service attack against another Web site (the hardware and bandwidth has a high capacity) or as a host for launching intrusion attempts against other networks.
2.2	Web server 1	Confidential information (source code, data files, system configuration information, and so on) stored on the server can be altered (appended, changed, or deleted).	H	A worse situation than being able to read the information, this will likely make the cleanup process messier. If access allows for the uploading of an attacker's toolkit, this breech may allow the attacker to escalate their privileges, ultimately taking full control of the server.

(continues)

Table 10.3 Assigning a Relative Business Impact to Threats (*continued*)

DEVICE/ THREAT ID	DEVICE DESCRIPTION	THREAT	RELATIVE BUSINESS IMPACT	COMMENT
2.3	Web server 1	Confidential information stored on the server can be deduced, viewed online, or downloaded.	M	It is suspected that developers may have hard-coded database userIDs and passwords into the application source code residing on this server. Also, the current (questionable) system design calls for caching in-progress financial transactions on the Web server.
2.4	Web server 1	An unauthorized process may be run on the server with limited privileges.	M	The Web server is in a DMZ and should only have marginally more access privileges to the inner network (application server and so on) than any other machine of the Internet. An intruder may be able to access confidential information and/or escalate his or her authority to a system administrator's level.
2.5	Web server 1	Access to the server's functionality is lost.	L	In the short term, spare capacity in other servers should be able to pick up the slack, assuming other servers are still functional. If all servers go down, the application is not mission critical and the organization can survive until the backup site comes online.

Note: The business impact assessment and comments in this table are intended to illustrate this process, not provide an assessment for every organization's Web site, as the consequences of a Web site being compromised will vary significantly from site to site.

Risk Likelihood

Some exploits are far easier to accomplish than others. For example, a remote port scan is a lot easier to run than trying to find and exploit a new application buffer overflow. The reward for some successfully executed techniques is much greater than for others. For example, correctly guessing a system administrator's userID and password combination is likely to be much more satisfying than reviewing the results of a ping sweep. In addition, in order to be successful, some exploits may depend on the existence of more than one security failing (such as a perimeter firewall permitting a DNS transfer to take place and the DNS server fulfilling this request). It is not surprising that intruders favor some exploits over others; therefore, the probability of different exploits being performed successfully will vary and this should influence the priorities assigned to the tests designed to detect the existence of these vulnerabilities.

Up until this point, the relative likelihood of each possible security failure occurring has not been considered (with the exception of ruling out threats that are so unlikely to happen that it would be a poor use of time to continue to include them in the risk analysis). Unfortunately, trying to accurately gauge the likelihood of one type of exploit over another is not an easy thing to do, especially when exploit popularity changes by the month. Fundamentally, this problem can be resolved in one of two ways: using metrics specific to the organization or using generic industry metrics.

Internal Metrics

The benefit of using information that is directly derived from an organization's own experiences is that it is theoretically a better gauge of the exploits that are likely to be employed by potential attackers against this specific system. Possible methods of collecting exploit likelihood metrics for a specific organization include the following:

- Reviewing an organization's own records of failed (and successful) exploit attempts. An example would be reviewing IDS reports.

- Reviewing the results of a honey pot project (see Chapter 8 for an explanation of honey pots).

- Extending the workshop used to identify security threats (described earlier in this chapter) to also include an estimation of exploit likelihood.

External Metrics

Unfortunately, gathering organization-specific metrics can be time consuming or impossible to calculate due to a complete lack of raw data or data that is too small a sample to be statistically valid. The latter would be the case if an organization were connecting a legacy system to the Internet for the first time and there had therefore never been an opportunity for an external intruder to attack the system. It is prudent to not only take into account any metrics collected internally, but also to consider externally gathered metrics. Possible avenues for externally researching exploit popularity include the following:

- Reviewing the exploit lists on Web sites that report on security incidents. Appendix B lists the top-20 critical Internet security vulnerabilities as identified by the System Administration, Networking, and Security (SANS) Institute (www.sans.org).

- Seeking the recommendations of external security consultants.

- Reviewing publications (such as the latest edition of *Hacking Exposed* by Scambray et al. (2001), which rates specific exploits by popularity).

Whether one (or more) of the previously mentioned methods of research is employed, or the security-testing team decides to rely on their own gut feeling, each identified exploit should be assigned a relative probability of being successful. This is assuming no additional security tests were to be done to determine the existence or nonexistence of the vulnerability.

Since assigning the relative likelihood is a subjective matter, using scales with many options, such as 1 to 100, may result in more time being spent debating whether or not a particular exploit has a relative probability of 66 or 67 than it helps with prioritizing the testing effort. (It may also lead the casual reviewer to believe that the rating is more precise than it actually is.) Instead, a simple categorization of *high*, *medium*, and *low* may prove to be sufficient. Table 10.4 depicts a portion of the inventory used to document the relative likelihood of specific exploits being successfully employed against some of the devices found in Table 10.2.

Calculating Relative Criticality

Once high, medium, and low values have been assigned to the likelihood of an exploit being successful, and the impact to the business should the event occur, it then becomes possible to combine these values into a single assessment of the criticality of this potential vulnerability. For example, assigning a numeric value of 3 to a high, 2 to a medium, 1 to a low, and then adding the two numeric values together will result in a criticality between 2 and 6, as depicted in Figure 10.3.

Regardless of whether addition or multiplication is used to combine the two variables, the resulting threat/exploit matrix can be sorted using the calculated criticality. Table 10.5 illustrates this for some of the threats and exploits mentioned previously.

This risk analysis approach has now attempted to sort into a *pecking order* the various threats that the system being tested may foreseeably be expected to face. This enables the security-testing team to identify the system's greatest exposures and therefore the areas that the testing effort should focus on.

If created before a system is built, this list may also be used by the system's designers to review their planned implementation, paying particular attention to ensuring that any highly critical threats are not solely protected by a single security measure (or single point of failure).

Identify and Assign Candidate Tests

Once an objective assessment of the relative exposures that threaten a system's security has been determined, it becomes much easier to decide which vulnerabilities should

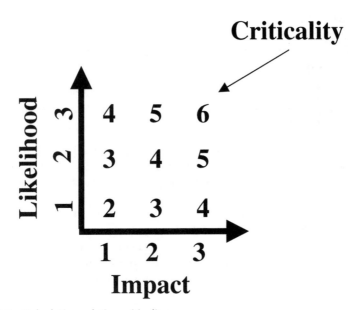

Figure 10.3   Calculating relative criticality.

Note that multiplying instead of adding the two variables will result in a scale of 1 to 9 and marginally increase the criticality of medium/medium pairs over low/high pairs.

ideally be tested for first. Tests can be designed to check for specific vulnerabilities and scheduled for execution depending upon the criticality of the vulnerability (or vulnerabilities) that the test is designed to expose.

It is possible that some threats will be ranked so low that they may not warrant any tests being assigned at all. Even if this is the case, the threat has still been identified, evaluated, and documented, enabling a future risk analysis to revisit any assumptions made and possibly change them in light of new information.

Priority Modifiers

The preceding steps are intended to help the security-testing team draft an outline of their security-testing schedule, the key word being *draft*. The output from this approach should not be regarded as the *final say* on which tests should be executed first, but rather a starting point from which other criteria can be applied. Some of the other factors that should be taken into account before finalizing the testing schedule (and will vary in importance from project to project) include the following:

Test cost and ease of implementation.   Some tests are extremely easy and cheap to run—for example, externally launched port scans using a freeware tool—while other tests may be quite expensive in terms of monetary cost, elapsed time, staff resources, or political capital—for example, purchasing some of the most sophisticated security assessment tools cost tens of thousands of dollars,

Table 10.4 Assigning a Relative Likelihood to Potential Exploits

DEVICE/ THREAT/ EXPLOIT ID	DEVICE DESCRIPTION	THREAT	EXPLOIT	RELATIVE LIKELIHOOD	COMMENT
1.1.1	Perimeter firewall	Legitimate network traffic is unable to pass through firewall.	Denial-of-service attack.	L	Large surplus network capacity means firewall not likely to be a bottleneck in a denial-of-service attack.
1.1.2			Physical theft or damage to the firewall.	L	Box is in a secured room.
1.1.3			An intruder changes the firewall rules to block everything.	M	Firewall may still have default account active.
1.2.1		Unauthorized network traffic is permitted to pass through the firewall.	Wrongly configured firewall rules.	H	Previous inspection of rules found several errors.
1.2.2			An intruder changes the firewall rules.	M	Firewall may still have default account active.
2.1.1	Web server 1	An unauthorized process may be run on the server using system-administrator-level privileges.	Vulnerable CGI script installed on Web server.	L	CGI capability (theoretically) disabled.

Table 10.5 Calculating Threat/Exploit Criticality

DEVICE/ THREAT/ EXPLOIT ID	DEVICE DESCRIPTION	THREAT	RELATIVE BUSINESS IMPACT	EXPLOIT	RELATIVE LIKELIHOOD	RELATIVE CRITICALITY
1.1.1	Perimeter firewall	Legitimate network traffic is unable to pass through firewall.	M (2)	Distributed denial-of-service attack.	L (1)	2 (1+1)
1.1.2			M (2)	Physical theft of or damage to the firewall.	L (1)	3 (2+1)
1.1.3			M (2)	An intruder changes the firewall rules to block everything.	M (2)	4 (2+2)
1.2.1		Unauthorized network traffic is permitted to pass through the firewall.	H (3)	Wrongly configured firewall rules.	H (3)	6 (3+3)
1.2.2			H (3)	An intruder changes the firewall rules.	M (2)	5 (3+2)
2.1.1	Web server 1	An unauthorized process may be run on the server using system-administrator-level privileges.	H (3)	Vulnerable CGI script installed on Web server.	L (1)	4 (3+1)

and manually identifying and validating every service running on the hosts being assessed can be quite time consuming.

Test dependencies.   Some tests only make sense to run if a previous test has already passed and should therefore be scheduled to occur after the former test is executed. For instance, there is little point in trying to run a brute-force, password-cracking algorithm against a product's password file if the vendor's default userIDs and passwords are found to be still active.

Pretesting dependencies.   It's quite probable that some components of the system will be available for testing before others, typically a reflection of development priorities and dependencies. It would be nice if the development team factored in the testing team's priorities when finalizing the development schedule, but unfortunately this is not always the case.

Post-testing dependencies.   If other (nontesting) project activities are dependent upon the results of a specific test, it may be more important to schedule that test early in the testing effort in order to help the project as a whole proceed more quickly. For instance, finding out that an organization's standard operating system install is missing a critical security patch is a lot more helpful *before* the organization deploys 200 machines to 3 different locations than afterwards.

Test coverage.   Some tests can be used to mitigate multiple exploits. For example, running a security assessment tool may check for the existence of numerous vulnerabilities.

Scheduling conflicts.   It could be that the DBA is going on vacation next week. Executing tests that focus on the database during this week may be less productive than waiting for the DBA to return.

Fragile application code.   Some parts of the application may be noticeably more complex, have more interfaces, have recently been significantly modified, or have a history of excessive defects. All these traits typically indicate that the application code is likely to be prone to future defects (functional or security related) and should therefore also be considered for more extensive testing.

Regression tests.   These tests consist of reviewing the test logs of earlier security assessments for security holes that were previously identified and may not have been adequately fixed.

Previous history.   If this consideration wasn't factored in earlier in the analysis, then memories of recent attacks, especially *accidental* intrusions by employees, should be considered.

Senior management's preferences.   For many security-testing teams, it's an unfortunate fact of life that testing priorities will be influenced to some degree by senior management's willingness to *invest* in certain types of testing more than others. For example, the CIO may be quite willing to write a one-time check for an external-penetration-testing firm to try and break into the organization's internal network, but be less willing to sanction tests designed to find vulnerabilities potentially available to internal employees, because "We trust everybody here." Although a well-documented risk analysis may help educate senior management and thereby reduce any irrational interference, this factor may not be completely eliminated.

Common sense.   This process should be a helpful guideline, not an inflexible mandate etched in stone.

Test Schedule

Once this set of factors has been evaluated and the test schedule has been updated to reflect these considerations, it becomes possible to determine the point where this phase of security testing will theoretically come to a close. This is typically due to funding, project deadlines, or some other project constraint, rather than the exhaustion of possible tests. Used wisely, a prioritized test schedule with a cutoff point showing where the resources will run out and which low-priority tests will therefore not be run can make a powerful ally when negotiating with senior management for additional funding.

In addition, if the test schedule has been front-loaded to perform the most critical tests first, an unplanned reduction in the time or resources available to conduct the testing can be handled by removing the less critical tests from the test schedule. This would not be possible if the tests' criticality was unknown or if the testing done to date had focused on the easy but less critical tests, which perhaps would be done in order to make a manager's "tests completed" metric look artificially better. Figure 10.4 summarizes all the steps performed in this process.

If warranted, this style of risk analysis can be used as a starting point for conducting a more rigorous analysis, such as a full-fledged FMECA.

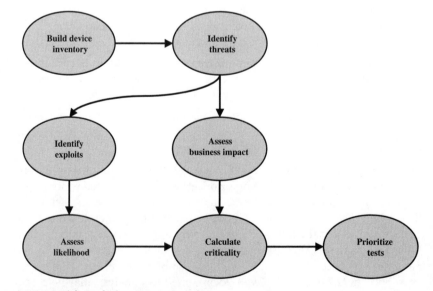

Figure 10.4   Risk analysis process overview.

Failure Mode, Effects, and Criticality Analysis (FMECA)

The Failure Mode, Effects, and Criticality Analysis (FMECA), or its abbreviated version, Failure Mode and Effects Analysis (FMEA), is a rigorous approach to quantifying and prioritizing the risks associated with a product. FMECA is extensively used by organizations with extremely low risk tolerances (such as the military, space agencies, and manufactures of medical devices) as a systematic process for identifying potential design and process failures before they occur, with the intent to eliminate them or minimize the risk. This approach can be adopted for analyzing the potential failure of a system's security defenses.

To quickly (if rather crudely) convert the information gathered by the risk analysis described in the previous section of this chapter to the format used by an FMECA study, you would perform the following steps:

1. Replace the term *likelihood* with *occurrence* and use a scale of 1 to 10 (1 meaning not likely to happen) instead of high, medium, and low.

2. Replace the term *business impact* with *severity* and use a scale of 1 to 10 (1 meaning negligible consequence) instead of high, medium, and low.

3. Add an additional variable, *detection* (described later), to the matrix, using a scale of 1 to 10 (1 meaning it is obvious and is therefore extremely likely to be detected and 10 indicating that the current detection mechanisms are extremely unlikely to detect this problem).

4. Multiply the three variables together to produce a risk priority number (RPN).

Detection (perhaps easier to think of as *detectability*) is an assessment of the likelihood that the current set of preventive measures (design reviews, unit testing, and so on) will detect the vulnerability, thus preventing it from reaching the production environment. The theory here is that it is more important to do additional testing for potential failures that are not likely to be caught using existing detection measures than for those that will probably be detected without further scrutiny. Unfortunately, in a security analysis, unless reliable metrics have been collected previously, relying upon a gut feeling to estimate this value is unlikely to be very accurate. For instance, most security testers would be hard-pressed to estimate the probability of a misconfigured firewall rule being detected before it is placed into service, or that a network-based intrusion detection system will not notice an intruder communicating to a compromised server.

If an objective measure of detection can be assigned to each vulnerability, then multiplying all three variables (occurrence, severity, and detection) together will generate a RPN, which may range from 1 (low significance) to 1,000 (fire alarm). The vulnerabilities with the highest score represent the greatest threats to the system and should therefore be given the highest priority for risk mitigation or reduction.

To reduce the risk posed by each of these threats, an organization could implement one (or more) of the following actions:

- Rework the design of the system to remove the threat. Unfortunately, it's not always possible to completely remove one threat without creating another.

- Reduce the likelihood of a failure (exploit) occurring. For instance, encrypting data being transmitted over the Internet or a LAN would reduce the probability of an external or internal eavesdropper acquiring sensitive information.

- Reduce the impact on the business should the failure occur. For instance, moving a database off the Web server would reduce the business impact of the Web server being compromised, or developing and testing a contingency plan that utilized a backup site could reduce the amount of time a compromised Web site was unavailable. A variation of this mitigation strategy is for an organization to transfer the risk to another entity. For instance, purchasing a cybercrime insurance policy would provide an organization with compensation to help reduce the impact of a successful attack.

- Improve the organization or system's detection capabilities. An example of this would be designing and executing additional security tests, or installing an intruder detection system on a critical server.

Typically, a combination of these solutions will be employed. Once the remedies have been successfully implemented, the RPN equation can be recalculated to identify the new *riskiest* threats and thereby enable continuous system and process improvement. McDermott et al. (1996), Stamatis (1995), the Haviland Consulting Group (www.fmeca.com), and Relex Software (www.relexsoftware.com) all provide additional information on the FMECA and FMEA techniques, while Relex Software (www.relexsoftware.com) and SkyMark (www.skymark.com) both offer tools (Relex and PathMaker, respectively) designed to support FMECA and FMEA deliverables.

Summary

In a well-funded security-testing project, without the prospect of truncating the period of time available for testing and consequently guaranteeing enough time to perform all the planned tests, the need to do a risk analysis for the purpose of scheduling tests will be less critical. Unfortunately, this is an unlikely scenario for the majority of security-testing teams, who must instead prudently decide how to best expend their limited resources in order to maximize the reduction in an organization's risk exposure. A risk analysis can go a long way toward facilitating a smart test schedule that gives testing priority to tests that are intended to detect vulnerabilities that pose the greatest risk to the organization early on in the testing effort and thereby ensure that the high-priority tests stand the best chance of being executed.

Additionally, using a systematic approach, such as a risk analysis, to put together a test schedule has the added benefit of providing the testing team with test traceability (answering questions such as "Why was this specific test needed?", "How did you test for X vulnerability?" and "Why didn't you check for Y?"). Such an approach may allow for better test coverage estimates, which are useful things to have if the testing team is required to show due diligence.

Epilogue

One thing that is certain about the future of Web security is that it will always be changing. If history is any indicator of the future, as soon as a technology matures enough for its weaknesses to become fully understood and avoidable, the technology will either mutate or be replaced by another newer technology. This metamorphosis can potentially create a whole new set of vulnerabilities waiting to be discovered and subsequently plugged.

At the time of this writing, the next anticipated technology shift is that of Web services. It still remains to be seen how secure Microsoft's .NET or Sun Microsystems's open network environment (Sun ONE) implementations will ultimately be, especially when implemented over a wireless network. When you consider how open and accessible this technology is designed to be, it doesn't take much creativity to imagine how an attacker could try to utilize it for some malicious purpose.

For example, many organizations are considering swapping their electronic data interchange (EDI) connections for simple object address protocol (SOAP) implementations. Effectively, this will replace cryptic and proprietary data formats transmitted over private networks with, self-describing industry-standard data formats, such as Extensible Markup Language (XML) and XML schemas, over the public Internet. Although one of the greatest benefits of using a standard format is that it simplifies the exchange of data between business partners, one of the greatest disadvantages is that an eavesdropper can easily intercept and (unless encrypted) interpret the data. Such an exploit is also made increasingly easier to perform with the continued, widespread adoption of wireless networks.

The intent of Universal Description, Discovery, and Integration (UDDI) online registries is to enable organizations to advertise the Web services they offer and to publish the technical specifications needed to connect to the applications that provide these services. However, it remains to be seen whether or not attackers will be able to utilize information specified in an application's associated UDDI registry entry to locate and gain unauthorized access to these applications.

As Web-service-related vulnerabilities begin to surface (such as CERT notification VU#736923, which relates to Oracles9iAS's implementation of SOAP), relying solely upon the good old firewall to protect an organization's Web services would be a precarious decision. One of the reasons why SOAP was designed to work using Hypertext Transfer Protocol (HTTP) is because HTTP network traffic is comparatively unfettered by many current firewall implementations, thereby making its deployment much easier. Instead, an organization would be well advised to consider a defense-in-depth approach for protecting its electronic assets and execute an associated testing strategy designed to validate that all these defenses have been correctly implemented (and maintained) using this new technology.

PART

Five

Appendixes

An Overview of Network Protocols, Addresses, and Devices

For the benefit of readers who may not be too familiar with the networking terms used in this book, this appendix provides additional background on the network protocols (and associated network addressing issues) commonly used by Web applications, and the network devices typically found on networks used to host a Web site. Lierley (2001), Northcutt et al. (2000), and Skoudis (2001) provide additional introductory explanations of networking concepts geared towards the security tester.

Network Protocols

To reduce network design complexity, the vast majority of modern networks use not one, but several network protocols to facilitate communication between two network devices. These protocols are organized as a series of layers (or levels), each layer building upon the functionality and capabilities offered by the previous layer. Conceptually, this collection of layers is often referred to as a stack of network protocols (or simply the *stack*). An analogy from the desktop PC world would be the way in which a user develops MS Office macros. He or she utilizes the functionality of MS Office, which in turn makes system calls to an operating system, which itself utilizes the desktop's basic input/output system (BIOS) to access hardware devices, such as a hard drive.

The number, names, and purposes of each network layer varies from network architecture to network architecture, which can make interfacing networks that use different protocols problematic. In 1980, in an effort to try and make network protocols more standard and thereby easier to integrate, the International Organization for

Standardization (ISO, www.iso.ch) proposed the Open Systems Interconnection (OSI) model. This model attempted to group the numerous tasks that needed to be performed on a network into seven reference layers, each layer being responsible for a set of specific functions. Ideally, each network protocol would be designed to perform all the functions that belong to a single layer (and no more). Protocols at the same layer would then (theoretically) become interchangeable, but they would not repeat any of the functionality being handled by another layer of this network stack, thereby improving network performance and reducing the complexity of each layer.

Unfortunately, some of the network protocols in use today date back to before 1980 and were therefore not originally designed with the OSI model in mind. In some cases, a protocol's owner (a proprietary vendor or industry committee) has tried to retrofit the protocol into one of the seven OSI layers. As can be seen from the comparison in Table A.1, the network model used by the Internet differs from the OSI model in that it

Table A.1   Internet-to-OSI Network Model Comparison

INTERNET NAME	LAYER	OSI NAME	EXAMPLE PROTOCOLS
Application	7	Application	BOOTP, FTP, HTTP, DNS, LPD, NFS, S-HTTP, SET, SMTP, SNMP, TelNet, and TFTP
	6	Presentation	ASCII, AVI, EDCDIC, GIF, JPEG, and MPEG
	5	Session	Secure Socket Layer (SSL)
Host-to-host	4	Transport	Transmission Control Protocol (TCP) or User Datagram Protocol (UDP)
Internet	3	Network	Internet Protocol (IP), Internet Protocol Security (IPsec), Internet Control Message Protocol (ICMP), Internet Group Membership Protocol (IGMP), Address Resolution Protocol (ARP), and Reverse Address Resolution Protocol (RARP)
Network Access	2	Data Link	ARCNET, Asynchronous Transfer Method (ATM), Compressed Serial Line Internet Protocol (CSLIP), Digital Subscriber Line, (DSL), Ethernet, Frame Relay, Integrated Services Digital Network (ISDN), Point-to-Point Protocol (PPP), Serial Line Internet Protocol (SLIP), Token Bus, and Token Ring
	1	Physical	IEEE 802.x, RS232, V.32, V.34, and V.90

conceptually only defines four separate network protocol layers, instead of the seven defined by the OSI model.

The following sections provide a brief summary of what each OSI layer is intended to accomplish.

Application Layer

The application layer is where all the programs that actually use the network typically reside, the Web being just one of the network applications that functions at this layer. Since this layer is at the top of the stack, its functionality is open-ended, permitting applications to offer services that range from supporting distributed databases to broadcasting live television shows.

Presentation Layer

The presentation layer is charged with transforming data into a format that an application layer program can understand. In effect, the presentation layer provides a

---

HTTP

The hypertext transfer protocol (HTTP) is the application-layer network protocol that is used to transfer Web content between a Web server and its client (typically a browser). Interestingly, a client can send information in more than one way to a Web server using HTTP. The following describes the two most common methods that are used for this purpose.

Get.   Initially conceived as a method to get information from a Web server, in the Get method, any associated data is added to the end of the URL and is transmitted as part of the Query component (note the ? in the following example). Aside from the fact that this information may be truncated when transmitted, it may also be readily seen by anyone viewing the client screen, reviewing their browser's history, or examining the target Web site's logs. Additionally, when the visitor leaves the Web site, this URL (with its embedded data) may be carried over to the next Web site where it can be viewed via the new Web site's logs (this is true regardless of whether or not the communication is encrypted). For example, the following URL's blatant exposure of the userID and password would make it easy for someone else to acquire this particular userID and password combination.

https://www.wiley.com/cgi/login.cgi?uid=888753369&pass=888424749

Post.   Initially conceived as a method for posting information to a Web server, Post is similar to Get but embeds any input information (such as data from a HTML form) into the HTTP body, rather than into the URL. Post thereby avoids the Web log and screen-viewing issues associated with the Get command, which is in part why the Web's governing body, the World Wide Web Consortium (W3C, www.w3c.org), recommends using Post over Get whenever possible.

translation service when the two machines that are trying to communicate with each other are using different data formats, such as EBCDIC and ASCII. Additionally, this layer may be enabled to compress large volumes of data and/or encrypt sensitive information.

Session Layer

The session layer opens a dialog (or session) between the sending and receiving machines. It accomplishes this by using three steps: connection establishment, data transfer, and connection release. Once the session has been established and data transfer has begun, the data can be passed to the presentation layer, where it can potentially be reformatted to make it ready for the application that is waiting to receive it.

The secure sockets layer (SSL) is typically considered to be a session layer in the OSI model, as it utilizes the functionality provided by the transport layer protocols to enhance the service available to the higher-level application layer protocols.

Transport Layer

The transport layer accepts data from the session layer and then chops it up into small chunks of information (typically known as datagrams) that can easily be sent over the network. Conversely, the transport layer is responsible for reassembling the datagrams that it receives, requesting replacements for any that appear to have gotten lost somewhere on their journey across the network.

The Internet uses two layer 4 protocols: the Transmission Control Protocol (TCP) and the User Datagram Protocol (UDP). The TCP protocol attempts to guarantee that any data sent over a network via TCP will ultimately get to its intended destination. It does this at a simplistic level by requesting that the recipient of the data send a confirmation that it has actually received the data (analogous to requesting a return receipt from the postal service when it delivers an item of mail). If no confirmation is received after a predefined period of time, the sender assumes the data was lost and resends it. In comparison, UDP is regarded as a *connectionless* protocol, which means that it effectively *sends and forgets*, offering no guarantee that the data will actually arrive at its intended destination. Such an approach typically allows data to be sent faster, since no confirmation messages are being sent or waited upon. UDP is typically used for streaming video and audio, where losing a few pieces of data here and there is a small price to pay for increased network speed. Web pages, on the other hand, typically use TCP as a means of ensuring that the entire page is received correctly.

Network Layer

The network layer handles the task of actually conveying network packets across the network, resolving issues such as converting logical network addresses (that are easy for humans to remember) into physical addresses, or determining the route a data packet should take across the network.

The layer 3 protocol used by the Internet is called the Internet Protocol (IP). Its specification can be traced back to a 1960s U.S. Department of Defense network research project called ARPANET. For a computer to be directly connected to the Internet, it must use IP as its layer 3 (network) protocol. However, it may potentially utilize the services of any of the lower-layer protocols (data link and physical) in order to support the various application layer protocols that it in turn must support. Figure A.1 illustrates how an Internet data packet might be composed of data from each of the various layers of a network protocol stack.

Data Link Layer

The data link layer organizes the data packets into a series of data frames, transmitting each frame sequentially between two network devices. It is this layer of the network model that is expected to correct errors caused by network *noise* (interference that causes some or the entire network frame to be lost) and negotiate a mutually acceptable transmission speed that both network devices can handle.

Physical Layer

At the physical layer, data is represented as electronic bits in the form of zeros and ones. Layer 1 protocols specify such fundamental communication requirements as when a zero is a zero and when a one is a one (or even what the difference is between two *ones* back to back, and a single *one*). This layer of the model to a large degree will be molded by the physical medium used to convey the data signal (for example, copper wire versus airwaves).

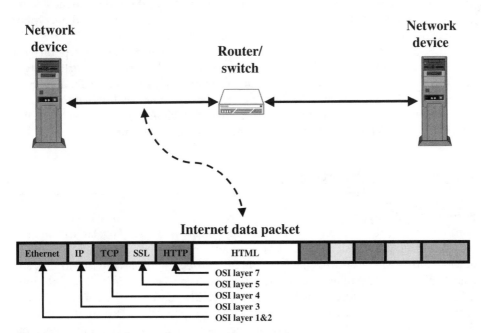

Figure A.1   Internet data packet composition.

Security-Minded Network Protocols

Several different network protocols have been specifically designed to provide secure communication over the Internet (or intranet) via encryption. Secure Hypertext Transfer Protocol (S-HTTP), SSL, and IP Security (IPsec) are three such protocols. The primary difference between these three protocols is the network layer at which that they work.

S-HTTP is a superset of HTTP and is designed to send individual messages securely by encrypting and decrypting the message at the OSI application layer (layer 7). SSL is designed to establish a secure connection between two machines, thereby protecting all communications (not just HTTP-based messages). It achieves this by working down the network *stack*, nearer to the *bits and bytes*, encrypting and decrypting the data at the OSI session layer (layer 5). IPsec is a standard for security at the network packet-processing layer or network communication layer (layer 3 of the OSI model). IPsec actually provides two choices of security service: authentication header (AH), which essentially enables authentication of the sender and integrity (but not encryption) of the data, and encapsulating security payload (ESP), which supports both authentication of the sender and encryption of the data as well.

Since each encryption method works at a different network layer and has slightly different goals, in theory it will be possible to simultaneously use all three to provide extremely secure transmissions. However, in practice the three methods are not equally well supported. First introduced by Netscape in its 2.x-generation browser, SSL has since been implemented in all the leading browsers and Web servers, as well as many other Web-enabled supporting tools. In contrast, S-HTTP is scarcely supported, and the Internet Engineering Task Force (IETF, www.ietg.org) is still working on IPsec. When you also take into consideration that each encryption and decryption increases network latency and places a heavier resource requirement on a CPU, it's understandable that a Web site designer would not want to use an over-engineered, multitiered encryption strategy that has issues communicating with some of its clients. This is why most Web sites today that want to transmit data securely rely upon SSL to do their encryption work directly, or via an application-layer secure protocol that builds upon the functionality of SSL. An example of this would be Secure Electronic Transaction (SET), a protocol designed to ensure the security of financial transactions over the Internet. Additional information on SET can be found at www.setco.org. Table A.2 lists some vendors that provide more background information on encrypting network traffic.

Network Addresses

Surprising as it may seem to many, each network device will typically have more than one network address (the reasons for this situation are many and to a large extent historical). At the most basic network layer (or bottom of the network stack), the media access control (MAC) address (such as aa-bb-cc-dd-ee-ff) enables devices to find and communicate to each other (over relatively short distances) using the Ethernet protocol. The IP network address (such as 123.456.789.123) permits messages to be reliably sent across multiple networks (including, of course, the Internet) using IP. Finally, a device's host name (such as web1.tampa) enables the machine to be more easily identifiable to humans and hence easier to remember and administrate.

Table A.2 Vendors Offering Encryption Solutions

NAME	ASSOCIATED WEB SITE
Baltimore Technologies	www.baltimore.com
Entrust	www.entrust.com
Microsoft	www.microsoft.com
RSA Security	www.rsa.com
ValiCert	www.valicert.com
VeriSign	www.verisign.com

Binding is a term used to describe the process of converting one network address into another. In the case of IP-to-MAC address conversions, this binding is performed using a network utility called the Address Resolution Protocol (ARP), while an IP address to host name conversion is typically performed using a request to a DNS server.

The following sections describe some of the network addressing scenarios that a testing team may encounter (and could possibly cause them confusion) while trying to build (or verify) an inventory of network addresses used by a Web site (often an initial step in conducting a security assessment).

Dynamic IP Addresses

In a dynamically assigned IP configuration (or a Dynamic Host Configuration Protocol [DHCP] implementation), as each network device is powered up, it requests and receives the IP address that it is expected to use while it is up and running. This address may or may not be the same IP address that it had the last time it was assigned an address and may therefore confuse an unsuspecting member of the testing team.

One of the reasons an organization may choose to use DHCP is to reduce the amount of administration needed to maintain a network, because it allows each DHCP device to automatically configure itself based on the values set in the DHCP controller. Although it's quite common for network administrators to assign IP addresses to desktop machines dynamically, it's much less common for servers, routers, and other server-orientated network devices (which are typically the focus of a security assessment) to have their IP addresses dynamically assigned.

Private IP Addresses

Rather than assign each network device an IP address that is universally unique (that is, no other device anywhere in the world has this IP address), many network administrators will configure their network devices which do not have direct access to the outside world to use IP addresses that are only unique on the network they reside upon. The Internet Assigned Numbers Authority (www.iana.org), the governing body that administers IP addresses, has set aside specific ranges of IP addresses for this purpose (such as the IP address range 10.0.0.0 to 10.255.255.255). This technique works because each of the gateways to the outside world can be configured to dynamically translate these nonunique (or private) IP addresses into globally unique ones, a technique normally referred to as network address translation (NAT).

Multiple IP Addresses

Although most network devices will typically only have a single IP address, some network administrators will assign multiple IP addresses to the same device. This can be done by either assigning multiple IP addresses to a single network interface card (NIC) or by installing multiple NICs and assigning each NIC one or more IP addresses.

IP-less Devices

It's possible that one or more of the devices connected to the network will not have an IP address. For example, a network-based intrusion detection system (IDS) appliance may not use an IP address. It may be impossible for an intruder to compromise these machines due to his or her inability to communicate with them remotely. However, these machines could still be compromised by an intruder walking up to the device and using its physical connection to the network for eavesdropping or other subversive purposes.

Misdirecting Host Names

Deducing the physical location of a network device based on its host name will be easier in some organizations than in others. For instance, a network address naming standard that embeds the physical location of a device (together with its primary function) into its *host name* provides an easy way of identifying exactly where the device is located and its primary purpose. For example, the Apache Web server in room 525, which has been assigned a host name of *apache525*, will prove easier to track down than an ad hoc standard. An example of such a standard would be a collection of servers named *ncc1701a, ncc1701b,* and *ncc1701c* (the network administrator who installed these servers is a Star Trek fan and named each server after the registration of a different version of the starship *Enterprise*).

Of course, making the network easier to comprehend for a legitimate network user may also make life easier for an intruder trying to figure out what each machine does. Therefore, a trade-off takes place between the ease of administration and an additional level of *security by obscurity*. One strategy that tries to take advantage of both approaches is to use a standard naming scheme but employ a misdirection strategy. For example, an Apache Web server would have the text *IIS* embedded within its host name, and an MS SQL Server database server would be named something like *oracleprime.*

Network Devices

The modern network is often compromised of many *faceless boxes*. To the casual user of a network, these boxes may seem to be rather mysterious in nature and their purpose may not necessarily be obvious. This section will endeavor to provide a short explanation of what each of these boxes does. It is intended to be a convenient reference, not a definitive, all-encompassing set of definitions. For such detailed descriptions, the reader should consider references such as one or more of the Web-based computer technology encyclopedias (such as www.webopedia.com or www.whatis.com).

Repeater

A repeater is a network device that can be used to extend the effective distance that data can be sent over a network connection. The repeater being used to boost a signal that has become weak because of the physical distance it has already traveled before reaching the repeater.

Hub

Hubs can be thought of as multiport repeaters. Instead of receiving and resending data between just two other network devices, a hub can be used to broadcast a message to several network devices that have been connected to a communal hub. Hubs are simple to implement but tend not to scale well because as data communication rates increase, so do data collisions and retransmit rates.

Bridge

A bridge is a network device that is typically used to connect two network segments together. The bridge blocks network traffic that is internal to one network segment from being forwarded (repeated) into the other network segment that the bridge is connected to. Howeever, a bridge will permit network traffic destined for a device located on another network segment to pass through the bridge to the other network segment.

Bridges can be used to segment a large network into several smaller ones, reducing the amount of network traffic collisions due to high utilization, while still enabling each network device to communicate to any other network device on any of the segments.

Gateway

A gateway is a network device that acts as an entrance to another network. Gateways are often used to restrict unauthorized traffic from passing through and/or for translating data from one network protocol to another (for example, from Ethernet to Token Bus).

SNIFFING SWITCHED NETWORKS

Although some advanced mechanisms can be used for sniffing switched networks, they are much harder for an attacker to use than eavesdropping on a simple hub-based network. Typical drawbacks to a switched network are the additional network administration complexity needed to implement the network and a potentially higher network hardware expense.

Switch (Switching Hub)

Switches differ from hubs in that they only resend (pass on) data to the data packets' ultimate destination. Other machines connected to the network are unlikely to *hear* the data being passed back and forth by two other network devices connected to the same network (a switch can be crudely thought of as a combination of a hub and a bridge). In addition to offering better performance, this approach also makes network eavesdropping (*sniffing*) less feasible, as the amount of data available for the eavesdropper to sniff is greatly reduced.

Router

A router is a network device that is used to connect two or more networks. Unlike many other network devices, the router tries to make intelligent decisions about which way to forward network traffic that it has received (rather than broadcasting it to every possible destination). The forwarding information is maintained in a routing table and is often updated dynamically to include the latest information on the health of the various networks the router is connected to as well as the other distant networks connected to the ones the router is immediately adjacent to.

Brouter

A brouter is a network device that combines the features of a bridge with that of a router.

Network Controller

Network controller is the name given to the device (or devices) that performs network administration tasks, such as detecting the presence of a new network device being added to the network or validating that a userID and password combination entered from any of the network devices it controls is valid.

Load Balancer

A network device is designed to spread the work of processing large amounts of network requests across two or more machines. Numerous strategies can be used to determine which request is sent to which specific destination (such as round-robin, IP multiplexing, and Domain Name System [DNS] redirection), each with its own set of pros and cons.

Servers

Servers typically run general-purpose operating systems (such as some variation of Windows or UNIX) and are loaded with one or more network-aware applications (although technically speaking, a server refers to any device that provides a service of some kind to another device, which is the client). Although such a device may be able to simultaneously run numerous different applications, only using a server to support a single application allows the underlying operating system to be tuned to provide better performance and tighter security. Examples of servers include the following.

Application Server

An application server is dedicated to running applications in a *batch-like* manner, typically any user-interaction component of the application is handled by another component of the application. Some application servers utilize special environmental software designed to share resources more effectively across numerous, small applications such as Enterprise JavaBean (EJB) implementations.

Database Server

For many Web applications, the database access component of a Web transaction is often the most resource-intensive and time-consuming portion of the request to fulfill. For this reason alone, many Web applications are architected with the database installed on a dedicated machine, a server that has been specifically tuned to handle database processing.

DNS Server

DNS is a network address translation program that converts domain names (such as www.wiley.com) into IP addresses (such as 123.456.789.123) and vice versa. This program may be installed on the device used as the network controller or on a separate dedicated machine.

File and Print Server

File servers provide network storage facilities that can be easily shared by all the network users, while print servers enable groups of users to share a scarce resource, such as a high-end color printer.

File Transfer Protocol (FTP) Server

The File Transfer Protocol (FTP) was designed and optimized to transfer large files across a wide area network (WAN) as quickly as possible without losing any data on the way. Standalone FTP servers are often used to isolate irregular network bandwidth utilizations (due to the large files typically associated with this application). They also are used to mitigate any security hole inadvertently left open that an attacker might be able to exploit by uploading a toolkit or downloading a sensitive file using FTP.

Web Server

A Web server uses the HTTP network protocol to *serve up* content to requesting users (typically via a browser).

Firewalls

From the security perspective, firewalls are perhaps the most exposed device on a network. For this reason, this specific network device will be expanded upon in much greater detail.

A firewall is a software program or hardware appliance that typically resides at the edge of a network or network segment and is used to protect resources located on the network. Not all firewalls are created equal; a firewall can be implemented in several different ways (the vendors of each approach typically claim their tool's approach is superior to their competitors).

Firewall Types

Firewalls can be grouped into two main categories: those that examine network traffic at the application layer of the OSI network model (layer 7) and those that work at the lower network layer (layer 3).

Application-Layer Firewalls

Application-layer firewalls (also known as application proxies, application forwarders, application gateways, or circuit-layer gateways) run on top of a general-purpose operating system such as UNIX or Windows. These firewalls base their decision of whether or not to permit or deny an entire group of network packets (which together comprise a single network message) to pass based on predefined security policies (typically established via a user-friendly software application). Application-layer firewalls can also maintain elaborate logging and auditing information on the traffic passing through them, and they are considered by many to be the easiest firewall to maintain, which in part is why their advocates consider them to be the most secure.

Network-Layer Firewalls

Network-layer firewalls (also known as packet filters) work at a more granular level than application-layer firewalls, typically examining each network packet in isolation. Each individual network packet is typically dropped, rejected, or approved based on comparing the source network address, destination network address, requested port number, or network protocol used, with a predefined set of security rules.

Dynamic packet filters (also known as *stateful filters*) are a more recent variation of network layer firewalls. Rather than relying on fixed (static) firewall openings, openings are dynamically created and closed for groups of packets based on the header information contained in the data packets. Once a series of packets has passed through the opening to its destination, the firewall closes the opening.

Network-layer firewall vendors claim that their approach allows for faster communication than an application-layer firewall, because the firewall's software is running at a lower network layer and therefore consumes a lower overhead. In the case of static packet filtering, the firewall can make its own decision of whether or not to forward a packet as soon as the packet has been received. It doesn't have to wait until an entire sequence of packets has been received (as is the case with application-layer firewalls) and therefore reduces the network latency for this network *hop*.

Unfortunately (from a categorization perspective), vendors are starting to incorporate several different strategies into the same product, blurring the lines between the capabilities of application-layer and network-layer firewalls.

When you factor in the cost of purchasing, installing, and maintaining these firewalls, it's not obvious which approach is best. *Best* may be based on purchase price (some software firewalls are available free of charge), performance, ease of use, and, of course, robustness to attack. Because there is not an outright winner, some organizations choose to implement one or more different types or brands of firewall on the same network. Table A.3 lists some sample firewalls.

Table A.3 Sample List of Firewalls

NAME	ASSOCIATED WEB SITE
BorderManager	www.novell.com
DI-701	www.dlink.com
e-Gap	www.whalecommunications.com
Firebox	www.watchguard.com
Firewall	www.netmax.com
Firewall-1	www.checkpoint.com
Firewall Server	www.borderware.com
FortiGate	www.fortinet.com
GNATBox	www.gnatbox.com
Guardian	www.netguard.com
Linux Netfilter	www.netfilter.org
MS ISA Server (Proxy Server)	www.microsoft.com
NetGap	www.sphd.com
NetScreen	www.netscreen.com

(continues)

Table A.3 Sample List of Firewalls (*continued*)

NAME	ASSOCIATED WEB SITE
PIX	www.cisco.com
SecureWay Firewall	www.ibm.com
Sidewinder	www.securecomputing.com
SonicWALL	www.sonicwall.com
StoneGate	www.stonesoft.com
SuperStack 3	www.3com.com
VelociRaptor	www.symantec.com
VPN Firewall	www.lucent.com
ZoneAlarm	www.zonealarm.com

Note: A more extensive list of firewalls can be found at www.firewall.com.

Upstream Firewalls

It may be possible to work with an organization's Internet service provider (ISP) to implement some network-filtering (firewall) rules, not just at the organization's own perimeter firewall(s), but also duplicated at the ISP's network routers that relay network traffic to the organization, effectively creating an additional *upstream* firewall. For example, the ISP router could be configured to drop all ICMP requests (*pings*) originating from the outside world (external ICMP requests are frequently used by attackers, but rarely used for legitimate purposes).

Downstream Firewalls

A machine such as a Web server located just behind a perimeter firewall could be configured to act as a *downstream* firewall. This could be achieved by configuring the Web server to perform a reverse DNS lookup. A reverse DNS lookup is a process where the source IP address of any incoming data is compared to the Web site's own DNS entries to see if the domain name resolved by the Web site matches the one contained in the incoming message. A discrepancy between the packet's alleged domain name and the locally derived one may indicate a *spoofer* at work, resulting in the message being discarded. Unfortunately, DNS lookups take time and slow down the performance of the Web server, once again creating a trade-off between being faster and being slightly more secure.

Firewall Configurations

The simplest firewall configuration is to place everything behind a single-perimeter firewall. Unfortunately, a network's security is only as good as its weakest link, so many network administrators will place applications particularly prone to compromise or subversion on a quarantined segment of the network. Web servers are considered by many to be the most vulnerable of all network devices, in part because they are designed with the intention of dispersing information to anyone and everyone. For this reason, Web servers are sometimes placed on the outward side of a firewall, isolated from the more valuable resources, consequently making these resources more secure, but making the Web server much more exposed. Figure A.2 depicts this *sacrificial lamb* approach.

The theory behind the sacrificial lamb approach is that the core network is made safer by placing the Web server outside the firewall, and the rules that the firewall can now impose are much stricter and therefore more secure. In the event that the Web server is compromised by an intruder (perhaps through a recently discovered vulnerability in the Web service that the webmaster has not had a chance to fix yet), the amount of damage that the intruder could inflict on the organization would be relatively minor compared to what the intruder could do if he or she had compromised a Web server sitting behind the firewall. For example, if the Web server is only displaying static information, the hard drive(s) of a compromised Web server could be swapped out for a clean set and then restarted, a much easier task than having to try to recover a corrupted database server or retrieving a stolen document. Unfortunately, the word relative, is just that, *relative*. The intruder could use the captured Web server to launch an attack against another Web site or upload some embarrassing graffiti-style graphics that the organization's legitimate visitors see and remember for a long time to come.

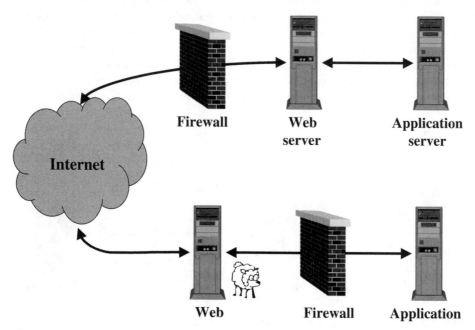

Figure A.2 Sacrificial lamb configuration.

DUAL NICS

An additional step that some network administrators use to make the core network a little more secure is to add a second network interface card (NIC) to the servers inside the DMZ. This gives each DMZ machine one network address for its outward bound (and therefore very public) network communications and a second (more private) network address for communicating to machines residing on the internal network, creating one more hurdle for an intruder to overcome.

Dual-Firewall Demilitarized Zone

A more sophisticated (and popular) approach to protecting the core network *and* the weak link(s) is to create what is commonly referred to as a demilitarized zone (DMZ). Rather than leaving the weakest links completely open to attack (as in the case of the sacrificial lamb approach), they are sheltered behind a liberal (or *thin*) firewall. The core network is then further protected by a more rigorous (or *strict*) firewall, imposing restrictions that could not be imposed on the servers in the DMZ without making them unreachable by their intended audience. In effect, the weak links are sandwiched between two firewalls (as depicted in Figure A.3). It is the area between the two firewalls that is considered to be a DMZ

Unfortunately, using two (or more) firewalls has some drawbacks. The extra hardware, system software licenses, and increased administrative maintenance will consume resources that could have been used elsewhere. For example, implementing a dual-firewall DMZ will require two sets of firewall rules to be maintained, one for the *liberal* firewall and one for the *strict* firewall, potentially increasing the chance of human error. In addition, adding an extra firewall will add one more *hop* to each network request, increasing network latency and slowing the overall performance of the network. On the plus side, using two different brands of firewall, one for the liberal and the one for the strict, means that an intruder who discovers a security hole in one firewall is unlikely to be able to use the same flaw to circumvent the second firewall.

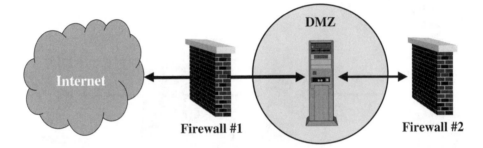

Figure A.3 Dual-firewall DMZ configuration.

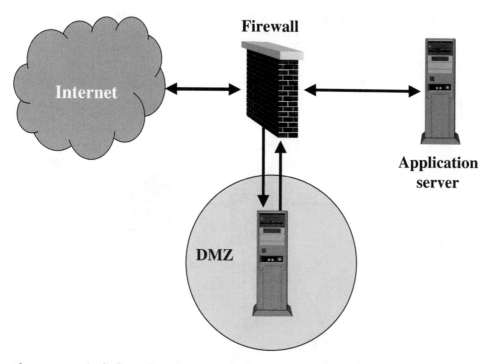

Figure A.4 Single-firewall DMZ configuration.

Single-Firewall DMZ

Using a single firewall to implement a DMZ is often a much more economical option. Instead of using two physical firewalls, a single firewall is configured to act as two virtual firewalls (see Figure A.4).

The single firewall uses a different set of firewall rules for network traffic attempting to access the machines in the DMZ than for the traffic destined for the core network. If the inbound traffic originating from the DMZ machines is subjected to the same set of rules that traffic from the outside world is subjected to, then compromising a DMZ machine will not increase the vulnerability of any of the machines inside the firewall.

The downside to a single-firewall DMZ configuration is that the firewall has to deal with increased network traffic, as the single physical firewall has to handle *external-to-DMZ* requests across the same hardware that is monitoring the *DMZ-to-internal* requests. This is not a problem if the firewall has plenty of spare capacity, but it is a potential performance bottleneck if the firewall is already exceeding 50 percent of its throughput capacity just monitoring one of these routes.

Combination DMZ

Perhaps the most secure configuration is to combine the concepts of both the single-firewall and dual-firewall DMZ configurations. Here the *outer* firewall supporting the devices located in the DMZ is backed up by a second *stricter* firewall, which in all likelihood is not only a different brand of firewall, but quite possibly working at a different OSI network layer. For example, the outer firewall might be a Cisco PIX router working at the network layer, while the stricter firewall may be a Microsoft ISA server checking network traffic at the application layer (see Figure A.5).

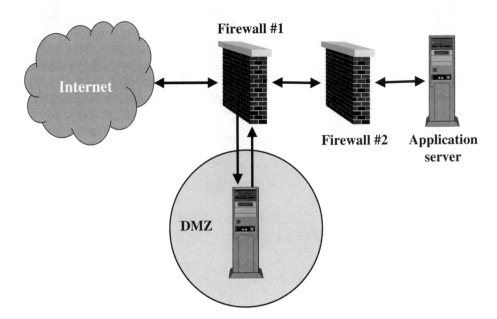

Figure A.5   Combination DMZ configuration.

SANS Institute Top 20 Critical Internet Security Vulnerabilities

The System Administration, Networking and Security Institute (SANS, www.sans.org) was established in 1989 as a cooperative research and education organization for security professionals, auditors, system administrators, and network administrators to share their knowledge.

In October 2001, the SANS Institute in conjunction with the FBI released a list summarizing the 20 most critical Internet security vulnerabilities (summarized in Table B.1). This new list updates and expands the Top 10 list released by the SANS Institute and the National Infrastructure Protection Center (NIPC, www.nipc.gov) in 2000. Thousands of organizations have used these lists to prioritize their testing efforts so they could detect and close the most dangerous security holes first. The majority of successful attacks on computer systems via the Internet can be traced to the exploitation of security vulnerabilities on this list.

Table B.1   The 20 Most Critical Internet Security Vulnerabilities

PLATFORM	VULNERABILITY
All platforms	Default installs of operating systems and applications
	Accounts with no passwords or weak passwords
	Nonexistent or incomplete backups
	Large number of open ports
	Not filtering packets for correct incoming and outgoing addresses
	Nonexistent or incomplete logging
	Vulnerable Common Gateway Interface (CGI) programs
Windows-specific	Unicode vulnerability—Web server folder traversal
	Internet server application programming interface (ISAPI) extension buffer overflows
	IIS Remote Data Services (RDS) exploit
	Network Basic Input Output System (NetBIOS), unprotected Windows networking shares
	Information leakage via null session connections
	Weak hashing in SAM (Security Accounts Manager)—LanManager hash
UNIX-specific	Buffer overflows in Remote Procedure Call (RPC) services
	Sendmail vulnerabilities
	Bind weaknesses
	Remote system command (such as rcp, rlogin, and rsh) vulnerabilities
	Line Printer Daemons (LPD) vulnerabilities
	Sadmind and mountd exploits
	Default Simple Network Management Protocol (SNMP) strings

Reprinted with permission: www.sans.org/top20.htm, last updated October 2001.

Test-Deliverable Templates

This appendix illustrates some example documentation layouts for the test deliverables previously described in Chapter 2, and may be used by the reader as templates for constructing their own customized testing deliverables. These templates are themselves loosely based on the structure defined by the Institute of Electrical and Electronics Engineers (IEEE, www.ieee.org) in their standard for Software Test Documentation (IEEE 829-1998). Nguyen (2000), Perry (2000), Stottlemyer (2001), and the Rational Unified Process (www.rational.com) provide additional test deliverable templates.

Template Test Status/Summary Report

A test status report is normally produced on a regular basis (weekly, for example) to summarize the progress of the testing effort to date. The very last test status report may become the test summary report for the entire testing effort (perhaps after a few cosmetic changes, such as changing the title of the document to *test summary report*, the names of the persons who will formally accept the report, and so on). The following sections describe some of the components that are typically found in a test status/summary report.

Test Status Report Identifier. For example, Application XYZ, build n.n test status report mm/dd/ccyy.

Status. Identifies the test items that have been tested (and optionally the items that have yet to be tested), indicating their versions (or build). This section may also highlight any major project management metrics that have been captured and that need to be reported, such as the number of tests completed, the percentage of tests failing, the total number of effort hours expended, and so on.

This section may also document any major issues that have impacted (or are expected to impact) the testing effort, supplemented with a brief description of how the closed issues were resolved and how the open issues could potentially be dealt with.

Variances.   Reports any variances of the test items to their (explicit or implicit) design specifications. Examples of variances include vulnerabilities in system software that have not been patched, buffer overflows in application code, on-duty security staff not responding appropriately to an intrusion detection system (IDS) alert, doors to computer rooms being left unlocked, and so on.

Comprehensive Assessment.   Documents the comprehensiveness of the testing effort compared to the testing objectives listed in the test plans. Identifies and justifies any aspects of the testing effort that have not yet been (or will not be) performed to the degree originally envisioned by the original version of the test plan.

Summary of Results (Incidents).   Summarizes the results of the testing done to date, itemizing all resolved and unresolved incidents, their resolutions (if resolved), and impact (if any) on the testing effort.

Evaluation.   Provides an overall evaluation of the items that have been tested, highlighting each of the vulnerabilities that have been detected and potentially rating their severity. These evaluations should be based on the test results and not any expectations that the test team may have based on hunches or gut feelings. If unsubstantiated suspicious are to be included (perhaps because time limitations prohibited sufficient investigation), then their inclusion should clearly indicate that the existence of these suspected vulnerabilities has yet to be established by impartial testing.

The evaluation may also include an estimate of the likelihood of a detected vulnerability being exploited by an attacker and the impact to the business should he or she be successful. This evaluation may then be used by the Web site/application's owner (or their proxy, such as a project manager) to decide what vulnerabilities need to be plugged before the product can be placed into production or, if already in production, the priority with which the vulnerabilities should be fixed.

Summary of Activities.   Summarizes the major testing activities and events that have occurred to date, providing an appropriate level of breakdown to justify the amount of resources that have so far been consumed by the testing effort.

Approval.   Specifies the names and titles of persons who must approve (accept) this status report.

Template Test Incident Report

Many organizations choose to skip writing a formal test incident report and instead enter equivalent information directly into a incident/defect tracking system, a system that typically provides a reporting feature that can, if so desired, produce actual test incident reports. The following sections describe some of the components that are typically found in a test incident report.

Test Incident Identifier. For example, Application XYZ, incident nnnn.

Summary. Provides a brief description of the incident that was observed. This would include pertinent information such as the item that was being tested when the incident occurred (including the exact version or build of the item), the test(s) that was being executed when the incident occurred (ideally cross-referenced to the appropriate test log entry, test case, and test plan), and the name of the person who observed the incident.

Incident Description. The following is a list of some of the additional attributes that an organization may wish to consider capturing at the moment (or shortly after) an incident was observed:

- The date and time when the incident occurred
- Contact information for the person who observed the incident (and, if different, the person who wrote up the incident), such as an email address or telephone number
- The phase of testing that the incident occurred in: unit level, system level, outsourced penetration test, production, and so on
- A description of the steps taken to create the incident (cross-referenced to any relevant test automation script)
- Whether or not the incident is repeatable
- Whether or not the incident will prevent, or inhabit further testing
- If detected by a tool, the name and version of the tool and, if relevant, any special configuration settings
- The initial estimate of the relative severity of the incident to the business
- The initial estimate of the relative likelihood (or frequency) of the incident reoccurring in production
- The initial (and subsequently refined) estimation of the cause of the incident, such as a defect in the testing tool, application software, system software configuration, testing procedure, and so on
- Supporting information, such as screen capture attachments or test output reports
- A detailed description of the incident

Additional attributes that may be added at a later date to facilitate better defect tracking include the following:

- A status, such as: new (unassigned), open (assigned), closed, unable to recreate, rejected, deferred, duplicate, and so on

- The date and name of the person closing out the incident (and, if authorized by a different person, their name and title)

- The priority given to the investigation effort

- Who the investigation is assigned to (and optionally the date by which they need to complete their assessment)

- The priority given to fix the defect

- An estimate of the effort needed to fix the defect

- Who the fix is assigned to (and optionally the date or version number by which he or she needs to complete the fix)

- Whether or not retesting will be required (and if not, why not)

- Who the retesting is assigned to (and optionally the date by which he or she needs to complete the retest)

- The root cause of the defect, such as: requirements, design, code, reference data, version control, environment, test tool, system software configuration, and so on

- Recommendations on how to avoid a reoccurrence of the same (or similar) incident

In addition, changes to any of this data may also warrant tracking.

Template Test Log

A test log could be as informal as the back of an envelope or as comprehensive as a series of screen captures that records every single interaction that the tester has with the system being tested. The degree of detail deemed appropriate for a particular set of tests will, to a large extent, depend on what this documentation will actually be used for. For instance, an outsourced testing firm conducting a security assessment may need to provide a very detailed test log to prove that they actually performed the work they were hired to do. On the other hand, an in-house security group conducting some exploratory penetration tests may just want to jot down some pointers that will be used to design more structured tests at a later point in the testing effort.

The following template should therefore not be regarded as *the* way to document a test log, but merely an example of how such information could be formally recorded for posterity.

Test Log Identifier.   For example, Application XYZ, build n.n test log report mm/dd/ccyy (and to mm/dd/ccyy if spanning multiple days).

Description. This section often includes information that applies to all the entries in the test log, such as the hardware and system software environment where the testing took place, or the test items that were the subject of the tests covered by this test log.

Activity and Event Entries. Documents the actual results of each test run, information that may be more easily documented using a landscape format such as the example layout depicted by Table C.1.

Table C.1 Example Test Log Layout

TEST IDENTIFIER AND TEST NAME	PASS/ FAIL	INCIDENT IDENTIFIER	BRIEF DESCRIPTION OF INCIDENT
		LOG AUTHOR:	**MARC SILVER**
		TESTER(S):	**MARY CATCHALL**
TESTING START TIME: 10.15AM **TESTING END TIME: 2.30PM**		**OBSERVER(S):**	
SysNet25: Port scan Web server #1 for unauthorized open ports	Fail	91	Port #139 (NetBIOS) found open
SysNet26: Port scan Web server #2 for unauthorized open ports	Pass		
SysNet27: Ping internal (private) network addresses from outside perimeter firewall	Fail	92	Response detected from IP address 123.456.789.123
SysNet28: DNS zone transfer	Pass		
SysNet29: Static network address entries in Web server #1's hosts file	Pass		
SysNet30: Static network address entries in Web server #2's hosts file	Pass		
SysNet31: Perimeter firewall blocks all outbound UDP network traffic	Pass		
SysNet32: Stress test perimeter firewall	Pass		
SysNet33: Wireless segment effective range	Fail	93	Connection to the corporate LAN (which has unfiltered network access to the Web application) was established from a hamburger restaurant's parking lot located half a mile away from the Web site's physical location.

Additional Resources

The subject matter for testing Web security is so vast that one book cannot hope to cover every facet of this knowledge domain in great detail. This section has therefore been included in this book to provide the reader with a consolidated list of book and Web sites that may be used to acquire additional information of the topic of testing Web security.

Books

This list of books not only serves as a bibliography of all the books referenced in this book, but also includes other books related to this book's subject matter and may therefore prove to be an additional resource for the reader.

Computer Forensics

Caloyannides, Michael A. *Computer Forensics and Privacy*. Artech House, 2001.

Casey, Eoghan. *Digital Evidence and Computer Crime*. Academic Press, 2000.

Kruse, Warren G., II, and Jay G. Heiser. *Computer Forensics : Incident Response Essentials*. Addison-Wesley, 2001.

Marcella, Albert J., Jr., and Robert S. Greenfield. *Cyber Forensics: A Field Manual for Collecting, Examining, and Preserving Evidence of Computer Crimes*. Auerbach, 2002.

Prosise, Chris, and Kevin Mandia. *Incident Response: Investigating Computer Crime.* Osborne McGraw-Hill, 2001.

Shinder, Debra Littlejohn. *Scene of the Cybercrime: Computer Forensics Handbook.* Syngress Media, 2002.

Vacca, John R., and Michael Erbschloe. *Computer Forensics: Computer Crime Scene Investigation.* Charles River Media, 2002.

Configuration Management

Brown, William J., Hays W. McCormick, and Scott W. Thomas. *Anti-Patterns and Patterns in Software Configuration Management.* John Wiley & Sons, 1999.

Dart, Susan. *Configuration Management: The Missing Link in Web Engineering.* Artech House, 2000.

Haug, Michael, Eric W. Olsen, and Gonzalo Cuevas (eds.). *Managing the Change: Software Configuration and Change Management.* Springer Verlag, 1999.

Leon, Alexis. *A Guide to Software Configuration Management.* Artech House, 2000.

Lyon, David D. *Practical CM: Best Configuration Management Practices.* Butterworth Architecture, 2000.

White, Brian A., and Geoffrey M. Clemm. *Software Configuration Management Strategies and Rational ClearCase.* Addison Wesley Professional, 2000.

Disaster Recovery

Maiwald, Eric, William Sieglein, and Michael Mueller. *Security Planning and Disaster Recovery.* Osborne McGraw-Hill, 2002.

Toigo, Jon William, and Margaret Romano Toigo. *Disaster Recovery Planning: Strategies for Protecting Critical Information Assets, Second Edition.* Prentice Hall, 1999.

Internet Law

Brinson, J. Dianne, and Mark F. Radcliffe. *Internet Law and Business Handbook : A Practical Guide.* Ladera Press, 2000.

Matsuura, Jeffrey H. *Security, Rights, & Liabilities in E-Commerce.* Artech House, 2001.

Saunders, Kurt M. *Practical Internet Law for Business.* Artech House, 2001.

Singleton, Susan *Ecommerce: A Practical Guide to the Law.* Ashgate, 2001.

Poindexter, Carl J., and David L. Baumer. *Cyberlaw and E-Commerce.* Irwin/McGraw-Hill, 2001.

Wright, Benjamin, and Jane K. Winn. *The Law of Electronic Commerce.* Aspen, 2001.

Miscellaneous

Hedayat, A.S., Neil J. A. Sloane, and John Stufken. *Orthogonal Arrays: Theory and Applications*. Springer Verlag, 1999.

St. Laurent, Simon. *Cookies*. McGraw-Hill, 1998.

Network Design

Brooks, Kari. *Networking Complete*. Sybex, 2001.

Dimarzio, J. F. *Network Architecture & Design: A Field Guide for IT Consultants*. Sams, 2001.

Oppenheimer, Priscilla. *Top-Down Network Design*. Cisco Press, 1999.

Risk Analysis

Chapman, C. B., and Stephen Ward. *Project Risk Management: Processes, Techniques and Insights*. John Wiley & Sons, 1996.

Friedman, M., and J. Voas. *Software Assessment: Reliability, Safety, and Testability*. Wiley-Interscience, 1995.

Grey, Stephen. *Practical Risk Assessment for Project Management*. John Wiley & Sons, 1995.

Koller, Glenn Robert. *Risk Assessment and Decision Making in Business and Industry: A Practical Guide*. CRC Press, 1999.

Leveson, Nancy. *Safeware: System Safety and Computers*. Addison-Wesley, 1995.

McDermott, Robin E., Raymond J. Mikulak, and Michael R. Beauregard. *The Basics of FMEA*. Productivity Inc., 1996.

Ould, Martyn. *Managing Software Quality and Business Risk*. John Wiley & Sons, 1999.

Palady, Paul. *FMEA Author's Edition*. PAL Publishing, 1997.

Peltier, Thomas R. *Information Security Risk Analysis*. Auerbach Publications, 2001.

Project Management Institute. *A Guide to the Project Management Body of Knowledge*. Project Management Institute, 2001.

Stamatis, D. H. *Failure Mode and Effect Analysis: FMEA from Theory to Execution*. American Society for Quality, 1995.

Wideman, R. Max (ed.), and Rodney J. Dawson. *Project and Program Risk Management: A Guide to Managing Project Risks and Opportunities*. Project Management Institute Publications, 1998.

Security

Allen, Julia H. *The CERT® Guide to System and Network Security Practices*. Addison-Wesley, 2001.

Anderson, Ross J. *Security Engineering: A Guide to Building Dependable Distributed Systems*. John Wiley & Sons, 2001.

Barman, Scott. *Writing Information Security Policies*. New Riders Publishing, 2001.

Bragg, Roberta. *CISSP Training Guide*. Que, 2002.

Brands, Stefan A. *Rethinking Public Key Infrastructures and Digital Certificates: Building in Privacy*. MIT Press, 2000.

Brenton, Chris. *Mastering Network Security*. Sybex, 1998.

Brenton, Chris, and Cameron Hunt. *Active Defense: A Comprehensive Guide to Network Security*. Sybex, 2001.

Burnett, Steve, and Stephen Paine. *RSA Security's Official Guide to Cryptography*. Osborne McGraw-Hill, 2001.

Canavan, John E. *The Fundamentals of Network Security*. Artech House, 2001.

Castano, Silvano, Maria Grazia Fugini, Giancarlo Martella, and Silvana Castano. *Database Security*. Addison-Wesley, 1994.

Chirillo, John. *Hack Attacks Denied: Complete Guide to Network LockDown*. John Wiley & Sons, 2001.

———. *Hack Attacks Revealed: A Complete Reference with Custom Security Hacking Toolkit*. John Wiley & Sons, 2001.

Cole, Eric, *Hackers Beware*. New Riders Publishing, 2001.

Cronkhite, Cathy, and Jack McCullough. *Access Denied: The Complete Guide to Protecting Your Business Online*. Osborne McGraw-Hill, 2001.

Endorf, Carl F. *Secured Computing: A Cissp Study Guide*. Trafford, 2001.

Erbschloe, Michael. *Information Warfare: How to Survive Cyber Attacks*. McGraw-Hill, 2001.

Feghhi, Jalal, Peter Williams, and Jalil Feghhi. *Digital Certificates: Applied Internet Security*. Addison-Wesley, 1998.

Forno, Richard, Kenneth R. Van Wyk, and Rick Forno. *Incident Response*. O'Reilly & Associates, 2001.

Garfinkel, Simson, Gene Spafford, and Debby Russell. *Web Security, Privacy and Commerce, Third Edition*. O'Reilly & Associates, 2002.

Ghosh, Anup K. *E-Commerce Security: Weak Links, Best Defenses*. John Wiley & Sons, 1998.

———. *Security and Privacy for E-Business*. John Wiley & Sons, 2001.

Harris, Shon. *CISSP All-in-One Exam Guide*. Osborne McGraw-Hill, 2001.

Hassler, Vesna. *Security Fundamentals for E-Commerce*. Artech House, 2000.

Hendry, Mike. *Smart Card Security and Applications*. Artech House, 2001.

Heney, William, Marlene L. Theriault, and Debby Russell. *Oracle Security*, 1998.

Herrmann, Debra S. *A Practical Guide to Security Engineering and Information Assurance*. CRC Press, 2001.

Honeynet Project (ed.), Lance Spitzner (Preface), and Bruce Schneier. *Know Your Enemy: Revealing the Security Tools, Tactics, and Motives of the Blackhat Community.* Addison-Wesley, 2001.

Huston, L. Brent (ed.), Teri Bidwell, Ryan Ruyssell, Robin Walshaw, and Oliver Steudler. *Hack Proofing Your Ecommerce Site.* Syngress Media Inc., 2001.

Klevinsky T.J., Scott Laliberte, and Ajay Gupta. *Hack I.T.—Security Through Penetration Testing.* Addison-Wesley, 2002.

King, Christopher (ed.), Ertem Osmanoglu, and Curtis Dalton. *Security Architecture: Design, Deployment and Operations.* McGraw-Hill, 2001.

Krutz, Ronald L., Russell Dean Vines: *Advanced CISSP Prep Guide: Exam Q&A.* John Wiley & Sons, 2002.

Krutz, Ronald L., Russell Dean Vines, and Edward M. Stroz. *The CISSP Prep Guide: Mastering the Ten Domains of Computer Security.* John Wiley & Sons, 2001.

Larson, Eric, and Brian Stephens. *Administrating Web Servers, Security, and Maintenance Interactive Workbook.* Prentice Hall, 1999.

Lierley, Mark (ed.). *Security Complete.* Sybex, 2001.

Loeb, Larry. *Secure Electronic Transactions: Introduction and Technical Reference.* Artech House, 1998.

McClure, Stuart, Saumil Shah, and Shreeraj Shah. *Web Hacking: Attacks and Defense.* Addison-Wesley, 2002.

McGraw, Gary, and Ed Felten. *Securing Java: Getting Down to Business with Mobile Code.* John Wiley & Sons, 1999.

Merkow, Mark S., Jim Breithaupt, and James Breithaupt. *The Complete Guide to Internet Security.* AMACOM, 2000.

Nanavati, Samir, Michael Thieme, and Raj Nanavati. *Biometrics: Identity Verification in a Networked World.* John Wiley & Sons, 2002.

Nichols, Randall K., Julie J. C. H. Ryan, and William E. Baugh, Jr. *Defending Your Digital Assets: Against Hackers, Crackers, Spies and Thieves.* Osborne McGraw-Hill, 1999.

Northcutt, Stephen, Donald McLachlan, and Judy Novak. *Network Intrusion Detection: An Analyst's Handbook.* New Riders Publishing, 2000.

Oppliger, Rolf. *Internet and Intranet Security.* Artech House, 2002.

———. *Security Technologies for the World Wide Web.* Artech House, 1999.

Parker, Donn B. *Fighting Computer Crime: A New Framework for Protecting Information.* John Wiley & Sons, 1998.

Peltier, Thomas, and Patrick D. Howard. *The Total CISSP Exam Prep Book: Practice Questions, Answers, and Test Taking Tips and Techniques*. Auerbach, 2002.

Peltier, Thomas R. *Information Security Policies, Procedures, and Standards: Guidelines for Effective Information Security Management*. CRC Press, 2001.

Phaltankar, Kaustubh M., and Vinton G. Cerf. *Practical Guide for Implementing Secure Intranets and Extranets*. Artech House, 1999.

Phoha, Vir V. *Internet Security Dictionary*. Springer Verlag, 2002.

Pieprzyk, Josef, Thomas Hardjono, and Jennifer Seberry. *Fundamentals of Computer Security*. Springer Verlag, 2002.

Proctor, Paul E. *Practical Intrusion Detection Handbook*. Prentice Hall PTR/Sun Microsystems Press, 2000.

Rankl, W., and W. Effing. *Smart Card Handbook*. John Wiley & Sons, 2000.

Rubin, Aviel D. *White-Hat Security Arsenal: Tackling the Threats*. Addison-Wesley, 2001.

Scambray, Joel, Stuart McClure, and George Kurtz. *Hacking Exposed, Third Edition*. McGraw-Hill, 2001.

Scambray, Joel, and Mike Shema. *Hacking Exposed: Web Applications*. Osborne McGraw-Hill, 2002.

Schneier, Bruce. *Secrets and Lies: Digital Security in a Networked World*. John Wiley & Sons, 2000.

Sherif, Mostafa Hashem, and Ahmed Sehrouchni. *Protocols for Secure Electronic Commerce*. CRC Press, 2000.

Shumway, Russell, and E. Eugene Schultz. *Incident Response: A Strategic Guide to Handling System and Network Security Breaches*. New Riders Publishing, 2002.

Skoudis, Ed. *Counter Hack: A Step-by-Step Guide to Computer Attacks and Effective Defenses*. Prentice Hall PTR, 2001.

Smith, Richard E. *Authentication: From Passwords to Public Keys*. Addison-Wesley, 2001.

Stallings, William. *Cryptography and Network Security: Principles and Practice*. Prentice Hall, 1998.

Stein, Lincoln D. *Web Security: A Step-by-Step Reference Guide*. Addison-Wesley, 1998.

Syngress Media (ed.), Ryan Russell, and Stace Cunningham. *Hack Proofing Your Network: Internet Tradecraft*. Syngress Media Inc., 2000.

Tiwana, Amrit. *Web Security*. Digital Press, 1999.

Traxler, Julie, and Jeff Forristal. *Hack Proofing Your Web Applications*. Syngress Media Inc., 2001.

Tudor, Jan Killmeyer. *Information Security Architecture: An Integrated Approach to Security in the Organization*. CRC Press, 2000.

Viega, John, and Gary McGraw. *Building Secure Software: How to Avoid Security Problems the Right Way.* Addison-Wesley Professional, 2001.

Wilson, Chuck, and Daniel Schillaci. *Get Smart: The Emergence of Smart Cards in the United States and their Pivotal Role in Internet Commerce.* Mullaney Corporation, 2001.

Winkler, Ira. *Corporate Espionage: What It Is, Why It Is Happening in Your Company, What You Must Do About It.* Prima Publishing, 1999.

Wood, Charles Cresson. *Information Security Policies Made Easy Version 8.* Baseline Software, 2001.

Zwicky, Elizabeth D., Simon Cooper, D. Brent Chapman, and Deborah Russell. *Building Internet Firewalls, Second Edition.* O'Reilly & Associates, 2000.

Software Engineering

Dunn, Robert H. *Software Defect Removal.* McGraw Hill, 1984.

Kan, Stephen H. *Metrics and Models in Software Quality Engineering.* Addison-Wesley, 1995.

Kolawa, Adam, Cynthia Dunlop, and Wendell Hicken. *Bulletproofing Web Applications.* John Wiley & Sons, 2001.

Moller, Karl-Heinrich, and Daniel J. Paulish. *Software Metrics: A Practitioner's Guide to Improved Product Development.* IEEE Computer Society, 1993.

Musa, John D., Anthony Iannino, and Kazuhira Okumoto. *Software Reliability: Measurement, Prediction, Application.* McGraw Hill, 1987.

Pfleeger, Shari Lawrence. *Software Engineering: Theory and Practice.* Prentice Hall, 2001.

Testing (General)

Beizer, Boris. *Black-Box Testing: Techniques for Functional Testing of Software and Systems.* John Wiley & Sons, 1995.

———. *Software System Testing and Quality Assurance.* International Thomson Publishing, 1984.

Black, Rex. *Critical Testing Processes.* Addison-Wesley, 2003.

———. *Managing the Testing Process: Practical Tools and Techniques for Managing Hardware and Software Testing.* John Wiley and Sons, 2002.

Buchanan, Robert W., Jr., *The Art of Testing Network Systems.* John Wiley & Sons, 1996.

Buwalda, Hans, Dennis Janssen, Iris Pinkster, and Paul A. Watters. *Integrated Test Design and Automation: Using the Testframe Method.* Addison-Wesley, 2001.

Craig, Rick, and Stefan Jaskiel. *Systematic Software Testing.* Artech House, 2002.

Culbertson, Robert, Chris Brown, and Gary Cobb. *Rapid Testing*. Prentice Hall PTR, 2001.

Dustin, Elfriede, Jeff Rashka, and John Paul. *Automated Software Testing: Introduction, Management, and Performance*. Addison-Wesley, 1999.

Graham, Dorothy, Mark Fewster (Preface), and Brian Marick. *Software Test Automation: Effective Use of Test Execution*. Addison-Wesley, 1999.

Hayes, Linda G. *Automated Testing Handbook*. Software Testing Institute, 1995.

Hetzel, William. *The Complete Guide to Software Testing*. John Wiley & Sons, 1993.

Jorgensen, Paul C. *Software Testing: A Craftsman's Approach, Second Edition*. CRC Press, 2002.

Kaner, Cem, Hung Quoc Nguyen, and Jack Falk. *Testing Computer Software*. John Wiley & Sons, 1999.

Kaner, Cem, James Bach, and Bret Pettichord. *Lessons Learned in Software Testing*. John Wiley & Sons, 2001.

Kit, Edward, and Susannah Finzi (ed.). *Testing in the Real World: Improving the Process*. Addison-Wesley, 1995.

Koomen, Tim, and Martin Pol. *Test Process Improvement*. Addison-Wesley, 1999.

Lewis, William E. *Software Testing and Continuous Quality Improvement*. CRC Press, 2000.

Musa, John D. *Software Reliability Engineered Testing*. McGraw-Hill, 1998.

Myers, Glenford J. *The Art of Software Testing*. John Wiley & Sons, 1979.

Patton, Ron. *Software Testing*. Sams, 2000.

Perry, William E. *Effective Methods for Software Testing, Second Edition*. John Wiley & Sons, 2000.

Perry, William E., and Randall W. Rice. *Surviving the Top Ten Challenges of Software Testing: A People-Oriented Approach*. Dorset House, 1997.

Rakitin, Steven R. *Software Verification and Validation for Practitioners and Managers*. Artech House, 2001.

Sweeney, Mary Romero. *Visual Basic for Testers*. Apress, 2001.

Tamres, Louise. *Introducing Software Testing*. Addison-Wesley, 2002.

Watkins, John. *Testing IT: An Off-the-Shelf Software Testing Process*. Cambridge University Press, 2001.

Whittaker, James A. *How to Break Software: A Practical Guide to Testing*. Addison-Wesley, 2002.

Wieczorek, Martin, Dirk Meyerhoff, and B. Baltus (eds.). *Software Quality: State of the Art in Management, Testing, and Tools*. Springer Verlag, 2001.

Testing (Web)

Dustin, Elfriede A., Jeff Rashka, and Douglas McDiarmid. *Quality Web Systems: Performance, Security, and Usability.* Addison-Wesley, 2001.

Gerrard, Paul, and Neil Thompson. *Risk Based E-Business Testing.* Artech House, 2002.

Marshall, Steve, Ryszard Szarkowski, and Billie Shea. *Making E-Business Work: A Guide to Software Testing in the Internet Age.* Newport Press Publications, 2000.

Nguyen, Hung Quoc. *Testing Applications for the Web: Testing Planning for Internet-Based Systems.* John Wiley & Sons, 2000.

Splaine, Steven, and Stefan Jaskiel. *The Web Testing Handbook.* STQE Publishing, 2001.

Stottlemyer, Diane. *Automated Web Testing Toolkit: Expert Methods for Testing and Managing Web Applications.* John Wiley & Sons, 2001.

Web Sites

The following tables summarize in a single consolidated section all the Web sites that have been referenced by this book. The chapter that references the site provides a more detailed explanation of the reason that the Web site was referenced. Note that, while these Web sites were accurate at the time this book was written, due to the constantly changing nature of the Web, some of these links may have since become broken.

Chapter 1: Introduction

PURPOSE	REFERENCED WEB SITES
Security vulnerability statistics and incidents	www.cert.org www.gocsi.com www.money.cnn.com www.reuters.co.uk
Testing terms and definitions	www.ieee.org www.pmi.org www.rational.com
CISSP Certification	www.cissp.com www.isc2.org

Chapter 2: Test Planning

PURPOSE	REFERENCED WEB SITES
Testing documentation or processes	www.ideahamster.org www.osstmm.org www.rational.com www.standards.ieee.org
Defect-tracking tools	www.avensoft.com www.elementool.com www.elsitech.com www.empirix.com www.fesoft.com www.hstech.com.au www.mercuryinteractive.com www.mozilla.org www.nesbitt.com www.novosys.de www.pandawave.com www.prostyle.com www.rational.com www.remotedebugger.com www.seapine.com www.skyeytech.com www.softwarewithbrains.com www.threerock.com www.visible.com
Configuration management tools	www.ca.com www.mccabe.com www.merant.com www.microsoft.com www.mks.com www.rational.com www.serena.com www.starbase.com www.telelogic.com www.visible.com
Disk replication tools	www.alohabob.com www.altiris.com www.highergroundsoftware.com www.ics-iq.com www.logicube.com www.storagesoftsolutions.com www.symantec.com
Project-scheduling tools	www.aecsoft.com www.axista.com www.gigaplan.com www.itgroupusa.com

PURPOSE	REFERENCED WEB SITES
	www.microsoft.com
	www.niku.com
	www.openair.com
	www.pacificedge.com
	www.patrena.com
	www.performancesolutionstech.com
	www.planview.com
	www.primavera.com
	www.projectkickstart.com
	www.rationalconcepts.com
	www.timedisciple.com

Chapter 3: Network Security

REASON	REFERENCED WEB SITES
IP-address-sweeping tools and services	www.deter.com
	www.eeye.com
	www.insecure.org
	www.ipswitch.com
	www.kyuzz.org/antirez
	www.nmrc.org
	www.nwpsw.com
	www.procheckup.com
	www.solarwinds.net
	www.trulan.com
	www.twpm.com
Network-auditing tools	www.ca.com
	www.centennial.co.uk
	www.dell.com
	www.eurotek.co.uk
	www.hp.com
	www.ibm.com
	www.lanauditor.com
	www.mfxr.com
	www.microsoft.com
	www.nai.com/magicsolutions.com
	www.trackbird.com
	www.vislogic.org
Domain name service (DNS) zone transfer tools and services	www.domtools.com
	ftp.cerias.purdue.edu
	ftp.technotronic.com
	ftp.uu.net/networking/ip/dns
	www.samspade.org
	www.solarwinds.net
	www.visi.com/~barr

PURPOSE	REFERENCED WEB SITES
Trace route tools and services	www.marko.net www.mcafee.com www.netiq.com www.network-tools.com www.packetfactory.net www.procheckup.com www.solarwinds.net www.trulan.com www.visualroute.com
Network-sniffing tools	www.distinct.com www.ee.lbl.gov www.eeye.com www.fbi.gov www.fte.com www.hackersclub.com www.microsoft.com www.ndgssoftware.com www.netgroup-serv.polito.it www.onenetworks.comms.agilent.com www.rootshell.com www.sniff-em.com www.sniffer.com www.tamos.com www.tcpdump.org www.zing.org
Denial of service emulation tools and services	www.antara.net www.caw.com www.exodus.com www.mercuryinteractive.com www.spirentcom.com
Traditional load testing tools	www.compuware.com www.empirix.com www.fiveninesolutions.com www.loadtesting.com www.mercuryinteractive.com www.microsoft.com www.radview.com www.rational.com www.redhillnetworks.com www.segue.com www.sourceforge.net www.technovations.com www.velometer.com www.webperfcenter.com

Chapter 4: System Software Security

PURPOSE	REFERENCED WEB SITES
System software products	www.apache.org www.bea.com www.lotus.com www.microsoft.com www.redhat.com www.symantec.com
Security certifications	www.commoncriteria.org www.defenselink.mil www.iso.ch www.itsec.gov uk
Bug- and incident-tracking centers	www.bugnet.com www.cert.org www.ciac.org www.csrc.nist.gov www.cve.mitre.org www.fedcirc.gov www.infosyssec.com www.iss.net www.nipc.gov www.ntbugtraq.com www.ntsecurity.net http://packetstorm.decepticons.org www.sans.org www.securitybugware.org www.securityfocus.com www.securitytracker.com www.vmyths.com www.whitehats.com
System software assessment tools	www.fish.com www.iss.net www.maximized.com www.microsoft.com www.nessus.org www.netiq.com www.shavlik.com
Operating system protection tools	www.bastille-linux.org www.engardelinux.org www.immunix.org www.watchguard.com

PURPOSE	REFERENCED WEB SITES
Fingerprinting tools and services	www.atstake.com www.bindview.com www.cerberus-infosec.co.uk www.foundstone.com www.insecure.org www.marko.net www.netcraft.com
Mapping services to ports	www.foundstone.com www.iana.org
Port-scanning tools	www.atstake.com www.bindview.com www.cerberus-infosec.co.uk www.cotse.com www.dataset.fr www.eeye.com www.foundstone.com www.freebsd.org www.insecure.org www.iss.net www.nai.com www.nessus.org www.ntsecurity.nu www.nwpsw.com www.packetfactory.net www.prosolve.com www.savant-software.com www.search.iland.co.kr www.wiretrip.net www.wwdsi.com www.www-arc.com
Port-scanning services	www.grc.com www.mis-cds.com www.norton.com www.securitymetrics.com
Directory and file access control tools	www.argus-systems.com www.armoredserver.com www.authoriszor.com www.entercept.com www.hp.com www.kavado.com www.okena.com www.sanctuminc.com www.securewave.com www.watchguard.com

PURPOSE	REFERENCED WEB SITES
File share scanning tools	www.atstake.com www.hackersclub.com www.nmrc.org www.ntsecurity.nu www.solarwinds.net
Password directories	www.hackersclub.com www.securityparadigm.com
Password-deciphering/guessing/ assessment tools	www.antifork.org www.bindview.com www.cerberus-infosec.co.uk www.hackersclub.com www.hoobie.net www.intrusion.com www.nai.com www.nmrc.org http://packetstorm.decepticons.org www.phenoelit.de www.securitysoftwaretech.com www.users.dircon.co.uk/~crypto www.waveset.com

Chapter 5: Client-Side Application Security

PURPOSE	REFERENCED WEB SITES
Providers of personal certificates and related services	www.btignite.com www.entrust.com www.globalsign.net www.openca.org www.scmmicro.com www.thawte.com www.verisign.com
Providers of smart cards and related services	www.activcard.com www.datakey.com www.ibutton.com www.labcal.com www.motus.com www.rsasecurity.com www.signify.net www.vasco.com

PURPOSE	REFERENCED WEB SITES
Providers of biometric devices and related services	www.activcard.com www.cybersign.com www.digitalpersona.com www.identix.com www.interlinkelec.com www.iridiantech.com www.keyware.com www.saflink.com www.secugen.com www.visionics.com
Link-checking tools	www.coast.com www.empirix.com www.mercuryinteractive.com www.rational.com www.trellian.com www.watchfire.com
Providers of encryption accelerators	www.aep-crypto.com www.andesnetworks.com www.cryptoapps.com www.ibm.com www.ncipher.co www.powercrypt.com www.rainbow.com www.safenet-inc.com www.sonicwall.com
ActiveX Control Safety Checklist	www.msdn.microsoft.com
Client-side script vulnerability demonstrations	www.guninski.com
Code coverage tool	www.mccabe.com
Personal firewalls	www.esafe.com www.f-secure.com www.infoexpress.com www.mcafee.com www.microsoft.com www.neoworx.com www.netfilter.samba.org www.network-1.com www.networkice.com www.seawall.sourceforge.net www.symantec.com www.zonelabs.com
Orthogonal array manipulation tools	www.argreenhouse.com www.lib.stat.cmu.edu www.phadkeassociates.com
Online advertisers	www.aol.com www.doubleclick.net

Chapter 6: Server-Side Application Security

PURPOSE	REFERENCED WEB SITES
CGI test harness tool	www.htmlhelp.com
CGI scalability	www.fastcgi.com
Sample CGI scanners	www.atstake.com www.glocksoft.com www.nebunu.home.ro www.nessus.org http://packetstorm.decepticons.org www.point2click.de www.sourceforge.net www.wiretrap.net
Sample dynamic code environments	www.chilisoft.com www.halcyonsoft.com www.macromedia.com www.microsoft.com www.php.net www.sun.com www.vignette.com
HTML squishing tool	www.imagiware.com
Tool libraries	www.acme.com www.davecentral.com www.download.com www.freeware32.com www.osdn.com www.shareware.com www.sourceforge.net www.tucows.com www.zdnet.com
Web site crawlers/mirroring tools	www.monkey.org www.samspade.org www.tenmax.com www.wget.sunsite.dk
Web-testing-based scripting tools	www.atesto.com www.autotester.com www.compuware.com www.empirix.com www.mercuryinteractive.com www.oclc.org www.radview.com www.rational.com www.segue.com www.soft.com www.wintask.com

PURPOSE	REFERENCED WEB SITES
Buffer overflow explanation	www.insecure.org
Buffer overflow protection tools	www.immunix.org www.securewave.com
Source-code-scanning tools	www.cigital.com www.gimpel.com www.ldra.co.uk www.parasoft.com www.programmingresearch.com www.reasoning.com www.securesw.com www.splint.cs.virginia.edu www.spidynamics.com
Buffer overflow generation tools	www.cenzic.com www.earth.li/projectpurple www.empirix.com www.foundstone.com www.microsoft.com www.perl.com www.radview.com
ASCII data input characters	www.ansi.org
Input data validation tools	www.elitesecureweb.com www.gilian.com www.microsoft.com www.stratum8.com
Data vaults	www.borderware.com www.cyber-ark.com
File encryption tools	www.bestcrypto.com www.cipherpack.com www.data-encryption.com www.easycrypt.co.uk www.f-secure.com www.gnupg.org www.gregorybraun.com www.hallogram.com www.pcguardian.com www.reflex-magnetics.com www.rsasecurity.com www.steganos.com
Database assessment tool	www.appsecinc.com www.iss.net

Chapter 7: Sneak Attacks: Guarding against the Less-Thought-of Security Threats

PURPOSE	REFERENCED WEB SITES
Manufactures or resellers of degassing devices	www.benjaminsweb.com www.datadev.com www.datalinksales.com www.datasecurityinc.com www.garner-products.com www.proton-eng.com www.veritysystems.com www.weircliffe.co.uk
Keyboard logging and screen reordering tools	www.computerspy.com www.enfiltrator.com www.internet-monitoring-software.com www.keykatcher.com www.snapshotspy.com www.spectorsoft.com www.webroot.com

Chapter 8: Intruder Confusion, Detection, and Response

PURPOSE	REFERENCED WEB SITES
Honey pot examples	www.nai.com www.netsecureinfo.com www.project.honeynet.org www.recourse.com www.snetcorp.com
Intrusion detection systems (IDSs)	www.ca.com www.cisco.com www.enterasys.com www.esecurityinc.com www.foundstone.com www.hp.com www.infinity-its.com www.iss.net www.microsoft.com www.nfr.com www.okena.com www.onesecure.com www.openwall.com www.psionic.com www.recourse.com

PURPOSE	REFERENCED WEB SITES
	www.snort.org www.statonline.com www.symantec.com
System event logging and reviewing tools	www.bluelance.com www.ca.com www.consul.com www.gfisoftware.com www.netforensics.com www.opensystems.com www.spidynamics.com
Tripwire and checksum tools	www.lockstep.com www.pedestalsoftware.com www.redhat.com www.resentment.org www.sourceforge.net www.tripwire.com www.tripwire.org
Virus, Trojan horse, and worm definitions	www.symantec.com
Antivirus products	www.agnitum.com www.antivirus.com www.ca.com www.commandcom.com www.f-secure.com www.lockdowncorp.com www.mcafee.com www.pestpatrol.com www.sophos.com www.symantec.com
Computer virus hoaxes and myths	www.vmyths.com
Mobile-code-scanning tools	www.ca.com www.esafe.com www.finjan.com www.trendmicro.com
Antivirus test file	www.eicar.org
Centralized security-monitoring tools and services	www.aprisma.com www.brinksinternetsecurity.com www.ca.com www.counterpane.com www.esecurityinc.com www.exodus.net

PURPOSE	REFERENCED WEB SITES
	www.farm9.com
	www.guarded.net
	www.guardent.com
	www.iss.net
	www.itactics.com
	www.metases.com
	www.mis-cds.com
	www.netiq.com
	www.nsec.net
	www.pentasafe.com
	www.redsiren.com
	www.riptech.com
	www.savvis.com
	www.secureworks.com
	www.trusecure.com
	www.ubizen.com
	www.verio.com
	www.verisign.com
	www.veritect.com
	www.vigilinx.com
Web log analysis tools	www.uu.se/software/analyze
Forensic data collection tools	www.accessdata.com
	www.dibsusa.com
	www.digitalintel.com
	www.dmares.com
	www.encase.com
	www.forensics-intl.com
	www.foundstone.com
	www.ics-iq.com
	www.ilook-forensics.org
	www.tucofs.com
Forensic consulting firms	www.all.net
	www.asrdata.com
	www.cryptec-forensic.com
	www.dibsusa.com
	www.forensics.com
	www.forensics.org
	www.forensics-intl.com
	www.lee-and-allen.com
Intruder coordination centers	www.cert.org
	www.sans.org

Chapter 9: Assessment and Penetration Options

PURPOSE	REFERENCED WEB SITES
Security testing firms	www.alphanetsolutions.com
	www.atstake.com
	www.baltimore.com
	www.boran.com
	www.cigital.com
	www.conqwest.com
	www.crg.com
	www.cryptek.com
	www.defcom.com
	www.emprisetech.com
	www.esmartcorp.com
	www.exodus.net
	www.ey.com
	www.farm9.com
	www.foundstone.com
	www.grayhatsecurity.com
	www.grci.com
	www.guardent.com
	www.hyperon.com
	www.ibm.com
	www.infidel.net
	www.infoscreen.com
	www.iss.net
	www.ixsecurity.com
	www.mavensecurity.com
	www.metases.com
	www.mis-cds.com
	www.nsec.net
	www.predictive.com
	www.procheckup.com
	www.rawtenla.com
	www.redsiren.com
	www.riptech.com
	www.secureinfo.com
	www.securityautomation.com
	www.sses.net
	www.sysinct.com
	www.systemexperts.com
	www.tescom-usa.com
	www.testpros.com
	www.tigertesting.com
	www.tritonic.com
	www.trusecure.com
	www.trustasia.com
	www.verisign.com
	www.veritect.com
	www.vigilinx.com

PURPOSE	REFERENCED WEB SITES
Insurance carriers offering cybercrime policies	www.insuretrust.com www.lloydsoflondon.co.uk www.safeonline.com
Security assessment tools	www.bindview.com www.cerberus-infosec.co.uk www.cisecurity.org www.eeye.com www.fish.com www.foundstone.com www.intrusion.com www.iss.net www.nai.com www.nessus.org www.netiq.com www.pentasafe.com www.sanctuminc.com www.search.iland.co.kr www.spidynamics.com www.statonline.com www.symantec.com www.vigilante.com www.wwdsi.com www.www-arc.com
Multiple O/S management tools	www.bootmanager.com www.ibm.com www.microsoft.com www.powerquest.com www.romtecusa.com www.v-com.com www.vmware.com
Tool libraries	www.acme.com www.atstake.com www.cotse.com www.davecentral.com www.download.com www.freeware32.com www.hackingexposed.com www.ideahamster.org www.insecure.org www.nmrc.org www.ntsecurity.nu www.shareware.com www.sourceforge.net www.tucows.com www.zdnet.com
Anonymous Web server service	www.anonymizer.com

Chapter 10: Risk Analysis

PURPOSE	REFERENCED WEB SITES
Information on fault trees	www.relexsoftware.com
Information on attack trees	www.cigitallabs.com www.counterpane.com
Security standards	www.bsi-global.com www.iso.ch
Information on gap analysis	www.greenbridge.com www.praxiom.com www.victoriagroup.com
Top 20 critical Internet security vulnerabilities	www.sans.org
Information on Failure Mode, Effects and Criticality Analysis (FMECA)	www.fmea.net www.fmeca.com www.relexsoftware.com www.skymark.com

Appendix A: An Overview of Network Protocols, Addresses, and Devices

PURPOSE	REFERENCED WEB SITES
Open Systems Interconnection model	www.iso.ch
HTTP usage recommendation	www.w3c.org
IPsec	www.ietg.org
Secure electronic transaction	www.setco.org
Vendors offering encryption solutions	www.baltimore.com www.entrust.com www.microsoft.com www.rsa.com www.valicert.com www.verisign.com
Internet number assignment	www.iana.org
Computer technology encyclopedias	www.webopedia.com www.whatis.com

PURPOSE	REFERENCED WEB SITES
Firewalls	www.3com.com
	www.borderware.com
	www.checkpoint.com
	www.cisco.com
	www.dlink.com
	www.firewall.com
	www.fortinet.com
	www.gnatbox.com
	www.ibm.com
	www.lucent.com
	www.microsoft.com
	www.netfilter.org
	www.netguard.com
	www.netmax.com
	www.netscreen.com
	www.novell.com
	www.pgp.com
	www.securecomputing.com
	www.sonicwall.com
	www.sphd.com
	www.stonesoft.com
	www.symantec.com
	www.watchguard.com
	www.whalecommunications.com
	www.zonealarm.com

Appendix B: SANS Institute Top 20 Critical Internet Security Vulnerabilities

PURPOSE	REFERENCED WEB SITES
Top 20 critical Internet security vulnerabilities	www.nipc.gov
	www.sans.org

Appendix C: Test-Deliverable Templates

PURPOSE	REFERENCED WEB SITES
Testing documentation standards	www.ieee.org
	www.rational.com

News and Information

The following Web sites have been included for those readers who want to stay abreast of the latest news and information in the field of Web security testing.

PURPOSE	REFERENCED WEB SITES
News and information	www.attrition.org
	www.astalavista.com
	www.esecurityonline.com
	www.hackersdigest.com
	www.incidents.org
	www.infosecuritymag.com
	www.infowar.com
	www.isalliance.org
	www.itsecurity.com
	www.iwar.org.uk
	www.phrack.com
	www.scmagazine.com
	www.searchsecurity.techtarget.com
	www.smarthack.com
	www.slashdot.org
	www.stickyminds.com

Index

A

Ambiguous requirements clarification, 16
access constraints, DBMSs, 177
account escalation, 97
ActiveX controls, client-side security, 130
all-pairs, 138
analysis of risk. *See* risk analysis.
anatomy of test plan, 18–19
  approach of test, 23
  approval options, 41
  change control process, 21
  configuration management, 33–35
  constraints/ dependencies, 40
  defect metrics, 29-30
  defect-tracking reports, 29
  document references, 41

features not to test, 22
features to test, 22
identifiers, 20
introduction, 20
levels of testing, 23
pass/fail criteria, 26
personnel responsibilities, 35
project closure, 38
project scope, 20
risk/contingency planning, 38
schedules, 37
staff/training needs, 36–37
suspension criteria, 27
terms used, 40
test deliverables, 27
test environment needs, 32
test incident reports, 28
test logs, 28
test summary reports, 31
what to retest, 25
when to retest, 24–25

when to test, 24
antivirus software, 211
application code
  client-side security, 119
  copyrights, 159
  security, 158
  session IDs, 119
application-level intruder detection, 179
approach of test, test plan anatomy, 23
approval options, test plan anatomy, 41
assailant, 9
assessing damage, 217
assessing security, 229
asset audits, 252–253
attack trees, 254–255
attacker, 9
audit trails, 207–208
auditing security, 229
automated approach to security testing, 241
automated user ID/ password guessing, 101

automatic updates, client-side security, 140

B

banner grabbing, 86–87
behavioral testing, 5
biometrics, client authentication, 114
black-box testing, 5
black-hat hackers, 9
brainstorming workshops, 257
browser security settings, client-side security, 137–138
brute-force attacks, 125
budget software, security testing, 247
building own tools, security testing, 246
business impact, security breaches, 262–263
BVA (boundary value analysis), 163

C

calculating relative criticality, test-prioritizing techniques, 267
CC (Common Criteria), 80
CCB (change control board/configuration control board), 21
certificate classes, 125
certification for secure software, 80
CGI security, 144
directories, 148
input data, 146
permissions, 147

scalability, 148
script language issues, 145–146
third-party scripts, 149–150
chain of evidence, 219
change control
process, test plan anatomy, 21
checklists
ActiveX control safety, 131
application
code, 161
intruder detection, 179
userID and password, 110
audit trail, 209
biometric device, 115
CGI, 149
client security, 141–140
client-side data, 124
confusion, 204
data disposal, 187
detecting Trojan horse mobile code, 136
DoS attack, 77
dynamic code, 157
IDS sensitivity, 207
illicit navigation, 121
inside accomplice, 191
intrusion monitoring, 216
intrusion response, 224
malware prevention, 214
network
address corruption, 71
design security inspection, 59
device inventory, 55

topology, 58
topology verification, 68
outside security testing firm consideration, 239
physical security, 196–197
protection from nature, 198
secure client transmission, 128–129
secure LAN communication, 72
secure token, 114
security-testing tool selection, 248
server-side data, 178
social engineering, 185
SSI configuration, 155
system software
directories and files, 97
hardening, 85
masking, 88
patching, 84
services, 94
user-group, 105
userIDs and passwords, 104
test-planning consideration, 43–44
third-party CGI script, 151
tripwire and checksum, 211
user permissions, 118
valuation routine, 172
verifying network device inventory implementation, 65
checksums, 209

CISSP certification (certified information systems security professionals), 11
clarifying system requirements, test planning, 16–17
classes of certificates, 125
cleanup after brainstorming, thwarting sneak attacks, 186
clear-box testing, 5
client adaptive code, client-side security, 140
client identification/authentication, 108
client security, 135
client sniffing, client-side security, 141
client-side application security, 107
client identification and authentication, 108–109
biometrics, 114
cross-related restrictions, 117
data restrictions, 117
functional restrictions, 116
has-something approach, 111
IP addresses, 113
know-something approach, 109
MAC addresses, 112
personal certificates, 111
smart cards, 112
telephone numbers, 113

user permissions, 115
code security, 119
HTTP header analysis, 118
illicit navigation, 118
client-side data security, 120
ActiveX controls, 130
automatic updates, 140
browser security settings, 137–138
client adaptive code, 140
client sniffing, 141
client-side mobile code, 139
client-side scripts, 132
code coverage tools, 134
code inspection and reviews, 133
code signing, 134
configuration management, 134
cookies, 121, 139
dedicated security servers, 127
digital certificates, 124
encrypted/non-encrypted content, 126
encryption capabilities, 139
encryption cards, 127
firewalls, 136–137
hidden fields, 123
Java applets, 130–132
local data files, 123
mobile application code, 129
multiple domains, 139
persistent cookies, 122

redirection, 139
scanning mobile code, 134
secure client transmissions, 124
session cookies, 122
small windows, 139
SSL, 125
Trojan Horse mobile code, 133
URLs, 123
client-side mobile code, client-side security, 139
client-side scripts, client-side security, 132
code coverage tools, client-side security, 134
code inspection and reviews, client-side security, 133
code signing, client-side security, 134
commercial network management tools, network security test design, 63
common sense testing guidelines, 272
compensation SLAs, security assessment companies, 235
compileable source code security, 158
computer hacker, 8
configuration management
client-side security, 134
test plan anatomy, 33–35

confirming intrusions, 217

constraints, test plan anatomy, 40

containing damage, 217

contingency planning, 40

controlling intrusion damage, 220

cookies, 121–122
  client-side security, 139
  encryption, 126

corrective measures for insider attacks, 190

cost of tools, security testing, 244

crackers, 8–9

cross-related restrictions, client authentication, 117

cybercrime insurance underwriters, 234

D

damage assessment, 217–219

damage containment, 217

damage control and recovery, 220–222

data, server-side security, 170

data input streams, escape characters, 169

data islands, server-side data security, 176

data restoration, 222

data restrictions, client authentication, 117

data security, 196
  ActiveX controls, 130
  automatic updates, 140

browser security settings, 137–138

client adaptive code, 140

client sniffing, 141

client side, 120
  mobile code, 139
  scripts, 132

code
  coverage tools, 134
  inspection and reviews, 133
  signing, 134

configuration management, 134

cookies, 121, 139

dedicated security servers, 127

digital certificates, 124

encryption
  capabilities, 139
  encrypted/non-encrypted content, 126
  encryption cards,127

firewalls, 136-137

hidden fields, 123

Java applets, 130–132

local data files, 123

mobile application code, 129

multiple domains, 139

persistent cookies, 122

redirection, 139

scanning mobile code, 134

secure client transmissions, 124

session cookies, 122

small windows, 139

SSL, 125

Trojan Horse mobile code, 133

URLs, 123

data vaults, server-side data security, 174

DBMSs, unauthorized access constraints, 177

deception, server-side data security, 175

deceptive defenses, 201

dedicated security servers, client-side security, 127

defect metrics, test plan anatomy, 29–30

defect-tracking reports, test plan anatomy, 29

degaussers, 187

designing tests for network security. *See* test design, network security.

detectability, 273

detecting intruders, 204

detection, 273

detective measures for insider attacks, 189

developer attacks, 133

device accessibility, network security test design, 56, 66

device inventories, 256
  network security test design, 53–55

device threats, 257

digital certificates, client-side security, 124

directory mapping, 96

directory security, 95

distributed copies, server-side data security, 176

DIY approach, security assessments, 230

document references,
test plan anatomy, 41
DoS attacks, 73
countermeasures, 74
detection, 74
emulation, 75
dual NICs, 92
due diligence, 231,
234, 249
dumpster-diving sneak
attacks, 185
dynamic code and server
security, 155
demo scripts, 157
error messages, 158
single points of
failure, 156
system command
tricks, 157
viewing templates, 156
dynamic defenses, mov-
ing targets, 200

E

ease of test implementa-
tion, 268
email sneak attacks,
182–183
employees and system
security, 103
encrypted/non-
encrypted content,
client-side security,
126
encryption
capabilities, client-side
security, 139
cards, client-side secu-
rity, 127
client-side security, 125
cookies, 126
server-side data secu-
rity, 175

equivalence partitioning,
163
escape characters, data
input streams, 169
ethical hacking, 8, 229
evaluating intruder con-
fusion, 203–204
exploratory test
approach, 24
external metrics, test-
prioritizing tech-
niques, 266

F

false acceptance
rates, 109
false rejection
rates, 109
fault trees, 253
features, test plan
anatomy, 22
file searches, 95
file security, 95
filenames, server-side
data security, 173
filtered indexes, Web
site access preven-
tion, 178
fingerprinting, 86
firewalls
client-side security,
136–137
myth, 4
FMEA (Failure Mode
Effects Analysis),
273–274
FMECA (Failure Mode,
Effects, and Critical-
ity Analysis), 252,
273–274
forensics
chain of evidence, 219
intrusion response, 218

fragile application
code, 271
fragmentation, server-
side data
security, 176
freeware, security test-
ing, 244–246
FTA (fault-tree/failure-
tree analysis), 253
functional restrictions,
client authentication,
116

G

gap analysis, 255
glass-box testing, 5
global intruder weather
maps, 203
global requirements
clarification, 16
gray-box testing, 6
gray-hat hackers, 8

H

hackers, 8
hardware
proper disposal to
thwart sneak
attacks, 186
security, 194
system restoration,
221
has-something user
identification, 111
hashing, 120
help desk sneak attack
calls, 182
heuristic test
approach, 24
hidden fields, Web
forms, 123
hiding client-side
code, 119

high-end software, security testing, 247
hijacking Web applications, 135
honey pots, intruder confusion, 201–203
hostname-to-IP address corruption, 69–70
hotel chain example, network security test design, 50
HTTP headers
CGI attacks, 147
client-side security, 118

I
identifiers, test plan anatomy, 20
identify/assign candidate tests, test-prioritizing techniques, 267
IDRSs (intrusion detection and response systems), 206
IDSs (intrusion detection systems), 205–206
IEEE 829-1998 standard, 19
illicit navigation, client-side security, 118
implementing tests, 229
implied requirements clarification, 16
in-house/outsourced combination security assessments, 240
in-person sneak attacks, 184
incomplete requirements clarification, 16

input parameters, ActiveX controls, 130
inside accomplices, sneak attacks, 188
insurance underwriters for cybercrime, 234
integration-level tests, 23
internal metrics, test-prioritizing techniques, 266
introduction, test plan anatomy, 20
intruders, 9
confusion, 200
deceptive defenses, 201
dynamic defenses, 200
evaluating, 203–204
honey pots, 201–203
detection, 204
application-level, 179
audit trails, 207–208
checksums, 209
monitoring, 213–214
tripwires, 209–210
intrusion response, 216
confirming intrusion, 217
damage assessment, 217–219
damage containment, 217
notification policies, 223
retaliatory action, 223
IP addresses
client authentication, 113
forwarding corruption, 70
IP address-to-MAC address corruption, 70

sweeps, network security test design, 61

J–K
Java applets
client-side security, 130–132
disability messages, 140
know-something user identification, 109

L
labels for network devices, 60
levels of testing, test plan anatomy, 23
link-level tests, 23
local data files, client-side security, 123
low-cost software, security testing, 247

M
MAC addresses, client authentication,112
magic cookies, 122
malicious mobile code, 212
malware, 210–211
manual approach to security testing, 240
manual network address confirmation, network security test design, 64
manual user ID/password guesses, 99
masking Web site systems, 86
mobile application code, client-side security, 129

module-level tests, 23

monitoring intrusion detection, 213–214

moving targets, dynamic defenses, 200

MTP (master test plan), 41

multiple domains, client-side security, 139

N

natural disaster recovery, 197

network addresses corruption, 69

network security test design, 62

network design inspections, network security test design, 59

network design reviews, network security test design, 58

network device locations, network security test design, 60

network security policies, 57

supplements, 68

network security test design, 47

commercial network management tools, 63

connections, 65

design inspections, reviews, 58–59

devices accessibility, 56, 66

inventories, 53–55

locations, 60

DNS zone transfers, 63

DoS attacks, 73

countermeasures, 74

detection, 74

emulation, 75

hostname-to-IP address corruption, 69–70

IP addresses forwarding corruption, 70

IP address-to-MAC address corruption, 70

sweeps, 61

manual network address confirmation, 64

network addresses, 62

corruption, 69

network segments, 49

network topologies, 56

scope of approach, 48

accounting company example, 51

furniture manufacturer example, 50

hotel chain example, 50

search engine example, 52

secure LAN communications, 71

suspension criteria, 53

test labs, 52

testing network-filtering devices, 67

validating network design, 57

verifying device inventories, 59

network topology, 65

wireless segments, 72

network segments, network security test design, 49

network topologies, network security test design, 56, 65

network under test, 47

noncompileable source code security, 158

nonspecific requirements clarification, 16

notification policies for intrusion detection, 223

null passwords, 101

O

Orange book, 80

organization of book, 6–7

orthogonal arrays, 138

outsourcing security assessments, 231

compensation SLAs, 235

comprehensiveness of coverage, 235

end point of tests, 237

reconfirming test results, 237

terms of engagement, 235

test location, 238

testing start point, 236

tools used, 236

trustworthiness of company, 233

P

paper disposal, thwarting sneak attacks, 185

pass/fail criteria, test plan anatomy, 26
passwords
  filenames, 102
  guidelines, 100
  security, 97–103
patches for secure software, 81–83
penetration testing, 229
persistent cookies, 122
personal certificates, 111, 125
personnel responsibilities, test plan anatomy, 35
PHF script attacks, 150
physical attack prevention
  cabling, 194
  facilities
    entrances, 193
    perimeter, 192
  hiding Web site location, 192
  room security, 193
  securing
    data, 196
    facilities, 192
    hardware, 194
    software, 195
platform for tools, security testing, 243–244
poisoning, 69, 170
port number assignments, 90
port scans, 90–92
post-testing dependencies, 271
postdeployment regression test set, 25
pretesting dependencies, 271

preventative measures for insider attacks, 188–189
preventing physical attacks
  cabling, 194
  facilities
    entrances, 193
    perimeter, 192
  hiding Web site location, 192
  room security, 193
  securing
    data, 196
    facilities, 192
    hardware, 194
    software, 195
previous history of attacks, 271
priority modifiers, test-prioritizing techniques, 268, 271
project closure, test plan anatomy, 38
project scope, test plan anatomy, 20
prosecuting intrusions, 223
prosecutive measures for insider attacks, 190
protecting
  cabling, 194
  facilities
    entrances, 193
    perimeter, 192

Q–R
quality trade-off triangle, 38
rating variance, 263
readership of book, 11

reconfirming test results, security assessment companies, 237
recovery
  from intrusions, 220
  natural disasters, 197
recycling earlier risk analyses, 252
Red team, 8
redirection, client-side security, 139
regression tests, 25, 271
remapping services, 92
remote access services, 94
responding to intrusions. *See* intrusion response.
restoring
  data, 222
  systems, 221
resumption of test requirements, 27
retaliation for intrusions, 223
reviewing security policies, 224
risk analysis, 251
  asset audits, 252–253
  attack trees, 254–255
  fault trees, 253
  gap analysis, 255
  recycling earlier risk analyses, 252
  test-prioritizing techniques, 256
    business impact, 262–263
    calculating relative criticality, 267
    device inventories, 256
    device threats, 257

external metrics, 266
identify/assign candidate tests, 267
internal metrics, 266
priority modifiers, 268, 271
risk likelihood, 266
test schedule, 272
risk likelihood, test-prioritizing techniques, 266
risk/contingency planning
assumptions, 40
test plan anatomy, 38
room security, 193
rootkits, 188

S
sabotage, 197
safe for scripting, ActiveX controls, 130
scanning mobile code, client-side security, 134
schedules, test plan anatomy, 37
scheduling conflicts, 271
scope of approach, network security test design, 48
accounting company example, 51
furniture manufacturer example, 50
hotel chain example, 50
search engine example, 52
script kiddies, 8–9
secure client transmissions, client-side security, 124

secure LAN communication, 71
securing
data, 196
hardware, 194
physical facilities, 192
software, 195
security
approach of book, 5
CGI server-side applications, 144
directories, 148
input data, 146
permissions, 147
scalability, 148
script language issues, 145–146
third-party scripts, 149–150
focus/goals of book, 4–5
server-side
applications, 143
application code, 158–160
application input data, 160
buffer overflows, 162, 166–168
code review/inspection, 164
compileable source code, 158
data input streams and escape characters, 169–170
diagnostics, 169
execution denial, 163
invalid application data types, 161
invalid range testing, 161
large-scale buffer overflows, 167

noncompileable source code, 158
observing buffer overflow tests, 168
old application components, 160
return leg buffer overflow tests, 168
small-scale buffer overflows, 167
testing buffer overflow, 164
viewing dynamic code templates, 156
server-side data, 170
data islands, 176
data vaults, 174
deception, 175
distributed copies, 176
encryption, 175
filenames, 173
fragmentation, 176
tripwires, 173
WORM devices, 174
server-side dynamic code, 155–158
SSIs, 151–153
system software. See system software security.
security assessment, 229
in-house/outsourced combination, 240
outsourcing
compensation SLAs, 235
comprehensiveness of coverage, 235
end point of tests, 237
reconfirming test results, 237

security assessment (*cont.*)
  terms of engagement, 235
  test location, 238
  testing start point, 236
  tools used, 236
  trustworthiness of company, 233
  test staffing options, 230–231
security audits, 229
  in-house/outsourced combination, 240
  outsourcing
    compensation SLAs, 235
    comprehensiveness of coverage, 235
    end point of tests, 237
    reconfirming test results, 237
    terms of engagement, 235
    test location, 238
    testing start point, 236
    tools used, 236
    trustworthiness of company, 233
    test staffing options, 230–231
security for services, 88–90
security of clients, 135
security policies, 57
  reviews, 224
  test planning, 17–18
security supplements for networks, 68
security testing
  automated approach, 241
  budget software, 247

building own tools, 246
freeware, 244, 246
high-end software, 247
manual approach, 240
shareware, 246
tool costs, 244
tool evaluation, 242
tool platforms, 243–244
security, client-side, 107
  client identification/ authentication, 108–109
  biometrics, 114
  cross-related restrictions, 117
  data restrictions, 117
  functional restrictions, 116
  has-something approach, 111
  IP addresses, 113
  know-something approach, 109
  MAC addresses, 112
  personal certificates, 111
  smart cards, 112
  telephone numbers, 113
  user permissions, 115
  code, 119
  HTTP header analysis, 118
  illicit navigation, 118
  security-by-obscurity, 120
security-related incident statistics, 3
security-testing firms. *See* security assessment, outsourcing.
senior management testing preferences, 271

server certificates, 125
server-side application security, 143
  application code, 158
  copyrights, 159
  error messages, 160
  application input data, 160
  buffer overflows, 162
  test logs, 166
  test optimization, 168
  test-entry criteria, 166
  calibrating buffer overflow test environment, 166
  CGI, 144
  directories, 148
  input data, 146
  permissions, 147
  scalability, 148
  script language issues, 145–146
  third-party scripts, 149–150
  code review/ inspection, 164
  compileable source code, 158
  data input streams and escape characters, 169–170
  diagnostics, 169
  dynamic code, 155
  demo scripts, 157
  helpful error messages, 158
  single points of failure, 156
  system command tricks, 157
  viewing templates, 156
  execution denial, 163

invalid application data types, 161
invalid range testing, 161
large-scale buffer overflows, 167
noncompileable source code, 158
observing buffer overflow tests, 168
old application components, 160
return leg buffer overflow tests, 168
small-scale buffer overflows, 167
SSIs, 151–153
testing buffer overflow, 164
server-side data security, 170
data islands, 176
data vaults, 174
deception, 175
distributed copies, 176
encryption, 175
filenames, 173
fragmentation, 176
tripwires, 173
WORM devices, 174
services security, 88–90
session cookies, 122
session IDs, client-side code security, 119
shadowed password files, 103
shareware, security testing, 246
shelfware, 231
SLAs, intrusion detection monitoring, 214
small windows, client-side security, 139

smart cards, 112
sneak attacks
cleanup after brainstorming, 186
dumpster diving, 185
email, 182–183
help desk calls, 182
in-person, 184
inside accomplices, 188
social engineering, 181
traditional mail, 183
social engineering, 103, 181
software
inspection, 229
security, 79, 195
certifications, 80
directories/files, 95
employees, 103
masking Web sites, 86
patches, 81–83
port scans, 90
services security, 88
social engineering, 103
stealth ports, 90
user IDs/passwords, 97–103
system restoration, 221
spoofing, 67–69
SSI (Server-Side Includes), security, 151–154
SSL (Secure Sockets Layer), client-side security, 125
SSO (single sign-on), 99
staff/training needs, test plan anatomy, 36–37
staffing options, security assessments, 230
stealth ports, 90
string-level tests, 23

structural testing, 5
supplemental network security, 68
suspension criteria
network security test design, 53
test plan anatomy, 27
system requirements, test planning, 15
system salvage/restoration, 221
system software security, 79
certifications, 80
directories/files, 95
employees, 103
masking Web sites, 86
patches, 81–83
port scans, 90
services security, 88
social engineering, 103
stealth ports, 90
user IDs/passwords, 97–103
system under test, 10
system-level tests, 23

T
telephone numbers, client authentication, 113
telephone sneak attack calls, 182
templates, test plan, 10
terminology
software testing, 9–10
test plan anatomy, 40
used in text, 7
terms of engagement, security assessment companies, 235

tests
  approach, test plan
    anatomy, 23
  case, 10
  cost, 268
  coverage, 271
  deliverables, test plan
    anatomy, 27
  dependencies, 271
  test design, network
    security, 47
  commercial network
    management
    tools, 63
  devices
    accessibility, 56, 66
    inventories, 53–55
  DoS attacks, 73
    countermeasures, 74
    detection, 74
    emulation, 75
  hostname-to-IP address
    corruption, 69–70
  IP addresses
    forwarding corrup-
      tion, 70
    IP address-to-MAC
      address corrup-
      tion, 70
    sweeps, 61
  manual network
    address confirma-
    tion, 64
  network addresses, 62
    corruption, 69
  network
    connections, 65
    design inspections, 59
    design reviews, 58
    device locations, 60
    segments, 49
    topologies, 56

  scope of approach, 48
    accounting company
      example, 51
    furniture manufac-
      turer example, 50
    hotel chain
      example, 50
    search engine
      example, 52
    secure LAN
      communications,
      71
  suspension criteria, 53
  test labs, 52
  testing network-filter-
    ing devices, 67
  validating network
    design, 57
  verifying
    device inventories, 59
    network topology, 65
    wireless segments, 72
  test environment needs,
    test plan anatomy, 32
  test implementation, 229
  test incident reports, test
    plan anatomy, 28
  test items, 10
  test labs, network secu-
    rity test
    design, 52
  test logs, test plan
    anatomy, 28
  test plan anatomy, 18–19
    approach of test, 23
    approval options, 41
    change control
      process, 21
    configuration manage-
      ment, 33–35
    constraints, 40
    defect metrics, 29–30

    defect-tracking
      reports, 29
    document references,
      41
    features not to test, 22
    features to test, 22
    identifiers, 20
    introduction, 20
    levels of testing, 23
    pass/fail criteria, 26
    personnel responsi-
      bilities, 35
    project closure, 38
    project scope, 20
    risk/contingency plan-
      ning, 38
    schedules, 37
    staff/training needs,
      36–37
    suspension criteria, 27
    templates, 10
    terms used, 40
    test deliverables, 27
    test environment
      needs, 32
    test incident reports, 2
      8
    test logs, 28
    test summary
      reports, 31
    what to retest, 25
    when to retest, 24–25
    when to test, 24
  test planning, 9
    clarifying system
      requirements,
      16–17
    security policies, 17–18
    system require-
      ments, 15
  test procedure, 10
  test run, 11

test schedule, test-prioritizing techniques, 272
test script, 10
test staffing options, security assessments, 230
test summary reports, test plan anatomy, 31
test-prioritizing techniques, 256
  business impact, 262–263
  calculating relative criticality, 267
  device inventories, 256
  device threats, 257
  external metrics, 266
  identify/assign candidate tests, 267
  internal metrics, 266
  priority modifiers, 268, 271
  risk likelihood, 266
  test schedule, 272
testing network-filtering devices, network security test design, 67
testing security
  automated approach, 241
  budget software, 247
  building own tools, 246
  freeware, 244, 246
  high-end software, 247

manual approach, 240
shareware, 246
tool costs, 244
tool evaluation, 242
tool platforms, 243–244
threats to devices, 257
Tiger team, 8
time bombs, 188
tool evaluation, security testing, 242
traceroute, 65
tracert, 65
traditional mail sneak attacks, 183
translucent testing, 5
tripwires, 173, 209–210
Trojan horses, 133, 188, 211
trustworthiness of security assessment outsources, 233

U
unauthorized access constraints, DBMSs, 177
underwriting for cybercrime insurance, 234
unit-level tests, 23
URLs, client-side security, 123
user groups, 103
user ID security, 97–103
user permissions, client authentication, 115

V
validating network design, network security test design, 57
verifying device inventories, network security test design, 59
verifying network topology, network security test design, 65
viruses, 211

W
wackers, 8
weak password protection, 98
what to retest, test plan anatomy, 25
when to retest, test plan anatomy, 24–25
when to test, test plan anatomy, 24
white-box testing, 5
white-hat hackers, 8
Windows Registry, client side security, 123
wireless segment security, 55, 72
WORM devices, server-side data security, 174
worms, 211